THE STRUCTURE OF LOVE

Yale University Press

New Haven & London

THE
STRUCTURE
OF *Love*

ALAN SOBLE

The author gratefully acknowledges permission to reprint from the following
copyrighted works: Excerpt from "Sonnet 43" from *100 Love Sonnets* by
Pablo Neruda. Copyright © Pablo Neruda 1959 and Fundacion Pablo
Neruda. Excerpt from "Sonnet #24" from *Berryman's Sonnets* by John
Berryman. Copyright © 1952, 1967, by John Berryman. Reprinted by
permission of Farrar, Straus and Giroux, Inc., and of Faber and Faber Ltd.
The last six lines from "For Anne Gregory" by William Butler Yeats are
reprinted with permission of Macmillan Publishing Company from *The
Poems of W. B. Yeats: A New Edition,* edited by Richard J. Finneran.
Copyright © 1933 by Macmillan Publishing Company, renewed 1961 by
Bertha Georgie Yeats.

Designed by Nancy Ovedovitz and set in Galliard type by the Composing
Room of Michigan. Printed in the United States of America by Book
Crafters, Inc., Chelsea, Michigan.

Library of Congress Cataloging-in-Publication Data

Soble, Alan,
    The structure of love / Alan Soble.
       p.   cm.
    Bibliography: p.
    Includes index.
    ISBN 0–300–04566–2 (alk. paper)
    1. Love. I. Title.
BD436.S59   1990
128′.4–dc20   89–16571
                                                  CIP

10   9   8   7   6   5   4   3   2   1

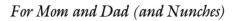

For Mom and Dad (and Nunches)

CONTENTS

PREFACE

An ancient philosopher has said that, if a man were to record accurately all of his experiences, then he would be, without knowing a word of the subject, a philosopher. I have now for a long time lived in close association with the community of the betrothed. Such a relationship ought then to bear some fruit. I have considered gathering all the material into a book, entitled: *Contribution to the Theory of the Kiss*.

—Søren Kierkegaard

In the final pages of *Pornography*, I asked whether photographs and films could represent and communicate the lovingness, if any, of sexual acts. More than a year after I began to write *The Structure of Love*, I noticed that I had finished *Pornography* by discussing love, and I wondered whether love's being the final topic in a book devoted to sexuality was an unconscious sign of my true interests or prejudices. But many books develop, either coincidentally or intentionally, the author's final thoughts in an immediately preceding book. Discussing love, even briefly, in a book on sexuality and sexual images is hardly surprising; subsequently writing a treatise on love is scarcely more so. That I have turned my attention to love (in a book that barely mentions sexuality) does not indicate that I think the theoretical problems in sexuality have been solved. It does show that concerns with the nature and significance of love have replaced concerns with sexuality in my intellectual life. The investigation of one set of social or scientific problems is often temporarily suspended, or permanently abandoned, even though they have not been solved, in favor of another set, for all sorts of reasons. The new questions may be more exciting because they are fresh and relatively unexamined, or because they are of more general interest, or because they present themselves as more urgent or merely as more manageable.

In the introductory note to his anthology *Prefaces and Prologues to Famous Books*, Charles Eliot proclaims a commonsensical view of the purpose of a book's preface: "No part of a book is so intimate as the Preface. Here, after the long labor of the work is over, the author descends from his platform, and speaks with his reader as man to man, disclosing his hopes and fears, seeking sympathy for his difficulties."[1] This view is by now discredited. The preface is very much part of the whole text, and the author can at best pretend to put aside his or her dictatorial tone. There are, of course, difficulties I could talk about here, but most are too mundane for print. The major intellectual obstacle I encountered was organizational: the concepts that surround love form a complex web, which makes dividing topics and issues into neat packages a constant headache. The final architecture of the book is, I think, adequate, but the reader will understand why I employ frequent cross-references. (Cross-references include chapter and section numbers; for example, "8.3" refers to chap. 8, sect. 3.) The major personal difficulties I encountered are just that: personal. I will say only that a scholarly life devoted to the philosophy of sexuality elicits reactions from people that are by now routinely predictable; what was amazing was that writing about love, instead, hardly changes matters. Imagine a psychologist testing his latest idea in bed with a beloved during their postcoital conversation: "The most striking distinction between the erotic life of antiquity and our own, liebchen, no doubt lies in the fact that the ancients laid the stress upon the instinct itself, whereas we emphasize its object. The ancients glorified the instinct and were prepared on its account to honor even an inferior object; while we, including you and I, liebliche, despise the instinctual activity in itself, and find excuses for it only in the merits of the object."[2] Liebchen must want to clobber, and not for the historical error about the Greeks.

Nevertheless, the perceptive or ingenious psychoanalyst should be able to read between the lines of my text to ferret out hidden details of my life—at least according to Peter Gay: "No matter how abstract or apparently rational their system, philosophers of love inevitably import their own erotic history into their theorizing."[3] If Kierkegaard is right, further, I should not even try to avoid exposing my life in the pages of *The Structure of Love;* a genuine philosophy of love would be a jargonless diary of my experiences with my betrothed. Some tiny details of my life, I admit, do infect the text, but I'll bet a dollar to a donut that no one will recognize them. They are too universal. (Or they will be recognized, but without curiosity, because they are universal.) Against Gay's charge I am of course defenseless. I am less worried, however, about an analyst's discerning anal-compulsiveness in my philosophical method or my tedious literature review than I am about a pundit reviewer's calling this book *The Love of Structure.*

I do not offer a grand theory of love, or of anything else, in this book. What the reader will find is detailed scrutiny of various claims that people (philosophers and others) make about love, of the logical relations among these claims, and of the arguments that are or could be used to defend them.[4] As a result, the book contains many small contributions to our understanding of love, tiny conclusions about its rationality and morality. The major questions concern the basis or ground of love (that is, its *structure*), the nature of what is loved, the roles of desires and beliefs in love, and whether love permits justifications as well as explanations. If my approach seems to slight love as a feeling, so be it; I will let the poets describe the inner phenomenology of love. Analytic philosophy (in the broad sense) speaks to a different ear, the ear that welcomes sustained logical probing of our beliefs and their grounds. My goal is to stimulate the reader into thinking more carefully about the nature and value of love. Hence, the book will neither help x catch and keep y nor inspire happy faces to smile into the void. Much of the book, I fear, will seem terribly dry on first reading. (Indeed, on first writing many of its sentences seemed to *me* as dry as sentences about love could be.) But when reread, these dry sentences reveal breathing truths about love. Like some beloveds, these sentences require perseverance to change them into vital beings.

I wish to thank many people for their help on this project. Most important are the people who labored, day in and day out, to do essential things: Jeannie Shapley, who typed the manuscript; and Jessie Hedman, Debbie Guidry (later Anderson), and Huey Henoumont, who ran to and through the library and photocopied until their eyes turned green. My colleagues in the Department of Philosophy, especially Edward Johnson, Norton Nelkin, and Carolyn Morillo, did everything that good colleagues are supposed to do, and then some. Many others contributed in various ways: teaching me Kierkegaard, reading chapters in progress, discussing tangles, corresponding at length about disagreements, sending me to books and articles. I appreciate the efforts of Céline Léon, Robert Perkins, Stephen Evans, Sylvia Walsh, Ronna Burger, Russell Vannoy, Irving Singer, James Nelson, Hilde Robinson, Neera Badhwar, Ursula Huemer, Stef Jones, Diane Michelfelder, Mark Fisher, Jean Braucher, and Nancy Muller. Jeanne Ferris, at Yale University Press, encouraged the project from the very beginning, and manuscript editor Karen Gangel did her job superbly in the face of my insufferability. A special word of thanks to Szabó Sára for her uplifting correspondence. My students as well as those attending presentations of sections of the book (at the Central Division meetings of the American Philosophical Association, April 1985; at Saint John's University, October 1985; at the UNO Philosophy Club, October 1986; and at four Tulane University Philosophy Research Seminars, 1987 through 1989) asked questions and made comments that improved my thinking on many issues.

The congenial people who work in the following establishments took some interest in my writing and did not rush me out: in New Orleans, Tastee

Donut and Burger King (both on Elysian Fields), and La Madeleine, Crois-
sant D'Or, Canal Pub, Maison Blanche Deli, Holmes Cafeteria, and the Yen
Ching Restaurant (all in the French Quarter); in Philadelphia, Burger King
(Welsh Road) and Popeye's (Goodnaw St.); in St. Joseph, Minnesota, Bo
Diddley's, Herk's, and Kay's Kitchen; and in Innsbruck, Max Kade Saal
(Studentenhaus), Unicafe, and Gasthaus Innrain.

The University of New Orleans—including, but not restricted to, my
chair, Edward Johnson, and the Dean of Liberal Arts, Dennis McSeveney—
more than any other university at which I have taught, has given my research
both moral and practical support. In the spring semester of 1988 my teaching
load was reduced to make time available for writing, and in the summer of
1988 I received the financial assistance of a UNO Research Council Award
and a Summer Scholar Award. The National Endowment for the Humanities
also played a crucial role. In the summer of 1985 I attended Sylvia Walsh's
Summer Seminar for College Teachers, on Kierkegaard, financially supported by the NEH; and in the summer of 1988 I received an NEH Summer
Stipend (FT–30486–88) precisely to work on this book.

THE STRUCTURE OF LOVE

CHAPTER 1   *Two Views of Love*

To the beloved and deplored memory of her who was the inspirer, and in part
the author, of all that is best in my writings—the friend and wife whose
exalted sense of truth and right was my strongest incitement, and whose
approbation was my chief reward—I dedicate this volume. Like all that I have
written for many years, it belongs as much to her as to me; but the work as it
stands has had, in a very insufficient degree, the inestimable advantage of her
revision; some of the most important portions having been reserved for a
more careful re-examination, which they are now never destined to receive.
Were I but capable of interpreting to the world one half the great thoughts
and noble feelings which are buried in her grave, I should be the medium of a
greater benefit to it, than is ever likely to arise from anything that I can write,
unprompted and unassisted by her all but unrivaled wisdom.

—John Stuart Mill, *On Liberty*

1. LOVE OSTENSIVELY DEFINED

More than eight centuries ago, Andreas Capellanus wrote in his treatise
on love that "love is a certain inborn suffering derived from the sight of and
excessive meditation upon the beauty of the opposite sex."[1] Something not
very different was expressed by René Descartes five centuries later: "Love is an
emotion of the soul caused by a movement of the spirits, which impels the soul
to join itself willingly to objects that appear to be agreeable to it."[2] Today we
are inclined to think of Capellanus' "suffering" (inborn or otherwise) as only a
contingent symptom or effect of love, not as love itself, and usually present, if
at all, only in the early sexual or romantic stages of a love relationship. Nor do
we take seriously the idea that love, suffering, or the response to beauty are
restricted to heterosexuals. But it is a defensible claim that beauty, or some
other attractive or admirable quality of the beloved, has something to do with
love. (I wonder, however, whether Capellanus means that the lover is in love
with the beauty per se or with a person who is beautiful.) When Descartes
writes that love is "caused" by a movement that "impels" the soul, yet the soul
joins "willingly" with its beloved object, I worry about his consistency. And
today we are not impressed with the idea that the soul is the seat of love, or of

1

anything else. Nevertheless, Descartes's claim that love is an emotion directed at things that are "agreeable" is plausible. His definition also has the merit of alerting us to the *intentionality* of love: the object of love (that which is loved) need not be actually agreeable as long as it at least appears, or is believed, to be agreeable. Moreover, even though Capellanus and Descartes disagree about the details, they are dealing with the same thing; we know what human phenomenon they have in mind, despite the fact that they have so far said very little about it.

I make this point as a mild warning, for I will indicate my object of study only negatively and ostensively; but if the reader is not confused by Capellanus or Descartes, he or she should not be confused by my procedure. My object of study is love, but that statement is unrevealing, for there are many kinds of love. My object of study is not the love of chocolate or of birds, parental love, filial love, sibling love, or love of country, although the love I am studying may have some of the features of these other loves. The loves that are most relevant to my study are, on the one hand, those within the *eros* tradition, comprising the eros of Plato's *Symposium*, sexual love, courtly love, and romantic love, and, on the other hand, those within the *agape* tradition, including God's love for humans and Christian neighbor-love. The love I am concerned with is similar to these loves and might be a combination of several either from the same tradition or from both traditions. It is probably a historical development of the loves in the eros tradition, but I do not want to rule out in advance that it displays some features of the loves in the agape tradition. Ostensively defined, my object of study is the love that one person has for another person (usually not a blood relation); that may exist between two people when it is reciprocal (which is often, but not always, the case); that today often leads to or occurs in marriage or cohabitation (but obviously need not); that often has a component of sexual desire (in varying degrees); and that occasionally, for heterosexuals, eventuates in procreation.

To clarify this ostensive definition of the love I am concerned with, I could mention examples of love from history and literature—say, the love of John Stuart Mill and Harriet Taylor, or that of Hack and Ray (in Marilyn Hacker's *Love, Death, and the Changing of the Seasons*). Referring to examples from life and literature will be helpful, but relying on them heavily while defining my object of study is dangerous, for I am not doing history, biography or literary criticism, but philosophy (by which I mean the conceptual and moral analysis of an idea and a practice). If I wanted to study the kind of love for which Mill and Taylor are a paradigm, I would proceed by dissecting that particular relationship (as Phyllis Rose did in *Parallel Lives*). Or if Shakespeare's love life is paradigmatic, I would proceed by rereading the sonnet sequence and doing close textual analysis (say, in the manner of Barthes on Balzac in *S/Z*). However, these historical and literary paradigms are firmly bound in time and place; therefore, what we can learn from them conceptually and morally about our concept and practice of love may be limited in unpredictable ways. And we have too many paradigms; emphasizing some cases from this embarrassment of riches, at the expense of others, would be arbitrary. These examples from life and literature, then, can serve as illustrations rather than as a foundation for a definition or theory of love. In *The Four Loves*, C. S. Lewis half-heartedly apologizes for his habit of referring to *King Lear* and the like: "I am driven to literary examples because you, the reader, and I do not live in the same neighbourhood; if we did, there would . . . be no difficulty about replacing them with examples from real life."[3] But I am able to define my object of study ostensively because my reader and I do live in the same neighborhood, and because, therefore, our experiences and observations about love are similar. (Lewis, after all, agrees; he can use literary examples only because he and his reader live in the same literary neighborhood.)

My purpose is served well enough by saying that my concern is the familiar, garden-variety love that we practice in our everyday lives, nothing esoteric; as Anthony Weston puts it, "a somewhat . . . settled condition, though one in which romance may of course play a part."[4] I mean the love that we imagine the couple upstairs has, based on their behavior in public; the love that in our happier moments we think we have and that we think the upstairs couple, behind closed doors, could never have. I will refer to the love I have in mind as "personal love"—but do not let anything hang on that phrase. (I find the expression "people love" ugly; otherwise, I would prefer it for its neutrality. The problem with the term "personal love" is that it is often a technical term describing "love for the person" rather than love for the properties of a person. It might be true that the love I am studying is "love for the person" in this technical sense; but my use of the term "personal love" does not imply that by definition the love I am concerned with is "love for the person.") I am not going to define love any further; the ostensive definition will have to suffice. I am not even aiming at a general definition of love. I assume that the reader knows what I am talking about. If, when reflecting on my claims, a reader cannot make any sense of my assertions, then my assumption will be proven false. How often this does not happen is the measure of my grasp of our concept and practice of love, of its underlying structure and morality.

One philosophical view of the love I am concerned with characterizes it in terms of a central thesis of the eros tradition; I will call this view "the first view of personal love," "view one," or simply "the eros tradition." In contrast to view one, there is a view of personal love that I will call "the second view,"

"view two," or "the agape tradition." I define "second view" as any view denying that the central thesis of the first view gives an accurate or complete account of personal love. What logical coherence there is in the second view is provided by a central thesis of the agape tradition. In working out the details of these two different characterizations of personal love, I am interested in several questions: What are the advantages and limits of these views in understanding the love I am concerned with? What would personal love look like if the first view, or the second, happened to be true? What do these two views presuppose about human nature and our ability to love? In particular, there are certain philosophical tangles that purportedly show that the eros tradition is inadequate and that personal love is poorly understood if analyzed by that tradition. Personal love, some have argued, can succeed (or be genuine) only if it is "agapized," that is, transformed by agape into a second-view ("agapic") love.[5] Much of the book defends the eros tradition (or "erosic" love) and argues that the agape tradition may succumb to similar tangles or objections when it is employed to characterize personal love. Does personal love need a dose of agape? Or at the theoretical level: Does conceiving of personal love in terms foreign to the eros tradition provide a better understanding of it? My eventual conclusion is "no."

2. PROPERTY-BASED AND REASON-DEPENDENT LOVE

In the first view of personal love (that derived from the eros tradition), love is in principle and often in practice comprehensible. In particular, love is what I will call "property-based": When x loves y, this can be explained as the result of y's having, or x's perceiving that y has, some set S of attractive, admirable, or valuable properties; x loves y *because* y has S or because x perceives or believes that y has S. These properties of y are the basis or ground of x's love and hence, in the first view, something about the object of one's personal love is a crucial part of the explanatory source of love; love is "object-centric."[6] In principle, x and y (and outsiders) are capable of knowing why x loves y—that is, of knowing which attractive properties of y, the object, have brought it about that x loves y. Further, personal love is "reason-dependent": when x loves y, x (given enough self-investigation) will be able to answer "Why do you love y?" by supplying reasons for loving y in terms of y's having S. Because the attractive properties of y figure both in the explanation of x's love and in the reasons x will give for loving y, I will use "property-based" and "reason-dependent" interchangeably. The central claim of the first view is that something about y is central in accounting for x's love for y; the emphasis is on the perceived merit of the object as the ground of love. Such is the structure of erosic personal love.

Several corollaries follow about personal love from the claim that it is property-based and reason-dependent. First, personal love, though susceptible to various kinds of irrationality, is not inherently irrational. If love is intentional—that is, if x loves y in virtue of x's believing or perceiving that y has S—then love is vulnerable to cognitive or psychological mistakes. X, for example, may be deluded in thinking that y has S; x might still love y in this case, even though the foundation of x's love is suspicious. But if personal love is in principle explainable in terms of y's having S, then love is not irrational at its core; it is not unpatterned, unprincipled, or unpredictable. Personal love is not one of the great mysteries of the universe. Second, the object's possessing properties that are unattractive ("defects") must play some role in determining the duration or intensity of personal love. Defects are not theoretically dispensable or ignorable; love exists, and is expected to exist, only up to a point. Third, that y loves x cannot ever suffice as a reason for why x loves y; that y loves x may contribute to the reasons in virtue of which x loves y, but it cannot be the original or the full reason. If y's loving x is allowed as the full reason that x loves y, and this particular reason can operate generally, then x might love y because y loves x—in turn because x loves y. This love is inexplicable.

The distinction between the first and the second view of personal love is not the same as that between "vulgar" love of the body and "heavenly" love of the mind, as described by Pausanias in Plato's *Symposium*. This is a distinction within the eros tradition itself, which in principle places little or no limit on what x may consider a valuable property of y; this is not what differentiates erosic love and agapic personal love. The second view of personal love (remember that the second view is not equivalent to agape but asserts the central thesis of that tradition) denies that personal love is property-based: the love of x for y is not grounded in y's attractive properties S or in x's belief or perception that y has S. If anything, the opposite is true: that is, x finds the properties that y has attractive, or x considers y to be attractive, *because* x loves y. The ground of personal love is not the perceived merit of the object but something about x, something in the nature of the lover; thus, personal love is subject-centric rather than object-centric. "It is not that the woman loved is the origin of the emotions apparently aroused by her; they are merely set behind her like a light."[7] Since x values y's properties in virtue of loving y, y's valuable properties cannot explain why x loves y. Love, then, is incomprehensible, insofar as the best candidate for the explanation of x's loving y (namely, that y has S) has been eliminated. If personal love is comprehensible at all, the explanation for x's loving y might be that y already loves x. (George Sand wrote in a letter, "If you want me to love you, you must begin by loving me. . . . [T]hen . . . anything you tell me will seem divine."[8] So x might find S in y to be valuable because x loves y, where x loves y because y loves x.) Alternatively, the explanation for x's loving y might be the nature of x (x is filled with love) or x's desire or capacity to love regardless of the object's merit. Further, personal love is not reason-dependent: x should not be called upon to explain or justify loving y by giving reasons in terms of y's attractive properties, or any reasons at all. Love is its own reason and love is taken as a metaphysical primitive.[9] Such is the structure of agapic personal love.

The intentionality of personal love, in the second view, is not an important feature. Since love is not a response of the subject to the attractive properties of its object, love is much less dependent on what x believes about, or perceives in, y; hence, cognitive mistakes play no role in this picture of personal love. (One exception is x's loving y because y loves x, which must be understood as x's loving y because x *believes* that y loves x.) Similarly, defects play no role in personal love. Because x's love for y is not grounded in y's attractive properties, y's having unattractive properties carries no weight; a personal love that does not arise as a response to attractive properties is not a love that is extinguished or prevented by unattractive properties. That x finds S in y valuable because x loves y even implies that there is no distinction between y's attractive and unattractive properties until x develops a loving attitude toward y. (Analogously, x's hating y would explain, instead of being explained by, the fact that x finds properties of y to be disagreeable or obnoxious.) This is why personal love in this view is incomprehensible, even irrational. But in this view love's being a mystery is no strike against love or against any theory that conceives of love this way.[10]

An important issue regarding the first view of personal love is the relationship between y's having S as the cause of x's loving y (and thereby y's having S being the explanation of x's loving y) and y's having S as x's reason for loving y. We might appeal here to the notion that the distinction between causes and reasons is artificial: x's reasons to do Φ *are* the causes of x's doing Φ.[11] This move does not entirely work. Even if x's reasons for loving y can be adequately conceived of as the cause of x's loving y (in which case love's being reason-dependent is primary, while its being property-based is secondary), there is still room to think of nonreason-causes as the explanation of x's loving y (in which case love's being property-based is primary and reason-dependence is secondary). Even if all reasons are causes (hence that x's reason for loving y is the reason-cause explanation), not all causes are reasons (when x's love is mostly explained by nonreason-causes).

The first view of personal love claims that in "ideal" cases either (1) x accurately believes that y has S, x provides without self-deception "y has S" as x's reason for loving y, and this reason is the sole cause of x's loving y (no other reason-causes or nonreason-causes are involved); or (2) x is caused (by non-reason-causes) to love y by x's accurate perception or belief that y has S, this causal mechanism is transparent to x, and x acknowledges y's having S also as x's reason for loving y.[12] (For example, x's being aware of the nonreason-causes operating on x, and x's allowing them to operate without resistance, is a way x acknowledges the nonreason-causes as x's reasons.) In the first case reason-dependence is primary, while in the second property-basedness is primary; but in both cases there is a convergence of x's reasons and the causes.

Divergence between the properties of y that cause x's love for y and the properties of y that x invokes as the reason for x's loving y can occur in several ways. Suppose that x's stated reason for loving y is that y has attractive property P, but that (unknown to x) y does not in fact have P; nevertheless, suppose in addition that x is caused to love y by y's having some other property Q. There are in this scenario two causes for x's loving y: x's (false) belief that y has P (the reason-cause) and y's having Q, which operates behind the scenes of x's consciousness as a nonreason-cause. Hence x's love is both reason-dependent and property-based, but x's love is nonideal because x makes two mistakes: x believes falsely that (1) y has P and that (2) y's having P totally explains x's love. The scenario can be altered to make it monocausal: suppose that x loves y because x believes (falsely) that y has P, that x's believing that y has P really is x's reason for loving y, and that there are no nonreason-causes at work. Now x's love for y is explained by x's belief that y has P, and this reason is the total cause of x's love. Here is another monocausal scenario: suppose that x believes (falsely) that y has P, that x offers y's having P as the reason for x's love, but that x is wrong about having this or any reason for loving y—the real cause being y's having Q, which generates x's love for y from behind the scenes. These loves are reason-dependent and/or property-based, as love is characterized by the first view, even though x falsely believes that y has P.

Now let us assume that x correctly perceives or believes that y has the attractive property P. The matrix below (in which "xLy" means "x loves y") further clarifies the first view of personal love and shows how it differs from the second. Category (A) includes one of the ideal cases of erosic love, in which y's having P causes xLy and x offers "y has P" as x's reason for xLy (because x realizes that y's having P causes xLy). But (A) also includes several nonideal cases. Without knowing that y's having P causes x to love y, x may offer "y has P" as the reason for xLy, in which case y's having P figures separately in both the reason-cause and the nonreason-cause of xLy. (The case is nonideal since it involves some lack of self-awareness on x's part.) Further, if x provides the reason "y has Q" for xLy, while y's having P operates as the nonreason-cause, then either (1) we have a case of dual causation of xLy (caused both by y's having Q as the reason-cause and by y's having P as the nonreason-cause), and again x lacks some self-awareness, or (2) y's having P is the only cause of xLy, and x has made two mistakes: thinking that y's having Q is x's reason for xLy and missing the fact that y's having P is the nonreason-cause.

	y's attractive P is a nonreason-cause of xLy	y's attractive P is not a nonreason-cause of xLy
x provides reasons for xLy that mention y's attractive P	(A)	(B)
x does not provide reasons for xLy that mention y's attractive P	(C)	(D)

Category (B) includes the other ideal case of erosic love: x's reason for xLy, that y has P, is the full and genuine reason-cause for xLy, and there are no other causes operating on x. But (B) also includes one nonideal case, in which x offers "y has P" as the reason for xLy when, in fact, x's real reason (hidden from x by self-deception or rationalization) is that y has Q.[13] Within (B) there is also one type of second-view personal love (although not an ideal agapic love): x believes that y's having P is x's reason for xLy, yet x has no reason at all for xLy that involves y's attractive properties. If some x can be mistaken in thinking that x's reason for xLy is y's having P (when x's real reason is that y has Q), then some other x can be mistaken in thinking that x has a reason for xLy (when in fact x has none). Since we assume in (B) that no attractive property of y plays a nonreason-causal role in xLy, this love is neither property-based nor reason-dependent and is therefore a second-view, or agapic, form of love.

Category (C) includes no ideal cases of erosic personal love. We suppose that y's having P causes xLy, but x does not offer any reason for xLy in terms of y's properties. If in fact x has no reasons for xLy, x is correct not to offer any, and x's only mistake is being unaware of the nonreason-cause working on x that x could embrace as a reason. Alternatively, x might not offer reasons for xLy because x is unaware of them, and here x makes an additional mistake.

Category (D) includes another nonideal form of erosic love, when x's reason for xLy is that y has P, but x is unaware of this reason and therefore cannot provide it. Indeed, because in (D) we are assuming that y's having P is not a nonreason-cause of xLy, it may appear to x that x's love for y is entirely agapic. For category (D) also includes the ideal form of second-view love. In this case y's having the attractive P is not a nonreason-cause of xLy, and x really does not have any reason that mentions an attractive property of y for xLy. Category (D), then, not only clarifies the difference between the ideal form of agapic personal love and the ideal forms of erosic love [found in categories (A) and (B)] but also suggests how x could be mistaken in believing that x is loving agapically when x is really loving erosically.

In the second view of personal love the attractive properties of y play no role in either the reason or the nonreason-causes of xLy (that is, personal love is neither property-based nor reason-dependent), but this does not entail that no causes or reasons figure into love. The second view does not require that x have any reasons for loving y; but if x does offer reasons, x need not mention y's attractive properties. Perhaps x loves y for the reason that y loves x, or because x believes that x has an obligation to love y. Similarly, the second view does not require that x's love for y be caused; perhaps x's love is a pure act of will. If x's love for y is caused, these causes are not y's having the attractive P or x's belief that y has P. For example, y's loving x could be the nonreason-cause for x's loving y, or perhaps something special in x's nature causally explains why x loves y.

3. OBJECT-CENTRIC AND SUBJECT-CENTRIC LOVES

We need to consider an objection to one way in which I have distinguished the first from the second view of personal love. I stated that in the first view love is object-centric, while in the second it is subject-centric; in the first view, a crucial source of x's love for y is y, and in the second the source is x. But there may be no firm distinction between love's being object-centric and its being subject-centric. We can formulate the objection as a dilemma: if we are talking only about the objective properties of y (those that are y's independently of y's being evaluated by anyone, that are in some sense inherent in y, and whose presence in y is publicly and empirically verifiable), then there is a clear distinction between an object-centric and a subject-centric view of personal love, although the second view at first seems bizarre or implausible (and hence is treated unfairly). If, on the other hand, we are talking only about y's subjective properties (those that are not inherent in y because their existence depends altogether on an evaluation by the perceiver), then the second view looks much better (and is treated fairly), but the distinction between object-centric and subject-centric largely collapses.

The details of the objection need to be filled in. Consider the first horn of the dilemma: assume that there is an objective property P (for example, beauty, wit, intelligence, or moral virtue) that y has or does not have.[14] In this case, it is coherent to say (as in the first view) that x loves y in virtue of responding to y, either when x correctly perceives P in y or when x mistakenly believes that y has P. This would be an object-centric love easily distinguishable from a subject-centric love in which P is irrelevant to the existence of x's love. But if we are considering an objective property P, it seems strange to say (as we would have to in the second view) that because x loves y, x attributes P to y. For x must be undergoing some suspicious psychological process; how else to understand x's love for y leading x to believe that y possesses some *objective* property? Think about x's believing that y is five feet tall because x loves y. Y might have P, but that is not why x believes that y has P. Thus, if we talk only about objective properties, we preserve the analytic distinction between object-centric and subject-centric at the cost of making the second view of personal love implausible. (It is said that when God loves humans, God confers objective value on His beloveds. Even if true, that fact would not save the second view. Although humans may be able to confer objective value on other humans, we are considering not the conferral of objective value *simpliciter* but the attribution of some specific valuable objective property P to the beloved.)

Now examine the second horn: assume that there is a subjective property Q (for example, beauty, wit, intelligence, or moral virtue). In this case the second view has no problem claiming that because x loves y, x attributes Q to y: because x loves y, x comes to value y's appearance or to believe that y's humor is entertaining. "To the lover the loved one is always the most beautiful thing imaginable, even though to a stranger she may be indistinguishable from an order of smelts. Beauty is in the eye of the beholder."[15] The psychology of this phenomenon does not strike us as unusual because the attributed property is merely subjective (attributions of these properties vary tremendously, according to taste, from person to person; the question of their possession cannot be resolved by straightforward empirical debate). Thus, the second view of personal love is not eliminated unfairly, in advance. But if we are talking about subjective properties, we lose the sense of object-centric that underlies the difference between the two views of personal love. For if x loves y because (or after) x attributes subjective property Q to y, then "equal contributions" are made to x's loving y by y's possessing Q and by x's evaluating y in x's idiosyncratic way. The ground of love is not simply y (if it is y to any extent) but rather x's nature that leads x to evaluate y in this way. Hence the first view must admit that love is subject-centric. Note that if x loves y in virtue of a subjective property, it makes no sense to say that x might love y because x is *mistaken* in believing that y has Q; mistakes can be made only about objective properties. If so, part of the intentionality of love, an important feature of the first view, drops out of the picture—which confirms the conclusion that no firm distinction exists between the two views of personal love.

One response to the objection would define the two views in such a way that in the first view only objective properties figure into love, while in the second only subjective properties count. This move is consistent with the spirit of each view as descendants of the eros and agape traditions, respectively: in eros love is elicited by the objective merit of the object, while agape is a freely given love that creates value in its object regardless of the object's objective merit.[16] The solution, however, is too timid: allocating objective properties to the first view, and subjective properties to the second, eviscerates these views. The trick is either to make room for objective properties in the second view or to make room for subjective properties in the first.

I prefer the latter solution. The distinction between the two views does not collapse if the first view allows that the lover may be responding to subjective properties. For the lover does not necessarily attribute any subjective property to the beloved because the lover already loves the beloved; only x's attribution of a subjective property to y on the basis of already loving y is a second view phenomenon. Further, in the second view *nothing* valuable, objectively or subjectively, about the object is the ground of love; whereas in the first view, whether the lover responds to the objective or to the subjective value of the beloved, *something* valuable about the beloved figures into the ground of love. Even if x loves y in virtue of subjective property Q, something about the beloved, some raw material, encourages the lover to find value in the beloved. The first view permits the lover to claim that his reason for loving is that subjective, valuable property of y; and as long as x can offer this reason for loving y, the first view does not collapse into the second, which makes no room for that reason. Thus, we might think of erosic personal love as partially subject-centric or partially object-centric, while agapic personal love is totally subject-centric or never object-centric. This terminology acknowledges that something about the lover, either preferences or evaluations, plays a role in the basis of erosic love along with the characteristics of the beloved.

Moreover, x's attributing subjective, valuable property Q to y because x loves y can occur even within the first view of personal love. In the second view, sometimes x finds a property of y's valuable just because x loves y; in the first view, x's finding Q in y to be valuable because x loves y is possible only if x's love for y is already property-based or reason-dependent, as long as the love-grounding properties do not include Q. What is ruled out by the first view is exactly what the second allows, namely, that x finds value in y's properties because x loves y, *and* the love itself is not property-based (see 7.6). In the first view, as long as x loves y because y possesses S, x's finding other value in y, merely because x loves y, is neither impossible nor unlikely. (Here is an interesting case to think about: suppose that because x loves y, x attributes subjective valuable Q to y, and then x's love is reinforced because y has Q. The case is easily handled as a complex erosic love if x's love for y is originally property-based. But if x's love for y is not originally property-based, then the case is an internally contradictory agapic personal love. Similarly, suppose that because God loves valueless humans, He bestows objective value on them; and suppose that God's love for humans is reinforced by His response to the value they now have.)

4. THE TWO TRADITIONS

I am more concerned with the two views of personal love than I am with eros and agape themselves.[17] Plato's eros and God's agape are important because what is central to each of the two views I described above is a thesis extracted from these paradigms: one view claims that love is property-based and reason-dependent, while the other view denies that love can be adequately understood if conceived that way. Plato's eros and Paul's agape serve as models in the sense that our major question might be formulated: Is personal love more like the love a person has for God (eros) or more like the love that God has for persons (agape)? (Compare this question with the variants proposed below.) In this section I discuss to what extent the loves I have assigned to the eros and agape traditions exemplify these central themes.

For loves within the agape tradition, the attractive and unattractive properties of the object, the object's value, are entirely irrelevant. This irrelevance of merit is clear in agape as God's (or Jesus') love for humans: "God does not love that which is already in itself worthy of love, but on the contrary, that which in itself has no worth acquires worth just by becoming the object of God's love. Agape has nothing to do with the kind of love that depends on the recognition of a valuable quality in its object; Agape does not recognise value, but creates it."[18] Why, then, does God love humans? "The 'reason' why God loves men is that God is God, and this is reason enough."[19] As Nygren says, "There is only one right answer. . . . Because it is His nature to Love. . . . The only ground for it is to be found in God himself."[20] But some Christians were drawn to the rationality of property-based love. Richard of St. Victor, for example, could not imagine that "the Divine person could . . . have the highest love towards a person who was not worthy of the highest love."[21] Humans, having no worth, could not therefore be the recipients of God's love; ergo the Trinity, a device that, for Richard, supplied God with objects worthy of His love. Should we ask: Is it God's nature to love erosically or agapically? Does God love humans agapically only because we have no worth—that is, is He forced to love us agapically if He is to love us at all?

Love's not being based on the merit of its object is also characteristic of agape as Christian love of one's neighbor, which demands that humans love the sinner, the stranger, the sick, the ugly, and the enemy, as well as the righteous and one's kin. Given this list of appropriate objects of love, individual attractiveness obviously plays no role in neighbor-love. Nevertheless, neighbor-love is interpretable not as agape but as an erosic love (see 9.9). For example, if humans are not worthless precisely because God has bestowed objective value on them, then neighbor-love could be construed as a property-based response to this value.[22] Or perhaps neighbor-love is a response to the piece or spark of God that exists in all humans.[23] Here we should distinguish the claim (about the basis of love) that x's neighbor-love for y is property-based, in that x loves y because y possesses the valuable property "contains a piece of God," from the claim (about the object of love) that in neighbor-love what one loves is not the human per se but that piece of God in the human.[24] Even this latter claim, however, implies that neighbor-love is an erosic love, if the human love for God is itself based on God's attractive properties and, therefore, the love of the piece of God in humans is based on the attractive properties of that piece. Perhaps we should ask: Is neighbor-love more like a love of humans for humans (a heavenly eros) or more like the agape of God for humans?

Erich Fromm has argued that mother love is an agapic love, whereas father love is an erosic love (or, better, that the idea of mother love, or mother love as a Weberian "ideal type," fits into the agape tradition).[25] In mother love the child is loved unconditionally, just because she exists; in father love, the child is loved when or because she fulfills the father's expectations, obeys his moral demands, and achieves worldly success in his eyes (that is, in mother love, the child's merit is irrelevant; in father love, merit is central). Fromm also claims that the Old Testament God is a projection of this idea of father love, and the New Testament God a projection of mother love.[26] Thus, the theory of human parental love is not derived from the idea of God's love, but the idea of God's love is modeled after recognizable features of human parental love. Irving Singer has claimed that Fromm's social psychology of religion is "hardly defensible" because "the distinction between mother's love and father's love cannot be upheld": mother love can also be conditional (she needs her children, and an "actual mother" also "imposes demands and expectations"), while in some cases a father's love is unconditional (Singer mentions the parable of the prodigal son).[27] However, these points do not undermine

Fromm's view. First, if mothers and fathers do not love in accordance with the "ideal types," that fact has no relevance to Fromm's social psychology of religion, since what people project onto God is their idea of the perfect mother or father, or the observed behavior of rare, exemplary mothers and fathers. Second, to point out that some fathers love unconditionally is not to destroy the distinction between (ideal) mother love and father love but only to challenge the claim (which might not be Fromm's) that styles of parental love are gender-linked.

Nevertheless, Singer's suspicion that mother love, or a genderless parental love, is even in its ideal form more erosic than agapic deserves consideration. First, parental love might fall within the eros tradition if the parent loves the child not on the basis of the child's mere existence but because the child has the property "is a child of mine," which is, from the parent's subjective perspective, a meritorious property. Because the parent loves the child in virtue of this property, the parent might then (consistently with the first view) attribute all manner of other properties to the child (beauty, intelligence, and so on). This common phenomenon of "seeing" these valuable properties in one's child does not, then, have to be explained as a second-view process. Second, the parent's reason for loving the child is both general and selective; if this is why the parent loves child x, the parent has equal reason for loving child y, yet has no reason for loving someone else's child. That is, parental love is preferential in a way that God's agape and neighbor-love could never be. Further, parental love is erosic if parents do not love all their children equally: if a parent loves child x more than child y, even though both have the property "is a child of mine," then some other (probably meritorious) properties possessed by child x are involved. (An example might be loving child x more than child y because the former has the property "first-born.") Parental love, then, differs significantly from agape in structure: God loves all His children, but everyone is one of His children (God's love is general but not selective), and God loves all His children equally (other meritorious properties are irrelevant). But does this imply that God's love is erosic after all?—God loves humans in virtue of their possessing the property "is a child, or creation, of mine," and that property is an attractive property. Perhaps, however, "is a creation of mine" does not register in God's eyes as a meritorious property or is not a reason why God loves humans.

Finally, consider friendship-love. In one version it exhibits the main feature of eros, arising in virtue of the attractiveness of the friend. For example, x and y are friends because they have common interests or goals that both see as valuable or because they respond to each other's excellence and character (more broadly, for Aristotle, "we do not feel affection for everything, but only for the lovable, and that means what is good, pleasant, or useful").[28] But opposed to this is Montaigne's friendship with Etienne de La Boétie, whose properties Montaigne claimed were irrelevant to, and afforded no explanation for, their love. Montaigne wrote of his beloved:

> It is not one special consideration, nor two, nor three, nor four, nor a thousand: it is I know not what quintessence of all this mixture. . . . If you press me to tell why I loved him, I feel that this cannot be expressed, except by answering: Because it was he, because it was I.[29]

Whether Montaigne is describing friendship is not important; what he wrote, however, arguably does capture the spirit of the second view of personal love and is for that reason illuminating. The Puritan Daniel Rogers held a similar view about friendship, in which a "secret instinct" ties two friends together: "A reason cannot be given by either partie, why they should be so tender each to other."[30] Edmund Leites comments that for some Puritans, the same "mystery [was] at the heart of marital love. Its causes are largely hidden and unknown, and hence beyond our control."[31] The scorching reply to Montaigne, Rogers, and St. Bernard (who said about charity, "I love because I love")[32] is "To say *you Love*, but you *know not why,* is more beseeming Children or mad folks" (than, for example, two people contemplating marriage).[33]

For the loves of the eros tradition, the attractive properties of the object account for the existence of love and determine its course. This is almost perfectly clear in Plato's eros itself, where the beauty or goodness of an object (body, soul, law, theorem) grounds the subject's love (although a case can be made that Plato considers beauty to be love's object, not merely its basis). In courtly love, the lover chooses "one woman as the exemplar of all significant virtues and [uses] that as the reason for loving her. . . . [T]he inherent excellence of her total personality . . . elicits his love,"[34] rather than his love eliciting her excellence. In sexual love, the properties of the object obviously play an important role, even if sexual desirability is subjective and some lovers are less discriminating than others. (Note that my term "erosic" is very far from "erotic," even though the structures of both loves are the same.) And in the love of humans for God, the fine qualities of the object, or the belief that God manifests perfection, is the ground of love (see sect. 6).

Romantic love is a special case. Because romantic love is often seen as a historical development of courtly love, it may fall within the eros tradition and have the main features of the first view of personal love: powerful passion for the object is generated by an accurate perception of its goodness or beauty, and the lover realizes that these properties are responsible for the passion. But romantic love may also exhibit features of the second view: it arises (and disappears) mysteriously, incomprehensibly; the lover is not always expected to have reasons for his or her passion; and the lover is only under an illusion that the beloved has attractive properties. Whether romantic love is to be classified with the eros or the agape tradition depends not on the mere fact that x has an illusion about y's having P, but on the relationship between the illusion and x's loving y. If x's loving y leads x to have the illusion that y has P, then romantic love is agapic; but if x has the illusion that y has P and, on the basis of this falsely attributed property, x loves y, then it is erosic. In the first view of personal love, there is no structural difference between x's loving y because x believes truly that y has P, and x's loving y because x believes falsely that y has P, whether the false belief is the result of deliberate deception by y or x's need or desire to believe that y has P.

It is not clear how Stendhalian romantic love in particular is to be understood. Peter Gay apparently would put Stendhalian love within the second view: "[For Stendhal] it is not that all beautiful creatures are loved, but that all loved creatures are beautiful," by which Gay means that x sees y as beautiful because x loves y.[35] Stendhal's statement that "from the moment he falls in love even the wisest man no longer sees anything *as it really is*"[36] would confirm Gay's impression, except for the fact that the passage leaves open the possibility that the love was earlier secured in a property-based fashion and only later encouraged "overvaluation." When Stendhal wrote that the lover will discover *new* perfections,[37] he seems to mean that x, already loving y in a property-based way, will find additional value in y. Furthermore, he also claims that admiration and other positive appraisals (for example, "how delightful it would be to kiss her") precede love,[38] in which case love itself does not generate all positive appraisals of the beloved.[39] Admiration is a property-based emotion, and if it plays a role in the genesis of romantic love, then love, too, is property-based.[40] Another issue is whether, for Stendhal, the discovery of new perfections by the lover is psychologically unsound (the result of deluded imagination or of wish fulfillment). There is no denying his remark that once x loves y, x "no longer sees" y as she "really" is. Although Irving Singer recognizes that this statement suggests psychological infirmity in the lover,[41] he argues that Stendhal had something else in mind: "The lover experiences no illusion in the sense of mistaken judgment: he merely refuses to limit his appreciative responses to what the rest of the world declares beautiful. . . . [T]he lover's act of imagination consists in bestowing value upon attributes of the beloved that he *knows* are not beautiful."[42] That x finds P in y to be valuable just because x loves y does not mean x is guilty of a cognitive mistake or psychological foul-up. As a result of loving y, x may merely imagine that y has attractive properties and be blind to y's defects (perhaps x rationalizes, seeking an ex post facto justification for loving y). But, more so-berly, x may deliberately bestow value on y or on y's properties because x loves y, without being driven by neurotic processes. After all, if God bestows value on otherwise unworthy creatures, in virtue of His love for them, God would not be accused of making a cognitive mistake or of being the victim of a vicious psychological mechanism. Hence, as Singer argues, a Stendhalian lover may confer value upon the beloved unsuspiciously. And this may happen whether the love is or is not property-based.

5. DERIVATIVE FEATURES OF LOVE

While arguing that personal love is adequately understood within the eros tradition, that we need not appeal to elements of the agape tradition to salvage personal love, I shall also argue that personal love should not be pictured as constant, exclusive, and reciprocal. Conceiving of personal love as axiomatically, constitutively, or by definition constant, exclusive, or reciprocal, or insisting that only genuine personal love is any of these, is a mistake; these features must be viewed as derivative. By this I mean three things. First, constancy, exclusivity, and reciprocity are contingent features of personal love; some cases of love will be constant, exclusive, or reciprocal, others not. Second, one goal of a theory of love is to explain why these features are present, when they are present. Constancy, exclusivity, and reciprocity are the *explananda* of a theory of love, not the fundamental *explanans*. Third, these features are to be derived logically from more basic features of love; they are not part of the definition of love.[43] Of course, we shall investigate exactly what constancy, exclusivity, and reciprocity are, and explore the logical relations among them.

To argue that constancy, exclusivity, and reciprocity are not axiomatic of love is to defend the first view of personal love against various objections. A common charge made against the eros tradition is that it does not secure any of these features of love. Briefly, a property-based love, so the story goes, will exist only as long as the beloved possesses her attractive properties; an erosic lover who responds to P in y will also respond to P in z and thus will not love y exclusively; and if both x and y are concerned only with merit, nothing guarantees that when x loves y, y also loves x. Failing to secure constancy, exclusivity, and reciprocity is a disadvantage of an account of personal love, however, only if these features are constitutive. Further, there may be ways of construing erosic love so that it does secure some constancy and so on. Finally, agapic personal love may not exhibit much exclusivity; if so, the second view of personal love will not fare any better in this regard than the first view. For example, Kierkegaard claims that "Christianity's . . . task is man's likeness to God. But God is love; therefore we can resemble God only in loving. . . . Insofar as you love [only] your beloved, you are not like unto God, for in God there is no partiality."[44] If God's agape extends to all humans, and if Christian neighbor-love, as a copy of God's agape, extends to all people without partiality, then any attempt to fit personal love within the agape tradition will have difficulty securing exclusivity.

None of this has any bearing on another disagreement between the eros and the agape traditions. I said above that in the first view personal love was object-centric, and in the second view subject-centric. I used these terms to describe the relative emphasis these views put on the object and the subject as the ground of love. But it is often claimed, against eros and in favor of agape, that the former is subject-centric in a different sense: one who loves erosically is egocentric or loves because doing so benefits her, while one who loves agapically is concerned with benefiting the beloved (hence agape, in this different sense, is object-centric). This charge must be taken seriously (see chap. 12). Does personal love include concern or benevolence in some form? If so, should concern be treated axiomatically or as derivative? Does the first view of personal love have sufficient resources to overcome the accusation that it portrays love as egocentric?

6. THE HUMAN LOVE FOR GOD

Suppose that by our psychological nature personal love was property-based and reason-dependent: we could love in no other way than on the basis of attractive properties. Or suppose that even if loving this way is not psychologically determined, people preferred to love, and to be loved, on the basis of attractive properties. Also suppose that people desire that the most important love experience in their life be reciprocal, constant, and exclusive. The problem is that these suppositions do not fit comfortably together. I do not mean that humans cannot hope both that their loves be property-based, on the one hand, and constant, exclusive, and reciprocal, on the other. Rather, it may not be possible to satisfy both desires. Let us imagine the worst. If x loves y on the basis of y's S, the love will be reciprocated only if y perceives valuable T in x; whether that occurs may be a matter of x's dumb luck. If x loves y on the basis of y's S, then why should y expect any constancy in x's love? A plain fact of human life is that we are always changing. The constancy of a property-based love is continually threatened not only by y's losing S, but also by x's no longer finding S valuable. And if x loves y on the basis of y's S, why expect any exclusivity from x when it is plain that other candidates for x's love have S or even have S to a higher degree?

Perhaps these difficulties explain why in the eros tradition we are often admonished to turn our attention away from the transient, physical aspects of human beings and toward their supposedly permanent, valuable properties— for example, their goodness or their souls. Hence, Pausanias in Plato's *Symposium* distinguishes "vulgar" from "heavenly" eros. But this solution is not radical enough, for no human is an adequate object of erosic love. "All luv is lost bot upone God allone,"[45] the point being that if we are going to abandon "vulgar" eros for "heavenly" eros, we should go whole hog and attend instead to God, love's only suitable object.[46] Indeed, the love that humans have for God may be the paradigm case of erosic love, because with God as its object eros is relatively problem-free.[47] In loving God, humans can focus exclusively on one object in virtue of its incomparable objective value. God has no defects that interfere with His attractiveness. God does not change or lose His perfections, and He is always available as an object of love. "It is wrong that anyone should become attached to me," writes Pascal, "even though they do so gladly and of their own accord. I should be misleading those in whom I aroused such a desire, for I am no one's goal nor have I the means of satisfying anyone. Am I not ready to die? Then the object of their attachment will die."[48] Pascal draws the conclusion: love God, who never dies.[49] Further, when God is the object, love is constantly reciprocated,[50] and all the emotional turmoils and psychological disasters of loving humans are avoided. Listen to St. Augustine:

> I went to Carthage. . . . I had not yet fallen in love, but I was in love with the idea of it, and this feeling that something was missing made me despise myself for not being more anxious to satisfy the need. I began to look around for some object for my love, since I badly wanted to love something. . . . [A]lthough my real need was for you, my God, . . . I was not aware of this hunger. . . . To love and to have my love returned was my heart's desire, and it would be all the sweeter if I could also enjoy the body of the one who loved me. . . . [I] fell in love. . . . My love was returned and finally shackled me in the bonds of its consummation. In the midst of my joy I was caught up in the coils of trouble, for I was lashed with the cruel, fiery rods of jealousy and suspicion, fear, anger, and quarrels.[51]

Although Robert Graves does not draw the conclusion that God is the only object suitable for erosic love, he repeats Augustine's wisdom for the twentieth century: "Love is a universal migraine."[52]

The lover of God, however, must make a concession in return for the unconditionality, constancy, and reciprocity of this love relationship: she must not hope for being loved exclusively or with special affection by the object of her love; she may love God with all her heart and soul erosically, but the love returned by God is nonpartial agape. Another problem is that because God is not merely the object most worthy of love, but the only object worthy of love, the love that a human has for God could entice humans away from meaningful, even if imperfect, relationships with other humans. Pascal seemed to recognize and rejoice in that consequence. But this rivalry between humans and God for the erosic loving attention of a person cuts both ways. The other reason that is commonly given for abandoning the love for humans in favor of the love for God is that eros for humans succeeds too well, rather than not well enough. Being powerfully in love with another person substitutes one devoted love in the place of a love for the only proper object of devotion. Even if one's erosic love for a human being does not fare well, even if it does not live up to its promise, the anticipated joys it brings to mind can tempt us away from God (as Augustine tells us). Some have suggested that loving God is fully satisfied as soon as one genuinely, agapically, loves one's neighbor.[53] Would it not be a convenient way of resolving the rivalry if loving humans erosically, instead, somehow exhausted what it meant to love God?

Note that if loving the Christian God is the most satisfying erosic love that humans can experience, that satisfaction cannot be attained through Plato's eros. The desire to possess the Good and the Beautiful eternally is fulfilled at the highest stage of the Ascent; the Forms in their constancy and perfection provide the most worthy objects of love, and the bliss of apprehending this perfection is infinite. Yet something is missing that comes with loving the personal God of Christianity: reciprocity. Nevertheless, note how much Andrew Greeley sounds like Plato: "The difference between God and Jessica Lange is not that God is less sensuous (less attractive to the human senses) but more. Ms. Lange's appeal, impressive as it is, is but a hint of the appeal of Ultimate Grace."[54] Thus, the similarity between a heavenly eros for God and a heavenly eros for a Platonic Form suggests that if Christianity wanted to make a total break with pagan philosophy, postulating that God (in contrast to the Forms) loves humans agapically may not be enough. What might be needed in addition is the doctrine that not even the love of humans for God is erosic. The most radical move is to jettison eros altogether in any relation between humans and God.

Conceiving of the human love for God as erosic is objectionable exactly for the reasons that Pascal recommended an erosic love for God. Loving God erosically, in virtue of the perfections that God has but humans lack, is merely to direct a human-type love toward God because that love cannot be satisfied by humans; it is a love directed at God just because it will be satisfied. This is a poor reason for loving God, but what is the alternative? Abelard, I think, tried to make the human love for God a species of agape: "Since loving God for his sake meant loving him regardless of rewards, Abelard argued that to love God properly one had to renounce even the desire for beatitude. . . . God must not be loved *because of any desire* for beatitude. Loving God should enable us to renounce *everything* for his sake—including the search for goodness."[55] No longer motivated by any anticipated happiness, the love for God in Abelard loses its odor of egocentricity. Yet there are enormous problems in thinking of the love of humans for God as agape, as was recognized by Abelard's predecessors. Paul, for example, "shr[a]nk from applying the term Agape" to man's love for God; "to do so would suggest that man possessed an independence and spontaneity over against God, which in reality he does not."[56] How, further, is a human able to bestow value on God, which is a central feature of agape? Finally, if agape involves self-sacrificial benevolence for the good of others (for example, the Crucifixion), how could a human act for the good of a God that is self-sufficient?[57]

For these reasons, Nygren developed an alternative account of the human love for God. Nygren's view is interesting because, even though for him the human love for God is not exactly agape (nor is it eros), it falls within the second view of love. The concept employed by Nygren is *pistis* (faith), which "includes in itself the whole devotion of love,"[58] for example, surrender to God and obedience "without any thought of reward."[59] But the most important aspect of *pistis* is that it is "a response, . . . it is reciprocated love."[60] Man is not to love God because He is great, that is, "more desirable than all other objects of desire. . . . He is simply not to be classed with any objects of desire whatsoever."[61] Nor is man to love God because doing so is more satisfying "than anything else." *Pistis,* as man's love for God, "is only his response to God's love for him. . . . Man loves God . . . because God's un-motivated love has overwhelmed him and taken control of him, so that he cannot do other than love God."[62] How is this a second-view interpretation of the human love for God? The obvious point is that the human being loves God just because God loves the human, not because the human responds to God's merit. Further, since God loves the human not for any reason invoking human merit, but because God is love or because God's nature is to love, the reciprocal love between God and human exemplifies the full inexplicable circle permitted only by the second view. Note that Nygren claims that the human's love for God is caused by God's love for the human, not that God's loving the human is the human's reason for loving God. Since God's love is the nonreason-cause of the human love for God, the following scenario is possible. While God's love causes the human to love God, the human may falsely *believe* that she loves God because God is great, and the human offers His greatness as her reason for loving God. Since this reason is not really why she loves God, her love for God is the nonideal version of second-view love described under category (B) in section 2.

Paul Tillich, perhaps with Nygren in mind, defends our initial erosic interpretation of the human love for God: "Without the *eros* towards truth, theology would not exist, and without the *eros* towards the beautiful no ritual expressions would exist. Even more serious is the rejection of the *eros* quality of love with respect to God. The consequence of this rejection is that love towards God becomes an impossible concept to be replaced by obedience to God."[63] He adds, contrary to Nygren, that "obedience is not love. It can be the opposite of love." Earlier I said that our central question might be formulated: Is the love that a human has for a human (personal love) more like the love of a human for God (eros) or more like the love of God for humans (agape)? But in light of this dispute among Augustine, Pascal, Nygren, and Tillich, if I were writing a different book the central question might be formulated: Is the human love for God more like the love of a human for another human (eros), more like the love of God for humans (agape), or is it something else? Nevertheless, this excursion into theology does more than illuminate the differences between the two traditions; it also suggests a question relevant to personal love. When Nygren uses the expression "Man is not to love God because . . . ," he (unintentionally) stimulates us to wonder whether humans could choose to love God either erosically or agapically (or pistiscally), and whether only one of these is the best way of loving God.[64] Accounts of the human love for God may not be describing the love for God; rather, they might be laying down what the love for God should be, in a moral or nonmoral sense of "should." We must keep in mind, then, that accounts of personal love may similarly be evaluative (see 6.4).

One final point. If the problems in the eros tradition mentioned above (for example, the tension between property-basedness and constancy) have suggested that remaining within the eros tradition entails loving God instead of humans, they have also suggested that if we want humans to be the objects of personal love, our loves must be fashioned to be consistent with the agape tradition. "Would it not be sadder still, and still more confusing, if love . . . should be only a curse because its demand could only make it evident that none of us is worth loving, instead of love's being recognized precisely by its *loving enough to be able to find* some loveableness in all of us," writes Kierkegaard.[65] This love is possible, he tells us, only because the lover "bring[s] a certain something with him," that is, only if the source of love is the lover himself. Given that "no one is worthy to be loved" (Oscar Wilde, *De*

Profundis), an erosic love will never get off the ground, or if it does it will soon come crashing down. Or even if humans have sufficient merit to warrant being loved, the fact that love occurs in virtue of changeable and repeatable merit implies a corresponding fragility in our loves. A dose of agape, so the story goes, must be added to erosic love to keep it flying; or the eros style must be repudiated altogether in favor of the agape style, if we want a satisfying love or, more ambitiously, the ideal love that is constant, exclusive, and reciprocal. I intend to refute this view about personal love.

7. RECONCILING EROS AND AGAPE

Accounts of personal love in the agape tradition are prevalent among contemporary philosophers. For example, at the beginning and end of his three-volume history of the idea of love, Irving Singer presents his own theory of love.[66] In arriving at his view about the nature of love, Singer embraces the metaphilosophical principle that "explaining the occurrence of love is not the same as explicating the concept. The conditions for love are not the same as love itself" (vol. 1, p. 13). Hence, the causal antecedents of love are not to be mentioned while "explicating the concept" of love. Clearly, I am meta-philosophically at odds with Singer: I have distinguished the two views of love by their different outlooks on the basis of love; a thesis about the explanatory ground of love is central to these accounts of personal love and must figure, therefore, into their respective concepts. Eros-style loves are not merely con-tingently based on the merits of the object; love's being property-based is part of the concept of erosic love. Similarly, love's not being property-based is part of the concept of agapic love. The point is that Singer's metaphilosophical principle rules out the eros tradition in advance as an adequate theory of personal love. How could erosic love ever be defined if the conditions of love must be kept distinct from love itself?

In Singer's analysis, all love includes, as a necessary condition, the be-stowal of value (vol. 3, p. 390). "In the love of persons," Singer writes, "people bestow value upon one another over and beyond their . . . objective value" (vol. 1, p. 6). And even more strongly, "love bestow[s] value without calculation. It confers importance no matter *what* the object is worth" (vol. 1, p. 10). Further, "loving another as a person means bestowing value upon his personality even if it is not virtuous" (vol. 1, p. 94); "love is a way of . . . over-coming negative appraisals" (vol. 1, p. 10).[67] This love sounds like agape or neighbor-love: for Singer, x bestows value on y even if y is not meritorious, or x bestows value on a meritorious y but not in virtue of that merit. Indeed, when Singer writes, "That love might be a way of bestowing value *upon* the object, taking an interest in it regardless of how good or bad it may be—this conception is as foreign to Aristotle as it was to Plato" (vol. 1, p. 90), he is in effect repeating Gregory Vlastos' criticism of the erosic loves of Aristotle and Plato,[68] the Vlastos who advances agapic love as the correct alternative (see 13.5). One might suspect that Singer is simply explicating agape and not offering an account of personal love. But he is certainly attempting primarily to shed light on that phenomenon: "Through [love] one human being affirms the significance of another. . . . But the beloved . . . is not static: she is fluid, changing, undefinable—*alive*" (vol. 1, p. 8). "To love a woman . . . is to desire her for the sake of values that appraisal might discover, and yet to place one's desires within a context that affirms her importance regardless of these values" (vol. 1, p. 6).

The preceding sentence suggests that Singer is analyzing personal love not as purely agapic, but as a reconciliation of eros and agape: personal love involves both a response to perceived value and a bestowal of value that occurs independently of perceived value. He writes, "Love is related to both [bestowal and appraisal]; they interweave in it. Unless we appraised we could not bestow a value that goes beyond appraisal; and without bestowal there would be no love" (vol. 1, p. 9). But to claim that appraisal is necessary for bestowal, and therefore for love, seems to contradict Singer's assertion that the lover bestows value "without calculation [and] no matter *what* the object is worth." How can appraisal be necessary if love, by including bestowal, can exist when the object has no merit or when the object's merit is irrelevant? "Love is a bestowal of value which supplements, and sometimes overrides, our attitudes of appraisal," he says (vol. 3, p. 393). In another passage Singer does claim that love is "primarily bestowal and only secondarily appraisal" (vol. 1, p. 13), but this is vague and hardly looks like a reconciliation of eros and agape. The issue is, in what way is appraisal, for Singer, operative in love? There are, based on what Singer has written, three different interpretations.

Singer comments on the song "Because You're You" by Henry Blossom:

> Not that you are fair, dear
> Not that you are true,
> Not your golden hair, dear,
> Not your eyes of blue.
> When we ask the reason,
> Words are all too few!
> So I know I love you, dear,
> Because you're you.

Singer rejects the reason offered in the last line (reminiscent of Montaigne's):

"[The song] seems to assert that the sheer *identity* of the beloved brings love into being. And this, I think, is highly implausible" (vol. 1, p. 150).[69] Loving "the lady *because* she's she" is "quite different" from the "bestowal over and beyond appraisal" (vol. 1, p. 149) that is a necessary component of love. For our purposes, Singer's remark about the last line of the song is important: it "makes it sound as if the delicacy of her complexion . . . had nothing to do with his loving her, which is most unlikely." He continues: "If all these endearing young charms were to vanish and fade away, would not the greatest of human loves vanish with them? We have every reason to think so, unless the lover cultivated new needs and desires." This amounts to saying (the first interpretation) that appraisal—finding valuable properties in the object—is essential for personal love, a necessary condition for humans to bestow value: "Wholly nonappraisive love is foreign to human nature" (vol. 3, p. 391). Apparently, Singer agrees with the eros tradition about the ground of love even though he insists again (among these passages) that the explication of the concept of love must not mention this fact. Yet, as we have seen, claiming that x bestows value on y only if x already perceives value in y contradicts the claim that the bestowal of value is independent of such evaluations. The very idea of agape is the idea of a love that is not grounded in the attractiveness of its object; hence claiming that appraisal is necessary for human personal love is not to reconcile the two traditions.

Perhaps this is why Singer occasionally claims (the second interpretation) that positive appraisal plays a facilitatory role in the genesis of bestowal: "For most men it is easier to bestow value upon a beautiful rather than an ugly woman" (vol. 1, p. 23); "by disclosing an excellence . . . appraisal . . . makes it easier for us to appreciate" the other person (vol. 1, p. 10).[70] His point might be that bestowal does not strictly require antecedent positive appraisal; bestowal after such an appraisal is merely psychologically "easier," and bestowals without positive appraisal are not impossible but only "unlikely" (vol. 1, p. 149). But to attempt to reconcile agape and eros by claiming that appraisal plays a facilitatory but not essential role in love is not convincing. If appraisal sometimes plays a role this means at best that some cases of personal love are erosic while other cases are agapic, not that personal love is a reconciliation in all its cases.

The third interpretation is that the bestowal of value occurs without positive appraisal. "In some circumstances the bestowing of value will happen more easily than in others; but *whenever* it happens, it happens as a new creation of value and exceeds all attributes of the object that might be thought to elicit it" (vol. 1, p. 13). The "whenever" here suggests that love can arise independently of any positive appraisal. Indeed, Singer seems to advance seriously this radical thesis: "Nothing can elicit bestowals" (vol. 1, p. 154). He continues, "Either [bestowals] come or they don't. This is the spontaneity in love, as it is in persons. Both defy our rational calculations." In this third interpretation, Singer's account of love is squarely within the second view of personal love. God, we can suppose, loves humans for no reason; His love is a sheer gift. And this is precisely what love's bestowal of value is, even when done by humans: "Love is sheer gratuity" (vol. 1, p. 15), hence love has no erosic basis. "It issues from the lover like hairs on his head." If so, love is a "sheer gratuity" and "spontaneous" in whatever sense hairs grow gratuitously and spontaneously. Nothing, apparently, about either the subject or the object figures into the ground of love, except that the lover's nature is to grow hair. Does this help us to understand these statements: "We instinctively bestow value upon persons . . . regardless of their utility" (vol. 2, p. 339), and "the act of bestowing is neither rational nor irrational. It is nonrational, and probably instinctual" (vol. 3, p. 158)? Consider how Singer describes God's love in similar terms: "Agapē is . . . spontaneous. It simply radiates, like the glorious sun or the universe at large, giving forth energy for no apparent reason" (vol. 1, p. 275).[71]

However, because Singer so often insists that appraisal plays a role in love ("appraisal may lead on to a further bestowal" [vol. 1, p. 10]), perhaps we should propose an account of love within the eros tradition that incorporates Singer's notion of bestowal. Love, in this proposal, would be defined as the property-based bestowal of value (this love is erosic, not a reconciliation), which is consistent with Singer's claim that "love would not be love unless appraising were accompanied by the bestowing of value" (vol. 1, p. 10). Singer should be open to the suggestion that "a property-based bestowal of value" is superior (as an account of personal love) to "an ungrounded bestowal of value," given his frequent assertions about the human psychological tendency to bestow value only after positive appraisal. Indeed, because he eventually asserts that "appraisal [is] a major ingredient within love, and not merely . . . a *causal* condition. . . . [T]he appraisive element [is] an ever-present constituent of love" (vol. 3, p. 394), Singer apparently agrees that love should be understood erosically as "a property-based bestowal of value." He refuses, however, to recognize the implications of his now calling appraisal a "constituent" of personal love, for he still insists that "in its mere definition love is not bound by any degree of worth in the object" (vol. 3, p. 402). But remember that Singer's metaphilosophical principle leads him to exclude only causal conditions from the analysis of love, but not its constituents; and he has just claimed that appraisal is "not merely . . . a causal condition." What would keep Singer from including this constituent of love, appraisal, in its definition? His argument seems to be that even though "human beings do not have this capacity," nevertheless "it is logically possible for love to bestow itself on an object that has no other worth" (vol. 3, p. 402), for we can imagine a being (the Christian God) that bestows value independently of appraisal.[72] But, then, appraisal is not a "constituent" of love after all, or it is a constituent only of personal love.

There is a deeper point to be made about Singer's claim that "in its mere definition love is not bound by any degree of worth in the object," that is, his insistence that appraisal is not part of the definition of love because "it is logically possible" to bestow independently of appraisal. His account of love amounts, as a result, to the thesis that all love involves, as a necessary common denominator, the bestowal of value (and not necessarily anything more than this). Hence, it is not unreasonable to think of God's agape for humans—the love that motivates Singer to exclude appraisal from the definition of love—as the paradigm case of love in Singer's view. Further, the claim that all love necessarily involves bestowal can be seen, because of its generality, as an umbrella account of love that applies to all cases. Thus, we could employ this umbrella account to analyze other loves, for example, parental love, the love of chocolate, patriotism; if these are genuine loves, they will all exhibit a bestowal of value even though they will be distinguishable by different causal conditions and, perhaps, by different effects. (In loving chess, the chess lover bestows value on the game beyond its perceived merit.) Singer's treatment of the human love for God confirms this interpretation: "God bestows value in loving man despite his imperfections. Man bestows value [on God] in recognizing the infinite goodness of God and delighting in it. They reciprocate within a community of bestowals" (vol. 1, p. 215). Again: "The Christians, who say God is perfect, believe that his being the creator gives a sufficient reason for man to love him. But creativity is no more reason than anything else. If the pious man loves God, he does so by bestowing a gratuitous value—as love always does" (vol. 1, p. 246). "As love always does" demonstrates that Singer, having analyzed all love as necessarily including the bestowal of value, must claim that even the human love for God includes bestowal.

Singer, then, runs into the same trouble that Plato does. The story about Plato usually goes like this: Plato's umbrella definition is that love is the desire to possess eternally the Good and the Beautiful. That is, love for a *thing*—the Form of the Good or the Beautiful—is the paradigm case of love. Hence, Plato must analyze even personal love as a case of loving only a thing. Thus, for Plato, when x loves y, x is loving only the beautiful properties (things) of y. Personal love is assimilated to the love of things, as being not essentially different from loving beautiful laws and theorems. The story concludes: to conceive of personal love in this way is to make a ghastly mistake. Singer, by analogy, is stuck with the disastrous result that the human love for God must be conceived of as including the bestowing of value on God by humans. But is it coherent to speak of humans bestowing value on God? (Recall sect. 6, above.) Consider again: "Man bestows value [on God] in recognizing the infinite goodness of God." Shouldn't Singer have written here, "Man positively appraises God in recognizing his infinite goodness"? "Recognizing the infinite goodness of God" becomes, for Singer, not an appraisal but a bestowal. But this expands unmercifully the notion of bestowal.

Singer eventually claims that he has driven too wide a wedge between bestowal and appraisal: "All appraisals must ultimately depend on bestowal since [appraisals] presuppose that human beings give importance to the satisfying of their needs and desires. Without such bestowal nothing could take on value of any sort. As a result, the two categories are not wholly separable" (vol. 3, p. 393). Thus, in personal love, x bestows value on y, the cause of x's love for y normally being x's positive appraisal of y; and x's positive appraisal of y depends on x's antecedent bestowal of value on x's desires that are satisfiable by these positively appraised properties in y. Hence, the bestowal of value occurs at two places in love—x bestows value on y (the top level), and x bestows value on x's desires (the deep level)—with appraisal sandwiched between.[73] Note that in this complex picture, the top-level bestowal is erosically grounded, while the deeper bestowal is ungrounded. (Singer never claims that the deeper bestowal is somehow dependent on a deeper appraisal. Hence, it must be spontaneous.) I believe Singer is right that an ungrounded bestowal of value must occur somewhere in love, but I will argue (13.9) that (1) x's bestowal of value on y is not the ungrounded bestowal of love, and (2) at the deepest level x bestows value on y's properties, not on x's desires. Claim (1) denies that personal love is best understood as an agapic phenomenon; the goal, then, is to explain how claim (2) is consistent with the eros tradition.

8. MILL'S DEDICATION

Let us return to John's praise of Harriet (see the epigraph). We can ask whether:

a. John loved Harriet because he believed truly that she possessed the fine qualities mentioned in the dedication;
b. John loved Harriet because he believed falsely that she had those fine qualities;

c. John found some of Harriet's qualities valuable because he loved her in virtue of her possessing other attractive properties; or

d. John found valuable qualities in Harriet only because he loved her (period), or because she loved him.

Which is true? According to Gertrude Himmelfarb, Mill's contemporaries "could only suppose that Mill was so besottedly in love with [Harriet] as to mistake her intellectual pretensions for intellectual distinction"—which suggests either (d) or a dismal version of (c). Himmelfarb also tells us that "Carlyle remembered [Harriet] as 'full of unwise intellect, asking and re-asking stupid questions,'"[74] which suggests (b). But was not Mill acquainted with Shakespeare's *Sonnet 17*?

> Who will believe my verse in time to come
> If it were filled with your most high deserts?
>
> .   .   .   .
>
> The age to come would say "This poet lies,
> Such heavenly touches ne'er touched earthly faces."
> So should my papers, yellowed with their age,
> Be scorned, like old men of less truth than tongue,
> And your true rights be termed a poet's rage
> And stretchèd meter of an antique song.

Yet Himmelfarb, though no fan of Harriet, did not belittle Mill as well; he "could attribute to his wife a large share in [*On Liberty's*] conception and composition, knowing that that attribution, however often and explicitly stated, would be largely discounted by his readers."[75] If Mill had enough wits to realize that, perhaps there is more truth in claim (a) than historians are pleased to admit.

I do not know which alternative is correct; but the example of Mill-Taylor shows why I would rather do philosophy. We cannot understand what is at stake in necessarily ambiguous examples until we do philosophy. Historical research into the Mill-Taylor relationship may explain why Mill praised Harriet in such fancy terms in the dedication. We might learn something from the fact that John never wrote "I love Harriet because she's Harriet." (But did he think it?) The problem is not only that in Mill-Taylor several of the alternatives may have been true at different times or that real examples are messy because they are real. The problem is also that, given any body of knowledge about Mill-Taylor, we could perceive John as loving Harriet either erosically or agapically, and this "underdetermination" of psychobiographical truth by the facts means we cannot rely heavily on examples to answer our intellectual questions. Even if John did write, in a still well-hidden diary, "I love Harriet, but I know not why. Probably because she's she, as Montaigne would have it," that would not necessarily tell us anything about his love for her, or about anyone else's love. Nor would it help us to make the distinctions relevant to the philosophy of love or to sort out the concepts that require analysis.

CHAPTER 2   *Love at Second Sight*

At our first meeting, . . . we found ourselves so taken with each other, . . . so
bound together, that from that time on nothing was so close to us as each
other.

                                                   —Montaigne, "Of Friendship"

Martha is mine, the sweet girl of whom everyone speaks with admiration,
who despite all my resistance captivated my heart at our first meeting, the girl
I feared to want and who came towards me with high-minded confidence.

                                          —Freud (letter to Martha Bernays, 1882)

1. GELLNER'S PARADOX

In a paper devoted to comparing existentialist and Kantian ethics, E. A.
Gellner begins by asking, "Is love at first sight *possible?*"[1] While sitting in his
dentist's waiting room perusing women's magazines, Gellner found that articles on love at first sight assumed it existed, the major question addressed being
empirical: How often does it occur? But for Gellner the issue is "in part or
wholly logical" (p. 158) rather than empirical; to support his suspicion he
constructed an a priori argument designed to show that love at first sight was
impossible (pp. 158–163). I will lay out in detail Gellner's argument that love
at first sight is as logically impossible as a round square (not that it is only
contingently nonexistent, like the unicorn). Because it throws into sharp relief
the problems attributed to erosic loves, Gellner's argument will haunt us on
almost every page.

Imagine that a person x has an encounter with a person y, the first contact
of any kind between them. (Gellner does not specify the length of this meeting
or what transpires between x and y.) We might even suppose that the encounter is at a distance and that x only catches sight of y without talking with y.[2]
After or during this encounter, x experiences some emotion, a feeling, or an
attitude toward y. (Gellner uses these terms interchangeably.) Also assume
that x's emotion arises in virtue of x's "noticing" a set S of y's attractive
properties. We can understand this in several ways. Does "x notices S in y"
mean that x correctly perceives S in y; that x falsely believes that y has S, either

because x hopes that y has S or because y pretends to have S; or that x perceives S in y only unconsciously? To get to the heart of Gellner's argument (Gellner does not say what he means by "x notices S in y"), let us assume that x consciously and correctly perceives that y has S, and x realizes that S is responsible for x's emotion. The unnamed emotion that x has, then, is property-based or reason-dependent.

Once we assume that x has an attitude toward y (xAy) because x notices a set S of y's properties, "first encounter" can be understood in two ways: we might be talking about (A) the emotion x has after x's first encounter *tout court* with y or (B) the emotion x has after the encounter with y at which x first notices S. Alternative (B) allows that x had earlier encounters with y during which x did not notice S and so did not experience any emotion toward y. But I am sure that Gellner means (A), in which "first sight" is meant literally. Alternative (B) is more complex and suggests a different phenomenon: x knows y, perhaps even loves y for some time, and x suddenly realizes that she loves y or suddenly notices that y has S and is quite lovable.

Suppose that some time after meeting and responding to y, x meets another person z. We are asked by Gellner to assume something interesting about z: he or she also has the set S that y has. Persons y and z, however, are not altogether identical; we assume only that x notices in z the same set S that x noticed in y and in virtue of which x has the emotion toward y. (We might be tempted to assume that z has no additional property P (beyond S), a property so annoying to x that S in z cannot have its effect on x; but to assume this only about z is wrong. Both y and z must lack this P, if S in y or S in z is to elicit x's emotion. We can include "lacks all such annoying properties" in the set S that both y and z have.) The likelihood that x will have an encounter with this relevantly similar z cannot be ruled out; after all, x noticed S in y during only one encounter. Now that x has met this similar z, there are only two, mutually exclusive possibilities. Either the emotional response that x had toward y occurs again toward z. Or x does not have that experience again (perhaps x has other feelings toward z, or none at all). Gellner proceeds to argue that the emotion x has toward y cannot be love and hence cannot be love at first sight, whether or not x has the same emotion toward z.

The argument is a classical dilemma and has two horns. First, if upon having the encounter with the relevantly similar z, x does have the emotion toward z that x has toward y, then x's emotion for y is not love. And, second, if x does not have the same experience toward z, then (nevertheless!) x's emotion for y cannot be love. Since there are only two possibilities, and each one implies that x's emotion for y is not love, Gellner's argument shows that it is impossible that the emotion experienced by x after the one encounter with y is love. (Note that Gellner must assume that whether or not x has the same emotion toward z, x is still experiencing the emotion toward y upon meeting z. For if x before meeting z no longer has that feeling toward y, or if during x's encounter with z the feeling evaporates, we might already be able to conclude that x's emotion for y was not love, and the rest of Gellner's argument would be superfluous.)

Our task is to substantiate the claims that if xAy and later xAz (x's unnamed attitude toward y is repeated toward z), then −xLy (the attitude is not love); and that if xAy and later −xAz, then still −xLy. Symbolically, Gellner wants to establish the following, when x notices S in both y and z:

1. (xAy & xAz) → −xLy
   or (xAy & xAz) → −(A = L); and
2. (xAy & −xAz) → −xLy
   or (xAy & −xAz) → −(A = L).

The first horn states that if x's attitude is repeated toward z, x's attitude toward y cannot be love. Gellner's reason is straightforward. Love is conceptually exclusive; it can have "only one object" (p. 159). The "very recurrence" of the attitude toward another person shows that it is not love. If x claims to have the same attitude toward both y and z, then x is wrong to think that the attitude is love; x cannot love both y and z—as a matter not of morality but of conceptual necessity.

Gellner's argument to establish the first horn seems awfully heavy-handed, as if Gellner defines love in advance as exclusive and uses this definition to proclaim that it could not possibly be true that xLy if x's attitude is repeated toward z. Do we not feel inclined to say that whether x's love turns out to be exclusive is an empirical issue? After all, many x's claim to love two people, and defining love as exclusive begs the question against them. Further, Gellner does not indicate clearly what the exclusivity of love means; "very recurrence" and "only one object" do not sufficiently nail down this idea (see chap. 9). Nevertheless, what Gellner is getting at makes good sense. If x meets y at t_1 and experiences A, and then x meets a relevantly similar z at some time t_2 after t_1, again experiencing A, we have good reason to doubt that xLy. (Try t_1 = noon, t_2 = 12:15 P.M.)

Note that Gellner's assumption that z, too, has S is not needed to establish the first horn. If the "very recurrence" of the attitude toward z shows that x does not love y, the exclusivity of love rules out x's loving both y and z even if xAy in virtue of y's having S and xAz in virtue of z's having some other set of properties T. Perhaps assuming that z also has S makes it more likely that x develops the attitude toward z. But assuming that z also has S allows the first horn to be defended independently of a claim about exclusivity—an alternative defense not considered by Gellner. For if x's attitudes toward both y and z are grounded in y's and z's having the same S, then perhaps x merely loves two tokens of the same type (9.10) or loves only S itself and not either y or z (13.5). Rather than appeal to the exclusivity of love to establish the first horn, we could appeal to what it means to "love the person" in some technical sense.

Having argued that if xAz, then it is false that xLy, Gellner seems unable to establish the second horn. After all, if the exclusivity of love entails that if x does have the same emotion toward z and y, then this emotion is not love, then the fact that x does not experience the emotion again when encountering z seems compatible with x's emotion toward y being love. Our friend x has met the z who also has S and has remained attitude-faithful toward y. So why does Gellner claim that even in this case x does not love y? Here is the argument (pp. 159–160):

> The alternative is that X does *not* have the same attitude . . . towards the new possessor of S as he had towards Y. But this equally constitutes conclusive evidence for X not really loving Y. For S is all he knows of Y; if . . . on reëncountering S the original emotion . . . is not reëvoked, this shows that it had not really been connected with its apparent stimulus and object, that it had been accidental, arbitrary, and without any of the significance which one normally attributes to [love].

We assumed that y's having S (or x's noticing S in y) explained xAy. So if x meets z and z also has S, then z's having S (or x's noticing S in z) should produce the same effect. The fact that x does not experience the same feeling toward z when presented with the same situation contradicts that assumption.[3] Hence, y's having S was not responsible for xAy after all. Further, since S fails to evoke xAz, why believe that during x's encounter with z the fact that y has S continues to evoke xAy? Or that S will evoke xAy well after x's encounter with z, or during x's second encounter with y? The fact that S failed to evoke xAz implies that S is not the ground of xAy initially or on a continuing basis. So what? Why conclude that if xAy in virtue of something other than y's having S, x's emotion toward y is not love? The point is that x's emotion toward y is due not to anything about y but to something about x.[4] If the ground of xAy is not y's having S, then y, it turns out, is incidental to the occurrence of x's emotion; and if so, x's emotion is whimsical ("arbitrary") in a way incompatible with its being love. There is no sense, for Gellner, in saying that x loves y unless some tight connection exists between y, or y's having S, and x's emotion. And it is the failure of z's having S to elicit xAz that shows that the required tight connection between y's having S and xAy is lacking. In a word: the second horn is established by assuming that love is property-based and reason-dependent, in which case Gellner's paradox derives from, or pre-supposes, the central thesis of the first view of personal love.

This, then, is Gellner's paradox: it is impossible that xLy after their first encounter, whether or not xAz when x meets the similar z. We might express it this way: if the connection between x's having an emotion and S is tight, then x does not love y because the tightness guarantees that x will also have the emotion toward others who have S; and if the connection between x's emotion and S is not tight (as shown by −xAz), then x does not love y because y's having S is not responsible for x's emotion. No third alternative can be squeezed between a "tight" and a "not tight" connection between x's emotion and S. Either y's having S accounts for xAy, as in the eros tradition, or it does not. And if we assume, as we did in the second horn, that the connection must be tight, then love at first sight is impossible.

2. KNOWLEDGE AND LOVE AT FIRST SIGHT

Gellner's argument is that love at first sight is impossible on the grounds that love is both exclusive and property-based. But there are other arguments against the existence of love at first sight that deserve consideration before we return to Gellner. One argument is that this phenomenon is unlikely because love is necessarily reciprocal (11.2) and during one encounter x's emotion will generally fail in this regard. Another is that love at first sight does not exist because when the phenomenon is occurring it has not yet proven itself to have the constancy required for love. Neither argument is very convincing; relying on claims about the reciprocity and constancy of love (or, as in Gellner, its exclusivity) is like hitting a cockroach with a sledgehammer. More interesting are arguments based on a claim about the relationship between x's knowledge of y and x's emotion toward y. There may be no such thing as love at first sight for any the following reasons: during x's first encounter with y (1) x is not in a position to believe anything about y, (2) x cannot reliably believe anything true about y, or (3) x cannot be believing anything significant (as opposed to trivial) about y. These arguments nip love at first sight in the bud at the place Gellner begins, by raising doubts about x's "noticing" S in y.

Montaigne might be a counterexample to the argument relying on claim (1), for Montaigne said that his love for Boétie was both "at first sight" and not reason-dependent: not only was his love not based on his beloved's properties, but also not possibly based on them. Claim (1), then, does not show that agapic love at first sight, in particular, is impossible; at most it shows that love at first sight cannot be erosic. On the other hand, Montaigne's experience may confirm the argument; he was wrong to call his emotion "love" at that early stage of his relationship with Boétie, just because it occurred at first sight and could not be based on anything about Boétie. To argue that love at first sight does not exist because x could not know anything about y, however, is implausible. I find it difficult to suppose that during a first encounter x has no beliefs about y or y's properties; even if x encounters y only at a distance, x will perceive some of y's properties.

An argument relying on (1) might be what Philip Slater had in mind when he wrote that love at first sight "can only be transference, in the psychoanalytic sense, since there is nothing . . . on which it can be based."[5] Slater's point, however, might not be that love at first sight cannot be based on x's knowledge of y because x could not have any knowledge of this unknown y; rather, he might mean that love at first sight cannot be based on x's knowledge of y because x's emotion is out of proportion to the information x has about y.[6] But let us assume that Slater means that love at first sight is only transference because x could not know anything about y. If so, the real object of x's emotion, for Slater, is not y; the "real object is not [even] the actual parent . . . but a fantasy image of that parent which has been retained, ageless and unchanging, in the unconscious."[7] Slater concludes that romantic love at first sight, being transference, is "Oedipal love," that is, still a kind of love, and hence that love at first sight exists even though disconnected from y, who is not "really" its object. Alternatively, we could say that love at first sight does not exist; it is only transference, not a kind of love at all. This transference is made possible, if not fueled, by the fact that x is not in a position to know anything about y. But neither account is compelling; the most sensible way to understand why x has the emotion now as a result of an encounter with y is to say that x notices some properties S of y, either consciously or unconsciously. Slater's Oedipal love at first sight is not disconnected from y; y's having the S that matches (or conjures in x's mind) the properties of the parent image is exactly why x has the emotion toward y. If y did not have properties approximating the "ageless and unchanging" image of the parent, not even the psychoanalyst could comprehend x's emotion. Slater's psychoanalysis provides a deep explanation of x's emotion: it tells us why S is attractive for x and why x will experience love toward persons having S.

On the other hand, x's not being in a position to know anything about y might allow x to imagine that y has S, and x's strong need to find a parent replacement induces x to do what is possible, so that x merely imagines (falsely) that y has S. Irving Singer interprets the psychoanalytic view this way: "No one can bring back the goddess of his childhood; and since that is how the Freudian lover must envisage his beloved, love can only involve illusion, even delusion."[8] One might argue against love at first sight, then, by relying on claim (2): since x's emotion occurs after one encounter, x cannot believe much that is true of y, in which case x's emotion is not love. But this argument, too, is unconvincing. First, x's having only one encounter with y does not entail that the beliefs and perceptions x does have about y are mostly false. X's beliefs, of course, might be true but incomplete; x sees some good but not yet the bad in y. But x's not having the emotion toward y when x finally sees the bad does not entail that earlier x's emotion was not love (chap. 10). Second, neither the eros nor the agape tradition insists that xLy entails that x has only true beliefs about y. In the eros tradition, the intentionality of love logically permits that xLy in virtue of x's believing falsely that y has P; x's loving y is explained by x's thinking that y has P, and why x thinks that y has P is (in this context) beside the point. The love that x has for y, if based on false beliefs, might be irrational, but it is still love (7.4). And if x's love is based altogether on illusions about y, then y may not be the emotion's object (or x may not be loving y "as a person"; 13.5), but the emotion is still love. In the agape tradition, x's believing falsely that y has P is no impediment to love; since x's love is not based on y's having P, x's believing falsely that y has P is irrelevant. Further, x might know little or nothing about y in the special case of agapic love for the stranger. When we assist the stranger who asks for help, we love her agapically "at first sight," even though we know nothing about her, may even falsely imagine that she is dangerous, or might be deliberately deceived by her as to her actual need.

However, we can interpret agapic love for the stranger not as loving despite having no knowledge about the strange person, but as loving when we do have knowledge. We know nothing in particular about the stranger, but these particularities are trivial. What we know immediately about the stranger is that he is a person, which is the only significant thing about him that we need to know. Erosic love at first sight might not exist, then, because even though x might know much about y, x does not usually know anything significant. Love, in this view, requires that x have not merely true beliefs about y but a deep knowledge of y; and this significant knowledge takes time to obtain.[9] This argument raises questions we will address: Is there a plausible way to distinguish between the beloved's significant and trivial properties? Is a love based on significant properties superior to a love based on the trivial (10.6; 12.9)? This question presupposes that love can be based on trivial properties; indeed, that is a clear empirical fact about personal love, as recognized by Plato's Pausanias. Hence, to argue that love at first sight is not love, because love is grounded in deep knowledge of the object, is too heavy-handed. If there are no a priori limits, or very weak ones, on what properties the lover finds attractive enough to ground love, we may be able to distinguish "bad" from "good" love (for example, vulgar versus heavenly eros) by distinguishing significant from trivial properties. But that is not the difference between loving and not loving.

When Descartes wrote to Chanut (June 6, 1647)[10] about "the reasons which . . . impel us to love one person rather than another before we know their worth," he was clearly asserting that one can love without perfect knowledge; but did Descartes intend "before we know their worth" to mean that x can love y without any beliefs about y, without true beliefs about y's worth, or without knowledge of y's significant (that is, worthful) properties? Regardless, his approach is more Skinnerian than Freudian: "When I was a child, I loved a little girl of my own age, who had a slight squint. The impression made . . . in my brain when I looked at her cross eyes became so closely connected to the simultaneous impression arousing in me the passion of love, that for a long time afterward when I saw cross-eyed persons I felt a special inclination to love them. . . . So, when we are inclined to love someone without knowing the reason [that is, before knowing their worth, which would be a reason], . . . this is because he has some similarity to something in an earlier object of our love, though we may not be able to identify it." Descartes, it seems, is a proponent of the first view of personal love.[11] Love can have both reason-causes (the object's worth) and nonreason-causes that exist in virtue of being psychologically associated with properties that have aroused "the passion of love." To Montaigne Descartes might have said: examine thyself, and you will find reasons and causes plenty for your loving Boetie. Further, Descartes claims not only that nonreason-causes need not remain unconscious (he figured out the influence of squints on his choice of beloveds), but also that nonreason-causes are controllable: "At that time I did not know that was the reason for my love; and as soon as I reflected on it . . . , I was no longer affected by it." The implication is that if Descartes did not wish to love on the basis of such a trivial nonreason-cause as squints, he was not locked into that pattern. Whether one can unencumber oneself of Freudian transference as easily as of Skinnerian associations is another question.

3. THE IMPOSSIBILITY OF LOVE

What, exactly, has Gellner shown to be logically impossible, if anything? There are three candidates: (a) love-at-first-sight; (b) love, at first sight (after one encounter); and (c) love (period). To defend the first horn of his dilemma, Gellner appealed to a claim about love: it is exclusive. I think this claim about love (that is, about love, period) might establish that (b) is impossible, but it does not establish that (a) is impossible; and to the extent Gellner establishes that (b) is impossible, he also shows that (c) is impossible.

We do refer to certain experiences with the words "love at first sight." Many x's have been instantly impassioned by y's with arousing S's, and they are hardly reluctant to call this experience love or love at first sight. One trouble with Gellner's relying on a claim about love (period) is that it prevents us from asking whether love at first sight might nevertheless be a form of love, even if it is not genuine love. And his argument misleadingly implies that there is no such phenomenon as that reported by all these x's; he seems to get an empirical conclusion (like the nonexistence of unicorns) from a priori considerations. (Both these problems also infect the argument that love at first sight does not exist because love requires deep knowledge.) An argument relying on a claim about love (period) touches only the possibility of "love, after one encounter." If we use the hyphenated expression "love-at-first-sight" to refer to x's experience, Gellner's argument does not show that (a) is impossible, only that the expression is a misnomer; we should call it "ψ" or "φ-at-first-sight." That conclusion is conceptual and not empirical; it permits us to concede the existence of the phenomenon and to inquire whether ψ is (vicariously) called love because it often becomes love.

Because Gellner uses a claim about (c), love (period), to show that (b), love after one encounter, is impossible, his argument also shows that (c) is impossible. Inspect the basic pattern of his dilemma:

  i. xAy in virtue of S (A = has an emotion toward)
  ii. xMz who has S (M = has an encounter with)
  iii. either xAz or −xAz
  iv. if xAz, then −xLy (L = loves)
  v. if −xAz, then −xLy

ergo, vi. −xLy

Nothing in this pattern relies essentially on x's emotion toward y arising after their first encounter. If so, Gellner has uncovered a full-blown paradox about love, period. This is an interpretation of his argument I think he intended and would endorse. For when Gellner attempts to solve the paradox, what he proposes encompasses not only love at first sight but also love, period.

Furthermore, there is no way to prevent the extension of the paradox to love, period. For Gellner has not told us what difference there is between xAy after one encounter and xAy after a second encounter. What is special about a second encounter with y that helps x avoid the catch-22 when xMz? How might love at second sight be possible while love at first sight is not? Gellner's dilemma depends only on assuming that x notices S in y and then again in z; whether x and y have had many encounters, or only one, seems irrelevant. Perhaps during a second encounter with y, x notices a larger or different set T of y's properties that is unlikely to be matched by z, and therefore xMz never occurs. But if T includes S, and S elicited xAy initially and still does so, then even though z has only the smaller set S and not the full T, xMz will still occur; that is, x will meet some z with the relevant emotion-eliciting properties. To say, instead, that T does not include S, is to say that after x's second encounter with y, xAy is based on different properties than it was initially; but if so, there is no warrant to suppose that, after the second encounter, xMz will not occur. For if there is a person z who, by having S, relevantly resembles y after the first encounter between x and y, there will also be a person w who, by having T, relevantly resembles y after the second encounter. This sort of answer, then, must say not only that T does include S, but also that the additional properties R in T are partly responsible for xAy after the second encounter (in which case T is sufficient for xAy; S is no longer sufficient but, like R, necessary), and that the additional properties R rule out xMz. Of course, with time x might acquire additional reasons for loving y. But this answer asserts that merely between the first and the second encounter of x and y, y's having S has (mysteriously) lost its power, having been demoted from sufficient for x's emotion to only necessary. We therefore have grounds for thinking (see Gellner's second horn) that S never had that power during the first encounter.

But the spirit of this answer is all wrong. For even if xAy on the basis of a larger set T after the second encounter, x's meeting some w who also has T is not logically ruled out, but only more unlikely than x's meeting some z who has S after x's first encounter with y. Whether Gellner's dilemma succeeds even when applied to x's first encounter with y depends, then, on murky matters of empirical possibility—that is, on how likely it is that x meets the z who also has S. This result is embarrassing to an argument purporting to establish an a priori conclusion. Now, since we have found no meaningful difference attributable to x's second encounter with y, the paradox applies equally to "love at second sight." By a sort of mathematical induction we can modify Gellner's argument against the possibility of love after one encounter into an argument against the possibility of love, period.[12]

4. NONGENERAL LOVE-REASONS

Gellner's solution to the paradox is that love is an "E-type" attitude. Some attitudes and emotions (for example, love, patriotism, religious commitment), according to Gellner, are "puzzling" in the way they attach to objects in a nongeneralizable ("nonuniversalizable") manner. "An agent acting in accordance with an E-type preference" for an object will not act or respond in the same way "with regard to another instance if one turned up" (p.

161). Suppose x notices S in y and on that basis xAy; later x encounters z and again notices S, but −xAz. Gellner claims that xLy after all: the facts −xAz and xLy are compatible because the reason that x has for loving y (namely, that y has S) is not generalizable to other persons. The lover operates according to a nongeneral reason, not according to a reason he would apply to relevantly similar cases. Thus the dilemma is solved by escaping along the second horn. For Gellner, love is reason-dependent, as in the first view of love, yet love is not the sort of emotion for which reasons are generalizable. Gellner does not, however, claim that love-reasons are perfectly nongeneral; his supposition that xLy continues on the basis of y's having S means that, for him, love-reasons are time-generalizable, even if they are not object-generalizable. Note that we could have stated Gellner's dilemma in terms of y's having S being the non-reason-cause for xLy rather than x's reason. Since nonreason-causes are perfectly general given the same initial conditions, S should induce both xAy and xAz, thereby violating the exclusivity requirement of the first horn; while xAy and −xAz, as in the second horn, would show that y's having S was not, after all, the nonreason-cause of xAy. Gellner's solution, that love involves nongeneral reasons, if transformed into a thesis about nonreason-causes, becomes the dramatic assertion that love (or exclusive love) is possible only by a miracle, a disruption of the regularity of causation.

Claiming that love-reasons are not general might seem to be an awful price to pay for a solution to the paradox, for E-type attitudes are irrational—consider the incoherence of "nongeneralizable reason"—in which case love is irrational if it exists at all. On the other hand, perhaps the solution is acceptable, given the result achieved. Denying the generalizability of love-reasons preserves the exclusivity of love at the same time that the basis of love remains the attractiveness of the object. Hence, the solution solves a major difficulty in the eros tradition by explaining how exclusive love is possible. However, concessions have been made; the problem is not merely that Gellner's solution entails that exclusive love is irrational but that it entails that love is necessarily irrational. The blame for love's irrationality falls squarely on the shoulders of x, the lover, for it is x who loves y on the basis of S and who fails to respond to z, or who refuses or is unable to love a similar z, despite having a quite adequate reason (as x himself has proven with respect to y) for doing so.[13] Lovers single out one person who has S to love, while not loving others who also have S, quite because lovers single out love-reasons as nongeneral, even though the logic of reasons requires that all reasons be treated as general. That is, the lover also has an E-type attitude toward love-reasons. (Solving the paradox by jettisoning the rationality of lovers yields this nice advice for beloveds: you remain rational as long as you do not reciprocate the love.)

There are two senses in which a reason might be nongeneral or nongeneralizable. First, a nongeneral reason could be a reason that is simply not applied in a general way by an agent. Nothing in the reason or in the situations encountered by the agent prevents the agent from reapplying the reason; the agent merely does not apply it again in a relevantly similar situation or would resist applying it again. In moral contexts, this failure or resistance is often taken as a blameworthy fault; in practical contexts, it is a sign of inconsistency. If this is the sense in which Gellner means that love-reasons are nonuniversalizable, then either lovers are irrational or the standards governing reasons are greatly relaxed for personal relations (versus morals and pragmatics). Second, a nongeneral reason could be a reason that logically cannot, in light of the form or content of the reason, be generalized to apply to more situations than the one in which it has been used; the reason is temporally or spatially indexed or it refers to a particular person. In moral contexts, offering a reason of this sort is either blameworthy or a violation of the logical requirements of moral discourse. If *this* is the sense in which love-reasons are for Gellner nonuniversalizable, then either the lover is guilty of a different kind of fault (for example, including a proper name in a reason) or love, unlike morality, permits indexed reasons. Gellner, I think, slides back and forth between these two senses of nonuniversalizable. Although some of his remarks imply that he favors the second meaning, the first meaning is more consistent with his treatment of love. Since in "y's having S" it is "having S," and not the fact that it is y who has S, that is x's reason for loving y, x's reason is not nonuniversalizable by including y's name; and "has S" is as generalizable (in the second sense) as a reason could be. Gellner never hints that Montaigne's "because it was he" is the sort of love-reason he has in mind.

In explaining how love is an E-type emotion, Gellner draws an analogy with patriotism (p. 160): if x is a loyal patriot of country C that has property set T (a great, freedom-loving country), x will not be a patriot of another country were it also to have T; likewise, if x loves y on the basis of S, x will not love another person who also has S. This analogy is supposed to reveal the essential feature of E-type attitudes: the reason x has for the attitude is nonuniversalizable in the sense that x is not prepared to apply it to another, relevantly similar object. The analogy between personal love and patriotism seems right to the point because patriotism is often conceived of as a kind of love. But notice that the patriot's reason might be, instead, nonuniversalizable in the second sense; the x who loves her country might give the reason "it is my country." By analogy, then, the lover's reason for xLy would be "y is mine" or "y is my beloved," which is either no reason at all or a poor one.

Gellner later (pp. 161–162) makes some remarks about the E-type patriot that further obscure the analogy. If x is a patriot of country C_1, says Gellner, then x cannot admit that some person w is justifiably a patriot of another country C_2. (If x is a patriot of C_1 because "it is my country," x will not allow w to defend her patriotism toward C_2 with "it is my country.") Patriotism, that is, exhibits another sort of nonuniversalizability. If x is a C_1 patriot, x cannot be a C_2 patriot even though C_2 might have the T in virtue of which x is a C_1 patriot; patriotism is object-nonuniversalizable. But in addition, patriotism is subject-nonuniversalizable: that x has reason R for being a C_1 patriot means that x cannot admit that w can rightly have reason R for being a C_2 patriot rather than a C_1 patriot. Now, if we maintain the analogy between personal love and patriotism, we should say two things about love. First, if x loves y on the basis of S, then x not only refuses to apply this reason generally so that xLz too but also cannot admit that w might have that or any reason for loving z. (The C_1 patriot will not be a patriot of C_2 and wants no one else to be a patriot of C_2.) Second, if x loves y, then x must claim that everyone else ought also to love y, and for the same reasons. (The C_1 patriot thinks everyone should be patriotic toward C_1, for the same good reasons he has, namely, it is a great country—not merely "it's mine.") Yet we do not want to say about the lover that if xLy, then x wants wLz to be false. The man who says "my wife is the best in the world" would not fight another man who says "*my* wife is the best in the world"; but the C_1 patriot will not remain silent when a patriot of C_2 says "*my* country is the best." Nor do we want to say that if xLy, x wants everyone to love y, or x believes that others should have the same good reasons for loving y; this would deny the role of subjectively valuable properties in love.

Gellner's most explicit definition of E-type states: "An agent acting in accordance with an E-type preference [is not] acting in accordance with some rule from which his preference follows as an instance, for he would not act in accordance with that rule with regard to another instance if one turned up" (p. 161). It sounds as if Gellner is defining an E-type attitude as one for which no rule is involved at all; the definition says "[not] acting in accordance with some rule." But the rest of the sentence confuses matters; it speaks of "that rule"— which suggests that an E-type attitude involves a nongeneral rule rather than no rule. Of course, we could equally characterize the E-type lover as acting according to no rule, *or* according to a nongeneral rule, if only because a nongeneral rule very likely does not even count as a rule. In either case something is amiss; x fails to recognize that rules are general, or x fails to abide by rules at all. Whichever is true, x displays arbitrariness or irrationality. But this issue is not a quibble. If Gellner means "nongeneral rule," then his solution to the paradox is that love is reason-dependent but love-reasons are not general, which is compatible with the eros tradition; and if he means "no rule at all," his solution is that love is not reason-dependent—that is, there are no reasons for love, which is incompatible with that tradition.

Because Gellner writes that "my distinction is between actions based on rules and those which are not" (p. 164), there is some evidence that he thinks of the E-type lover as acting according to no rule at all. And he characterizes E-type attitudes as involving a Kierkegaardian leap. But other passages imply that he means "nongeneral rule" rather than "no rule." (Kierkegaard's leap can be accomplished quite well with a nongeneral rule—just refuse to apply the rule again in a situation to which it applies.) The sentence I quoted just above begins, "Roughly speaking, my distinction is . . . ," a qualification that does not force us to take literally the claim that follows. Further, Gellner claims that it is "analytically true that all actions are based on a rule" (p. 158). If so, the only way to characterize the E-type lover is to say that he is acting according to a nongeneral rule. And what Gellner means throughout his paper by "acting according to a rule" is "acting according to reasons." The significant point to make about the E-type lover should be cast not in terms of rules but in terms of reasons: x is acting on the basis of a nongeneral reason, and the fact that x has reasons for loving y that are not applied to the similar z makes us doubt x's consistency. Finally, Gellner claims at the very beginning of his paper (p. 157) that there are two kinds of reasons for acting, distinguished by their logical forms. One kind of reason is "impersonal, general, abstracted," exactly what we expect reasons to be. The other kind of reason, then, must be nongeneral, the sort Gellner eventually attributes to E-type lovers. Gellner's description of this second kind of reason is imprecise: these reasons "include a . . . reference to some privileged person, thing or event, privileged in the sense that quite similar . . . persons, things or events would not by the agent be counted as equally good grounds for the relevant action." I would have said: "These reasons pick out some privileged person, privileged in the sense that these reasons would not by the agent be counted as grounds for acting in the same way toward a similar person." At least, I would have put it that way if I wanted to make it very clear that I was thinking of "nongeneral reason" (in the first sense) rather than "no reason."

The "blind self-assertion" (p. 165) of the E-type lover, then, is probably a failure to recognize that reasons are general (which is a kind of irrationality that is compatible with the eros tradition) rather than a failure to have reasons for one's behavior or preferences (which is a different kind of irrationality that is consistent with the agape tradition). Gellner, however, is not convinced of the appropriateness of calling E-typers "irrational." He says that E-typers are "often lumped together as modern irrationalism" (p. 165), most notably by contemporary "liberalism," toward which Gellner has a mocking attitude. And he sympathizes with existentialists who claim that E-type action is an assertion of the individual's freedom (p. 176). One might conclude that E-typers, given the truth of some bold metaphysical theses about the world and human nature, are actually rational in a more meaningful way. But there is a difference between wanting to be free from nonreason-causes, or from causal determination, and wanting to be free *tout court,* including being free from the demand that reasons be general. The desire to be free from causes, perhaps satisfied when one discovers and acknowledges their existence and tries to control them, seems laudable. (Recall Descartes to Chanut.) I cannot make sense of the idea, however, that we should take another step and free ourselves from the generality of reasons, not even for the sake of exclusive love.

5. THE SUBSTITUTION PROBLEM

After Gellner's paper was published in 1955, other versions of the paradox ("the substitution problem") appeared in the literature (as far as I can tell, independently of his article).[14] Typically, the substitution problem is used to show that personal love is not property-based or reason-dependent. One of the most bizarre versions is Mark Bernstein's:

> I have a wife, Nancy, whom I love very much. Let us suppose that I were informed that tomorrow, my wife Nancy would no longer be part of my life, that she would leave and forever be unseen and unheard of by me. But, in her stead, a Nancy* would appear, a qualitatively indistinguishable individual from Nancy. Nancy and Nancy* would look precisely alike, act precisely alike, think precisely alike, indeed would be alike in all physical and mental details.[15]

Nancy and Nancy* are not numerically identical, but qualitatively indistinguishable (which includes memories); Bernstein asks us not to "overestimate" any differences between them that follow from their numerical separateness (for example, that Mike was the father of Nancy and Mike* was the father of Nancy*). Bernstein claims that he would be grief-striken by the loss of Nancy, even though Nancy* is right by his side, and that he would not, at least not immediately, love Nancy*.[16] His argument is simple: "I love and only love Nancy, Nancy* ≠ Nancy, so I don't love Nancy*."[17] The argument begs the question; if Bernstein assumes that he loves only Nancy, he will of course not love Nancy*, or anyone else for that matter. He should instead be asking what follows from (1) I love Nancy and (2) Nancy* = Nancy (qualitatively). Regardless, Bernstein concludes from this thought-experiment that "no informative list of necessary and sufficient conditions for 'x loving y' can be given," since he would not love the identical Nancy*.[18] Further, he explains his grief by invoking the effect that the loss of Nancy has on his "sense of uniqueness or identity." For "loving someone is . . . an expression of our identity, of our uniqueness in the world."[19] But to argue that "if the object of our love vanishes . . . our own status as a unique individual is threatened," one need imagine only that Nancy dies, not that she is replaced by Nancy*. Bringing in Nancy* is not only quite beside the point, it is also queer, for the existence of a perfect copy of Nancy threatens everyone's status as "a unique individual," even if Nancy does not die.

I want to focus on Bernstein's assumption that x encounters not merely a person who duplicates the S that x's first beloved has (Gellner's strategy) but a perfect copy who replaces x's beloved in the furniture of the universe. If x does not know that the y he went to sleep with is not the y* he wakes up with the next morning, Bernstein's thought-experiment does not permit the conclusion that love is not property-based. In Gellner's version we were not considering x's meeting y, her later meeting z, and falsely believing that z is none other than y. That scenario illustrates only the intentionality of love. (If xLy and x believes that z is y, should we expect xLz? Yes.) If x does not know about the Bernstein replacement of y by the indistinguishable y*, x will feel no grief and will love y* as she had loved y. (Suppose I am making love in the garden during the blackness of midnight with a woman whom I believe to be my beloved but who is an imposter, yet I enjoy the events as I ordinarily would.)[20] More precisely, x's loving y* because x loves y and because she does not know that y* replaced y actually refutes the claim that "no informative list of necessary and sufficient conditions for 'x loving y' can be given" and confirms the thesis that personal love is property-based. In Mark Fisher's version of the substitution problem, y* has replaced y for five years without x's knowledge;[21] but that x has loved y* for so long as if y* were y is fully explainable and expected in the first view of personal love. Now, if x is informed that her beloved is really y* (Bernstein) or if x finally discovers she has been living with and loving an imposter (Fisher), x's reactions—grief, anger, withholding affection from y*—are readily explainable as reactions to one's being tricked, manipulated, or deceived and therefore do not entail anything about the ground of love.[22]

If x's not knowing that y* has replaced y leads x to love y* as if x were loving y, and that confirms that love is property-based, then why take seriously the claim that x's not loving y*, when x is informed or discovers that y* has replaced y, shows that love is not property-based? Those who employ the substitution problem against the thesis that love is property-based have not acknowledged that x's loving y* when x does not know that y* has replaced y actually confirms that love is property-based, and as a result they have not adequately explained why the fact that x does not love y*, when x knows that y* has replaced y, shows that love is not property-based. In Gellner's dilemma, the challenge to the view that love is property-based arises exactly when we assume that x *notices* that z, too, has S; then we need to worry about x's loving, or not loving, z. In the Bernstein-Fisher variant, the challenge arises when it is assumed that x *knows* that y* has replaced y. But the analogy between x's noticing and x's knowing is not a very good one. If, in Gellner's paradox, x does not notice that z, too, has S, we have no reason to expect that x will love z. But when x does not know about the Bernstein-Fisher replacement, we have every reason to expect x to love y*. This dissimilarity explains, I think, why the Bernstein-Fisher variant does not damage the view that love is property-based, or why Gellner's paradox is a better vehicle for posing the theoretical problem.

Gellner makes a reasonable assumption when he supposes that x encounters a second person z and notices that z has the small property set S in virtue of which x loves y. But the Bernstein-Fisher variant asks too much of us—that is, to imagine that x knows that a qualitatively identical y* has replaced y. How could x know that y* has replaced y when they are qualitatively indistinguishable? I can think of no reliable test that permits x to know this; no examination of fingerprints, no questioning y* about the intimate details of x's sex with y, no confrontation with Mike* (about whom the same problem arises), could provide evidence of the replacement. Bernstein claims that x is "informed" that y* replaces y. But who informs x that he has lost y and now has y* instead? If x is not in a position to know about the replacement, then for the same reasons no one else could know and inform x. But perhaps y* knows (how? her memories are identical to y's) and informs x: "See here, x, I am Nancy* and not Nancy." What would x's reaction be to being informed by y* that y* has replaced y? Undoubtedly, utter disbelief; x will think his beloved y has gone off her rocker. Should we just assume that x is informed by an authority (God) whom x considers infallible? Further, even if x were to suspect, or come to believe, that y* has replaced y, his reaction would not be grief over the loss of y but profound cognitive dissonance. In the meantime, we are not likely to learn anything about love when we deliberately proceed, as Bernstein does, to destroy x's world. Suppose that x watches as y is killed after serving as the source of clone y*.[23] Here x does know, by observation rather than by being informed, that y* has replaced y. But this situation is too weird to permit us to draw conclusions about love. While we are imagining that we live in the age of everyday cloning, still we have no idea *now* what our (or their) conception of love would look like; it might be quite different precisely because of the possibility of cloning. Would x suffer terribly as y dies, even though y* exists (as Bernstein would say, extrapolating his claim into the future), or would x rejoice as the identical y* emerges from the dust?

CHAPTER 3 *The Uniqueness of the Beloved*

I hunt for a sign of you in all the others,
in the rapid undulant river of women

. . . .

I searched, but no one else had your rhythms,
your light, the shady day you brought from the forest;
nobody had your tiny ears.

—Pablo Neruda, *100 Love Sonnets* (XLIII)

Love is the delusion that one woman differs
from another.

—H. L. Mencken

1. A STRANGE MUSIC LOVER

In *Sexual Desire,* Roger Scruton presents a thesis that can be interpreted as a solution to Gellner's paradox; he uses an analogy with aesthetic appreciation to argue that love can be reason-dependent yet exclusive.[1] An aesthetic interest in Beethoven's Violin Concerto (BVC), claims Scruton, is "reason-based" (his term): someone who enjoys the BVC must answer "Why do you enjoy it?" by referring to its properties. Yet this person may enjoy no other music and even dislike all other compositions. For Scruton, the *possibility* of this person shows that aesthetic reasons are not general; if so, neither are love-reasons. Hence, there is no contradiction in an exclusive, reason-based love: x may love y, answer *why* by referring to y's properties, and love only y.

Gellner's E-type lover reappears as Scruton's odd person who has excellent reasons for enjoying the BVC, yet enjoys no other music. I think Scruton's analogy, instead of confirming Gellner's picture of the lover, demonstrates its absurdity. The BVC fanatic is pathologically obsessed; the D-major strains of her beloved concerto float morning, noon, and night from her flat, even at Christmas when the neighbors would welcome Handel. But a theory of personal love is deficient if the lover is modeled after a person who relishes shrimp cocktail, has impeccable reasons for this preference, yet obstinately

48

refuses to understand that scallops or lobster might be as enjoyable, in part for the same reasons. Portraying the lover as a monomaniac is too high a price to pay for explaining exclusivity.

Scruton's thought-experiment, however, does not show that love-reasons or aesthetic reasons are not general. Indeed, Martha Nussbaum argues that because aesthetic reasons *are* general, what Scruton must conclude about love from his analogy (that is, nonexclusivity) is the opposite of what he wanted to conclude.[2] Scruton overlooked that after we ask the BVC lover why she enjoys it, we want to ask a second question: "Why do the reasons given for enjoying the BVC not imply that you should also enjoy Beethoven's Quartets or Sibelius's Violin Concerto?" Assume, with Scruton, that the BVC lover does not enjoy any other music. Even so, she must say why not, especially after she has given reasons for enjoying the BVC. If the BVC lover is confronted with a piece of music that apparently satisfies her reasons for loving the BVC, she must point out a difference. If she cannot, she is guilty of some sort of irrationality. Or she lacks self-awareness: her stated reasons for enjoying the BVC are not actually her reasons. The truth is that she does not, after all, understand why she enjoys the BVC. These features of her appreciation of the BVC are brought to light only if we supplement Scruton's "Why this?" with "Why not others?"

Note that Scruton's odd person might very well respond to our second question by pointing out a difference between the BVC and the Sibelius; and if the BVC lover can find a difference when comparing the BVC with all other music, her love of the BVC has been vindicated. In other words, the BVC lover can claim that her reasons for loving the BVC exclusively *are* general but happen to apply to only one case; she enjoys the BVC in virtue its properties, which no other composition has. She enjoys the BVC exclusively because it is unique, and she does not abandon reason-dependence or the generality of reasons. Scruton never assumes that the BVC lover's reasons pick out the BVC uniquely. But if the BVC lover believes, truly or falsely, that the BVC is a unique piece of music, her exclusive enjoyment becomes much less queer.

It is often asserted that every person is unique.[3] If so, all beloveds are unique, and the uniqueness of the beloved may reconcile the reason-dependence and exclusivity of love—that is, solve Gellner's paradox. As promising as this solution looks, ultimately it falls short. I will argue that the uniqueness of the beloved is in an important sense a derivative feature of love: love explains why the lover treats the beloved as unique, rather than uniqueness explaining love. Note that I deny that the beloved's uniqueness is the basis of love, which is compatible with claiming that the object of love is a unique person.

2. COUNTERFACTUAL MEETINGS

The proposal is that if x loves y in virtue of y's possessing a property-set S that makes y unique (no one else has S), then x will love y exclusively.[4] That love is reason-dependent implies that if x loves y in virtue of S, then x has equal reason for loving any z who also has S; but since there is no such z, x loves only y. But some tension remains between reason-dependence and exclusivity, for exclusivity implies that x would not love a similar (or different) z if z existed, and reason-dependence implies that x would love a similar z if z existed. Hence the BVC lover must admit that if someone were to write another piece of music having the relevant qualities of the BVC, she would also enjoy that now nonexistent composition. Analogously, x's loving y exclusively will result only from x's never meeting persons who are relevantly similar to y (perhaps, but not necessarily, because they do not exist). What some people mean by saying that their beloveds are unique is "unique in my experience," not "absolutely unique." But this implies an inverse relationship between the likelihood that one's love is exclusive and the extent of one's experiences. Hence, invoking the beloved's uniqueness to explain an exclusive love solves the paradox by claiming that exclusive lovers are contingently never in a position to apply their reasons for loving to another person. Gellner, recall, assumes that x meets z, who has the relevant properties, in order to generate the paradox; the uniqueness solution solves the paradox by simply denying one of its conditions.

But Gellner need not assume that x does meet the similar z; the problem about love to which he is alerting us has nothing to do with x's actually meeting z. If x loves y in virtue of S, then x has reason, both in advance of meeting z and in the absence of meeting z, for loving z. Reasons operate not only at the moment of contact with a similar case but also dispositionally. And if reasons are timeless in this way, the problem of reconciling exclusivity with reason-dependence does not turn on x's actually meeting z. The problem is posed when we ask x, who loves y on the basis of S, what x would feel upon meeting z. The lover must be able to imagine his reaction even if he is convinced that the meeting will not occur because y is unique. Since assuming that xMz is not required to lay out the theoretical problem, the fact that the uniqueness solution depends on denying xMz implies that it cannot be a full reconciliation of exclusivity and reason-dependence.

Suppose a lover cautiously conducts his daily activities in order to avoid encounters with persons he knows have the relevant S; or imagine a domineering spouse who locks up y in the house in an attempt to ensure their love by preventing y from having such encounters.[5] These maneuvers may work to preserve the appearance of exclusivity, but they miss the point. To claim that love is exclusive is not only to make a claim about what x does when xMz occurs, but is also to make a claim about x's mental state, about what x thinks he would do, even if xMz never happens. The man who locks up his wife under-estimates her mental life, which might love some z had she the opportunity. The man who deliberately avoids conversation with attractive persons might do so precisely because he realizes that he cannot satisfy what the exclusivity of love demands. (This is the grain of truth, differently expressed, in the idea that a married man who lusts after another woman in his heart has committed adultery.) The psychological attraction of thinking that one's beloved is unique may be: if x does not meet z just because y is unique, x does not have to feel responsible for preventing xMz or for foolishly trying to prevent it; xMz never occurs "naturally." Neruda can hunt and search for more tiny ears all he wants, secure in the thought that he will not find any.

In this way, thinking of the beloved as unique makes self-deception possible. The lover x might prevent xMz by falsely attributing uniqueness to y or by unconsciously overlooking that z, too, has S, and she might do so because she is not sure what she would feel or do were she to meet z. If the question about x's love—or specifically its exclusivity—depends only on x's behavior when she meets z, then x is allowed to avoid a confrontation with herself about her attitudes toward that situation, because x can either hope or arrange that a meeting with z never occurs; x can thereby postpone indefinitely this soul-searching. If x thinks that her exclusive love for y is secured by y's uniqueness, x has no inducement for engaging in reflection about her attitudes toward exclusivity. But patiently probing one's thoughts about exclusivity may be as much a mark of love as exclusivity itself; getting clear about why and when (or why not and when not) one will love exclusively is not merely a preparation for love.

3. DEFENDING UNIQUENESS

The uniqueness solution works only if people *are* unique. Clearly, people are trivially unique in being numerically distinct, in having their own genetic and historical properties. In a substantive sense, however, people are not nearly as different as the doctrine of uniqueness makes them out to be. At least I have found little reason to suppose they are. The doctrine of universal uniqueness is asserted so frequently by philosophers, poets, theologians, psychologists, and ordinary folk that we might be tempted to think there is something to it. Of course, Jesus was nontrivially unique, and so were Ghandi, Moses, Cyrano, Othello. Alcibiades loved Socrates, and only Socrates, because "he is like no other human being, living or dead. If you are looking for a parallel for Achilles, you can find it in Brasidas and others; if Pericles is your subject you can compare him to Nestor and Antenor" (*Symposium* 221c–d). But substantive uniqueness is not very common. Most of us draw on the same stock supply of merits and defects, good traits and bad traits, in building our personalities or characters—whether we are persons creating ourselves or writers creating protagonists. Our mannerisms, physiognomy, ways of walking, sense of humor, and linguistic habits are close copies of the traits of our parents, siblings, peers, and other models. A reasonable hypothesis is that the more places x has traveled to, the older x gets, and the more people x has encountered, the less x is convinced of uniqueness. Facial and personality types start to emerge and repeat themselves, and uniqueness is replaced by family resemblance.[6] Perhaps we should live in small towns. But, then, would we achieve exclusivity through artificial uniqueness or through there not being enough people for multiple loves?

Indeed, worries about the homogenization of personality and the conformity fostered by the media and schools presuppose that substantive uniqueness is rare enough to be a matter of social concern. The doctrine that we are unique might be only an attempt to create something by the bootstrap operation of pretending it already exists. Recall that John Stuart Mill complained over a hundred years ago (in *On Liberty*) about the lack of individuality; contemporary talk of uniqueness may be the exaggerated form this sort of discourse takes when the promises of individualism have worn thin. Another social critic, Erich Fromm, looking at more recent Western culture, found no genuine individuality.[7] Since Fromm claimed that "a part of love" is being aware of the beloved's "unique individuality,"[8] he might have drawn the conclusion that Western society contains little love *because* there are few appropriate objects.[9] Similarly, if people are not substantively unique, there should not be much exclusive love—unless lovers deceive themselves that their beloveds are unique.

Let us examine three arguments in defense of the doctrine of uniqueness:

A) William Galston writes that "we view human beings as unique . . . [because] even though every quality an individual has is possessed by others to some extent, the manner in which qualities are combined and emphasized . . . is distinctive."[10] But I find little evidence for sufficiently different combinations or emphases, but only evidence for a set of family resemblances.[11] Galston's argument is mathematical: "Imagine a many-dimensional space, each dimension of which can take on a very large number of discrete values. The number of combinations specifying distinguishable single points will be very large." Given a set of properties (dimensions), and given fine gradations within each property (different kinds or degrees of wit or beauty are the discrete values of those dimensions), the number of combinations will be huge. But the defender of uniqueness should not jump for joy. First, many combinations are only trivially different from others. Galston's assertion that these points will be "distinguishable" is mathematically true, but false when the model is applied to human beings; persons near each other on the various dimensions will not be significantly distinguishable. Second, Galston's assumption that each dimension takes on "a very large number of discrete values" is questionable. How many different kinds of wit or beauty are there? If the number of properties to begin with is only a dozen or so, the number of combinations is not "very large." Third, and most important, the mathematical model tells us only what is possible: given D dimensions, each dimension having V discrete values, we can calculate the maximum number of combinations. But the number of combinations among people approaches this maximum only if properties and their values are distributed randomly. Galston forgets that social factors operate to destroy randomness and make people congregate at specific locations. These factors, as recognized by Mill and Fromm, effectively prevent humans from reaching the variability permitted by the mathematics.

B) C. S. Lewis suggests another argument. "We may say, and not quite untruly, that we have chosen . . . the woman we love for [her] various excellences—for beauty, frankness, goodness of heart, wit, intelligence. . . . But it had to be the particular kind of wit, the particular kind of beauty, the particular kind of goodness that we like, and we have our personal tastes in these matters."[12] What is beautiful for me is not what is beautiful for you, or for the next guy. Since the properties of beloveds in virtue of which we love them are only subjectively valuable, beloveds vary to an extent even greater than Galston imagined. But invoking differences among lovers (beauty-for-x, beauty-for-w) does not work, even if we grant that subjective properties play a large role in love. For the argument assumes the uniqueness of persons qua lovers in order to demonstrate the uniqueness of persons qua beloveds, thereby begging the question. If there is little reason to think that individuals as beloveds are unique, there is little reason to think that individuals as lovers are unique. To show that lovers are unique requires showing that lovers are sufficiently idiosyncratic in their tastes that they are more than trivially unique. "We judge another's value in terms of preferences that are uniquely our own"[13] is too strong; I have never pretended that most of my preferences were unique to me and not shared widely by others. "Beauty is in the eye of the beholder" may be true, but it does not entail diversity in what counts as beautiful if the various eyes have been molded by the same social influences.

C) A third argument is suggested by R. Meager.[14] Imagine that John loves Rosie and wants to understand his love rationally, yet he does not like the reason "because she has S" since it implies nonexclusivity. John therefore provides the reason "because she is Rosie," which Meager unpacks: "It is the particular form in which Rosie manifests" S that makes her lovable. The idea is that xLy not in virtue of y's having S but in virtue of y's having S-as-manifested-by-y or S-as-embodied-in-y (for short, S-in-y). Meager claims that John's reason is "perfectly rational" even though it is nongeneral; "S-in-y" refers to and is logically applicable only to y.

The proposal is that instead of distinguishing properties with respect to lovers (P-for-x), we should distinguish them with respect to beloveds (P-in-y). The difference between y and z, when both have P, is that y really has P-in-y and z really has P-in-z, which indexed properties make each of them unique and give x reason to love y but not z. But indexing properties with respect to beloveds either begs the question or establishes only trivial uniqueness. How does P when embodied in y become the new or different property P-in-y? Or why is P-in-y different from P-in-z? One answer is that the two instances of P are qualitatively indistinguishable, and merely the fact that one instance of P appears in y and the other appears in z creates distinct properties P-in-y and P-in-z. In this case, the indexed properties are different only because y and z are numerically distinct; hence, in virtue of these indexed properties y and z are not more than trivially unique. Y is unique because only y logically can have P-in-y. The other answer is that P is qualitatively different from P-in-y; when P interacts with y and z two new properties exist, P-in-y and P-in-z. Having P-in-y makes y unique, since the property is qualitatively (not merely numerically) distinct from any instance of P in another person. But why think that because P interacts with y, P-in-y will be qualitatively different from P-in-z? The answer must be: P-in-y is different from P-in-z because y is already qualitatively different from z. Invoking the difference between P-in-y and P-in-z to explain the uniqueness of y and z is backward, for the other differences between y and z account for the difference between P-in-y and P-in-z.[15]

The uniqueness solution cannot claim merely that x loves y exclusively just because y is unique, for if the doctrine of universal uniqueness is correct, then x would have the same reason for loving z and others. The proposed solution must be that xLy exclusively because xLy in virtue of a property-set S that only y has. The problem with claiming that this uniqueness of the beloved grounds exclusive love is that many properties are unique to a person but not valuable or admirable, and many properties are valuable but not unique. The solution works only if some properties, the ones that ground love, are independently both valuable and uniqueness-making. But finding such a class of properties is futile. The properties we find lovable are widely shared: beauty, kindness, humor, moral virtue, intelligence, and courage. Properties that make a person unique—fingerprints, teeth and bite patterns, moles and scars, small details of the face, most of a person's biography—are not properties that ground love. Anthony Quinton claims that "persisting character and memory complexes" (as opposed to body types, which "have a large number of instances") confer uniqueness on everyone, and he implies that the *object* of love is this "unique cluster of character traits and recollections."[16] In defense of his claim about what makes us unique, he writes: "The memories of individual persons cannot be exactly similar, since even the closest of identical twins must see things from slightly different angles; they cannot be in the same place at the same time" (p. 404). This kind of uniqueness may be sufficient for discrete personal identity and hence might constitute the uniqueness of the object of love; but it is a trivial uniqueness and surely not a kind of valuable uniqueness that serves as the *basis* of love.

Further, even if we did love on the basis of a host of trivially unique properties (for example, being born in Muncie on March 4, 1950, at 12:03 in the morning) and not because of valuable widely shared properties, one could still argue: we *should* love for moral virtue and intelligence, even though these properties are not uniqueness-making. Nor does the beloved's uniqueness consist of his exhibiting fine qualities to a high degree; excellence may be statistically unusual but not rare enough to generate the required class of properties. Moreover, if the remonstrations of moralists (and the physical fitness priests) were heeded, moral (and physical) excellence would be the statistical norm, yet not any less effective or less worthy a basis of love.

Suppose that only y loves x. Then y has the property "the only person who loves x," which is uniqueness-making and (let us grant) valuable, in which case x might love y exclusively in virtue of this property. The exclusive love of x for y is explained in terms of a property that satisfies our desiderata. Can this uniqueness-making, valuable property provide a general account of exclusive love? To achieve that, we must be able to assume that y might love x also because x is the only person who loves y. Then xLy because only y loves x and yLx because only x loves y—their reciprocal love is incomprehensible and circular. Further, x's loving y altogether because (only) y loves x is psychologically suspicious: x's emotion for y is totally divorced from y's character. This version of the uniqueness solution abandons the attempt to solve the paradox within the eros tradition. Nevertheless, it is interesting insofar as it suggests that relational properties might satisfy our desiderata.

4. SHARED HISTORY

Some important relational properties might derive from love's history. For example, in Gellner's scenario xMy occurred before xMz ("primacy of encounter") and is part of the love's history. This historical property confers uniqueness on y, but "coming first" is a "thin" property (see chap. 4). Instead, exclusive love might be explainable in terms of the "thick" pleasurable or meaningful shared history that x and y have had together over some period of time. The shared history is not strictly a property of the beloved in virtue of which she is loved. Rather, she is loved for her "second-order" relational properties of having contributed to, and having the capacity and willingness to continue to contribute to, that shared history. X loves y not only in virtue of y's "first-order" properties (beauty, wit, charm, virtue) that elicited x's love originally and have made the shared history pleasurable and meaningful but also in virtue of y's ability and intention to extend that history—perhaps, in part, by changing, maintaining, or improving her first-order properties.[17] More exactly, y's first-order properties for which x originally loved y might not be the same as the first-order properties that account for y's contribution to their pleasurable shared history. X might come to love y also in virtue of the latter properties because x realizes that they underlie y's second-order properties.

Because the shared history of x and y is unique, the ability and willingness of y to contribute to its continuation is a valuable property that apparently only y could have.[18] Thus, the proposal is that second-order properties satisfy our desiderata and explain exclusivity. I do not doubt that second-order properties are an important factor in maintaining love; these relational properties might also help to explain love's constancy. Further, we can now understand why lovers wrongly attribute first-order uniqueness to beloveds: sensing that something unique about y explains her exclusive love, x overlooks uniqueness-making second-order properties and assumes that y's first-order properties make y nontrivially unique. That we are not significantly first-order unique but share the same stock supply of valuable first-order properties is why mail-order, contract, and arranged marriages can work as well as self-selecting marriages: both end up at the same place, love in virtue of shared history.

Despite the role that second-order properties play in love, their usefulness in solving Gellner's paradox is limited. Notice that x probably had to be loving y exclusively before this specific foundation for x's now exclusively loving y could emerge; if x has been loving both y and z, then the x-y relationship might not be, from x's perspective, sufficiently unique to make y's second-order properties both valuable and uniqueness-making. Thus, there is room to argue that the shared history of two lovers has been pleasant or meaningful because they have been loving each other exclusively, rather than vice versa. Let us proceed, however, to a different problem. Do second-order properties—having contributed to a pleasurable shared history and being willing and able to continue to contribute—make the beloved unique? At first glance the answer is yes, for x has shared a historically unique relationship with y, and y is therefore in fact the only person who has the property of having contributed to that history. But it is not strictly true that only y has the property of having contributed to the x-y shared history; x, too, has that property. Indeed, both x's and y's having the same second-order property might explain the reciprocity of their love (or its mutuality; 11.5). Should we protest that if y's having this second-order property is x's reason for loving y, then x has equal reason for loving x himself? Should we object that if both x and y have this second-order property, then this property makes neither x nor y unique? No. The fact that x, too, has this property does not mean that y is not unique as x's beloved. And why complain that while loving y, x is also given a reason to love himself?

Nevertheless, people other than x and y can have the property of having contributed to the x-y shared history and of being able and willing to continue to contribute. A person z might financially support x and y so that their shared history can be extended; or z might remove herself from the company of x and y because her passion for x would disrupt the x-y shared history; or z might babysit for x and y so they can enjoy intimate dinners out. We do not want to say of these people, in virtue of their having the same second-order properties as y, that they are for x equally as lovable as y and that, therefore, exclusivity has not been preserved; for x might *appreciate* these z's for their contributions to the x-y shared history, while x *loves* y for having made her contributions to their history. But how can we avoid this unwelcome implication? We might explain why x loves y in virtue of that second-order property while only appreciating z in virtue of that same property, by referring to first-order properties that y, but not z, has. But this move concedes that y's uniqueness does not consist in y's second-order properties and thrusts us back into Gellner's paradox. Alternatively, we could distinguish between direct and indirect contributions to the x-y shared history, or between contingent and necessary contributions, in order to assert that x loves y for a more specific second-order property that makes y unique. But to say that y is unique in possessing the property "is willing to contribute *directly* to the x-y shared history" will succumb to the same objection. If the x-y shared history were to be dashed on the rocks by z's withdrawal of financial support or dramatic expression of passion for x, then z's contribution is as direct or necessary as y's. I suspect that any attempt to describe y's second-order properties more specifically in order to make y unique relative to z will amount (in masquerade) to the claim that x values y's contribution to the x-y shared history in a different way (or more) than z's contribution *because* x loves y and *because* x only appreciates z. Either x values y's contribution to their shared history because x loves y for no reason having to do with y's first-order properties (which means the solution falls within the second view of personal love), or x loves y for his first-order properties alone, which is exactly what this solution wanted to avoid.

Even if we ignore these analytic tangles posed by "contributed to the x-y shared history," there is another reason second-order properties do not solve the paradox. Consider W. Newton-Smith's proposal that x exclusively loves y in virtue of "what y has done for x,"[19] a historical property referring to x's interaction specifically with y and apparently making y unique. But the property is ambiguous; it can figure into three distinct reasons x might have for loving y. One is that certain things were done for x and that x as a result experiences pleasurable or meaningful states. The point is that x values the fact that these things were done or these states experienced *simpliciter*. Y's being responsible for their occurrence is irrelevant; the reference to y's having done them is only contingent. Second, the reason x loves y might be that x experienced these states and that y in particular was responsible for them. Finally, the experienced state might not matter at all to x; x loves y just because y produced the states, as if x's only desire is to be attended to by y in whatever manner y chooses.

If the fact that x experienced certain states *simpliciter* is x's reason for loving y, then as long as these states are producible by z, y does not uniquely have the basis of x's love. If x loves y, instead, because y in particular produced these states, y is unique because no z can produce a state that is defined as "produced by y." But this is an unsatisfactory way to resolve Gellner's paradox: the reason invoked by x is nongeneral, since it mentions y. Further, why does the experienced state have significance only when it is produced for x by y? Why does x prefer the state-produced-by-y to the state-produced-by-z? Here we cannot say (which would be perfectly natural) that x wants only y to produce the states because x loves y and does not love z; for what we want to explain is why x loves y but not z. The third interpretation of x's reason falls to the same objection.

Identical considerations apply to the proposal that y's uniqueness consists in the second-order property "having contributed to the x-y shared history and being able and willing to continue to contribute to it." The reason x has for loving y could be either that (1) x has experienced a pleasurable or meaningful shared history contingently contributed to by y or that (2) x has experienced a pleasurable-shared-history-contributed-to-by-y. In the first case, x could have had, and can now have, a qualitatively similar shared history produced by z if z has y's first-order properties that account for y's second-order properties. Indeed, the pleasurable shared history x has had with y could continue if z replaced y—for the states of this history were only contingently produced by y, and z might be happy to contribute to the extension of x's pleasurable states. Z can even plausibly claim that he or she would do a better job of it than y. And since x had earlier given y the opportunity to produce a pleasurable shared history on the basis of y's first-order properties, x has equal reason to give z this opportunity. Nor will it do to say that y's uniqueness consists in her "*proven* ability and willingness to contribute to their shared history," for depending on how the "proof" of such a thing is construed, some z's will have the same property. So on reading (1) of x's reason for loving y, y is not significantly unique and exclusively is therefore not preserved. On the other hand, if x loves y for having contributed to the pleasurable-shared-history-as-produced-by-y, then y's second-order properties do make y unique, but we have no explanation for why x loves y exclusively. Why does x prefer pleasurable-shared-history-with-y to pleasurable-shared-history-with-z? Because x loves y. That x wants only the shared history as-produced-by-y is better understood as the *explanandum* of xLy rather than its *explanans*.

5. DYNAMIC LOVE

This sophisticated uniqueness view does not solve Gellner's paradox, but it provides insight into one role played by time in love. The point of this view is that love must be understood historically, not as a static phenomenon, because properties develop in love that sustain it. It is worthwhile to clarify this lesson by discussing another role for time.

A person's uniqueness might consist of (as Quinton suggested) a unique set of mental properties, broadly conceived to include character traits, that x discovers only after interacting with y for a long time. Over the years, y reveals more and more of this "deep self" to x, or x is eventually able to perceive it. As x and y continue their relationship and extend their knowledge of each other, they come to appreciate each other's richness of being.[20] The proposal is that x exclusively loves y in virtue of y's deep self, which makes y unique and can be known only after many years. But the solution fails. First, deep-self properties might not confer uniqueness on anyone; perhaps Fromm is right that "in essence, all human beings are identical"[21] at that level of being. Second, deep-self properties may confer only trivial uniqueness; there is little reason to assume that the depth of a trait makes it interesting.[22] Finally, deep-self properties might not be the kind of valuable or admirable properties that could ground love. What we find in the deep self—a deposit of repressed violence and perverse sexual urges—may repulse and revolt us. If what I argued earlier, that it is difficult to find a class of attractive and uniqueness-making, first-order properties, was convincing, an appeal to the deep self will not work. The properties of the deep self are simply first-order properties that are temporarily undisclosed. In a long relationship, x will come to know all the minute details of y's unique character, but there is no reason to think the sum of these details constitutes a significant, lovable, unique basis for love.

In this view time affords x the opportunity to perceive, or y to reveal, y's hidden first-order properties.[23] This is different from attributing to time the role of affording x and y the opportunity to create a shared history so they can develop valuable second-order properties and improve their manifest first-order properties. That is, the "richness-of-being" view is only superficially a dynamic view of love. A process of coming to know y's deep self over time presupposes that y's deep self remains the same. But the deep self of the lover or the beloved in a long-term relationship has likely undergone changes (even as a result of love itself). In contrast, if time permits the development of first- and second-order properties, then coming-to-be, rather than coming-to-know, is the dynamic component of love. Time plays an essential role in the development of second-order properties, only a contingent role in coming to know a deep self. In principle, deep selves need not take years to reveal or perceive. Indeed, those people who believe that the deep self exists and is the ground (or object) of love might attempt to get to the deep self posthaste, exposing their most intimate thoughts over a beer at the local tavern. The continual search for the other's deep self is, moreover, a comprehensible project if (perhaps only if) x already loves y. Given the prior development of second-order properties, the motivation required for revealing or discovering the deep self is present. Knowledge of the deep self, then, is the fruit of love, not its ground; knowing it might represent the profound intimacy of love in its advanced stages, but it is not the relationship's origin.[24] (See 9.5.) If both x and y change, in part as a result of their love, and these changes permeate the deep self, then discovering these serial deep selves is possible given the constancy implied by unwavering second-order properties. Reknowing the other depends on time, not knowing more deeply.

6. METAPHYSICAL UNIQUENESS

The biologist Peter Medawar writes that "philosophers and common sense . . . have long agreed about the uniqueness of individual man. . . . Science now makes it a trio of concordant voices, for the uniqueness of individual . . . men is a proposition which science can demonstrate with equal force, perhaps with deeper cogency, and certainly with a hundred times as much precision."[25] The medical study of skin grafts teaches us that all humans are immunologically unique (except identical twins), because immunological differences are combinational and "the combinations are so diverse that there is an almost continuous range of variations."[26] Of course, all persons are unique in this physical sense, but immunological properties are not the basis of love. Other empirical properties, such as personality and character, do not confer substantive uniqueness, and appealing to an empirical deep self fails. How, then, can a philosopher defend universal uniqueness? A distinctively philosophical account of uniqueness would avoid empirical objections by elaborating a metaphysics of the person, aiming at an absolute truth about uniqueness, not a likelihood (or unlikelihood).

While arguing that agape is the only genuine love, W. G. MacLagan posed a problem for the viability of romantic love, a variant of Gellner's paradox.[27] In romantic passion x loves y exclusively, which is possible only if the lover conceives of the beloved as "unique and therefore irreplaceable." But, claims MacLagan, the lover can conceive of the beloved as irreplaceable only if the lover refuses to reflect on the grounds of her preference, to ask why this particular person is the object of her attention. Romantic love, as a result, is irrational: at some level the lover realizes that were she to inquire about her preference, she would find only an unsatisfactory answer, and in order to save her love she must go through evasive mental gymnastics. The only answer to the repressed question is unsatisfactory because it provides no warrant for asserting the irreplaceability of the beloved and for loving exclusively. The answer is that the beloved instantiates a set of attractive properties; but if so, the beloved is not unique and the lover should feel passion toward others. The romantic lover, according to MacLagan, is forced to admit that she has no reason for her preferential love—which is contradictory, given what a preference is.

But the romantic lover who has read Leo Buscaglia is prepared to respond to MacLagan: "It seems to me that . . . we have not sufficiently celebrated the wonderful uniqueness of every individual. I would agree that personality is the sum total of all the experience that we have known since the moment of conception . . . along with heredity. But what is often ignored is an X factor. Something within the *you* of *you* that is different from every single human being."[28] This metaphysics of personal uniqueness is formulated slightly less obscurely by the philosopher Robert Ehman: "Given all of his universal attributes and values, he has in addition a distinctive value of his own that is more than a mere resultant of the sum of his universal traits. Apart from his virtues and general excellences, he might be worthless, but he nevertheless might have a personal value that is more than the sum of the values of his virtues."[29] And Mark Fisher argues (in effect) that Gellner's paradox can be solved only by postulating the existence of a "transcendental self," something beyond (the summation of) empirical qualities.[30] If the transcendental self is the seat of the beloved's value (and hence is lovable) and is unique to each person (even though we all are, or have, a transcendental self, all such selves, like the soul, are unique), the transcendental self, as either the object of love or that in virtue of which we love, satisfies our desiderata. But to say that x exclusively loves y because x loves y's unique transcendental self is simply to say nothing more illuminating than that x exclusively loves y because y has the property "is y" and that no one else has that property.

Few lovers ignore altogether the beloved's empirical properties in favor of a metaphysical abstraction, and beloveds are not pleased to think of themselves as being loved qua transcendental self. Both lover and beloved, confronted with a philosophical proof that love entails a transcendental self as its object or ground, may very well interpret that proof as a *reductio ad absurdum*. Despite the fact that our romantic lover quickly, if not in desperation, embraced Buscaglia's Cartesian "something within the *you* of *you*" to protect himself from MacLagan's charge of camel-bird irrationality, he now regrets becoming an accomplice in promoting a view that is difficult not only for him but also for the philosopher to express. Listen to Ehman: "There is a *certain* order and meaning in the personality of the individual that is his alone, distinctive, unique, original, in some measure creative. . . . [Personal love] focuses upon the *ineffable* individuality of the individual."[31] Even if we forget the vagueness of "certain" and the tautological "individuality of the individual," Ehman's "ineffable" is revealing. This is the philosopher's rendition of Buscaglia's "something within the *you* of *you*." But to say that metaphysical uniqueness is ineffable is to abandon ship, or to flee from eros to agape. "We know that the individual is unique," says Sartre, "but how can we say so?"[32] I should think that if we cannot say so, we should be reluctant to use metaphysical uniqueness as a solution to a philosophical puzzle and be quick to doubt that we do know that everyone is unique. Yet I suspect that some philosophers who fall back on the ineffability of personal uniqueness believe that this collapse is a virtue, not a defect, of their philosophy. If love is an elusive mystery, then it is fitting that at some point in our (necessarily futile) attempts to get a rational grip on it we fall back on ineffability.[33] Robert Solomon believes that "to say love is 'ineffable' or a 'mystery' is a dangerous bit of nonsense,"[34] but he does not explain why. The answer, I think, is that conceiving of love in this way prevents self-knowledge; it serves as an excuse for not reflecting on the grounds of our preferences, in the manner of Mac-Lagan's irrational lover (see 8.4 and 8.6).

I wanted to know, however, not only what sort of doctrine of uniqueness a philosopher might offer but also how that doctrine could be defended. Ehman argues for the "ineffable individuality of the individual," upon which the lover focuses, in part by appealing to an analogy between art and persons: "In personal love, we . . . approach other persons as we approach works of art, with an openness and sensitivity to what is unique and novel in them."[35] Works of art are unique and, by analogy, so are people. The argument begs the question; at most it establishes the possibility of personal uniqueness: if works of art are unique in an interesting sense, then the world contains some uniqueness, in which case persons might be unique in the same way. Not much more convincing is Ehman's other defense; since a work of art is unique, its creator must also be unique: "In his act, the artist creates something as distinctive and individualized as he himself."[36] This argument shows, if anything, only that an artist—one who does or could create a unique work of art—is unique; it does not establish a general metaphysics of personal uniqueness. We catch Ehman illegitimately sliding into the more general conclusion when he repeats the argument: "The originality and individuality of works of art are simply manifestations of the originality and individuality of *the human self*. In art the self reveals more clearly than in any other product . . . its own distinctive individuality."[37] Maybe the artist's self thereby reveals its uniqueness; but how does this show that human selves in general are unique?

Arguments for the existence of a transcendental self are usually exciting. Mark Fisher offers three novel ones, based upon claims about love. His first argument is a response to a version of Gellner's paradox: "If it is true that the reasons why one person loves another are to be found in the beloved's empirical qualities, then another man might have the same qualities. . . . On the assumption that the reason for love is to be found in the beloved's empirical qualities, . . . she would love [such a] substitute just the same. She would love them both. That this would undoubtedly not be [true] . . . cannot . . . be written off as some odd quirk in human psychological nature, some odd irrationality in us that we are unable to love a second person, no matter how like the first."[38] Fisher's solution is that the assumption is false: we do not love in virtue of empirical properties. Yet we love in virtue of something, and the remaining candidate is the nonempirical transcendental self. Fisher has not hereby solved Gellner's paradox in its pure form, for earlier in his paper he rejected Gellner's first horn: "Love often is, but need not by its nature be, exclusive, even serially."[39] His point is not that if x loves y on the basis of an empirical S, then x cannot love any z who also has S, but rather that x's loving y for S will not guarantee that x loves any z who also has S. The fact that it would not be "psychologically odd" if x did not love the similar z shows, for Fisher, that the basis or the object of love must be nonempirical, something not repeatable in z—that is, the transcendental self that is y.

This argument will not do. First, some particular x might love z for S just because x loves y for S, in which case this particular x, or any person psychologically similar to x, does not love a transcendental self. Or such a case shows that the transcendental self is not always the object or the basis of love. Second, even though it strikes me, too, as plausible (given "human psychological nature") that x will not necessarily love a person z who has the same S as the person y that x loves, the additional psychology implicit in Fisher's claim that something nonempirical must be the basis or the object of love seems far-fetched. How does x come to know, to touch, or to feel passion for a transcendental self? If x loves y but not z when y and z are in the relevant ways empirically indistinguishable, then how is x able to distinguish their transcendental selves? Recall that x had been deceived into thinking that y* was y in Fisher's version of Gellner's paradox—x confused their transcendental selves just because he "confused" their empirical qualities (see 2.5).[40]

In his second defense of the transcendental self, Fisher again radically divorces the empirical from love: "Surely the nature of love is to transcend these"—by which Fisher means *all*—"empirical changes [in the object of love]."[41] Fisher's point is that if x loves y, then x will continue to love y no matter what empirical changes y undergoes (as in the agape tradition?). And if x loves any empirical version of y, nothing empirical about y can be the basis of x's love. The argument, however, overlooks at least this: if y undergoes severe empirical changes (for example, metanoia), then y has become a different person. In such a case, claiming that x loves y only if x's love continues is unconvincing—for there is now no y for x to love. If x does not love the "new" y, x's love for y has not failed to be constant through y's empirical changes. If so, we cannot conclude that x must have loved something nonempirical. One might respond that no empirical change, not even a drastic one like metanoia, entails a change in identity, for underlying all such empirical properties is the persisting transcendental self. Perhaps. But now its existence is merely being asserted, not argued for.

Another fault with the second argument is that it assumes that love is constant. Why does Fisher, who concedes that love is not "by its nature" exclusive, retain this equally suspicious thesis? His argument is: love must persist through all empirical changes in the beloved, "for if it did not it would . . . be . . . conditional upon certain requirements being met. But conditional love . . . is not what it proclaims itself to be."[42] The weak link in the argument, I think, is Fisher's claim that love is perfectly unconditional. As we shall see later (8.8; 10.2), the conditionality of an emotion does not contradict its being love. Any reasonable view of love must allow that the ending of an emotion because of certain changes in the beloved does not preclude love as the emotion.

Fisher's third argument is this: "By another route we can reach the same conclusion. There is a difference between loving a person's beauty or wealth or power . . . and loving *that person himself*. . . . [T]he absurdity of loving a second person however like the first suggests that the idea of loving someone *for* his [empirical] qualities involves mistaking love for . . . things that can precede or go along with it, such as expectation of benefit."[43] As I understand the argument, it says: if x loves y's property S, then x does not love y "the person"; to achieve love "for the person" (rather than love of properties or "instrumental" love, which are impostors), one must be loving the transcendental self. Let me suggest that we have three notions here: (a) loving someone's empirical properties; (b) loving someone in virtue of their empirical properties; and (c) loving someone "as a person" in some technical sense.[44] Surely (a) seems incompatible with (c), but because (a) and (b) are quite different, it does not follow that (b), too, is incompatible with (c). Similarly, even if (a) is not genuine love, it does not follow that (b) is not genuine love. Since (b) is not necessarily incompatible with (c), we have no reason so far to think that only loving a transcendental self amounts to "loving the person" (see 13.5).

7. UNIQUENESS AND EXCLUSIVITY

There is a final reason why appealing to the uniqueness of the beloved cannot solve Gellner's paradox. Even if the beloved is in some nontrivial way unique, that fact could not reconcile the reason-dependence and exclusivity of love. Gellner summarizes his paradox by saying that it exposes a puzzle: love is exclusive yet there is "no guarantee"[45] the beloved is substantively unique. He seems to assume, that is, that the puzzle would disappear if the beloved were unique; that the uniqueness of the beloved, if there were such a thing, would account for exclusivity in a property-based love. It is time to challenge that assumption. Recall that in the second horn of his dilemma, Gellner claims that if x loves y in virtue of y's having S, and if love-reasons are general, then x will love z if z, too, has S. (The uniqueness solution escapes along the second horn by claiming that only y has S.) Yet Gellner's second horn is altogether silent on what is implied, *by* the fact that x loves y in virtue of S, *about* x's attitude toward z when z does not have S. The second horn's assumption that love is property-based is compatible with x's loving y in virtue of y's having S, while x loves z in virtue of z's having T, even if Gellner is right that love-reasons are not general.

The thesis that love is reason-dependent is not that one particular set of properties is both necessary and sufficient for x to love anyone at all. Rather, if x loves y, x's love is explainable by pointing out those properties of y in virtue of which x loves y. That x loves y in virtue of these properties does not mean that x will love only someone having the same set. Love's being property-based allows that y's having set S is sufficient for x to love y, and z's having set T is sufficient for x to love z. For a given x there may be a fixed number of sufficient sets, but this limit is not placed by the reason-dependence of love. Furthermore, a beloved's possessing a specific property P will be a necessary condition for x's loving anyone at all only if every property-set that is sufficient for x to love includes P; otherwise, no specific property will be necessary, which allows x to love y for properties A, B, and C and to love z for D, E, and F. It follows that unless the possession of a specific property P or a specific set S is both necessary and sufficient for x to love anyone at all, the fact that y's having S secures xLy has no bearing on whether xLz when z does not have S.

The upshot is that even if y is unique, and even if the basis of x's love is y's unique S, this does not guarantee the exclusivity of x's love. Exclusivity is secured by the uniqueness of the beloved only when (1) x loves y in virtue of y's having S, (2) the possession of S makes y unique, and (3) the possession of S by a person is necessary for x to love anyone at all. How likely is it that the possession of a specific property P is absolutely necessary for x to love anyone at all? Most unlikely. An exception would be a property such as "has never maliciously killed my cat,"[46] but these properties are widely shared and rule out few potential beloveds. Uniqueness, then, cannot be appealed to generally in accounting for exclusive love. This result is not avoided if x loves y in virtue of y's second-order properties, for x will love y exclusively only if y's second-order properties are necessary for x to love anyone at all. But how could "being willing and able to contribute to the continuation of the x-y shared history" be necessary for x's loving anyone at all? If it is a necessary condition, x, in considering that property necessary, was probably an exclusive y-lover already; that this property is necessary for x to love anyone at all is explained by, rather than explains, the fact that x loves y exclusively. It is no more illuminating than saying that "being y" is a necessary condition for x's loving anyone at all and that is why x loves only y.

If there is no foundation for a belief in substantive uniqueness, the belief may still be a psychologically useful self-deception. If x could not believe in his beloved's uniqueness, x might have to abandon the feeling that she is not replaceable or the belief that she is lovable in virtue of her prized properties.

We do not want to hear that we are loved exclusively, for example, because our lovers have a queer notion of what "having reasons" means. We want to be loved because we stand out from the crowd and are considered especially lovable. Or we know at some level that we are members of the homogeneous mass and still want our lovers to assert (falsely) our uniqueness and superiority. Thus, the belief in uniqueness may sustain our self-respect and help to preserve love. Such lovers and beloveds are not fully rational, but perhaps that is not to be condemned, given the love they secure through their mental gymnastics.

Lovers, however, can avoid irrationality by treating uniqueness as derivative. There is nothing incoherent in x's saying to y (as a greeting card does): "You're not like any other man" because "you're my man." X acknowledges that y is unique only insofar as y has the property "is loved by x" and no one else has that property; no pretensions are made that y is unique in any other way. But saying that x's loving y exclusively makes y unique is quite different from claiming that x loves y exclusively because y is unique. Uniqueness is the *explanandum*, not the *explanans*.

As a criticism of men who search for the woman with the perfect set of properties, Shulamith Firestone writes (sounding, ironically, like H. L. Mencken in the epigraph to this chapter) that these men never realize "there isn't much difference between one woman and the other."[47] Instead, "it is the loving that *creates* the difference." In this view, y's uniqueness does not consist in having a nonreplicable set of properties, nor does it consist in the fact that x loves only y. Rather, y's status as unique is a gift bestowed by x because x loves y. X may assent to the uniqueness of y counterfactually but not self-deceptively. X knows that y is not unique, but x acts as if y were. This bestowal of uniqueness is not automatically overestimation or the wish-fulfilling attribution to the beloved of excellences she does not have. Nor must it take the form of pedestalism or of denigrating other possible beloveds in order to think highly of one's actual beloved. The lover embellishes the beloved's merits to express the special meaning the beloved has in the lover's life. Treating the beloved as unique manifests itself as treating the beloved as the special object of one's concern (see 12.8). This bestowal of value need not represent an agapic tendency in personal love; after all, to treat the beloved as special is to treat him preferentially. Such preferential treatment may even be partially constitutive of love. But whether this preferential treatment is part of love or only a causal result of love, the question remains open as to why x loves y or, equivalently, why x bestows this preferential treatment on y, and perhaps only on y.

CHAPTER 4 *Coming First*

It was true, he realized with a terrible new pain, that if he had met Lisa first he would have married her.

—Iris Murdoch, *Bruno's Dream*

There is a wretched unbelief abroad. . . . It thinks it an accident that the lovers win one another, accidental that they love one another; there were a hundred other women with whom the hero might have been equally happy, and whom he could have loved as deeply.

—Kierkegaard, *Either/Or*

1. THE DEMOCRATIZATION OF LOVE

We attempted to solve Gellner's paradox by invoking uniqueness, looking for properties that were both love-grounding or valuable, yet not widely shared. That solution failed, however, in part because valuable properties are not rare enough to produce uniqueness, and rare properties are not the valuable ones. But given certain contingent facts, the uniqueness solution can explain some exclusivity. If people have an overly narrow conception of what counts as a valuable property and respond to such a property only if it is possessed to a high degree, then there might be a set of lovable, uniqueness-making properties. The uniqueness of beloveds derives not from a proliferation of properties or fine gradings within property groups (3.3) but from a reduction of lovable properties.

Imagine an "aristocratic" eros-style courtly love in which unblemished beauty, untainted moral virtue, the ownership of land and jewels, the performance of heroic deeds, and political or clerical power are the only properties considered valuable enough to ground love. In this courtly love beloveds could be unique and receive the exclusive attention of lovers, but few would be worthy of love,[1] few would therefore be the object of love, and few love relationships would exist.[2] Many lovers would not achieve reciprocity. Unrequited love would be an expected occurrence; it might even be transformed ideologically from a disadvantageous necessity into an ideal. If this aristocratic love were the norm, yet those unqualified for it embraced its standards, these masses would have good reason for turning their erosic attention to God: the high standards of aristocratic love would be satisfied (God is more worthy of love than the most worthy human), while the nonreciprocity of the aristocratic pattern would be overcome. The love for God would be not a second-rate alternative but a superior article.[3]

Imagine now that social, political, and economic upheavals have democratized love. The qualities of the object are still the basis of love, but love becomes more widely distributed because standards have been lowered. Some beauty, or some beautiful feature, suffices, rather than stunning beauty; some measure of intellectual or moral excellence is found attractive, rather than brilliance or saintliness. At the same time, a new individualist philosophy proclaims the subjectivity of value judgments, which contributes to the proliferation of lovable qualities. Many people become worthy of love, and unrequited love is no longer the expected course of events. Further, there is much less reason for people to prefer loving God—who languishes and then dies as humans increasingly love only each other. (Note that a wider distribution of love can be achieved also by eliminating altogether the role of meritorious properties, as in agapic love, rather than by lowering the standards of merit.) But along with the lowering of standards that increases the number of potential beloveds comes a leveling among people that destroys substantive uniqueness. This embarrassment of riches makes choosing a beloved from among so many qualified candidates difficult. When people share the same valuable qualities, what is there to latch onto in making distinctions? To say that no basis for distinguishing among potential beloveds exists and, therefore, selection must be arbitrary is (as Gellner suggested) to trivialize love. What is to be done?[4]

One answer is provided by another solution to Gellner's paradox. Suppose that x loves y in virtue of y's possessing S. Later x meets a person z who also has S (very likely after the democratization of standards). Gellner's paradox can be solved by escaping along the second horn: x does not love the relevantly similar z simply because x met y before meeting z. "In practice," Gellner claims, people sidestep the paradox by appealing to "primacy."[5] The time of x's meeting y is crucial not only in bringing about x's love for y but also in explaining why x loves y but not z. In chapter 3 (sect. 4) we examined whether a historical property—what y has done for x, or y's contribution to the x-y shared history—could make y both lovable and unique. In chapter 6 we will discuss another historical property: the satisfaction of x's desires by y. Here we consider one more historical property—namely, the spatiotemporal parameters of the encounters that x has with y and z.[6] That x met y before x met z—what else could the solution be for democratic love?

The time and place of x and y's first encounter may have a mysterious quality. In contrast to encounters deliberately arranged by third parties (matchmakers, mutual friends, the person who decides the seating at a dinner party), accidental meetings[7] that lead to something as significant in a person's life as love can be seen as the result of the inexplicable, supernatural manipulation of fate or an incredibly felicitous chance event; but both are imbued with deep mystery. Love arises like the discovery of penicillin: "How wondrous it is that if my date with the other woman hadn't been broken at the last minute, I wouldn't have been eating dinner alone. If it hadn't been raining, I would have walked another block instead of stopping at the first restaurant. If someone hadn't been sitting at the corner table, I would have sat there, isolated with my book. If someone hadn't accidentally brushed the window, I wouldn't have had an excuse to start a conversation. And we wouldn't now be experiencing this bliss (or horror)."

Some lovers have difficulty recalling these early moments of their love relationship and regret their weak memory. Consider these lines from Christina Rossetti's "The First Day":

> I wish I could remember the first day,
> First hour, first moment of your meeting me;
>
> . . . .
>
> So unrecorded did it slip away,
> So blind was I to see and to foresee,
>
> . . . .
>
> If only I could recollect it! Such
> a day of days! I let it come and go
> As traceless as a thaw of bygone snow.
> It seemed to mean so little, meant so much![8]

Other lovers engage in cynical or gamelike postmortems: "I thought you didn't like me" (see Jane Austen, *Pride and Prejudice,* chapter 60). But many lovers joyfully relive their first meeting, making it special, embellishing its lovely details.[9] They cherish the narrative, even relying on its power to get them through rough moments. They talk about first impressions, about when they first realized they had a loving interest, and about which statements, actions, mannerisms, and characteristics of the other produced these feelings. Children, curious about such things, persistently ask questions about how and when their parents met, what they did on their first date, how their joint history progressed. But I doubt that answering these questions or reliving in detail the first days gets to the heart of the matter: namely, why they love each other, the reasons for their love. As Gellner claims, lovers do often cite the fact that x encountered y before z, or that x developed an emotion toward y first, in explaining why x loves y but not z (whether or not z has the S in virtue of which x loves y). How seriously should we take this?

In the worst-case scenario, the fact that x loves y rather than z (or that x loves y at all) because x met y at a certain time or place is objectionably arbitrary. If x is in a hating mood and expresses this hatred toward y but not z merely because y wanders into x's sight first, x's hating y has everything to do with x and nothing to do with y. Because x's hating y is independent of y's having a hate-inducing property, we are not reluctant to judge x unreasonable or even irrational. If this is what is going on when x loves y because x met y first, y's properties are quite beside the point. X's love exhibits the subject-centricity of the second view of personal love; and to the extent that the primacy solution to Gellner's paradox makes love more a matter of the right time than of the right person, it makes love a psychologically suspicious agapic phenomenon. Since the beloved is only the recipient of a love lottery, the primacy solution does not solve the problem of how to select, on a reasonable basis, a beloved from the mass of indistinguishable candidates. But perhaps, because either metaphysically or democratically we are all basically the same, it does not matter one whit whom we love or marry; tossing a coin is as reasonable or unreasonable as any other method.[10]

On the other hand, in other scenarios the primacy solution seems acceptable. For example, x and y meet by chance at a coffee shop and are attracted to each other in virtue of their respective properties. It is not necessarily true that x would have been attracted to any person who happened to sit at the next table, let alone simply because she was sitting at that table. Nor will x be interested in the person z who would have sat at that table had she been a little quicker on her feet. Thus, appealing to y's coming along first might reconcile the exclusivity and reason-dependence of love, for the second horn of Gellner's paradox, by maintaining a tight connection between xLy and y's having S, while explaining why z's having S does not lead to xLz. The fact that x encountered y before z is not a characteristic of y and cannot be included in the set S of y's attractive properties that account for xLy; time and place are therefore a type of reason for or cause of xLy countenanced only by the second view of personal love.[11] But suppose that "met x at t_1" is a relational or historical property that the beloved y could have and counts as one of x's reasons for xLy. A later-encountered z does not have this property and it thereby distinguishes y from any z who is otherwise relevantly similar to y; moreover, this historical property makes y unique.

Of course, "met x before z met x" is a trivial uniqueness-making property, and it is not valuable or lovable. Nevertheless, if y's having this property is one reason for x to love y but not z, x is not guilty of the irrationality of the E-type lover. At least x can say what the BVC-lover said (3.1), that x's reason for loving y is perfectly general even though it now applies to only one case. X's reason for xLy is perfectly general as long as x says that x would have loved z rather than y had x met z before meeting y. X's total reason for loving someone might be "has S and is the first person having S that I encounter." This reason contains no proper names and mentions no particular time or place. Hence it does not rule out in advance z or anyone else who has S as a beloved. Never mind that as soon as y satisfies these conditions, no one else can; for before anyone in particular does satisfy them, anyone at all having S could satisfy them. Thus the primacy solution is an interesting reconciliation of the two love traditions: x's reasons for loving y include y's having S (from the first view) and y's coming along first (from the second view). The element of chance need not undermine the significance of the emotion or the reasonableness of the choice, for the emotion and the choice are both tied to y's having S.[12]

Gellner rejects the primacy solution by denying that x can rightly say that x would have loved z rather than y had x encountered z first: "The genuine lover cannot admit that his love would have had a different object had the order of his encounters been different."[13] Similarly, one who truly believes in Roman Catholicism cannot say that her religious commitment is merely a function of the accidents of time, place, and birth; the genuine Catholic cannot assert that she is a Catholic because her beliefs were learned before and instead of some other religious doctrines. The Catholic is conceptually forbidden from saying that she would properly be committed to Taoism had that religion come into her life first. Roger Scruton, whose solution to the paradox is the same as Gellner's (3.1), agrees: "Love [is] characterized by the fact that . . . this counterfactual substitution is ruled out. Any object that 'would have done just as well' as the object . . . would also be *identical* with that object."[14] The logic of love, or the logic of E-type emotions, entails that x cannot entertain the thought that x would have loved z, rather than y, had z come along first; it is a conceptual point that y's being the object of x's love can have no connection with when x encountered y and z.

If people believe, with Gellner, that genuine love rules out the counterfactual substitution, that would explain why many lovers tell themselves that the emotion they have today toward y is love, while the emotion they had last year toward z was not the genuine article, but instead infatuation or some other emotion (for example, sexual desire) pretending to be love.[15] (See the romanticism described by Doris Lessing in 9.8.) The phenomenon is also psychologically comprehensible. There is a mental tension between our realization that spatiotemporal factors have played a large role in the history of our love and our inability to admit that fact (psychologically, not conceptually). The logic of love might not prevent x from saying that x could very well have loved z had z come along first; but psychological factors do impede that admission. Callous lovers might quite easily proclaim that xLy just because x met y first, perhaps to remind y of her vulnerable position. But ordinarily, lovers have difficulty saying to themselves, and to their beloveds, that a crucial reason for xLy was the timing of x's meeting y. Beloveds do not want to hear from their lovers that x's meeting y before z explains why x does not love z; y derives no security from that explanation. Saving face, expressing respect, and being convincing require that lovers mention only other reasons for loving, primarily that y has S.

2. WHY PRIMACY MUST FAIL

Even if it is wrong to insist that for either conceptual or psychological reasons the counterfactual substitution is ruled out, the primacy solution is unsatisfactory. X's meeting y before meeting z cannot in general explain why x loves y but not z, simply because there are too many cases in which x meets z second and loves z rather than y. Or, more likely, x meets both y and z at roughly the same time and only later comes to love one and not the other, even though both might have S. In this case, the order of meeting is not as important as the point at which x's love for one or the other began. In understanding that, primacy of encounter is irrelevant. To say that x loves y and not z just because x's emotion toward y occurred before x's emotion toward z—taking it one stage beyond the physical encounter itself—is not to answer the question but to pose it again. (Note that primacy factors, despite Gellner's rejection of this solution as violating the conceptual ban on counterfactual substitution, figure into Gellner's own solution. For Gellner, why does x love y but not z? X is an E-type lover who fails to apply his reasons for loving y (who came first) to the later-encountered yet relevantly similar z. How can x make comprehensible his not applying his love-reasons in a general way, unless x says that y's having come first makes the difference or that because x has already applied his reasons to y, they can no longer be applied to the later-appearing z?)

Further, temporal priority per se cannot explain why xLy but not xLz, for much the same reason that time and place per se are, in moral contexts, irrelevant. "What makes it one rather than the other of a pair of identical twins that you are in love with? . . . no more than this: it was one of them and not the other that you have met."[16] But what if you do eventually meet the second?

Can you appeal to primacy per se to explain why you love the first? To have any effect on the course of your love, temporal priority must have some consequences; these mediating consequences, which explain the power of temporal priority, are really the ingredients of the intended solution to Gellner's paradox.[17] Favoring the firstborn son makes no sense if the son is favored merely because of birth order; something else about this son, which he has because he is firstborn, accounts for his special position. Another example: x meets y before meeting z, x begins to love y and promises to love no one else. Here x loves y and not z not merely because y came along first, but because of x's earlier-made promise. Temporal priority has to work through something; alone it has no effect.

Suppose that x loves y in virtue of y's having S and that x then meets z, who also has S. If x loves only y but not z, even though z has S, then S in z is not having the effect on x that S in y has. If reasons and causes are general, the failure of S in z to elicit x's love must be because of some difference in the total situations confronted by x. By hypothesis, there is no relevant difference between y and z; yet the difference in time per se cannot explain why the reason or cause works with respect to y but not z. Some difference in x, therefore, makes the situation xMy different from xMz and accounts for xLy because of S but not xLz. Temporal priority is relevant only if it contributes to this change in x, and it contributes to this change through some mediating factor.

Whatever this mediating factor is, the fact that time and place work in virtue of it has important theoretical implications. First, the acknowledgment of mediation avoids the arbitrariness of selecting on the basis of temporal priority per se. Something about the mediating factor might make the choice among similar potential beloveds more rational or reasonable than it would be if time per se led to the choice. Second, the mediating factor may be such that this solution to Gellner's paradox is no longer a reconciliation of the eros and agape traditions: the mediating factor may entail that love is entirely property-based. One mediating factor is discussed now; a more interesting factor, in chapter 6.

W. Newton-Smith has proposed a solution to Gellner's paradox about love at first sight.[18] The generality of reasons, he claims, does not require that xLz, when xLy because y has S and z, too, has S, if xLy *also because* "it was [y] that first excited this passion in [x]." The solution is plausible because included in x's reasons for loving y but not z is a mediating factor through which primacy of encounter has its effect. Yet Newton-Smith's solution, that after one encounter xLy (but not xLz) because y "first excited this passion" in x, is ambiguous, admitting of four interpretations.

Consider these readings: (i) y excited in x a passion that x never experienced before; x is experiencing "first love." Since "first love" is logically exclusive, the later-encountered z cannot elicit it in x once y has done so. (ii) Y excited a passion in x, before z could do so, that x has experienced before but that is now directed at y as the person who is currently eliciting it; x is experiencing a particular passion-token, one occurrence of a repeatable passion-type that is contingently tied to y. That y elicited this passion in x before xMz is compatible with the fact that had z come before y, z could have produced in x a passion-token qualitatively identical to the one that y produced. (iii) Y excited in x *this* passion-token, this specific instance of the passion-type; x is experiencing one occurrence of a repeatable feeling contingently tied to y. But x especially values *this* passion-token; z could at a later time elicit a passion-token of the same type, but x would not especially value it. If z had come before y, there are two possibilities. One, that the passion-token elicited by z would have had this special value for x; two, that it would not, but the later passion-token produced by y would have. Newton-Smith is ruling out the second possibility; in his view, xLy but not xLz because y came first. Finally, (iv) y excited in x the passion-for-y, a passion for a particular person. Since this is x's first encounter with y, x is experiencing something *logically* similar to "first love." X's experience is essentially, rather than contingently, tied to y; for x is experiencing a passion-token of the type "passion-for-y." This is a repeatable passion, but y is necessarily its object. Because the passion is indexed, z could never elicit this passion in x. At least, z cannot elicit it toward z (z might be able to elicit in x the passion-for-y, toward y, through a devious or complex causal mechanism).

Do any of these readings solve the paradox? I think (iv) can be eliminated immediately. It is superfluous to claim that xLy but not xLz *because* y came first, when even if z had come first z could not have elicited the indexed passion-for-y toward z. The fact that the passion is indexed means that the temporal relationship between the two encounters is irrelevant. Furthermore, if y can elicit in x the passion-for-y, z can elicit in x the passion-for-z; the fact that y elicits the passion-for-y first does not explain how its occurrence prevents the qualitatively different passion-for-z, or why x might prefer the passion-for-y to the passion-for-z when both y and z have S. Finally, why index passions this way? For some philosophers, that there is a distinct feeling, a passion-for-y, which is different from the passion-for-z, is the most natural way to conceptualize these things. But I doubt that the phenomenal nature of the passions provides clear evidence that the passion elicited in x by y is qualitatively different from the passion elicited by z, especially if we are considering emotions "at first sight."

Reading (i) does not solve Gellner's paradox because it covers only those cases in which xLy is x's first experience of love; the paradox is about "love at first sight," not "first love," which may not occur at first sight. But "first love, at first sight" does fall within the scope of the paradox. Does this reading provide a solution for this smaller set of cases? I think not. If xAy because y has S, then the generality of reasons implies xAz, because z also has S; we should expect, that is, a qualitatively similar response to z even though we cannot *call* that response "first love." The fact that first love is logically exclusive entails that it can be directed at only one person; it does not entail that x will not respond in a qualitatively identical fashion to z or that because we cannot describe xAz as "first love" xAz does not occur at all. Gellner's paradox remains, differently phrased: if xLy in virtue of y's having S, where xLy is the first time x has experienced love, why won't x experience "second love" when encountering the z who also has S?

We might say here that because xLy is x's first love experience, x is "overwhelmed" and cannot respond the same way toward z. X has changed between meeting y and meeting z, so we do not expect the later exposure to S in z to have the same effect. Because the initial conditions have changed, we can escape along the second horn without violating the generality of reasons or causes. Perhaps this solution works for cases of "first love, at first sight," but it will not work generally for cases in which xLy is not x's first love experience. There is no guarantee that x is so overwhelmed that x has significantly changed before meeting z.

A general point can be made here that applies to readings (i) and (ii), which is the most natural interpretation of Newton-Smith's solution. Suppose x is overwhelmed, either by "first love," as in reading (i), or by the passion elicited by y's having S, before z could elicit this passion in x, as in reading (ii). Why is it that y's S elicited a passion in x, but the later exposure to S in z does not do so? The answer must have this form: x has changed in such a way that having experienced one instance of the passion elicited by S, x is no longer able to experience another instance of the passion elicited by S. But why should one instance of that passion prevent the same passion from occurring again? What kind of change in x explains why x's having experienced this passion prevents x's experiencing it not merely a second time, but a second time in response to a cause (namely, S) that has already proven itself efficacious? In general, having a feeling at time t_1 does not prevent having it again at the later t_2; not even the physiology of the emotions makes it likely that one instance of an emotion prevents a later instance of the emotion. (X may hate y at t_1 in virtue of T and experience hate soon again at t_2 toward z who also has T; nothing about the emotion implies that x is likely to be hate-exhausted.) In order to argue plausibly that temporal priority works through the fact that x's passion for y was elicited before x met z, one must show that x has changed in some specific way. But to say that x is "overwhelmed" by the first passion explains nothing: that phrase only restates that x's experience of the passion at t_1 prevents x from experiencing it at t_2. Unless some specific mechanism is mentioned, "overwhelmed" only *means* "unable to respond again." Further, it is false that x's experiencing the passion in response to the earlier encounter with a person having S has changed x in such a way that x can no longer respond to a later exposure to S. For x is still experiencing the passion in response to y's S, and so one instance of the passion due to S is *not* preventing the occurrence of later instances of the passion due to S. If S in y still has the power to invoke this passion in x, x's sensitivity to S has not changed and x should respond the same way to S in z.

To claim that xLz is ruled out because y first elicited a passion in x is therefore to leave mysterious why temporal priority makes a difference. Reading (iii) fares no better: it will be futile to rely on the special value of the particular passion-token elicited by y, if one cannot explain why it is special. To say that it is special merely because it is first does not explain how temporal priority makes a difference. If, by having S, y can elicit a passion-token that is special, then z (who also has S) can elicit another special passion-token, and we still have no explanation why the first is a *special* special passion-token and the second only a special passion-token. If the passion-token elicited by y is special, this fact seems an *explanandum*, rather than the *explanans*, of xLy. Of course, we could say that y's coming along first influences x to discount, ignore, or be blind to the manifestation of S by z (that being the change in x), while x still responds to y in virtue of S. But this move abandons the generality of reasons or the rationality of the lover, exactly what Newton-Smith wanted to avoid.

CHAPTER 5 *Aristophanic Love*

Man had become . . . a thinking being. He had come to know enough about
permutations and combinations to realize that with millions of . . . females to
choose from, the chances of his choosing the ideal mate were almost zero.

—Thurber and White, *Is Sex Necessary?*

Somewhere in the world each of us has a partner who once formed part of
our body. . . . The trouble is, man does not find the other part of himself.
Instead, he is sent a Tereza in a bulrush basket. But what happens if
he . . . later meets the one who was meant for him, the other part of himself?

—Milan Kundera, *The Unbearable Lightness of Being*

1. ARISTOPHANES' MYTH

Exclusivity, constancy, reciprocity, and "love for the person," as I have
mentioned, present difficulties for the eros tradition. But there is a view of love
that may solve these problems at a single stroke: by cutting whole persons into
half persons, Zeus created love as well as the conditions that make it exclusive,
constant and reciprocal. In Plato's *Symposium,* Aristophanes tells this story:
originally, humans were circle-people, having four arms, four legs, two faces,
and two sets of genitals. Male circle-people had two sets of male genitalia,
females had two sets of female genitalia, and androgynes had a set of each.
These people were strong and vigorous and had the hubris not to think highly
of the gods (original sin). Zeus therefore sliced them in half. Thereafter,

> man's . . . body having been cut in two, each half yearned for the half from
> which it had been severed. When they met they threw their arms round one
> another and embraced, in their longing to grow together again. . . . It is from
> this distant epoch, then, that we may date the innate love which human beings
> feel for one another, the love which restores us to our ancient state by attempting
> to weld two beings into one and to heal the wounds which humanity suffered.
> Each of us . . . is the mere broken tally of a man, . . . and each of us is per-
> petually in search of his corresponding tally.[1]

Aristophanes' myth reappears, in different versions, throughout Western love
literature and popular culture.[2] Paul Tillich even surmises that "love in all its
forms is the drive towards the reunion of the separated." Under this umbrella

definition, both "infinite passion for God" and "sexual passion" are "a consequence . . . of the state of separation of those who belong together and are driven towards each other in love."[3]

Originally, x and y were the circle-person xy, but then they were separated from each other, and from the whole of which they were parts, by Zeus' fission. They now desire to unite, or reunite, with each other, to return to their "primitive condition when [they] were whole" (192e). Why do x and y love each other, that is, desire to join together? X desires y because y is x's other half; y desires x because x is y's other half. The property in virtue of which they love each other is "my other half," which makes each of them unique. In this case the uniqueness of the beloved does yield exclusivity. Recall that x will love y exclusively if (i) xLy because y has S, (ii) only y has S, and (iii) a person's having S is necessary for x to love anyone (3.7). Given Aristophanes' story about x and y originally being a single circle-person, all three conditions are satisfied. Indeed, given this story y's property "is x's other half" is both necessary and sufficient for x to love y and guarantees that no one else loves y.

Reciprocity occurs automatically: if xLy because y is x's other half, x is necessarily y's other half, which is sufficient for yLx. Constancy is also secured: if xLy because y is x's other half, x will always love y because y always has the property sufficient for xLy. Further, there seems to be no room to criticize Aristophanic love for involving only love for y's properties themselves. That problem in Plato's eros is avoided because "the objects of these creatures' passions are whole people"—not a set of valuable properties, but "entire beings."[4] (Note the irony of saying that x loves y the "whole" person when x loves y because y is x's other half.) Thus, Aristophanic love solves the problems of the eros tradition. But is Aristophanic love even an erosic love, or is it agapic?

2. THE STRUCTURE OF ARISTOPHANIC LOVE

There are many reasons to think that Aristophanic love is erosic. Aristophanes' speech is delivered during a banquet at which all the speakers praise eros. The *Symposium*, written around 385 B.C., is hardly a treatise on agape. Aristophanes' account of love ("the name for the desire . . . of the whole" [192e]) is not far from Diotima's account of eros ("love is desire for the perpetual possession of the good" [206a], a different sense of "wholeness"). And Aristophanes' desire for union is a precursor of a main feature of the romantic view of love. But none of these reasons for placing Aristophanes' myth within the eros tradition is compelling. Aristophanes' use of the word "eros" means nothing; he may be informing the banquet guests that eros is quite a different kind of thing than they are accustomed to think ("I shall . . . initiate you into the secret" of love [189d]). Aristophanes' account of love may be an unintended anticipation of the agape tradition.

The main reason for thinking of Aristophanic love as agapic is that one's other half "has no specific qualities of goodness or badness, beauty or ugliness, brown or red hair. . . . We do not desire union with the other because he or she is beautiful"[5] but simply because he or she is our other half. Thus, x does not love y in virtue of y's outstanding properties; moreover, x loves y even if y is objectively unattractive. The point is not that y's property "x's other half" outweighs, in a comparison of the good and bad properties of y, y's defects; if that were so, Aristophanic love would be erosic. Rather, defects do not count at all against x's loving y: Aristophanic lovers "overlook all that is ugly and grotesque."[6] There is no balancing, but rather an insensitivity to both merits and defects compatible only with the second view of personal love. Further, because x is overwhelmed with joy when reuniting with y (192b, c), x probably finds y's properties to be wonderful just because they are y's, transforming even y's flaws into beautiful things.[7] If so, Aristophanic love is agapic—x finds P in y to be valuable because xLy—since xLy is not in turn a response to y's other valuable properties. Aristophanic love is exclusive, constant, reciprocal, and "love for the person" because it is not erosic; the myth does not defend eros but abandons it.

Nevertheless, Aristophanic love is erosic after all, because "my other half" is a meritorious second-order or historical property. Why does x seek the y who is x's other half? X has been wounded by the fission (191d), or the whole of which x had been a part has been wounded, and as a result x suffers (as does y). X had been happy as a part of a whole, because the whole circle-person had been happy. But now x is a "broken tally," seeking her other half in order to re-create the happy whole. Y, in virtue of being x's other half, is the only one who can restore x to prelapsarian bliss. X therefore desires y because y can heal x and make x happy again. In other words, x desires y as having the property "my other half" because x desires y as having the property "can restore me to happiness." If this is what grounds x's love, we have a whole new can of worms.

First, Aristophanic love is property-based; "has the ability to make me happy again" is certainly a valuable property from x's perspective. Second, either x finds y's other properties attractive because x loves y, which in turn is grounded in y's most important valuable property, or y's property "can restore me to happiness" always outweighs y's defects. Third, even though this erosic love for y will be exclusive and constant (only y has, and will always have, the property "can restore x to happiness"), Aristophanic love introduces another problem: egocentricity. Aristophanic love is exclusive, constant, and reciprocal just because x and y desperately need each other to heal their wounds. X wants to join with y because that union will benefit x. Surely, when x and y reunite, y is also made happy by being healed, but x does not join with y precisely in order to make y happy. Y, not y's happiness, is necessary for x's happiness. And y's happiness is produced automatically, without x's doing anything (and without doing anything intentionally) to promote it. Aristophanic reciprocity is the result of the dual benefits derived by two self-interested parties who are forced together by circumstances.[8] And, fourth, even though x does not love y's first-order properties, Aristophanic love still does not involve "love for the person" in any robust sense. X does not desire y, but desires the union itself, the reestablished whole of which x wants to be again a part; x loves y only qua contributor to what x ultimately wants. What I earlier said was ironic is the truth: x does not love y the whole person but only y the half, as the other piece that with x comprises the whole circle-person that x wants to reestablish.

3. THE FIRST GENERATION

Reading the myth, we might conclude that the halves x and y will be lucky if they encounter each other and rejoin. What guarantees that x will meet the y who is x's other half and that x knows, on meeting y, that y is x's other half? "The encounter with our true mate occurs by chance," writes Arlene Saxonhouse; it "is not predetermined and we may spend our whole lives searching in vain."[9] Martha Nussbaum also attributes the encounter's happening to "luck"; love "comes to the cut-up creatures by sheer chance, if at all." The lover's "other half is somewhere, but it is hard to see what reason and planning can do to make that half turn up." Further, even if one encounters his other half, it is "mysterious still how you come to know that."[10] But even though Aristophanes does speak of the "good fortune" of finding one's other half and hints that the two halves recognize each other merely by an "overwhelming" feeling (192b, c), Aristophanic love is not a rare or lucky event radically contingent on time and place.

First, why agree with Nussbaum that x's other half is "somewhere" in the world and must be found? If x and y are halves of a circle-person split by Zeus, immediately after fission they will be sitting, or standing, next to each other. Aristophanes never says that after fission Zeus dispersed the halves as if tossing dust into the wind. Second, even if the halves are immediately scattered after fission and must search for each other, they will probably find their other half and know (unmysteriously) they have done so. At the very least, because they originate from the same circle-person they have certain traits in common and resemble each other like twins; Aristophanes even says (190a) that they have "identical faces." (Hence, x has another reason to find y's properties beautiful: in a sense y is simply another x, and x's loving y is a type of narcissistic self-love.) The main point, however, is that the two halves knew each other intimately when they existed as the circle-person xy; x and y know each other by acquaintance and therefore should, when they later meet, recognize each other on the spot. I do not mean this metaphorically, as if to suggest that they will recognize each other by having a *feeling* that the person is their other half. Their recognizing each other is a result of remembering earlier knowledge. Maybe the halves of a circle-person that is cut up when it is young will have trouble coming together, but we should not conclude that in general Aristophanic love is rarely consummated. To think otherwise is to insert complications into the myth that have little textual support.[11]

Let us not forget the sequel to Zeus' splitting the circle-people: he then created sexual intercourse as a mechanism both for physically uniting the severed halves and (in halves originating from androgynes) for the reproduction of the species (191c, d). The humans resulting from sexual intercourse engaged in by half-persons of the first generation were not at any time circle-people; they were, like their parents, only half-persons. But these second-generation half-persons are different: they are half-persons by their nature, born as "halves." They are half-persons only in form. Never having been severed from another part, they have no "other half" at all, and hence they are not genuine half-persons.[12] (Aristophanes never suggests that the genuine half-person nature of first-generation halves is biologically transmitted to the second generation or that even though they did not originate in a whole, somehow they still have other halves. Nor is there any hint in Aristophanes' myth that the progeny of first-generation heterosexual halves are born as wholes that Zeus cuts into two.)[13] Thus, Hume's interpretation is inaccurate: "Each of these halves is continually searching through the whole species to find the other half, which was broken from it; . . . it *often* happens, that they are *mistaken* in . . . [taking] for their half what [in] no way corresponds to them; and . . . the parts do not meet nor join in with each other, as is usual in fractures. In this case the union is soon dissolved, and each part is set loose again to hunt for its lost half."[14] If we are talking about first-generation half-persons, mistakes as to the identity of one's other half are not likely (given what I said above); and if we are talking about second-generation "half"-persons, such mistakes are not possible, since no one in this generation has an other half to begin with. Similarly, to claim that love will be a lucky or rare event for second-generation Aristophanic humans *because* finding one's other half, and knowing that one has found it, are difficult is to overlook that these "half"-persons do not have any other halves that it would be difficult for them to find.

Second- and later-generation humans who have no other halves might either falsely believe they have them or realize they do not. If they are aware of not having other halves, they will not embark on necessarily unsuccessful searches. On the other hand, if they believe they do have other halves, they will surely have difficulty knowing they have encountered what does not exist and may wander throughout the world in a perpetual search for it. Hence, consummation of love might very well be rare, although it is still conceptually incorrect to speak of "mistakes." But the fact that Aristophanes is initiating his audience into the secret of love implies that contemporary "half"-persons do not even know that humans were originally circle-people. More to the point: even if later-generation persons know the story, to suppose that they incorrectly conclude that it also applies to them is farfetched. Why should they believe that they have (and are) genuine other halves, just because there had been one generation like that; and is it not plain to them that they are full-born as halves? I do not conclude that I was parented by apes because humans long ago came from apes.

4. LATER GENERATIONS

A plausible reading of Plato's Aristophanes must keep separate his claims (or their implications) about the first generation and those about subsequent generations. Indeed, because Aristophanes is speaking to his contemporaries about their loves, our task is to make sense of his account of love as it pertains to post-first-generation "half"-persons. In doing so, it is useful to reconstruct Aristophanes' account of first-generation love as a set of five claims:

a. x and y were severed from the original xy whole;
b. y has the property "x's other half";
c. y is x's ideal mate (that is, the one and only person for x);
d. x desires to join with y; and
e. y makes x happy.

For first-generation half-persons, claims (a) and (b) entail each other and explain (c), (d), and (e). But when claims (a) and (b) are dropped for later-generation "half"-persons, that which ties (c), (d), and (e) together is no longer available. We are thus able to fashion three different accounts of later-generation love from Aristophanes' myth, depending on whether (c), (d), or (e) is emphasized.

First, if we were to continue talking about other halves for later-generation humans who do not actually have other halves, such talk could only be elliptical for the doctrine that one absolutely right person exists for each of us.

This "ideal mate" theory drops claim (a) but retains claim (c), that only one person is our perfect partner.[15] Consider two strategies for finding love, both of which illustrate the chanciness of love if (c) is true. In the first, one patiently waits for the right person to appear, preparing oneself for that momentous occasion by educating oneself, remaining chaste, forsaking superficial relationships. One passively searches by deliberately not searching, believing love will happen without prodding. In the second, one actively searches by forming many relationships, and perhaps by engaging in promiscuous sexual activity, until one finally finds the ideal. Both strategies are unreliable. The one who waits never knows if she has waited long enough; the next person—the one not waited for—may be the ideal. The one who examines and examines never knows that the ideal is not the next unexamined person. The problem is not exactly the methodology but the assumption that only one person is "right."[16] In this case, love *will* be a rare or lucky event.

Nevertheless, if the ideal is understood as the person having the best set of properties, then a perpetual waiting or search almost necessarily follows, for outside the circle of one's acquaintances there likely is a person, closer to the ideal, who has better properties. If the ideal mate theory were construed, instead, as falling within the agape tradition (in which case "ideal" has no connection with superlative properties), then neither waiting nor searching makes sense. Since the ideal person cannot be identified by properties, then (as Nussbaum said about Aristophanic first-generation love) "it is hard to see what reason and planning can do to make [the ideal] turn up." But if the ideal mate theory is construed erosically, the reason and planning involved in waiting and searching have lots of room to operate, indeed too much room, since their demands are never fully satisfiable. Because the next person might be the ideal, not much if any exclusivity or constancy is secured. The eros tradition, of course, is under no compulsion to embrace claim (c). And why would anyone believe (c) and conduct her love life accordingly? Perhaps because she believes that Aristophanes' myth applies per force to later-generation humans or because she is entranced by some other metaphysical delusion (for example, x and y—as in Schopenhauer—experience a unique animal magnetism for each other and only each other, which mechanism is the product of evolution). Regardless, I find no reason to think that (c) is Aristophanes' account of love for later-generation humans. He knows that he has dropped (a) for later generations, and that when (a) is dropped (c) is untenable.

Second, we can, instead, retain claim (d). Whereas finding support for (c) when (a) is abandoned is difficult, claim (d) may be defensible without (a). Why does x want to merge with y? ("This is what everybody wants, and everybody would regard it as the precise expression of the desire which he had long felt" [192e].) Even though having actually been separated from y is sufficient for a first-generation x to feel incomplete and unhappy, or to judge himself deficient, and hence sufficient for his desire to merge, that motivating feeling or judgment could arise in a later-generation x in some other way. Genuine first-generation half-persons feel incomplete because they really are incomplete; later-generation "half"-persons, not being halves of a whole, must feel deficient for some other reason, if they feel deficient at all. Descartes suggests that "nature has . . . implanted certain impressions in the brain which bring it about that at a certain age and time we regard ourselves as deficient—as forming only one half of a whole, whose other half must be a person of the opposite sex."[17] Perhaps x feels deficient and hence desires to merge in order to overcome this unpleasant feeling, because x notices the anatomical or psychological differences between himself or herself and persons of the other sex (penis- or vagina-envy?) or because sexual desire, which x cannot quiet without the cooperation of another person, makes x feel less than the captain of his own ship.[18] Or perhaps in virtue of being born "half"-persons in form, later generations are "permanently incomplete" in not having the original full measure of arms, legs, genitals.[19]

The first explanation (we want to merge with others because we feel deficient upon noticing sexual differences) does not explain what was obvious to Aristophanes—that some males desire to merge with males and some females with females.[20] The second explanation (the experience of sexual desire makes us feel deficient) reduces the desire to merge to the desire to engage in sex, which is not only phenomenally questionable but also inconsistent with the spiritual nature of the union sought by Aristophanic lovers (191c, d). The third explanation (we are deficient in form and therefore feel deficient) might seem to be what Aristophanes claims about later-generation humans. But even though this deficiency can account for the desire of first-generation half-persons to merge, it does not work for later generations. A later-generation human, given *his* nature, *is* complete; or he is as complete as he *could* be, for he has no more complete state to which he could aspire. By contrast, a first-generation human, given *his* nature, is incomplete; or he is not as complete as he *could* be, for he does have a more complete state to which he can aspire. Not originating from a larger whole, later generation "half"-persons are already whole. (The notion that Socrates, later in the *Symposium*, takes up and improves the "desire as lack" view of love from Aristophanes must therefore be qualified. If he takes it from Aristophanes, it is from the account of first-generation love, not from the account of later-generation love.)

Theorists of a liberal bent might claim either that people by and large do not judge themselves deficient—and hence desire to merge with others for other, more positive reasons—or that if people do feel deficient, this is a cultural artifact having no essential connection with love. Yet Erich Fromm, who (as a member of the Frankfurt School in his early days) might have been expected to take such a stance, contends that "the awareness of . . . separateness" is a timeless truth, "the problem of human existence." The experience of this "separateness" is "the source of all anxiety," and humans can "leave the prison of [their] aloneness" only "in the achievement of interpersonal union, of fusion with another person, in *love*."[21] Theodor Reik develops this psychoanalytic explanation: "We have discovered some strange things concerning the origin of love: the preliminary state of discontent . . . with oneself, the inner tension resulting therefrom, the attempts to remove it or ease it. Before he fell in love the person is not in an enviable psychical condition but in emotional distress. . . . [L]ove does not spring from abundance and richness of the ego, but is a way out of . . . poverty."[22] In contrast to Reik and Fromm, who claim that our deficiency makes love possible, Robert N. Bellah and his colleagues claim that deficiency prevents love. Lightly chastising people who search for the "person who is going to stop making them feel alone," they write that "this search . . . cannot succeed because it comes from a self that is not full and self-sustaining. [Their] desire for relatedness is really a reflection of incompleteness."[23] Bellah concludes that "before one can love others, one must learn to love one's self."[24] In a sense, one must be "whole" to love others (in contrast to Aristophanes' claim that wholes, that is, circle-people, do not love anyone). Defenders of the agape tradition would reply to Bellah with their own platitude: "Self-love is man's natural condition," not something to be nurtured in order to attain the ability to love others but something to be vanquished in developing that ability.[25]

Experimental social psychologists are still debating whether deficiency can explain love.[26] In the meantime, there is another possibility: x wants to merge with y in order to share in y's admirable properties, even if only vicariously.[27] Although some admiration might result from x's comparing herself with y and judging herself not to measure up, admiration need not be backhanded criticism of the self or a sign of a defect in one's ego. Thinking within the eros tradition, we could say that y's properties are highly valued by or attractive to x and that x desires that these properties be her own; to achieve this feat, x joins herself to y by conversing with y, sleeping with y, emulating y. On the other hand, the desire to merge may be consistent with the agape tradition. In a nonideal case of second-view love, x has such low self-esteem that x needs the companionship and support of y; there is nothing special about y, beyond the fact that y is a human being, that figures into x's desire to spend her life with y.[28] If Aristophanes' account of later-generation love involves the desire to merge, then, this would not by itself indicate whether it falls within the first or second view of personal love. Both the erosic and agapic interpretation of the desire to merge imply that love might not be constant. If x no longer feels deficient (perhaps because y has supplied x with the support x needed) or no longer admires y, then x will no longer desire to merge. And if this desire is necessary for love, x will no longer love.

Third, recall that for genuine, first-generation half-persons, an object's having the property "my other half" is necessary for x to love anyone at all. If this condition is retained, then later-generation "half"-persons will love no one, since they have no other halves. Love is impossible for later-generation humans, since they have no suitable objects, and therefore the only thing left for humans is sex. Sexual activity becomes a substitute merging that takes the place of the merging of love.[29] There is some support for this reading of Aristophanes. At 191d, Aristophanes says that everyone, including later-generation humans, carries on a perpetual search for his other half; but why "perpetual," unless the search is necessarily futile? And Aristophanes immediately follows this with descriptions of sexually promiscuous men and women.

Nevertheless, what Aristophanes says at 193c pertains directly to later-generation humans: if the ideal is to join with a literal other half, but doing so is impossible, "it follows that it is best for us to come as near to it as our present circumstances allow; and the way to do that is to find *a sympathetic and congenial object* for our affections." What Aristophanes is doing in 193c is dropping the assumption, for later-generation humans ("our present circumstances"), that "my other half" or "can restore me to my earlier state" is a property y must have for x to love y or anyone else. It is crucial to note Aristophanes' remark about first-generation half-persons: "When one member of a pair died and the other was left, the latter sought after and embraced another partner" (191b). What Aristophanes does not say here is revealing. He does not say that because x's other half has died—and therefore x, just like later-generation humans, has no actual other half (that is, no longer has one)—x is cut off forever from love, must replace love with sex, or cannot achieve happiness. Rather, he allows that x will find another beloved, presumably one who is "sympathetic and congenial" and who can bring x as close to the happiness x had with his actual other half. The core of Aristophanic love for later generations, then, is captured by claim (e). Since a later-generation x will not be able to find the nonexistent person who has the property "the only one capable of restoring me to my original condition of happiness," x does best to look for a person who has the property "can make me as happy as anyone else could" or "can bring me as close to happiness as realistically possible."

Aristophanes is not saying, however, that later-generation humans *settle* for such a person and for that "lesser" degree of happiness; they have no actual other half with whom they could, by comparison, find perfect happiness. To say that later generations must settle for something other than an actual half is to imply that they could do better than that. But they cannot. There is still a difference between a later-generation x who has never had an other half, and a first-generation human whose other half has died. The latter must settle for less than perfect happiness because she had her ideal mate, and no one else can totally replace him (see chap. 13). Later-generation humans, never having had ideal mates, cannot be thought of as settling for second best. Given their nature, the best they can do is find some happiness with a sympathetic and congenial mate. Note that once we abandon the assumption that x will love only someone who has the property "my other half," the exclusivity, constancy, and reciprocity of love are no longer secured. Love will not necessarily be any of these things (but not because sexual desire now looms larger than love). Indeed, Aristophanic later-generation love looks quite mundane, not like something as esoteric as implied by his myth.

5. MATCHING THE LOVER'S NATURE

Aristophanes advises a later-generation human to "find a sympathetic and congenial object for [his] affections" (Hamilton), a beloved "who is of like mind to oneself" (Groden), or a person "who matches his nature" (Larson). These descriptions of suitable beloveds are not equivalent. "Like mind" suggests that one's beloved will be someone similar to oneself in beliefs, temperament, and interests (perhaps because genuine half-persons, coming from the same circle-person, were similar).[30] If this is Aristophanes' point, his model of love may be a predecessor of Aristotle's view that friendship occurs between good men of similar character (although Aristophanic love, unlike Aristotelian aristocratic friendship, is democratic). Or perhaps Aristophanes is claiming that some type of equality (see 11.5) is essential for love.[31] The term *matches* is ambiguous; it might mean "similar to," but it also suggests a beloved who completes the nature of the lover (perhaps because genuine half-persons were more like yin-yang complements than replicas of each other). If so, Aristophanes is asserting that "opposites attract," rather than "birds of a feather flock together," and his thesis confirms Pausanias' ideal—that of love between an older man and a boy. But "matches" might be tautological: y matches the nature of x when y is a fitting or appropriate object for x's affections. For similar reasons, to say that one's beloved should be "sympathetic and congenial" is not very helpful. Other than telling us to find someone with whom

we can be happy, Aristophanes apparently provides little guidance for selecting a beloved.[32]

If "x loves y because y makes x happy" is all that his account of love
amounts to, why does Aristophanes meticulously lay out the prefatory material
about the circle-people? Consider Aristophanes' claim (at 192e) that we, or his
comrades, desire to merge with our beloveds because "this was our primitive
condition when we were wholes." This must be reinterpreted as saying that a
later-generation human can attain happiness by joining with a person who, by
matching her particular nature, *could* have been her other half *if* she had one.
And Aristophanes seems to suggest that our beloveds now will at least appear
to be other halves even though they couldn't actually be other halves. Thus the
myth about "our" distant origin as circle-people might be meant to give us
some signs as to what now counts as a sympathetic and congenial mate. This is
Aristophanes' unromantic message: *we* do not have other halves or ideal mates,
despite the fact that we often feel and behave as if we do. If we believe that we
have ideal mates, we only create problems for ourselves. And if we recognize
that we don't have them (by listening carefully to the myth and noticing the
difference between first- and later-generation humans), we can go about finding happiness anyway. Now "reason and planning" do play a role in love, in
seeking a congenial mate with whom one can be happy; for later-generation
humans, unlike the first generation, have freedom in selecting a beloved (see n.
8). But later-generation humans have no guarantee that they will find love or
that it will turn out to be wonderful.

"It has taken many accidents, many surprising coincidences (and perhaps
many efforts), for me to find the Image which, out of a thousand, suits my
desire," writes Roland Barthes.[33] "Herein a great enigma, to which I shall
never possess the key: Why is it that I desire So-and-so?" Aristophanes gives
Barthes the key to the puzzle. Indeed, Aristophanes promises to answer, with
one bold, unifying principle, a whole slew of questions: why anyone desires
another person at all (every person used to be tied to someone else); why x
loves y in particular (y is x's other half); why x loves the kind of person y is (that
is, x's sexual-object preference); why x feels joy when encountering y (the spurt
of happiness upon reuniting); why x believes that y is the only person for x
(they are two halves of the same whole); why x does not consciously account
for loving y in ordinary terms (for example, by mentioning y's properties that x
finds valuable). In retrospect, however, Aristophanes cannot explain these
things, for there is no metaphysical or biological transmission of the genuine
half-person nature of the first generation to later generations. In response to
the question, "Is love exclusive, constant, and reciprocal?," Aristophanes can

answer "yes, because lovers are two halves of the same whole"—although only for the first generation. For later generations all Aristophanes can say is "maybe." When later-generation love is exclusive, constant, and reciprocal, what would be Aristophanes' explanation? X and y make each other sufficiently happy. In the other cases they do not. This truism is not very illuminating: some loves are exclusive and constant because they work out well; other loves are not because they do not work out well. Yet an intuitively acceptable solution to Gellner's paradox builds on claim (e). To this solution we now turn.

CHAPTER 6 *The Satisfaction of Desire*

The woman will . . . try to believe herself indispensible . . . and she derives her own value from that. Her joy is to serve him. . . . [But] a woman with a scrupulous mind is bound to ask herself: does he really need *me*? . . . would he not have an equally personal feeling for someone else in [my] place?

—Simone de Beauvoir, *The Second Sex*

1. THE MISSING LINK

From several directions, we have arrived at a commonsensical solution to Gellner's paradox. I earlier discussed Newton-Smith's proposal that x loves y but not z, when both have the attractive S, in virtue of y's historical property "what y has done for x" (3.4). We can now interpret this property more specifically in light of Aristophanes' account of love for later-generation humans: x loves y because y makes x happy. I also argued that y's coming first cannot, by itself, explain why x loves y but not z when both have S; some mediating factor must allow time to make a difference (4.2). A modification of Aristophanes' claim (e) supplies the connection: x loves the earlier-encountered y rather than the latecomer z because y already satisfies x's desires or fulfills x's needs, thereby making x happy.

This solution to Gellner's paradox (call it the D-S solution, or the D-S model, after "desire-satisfaction") can be understood in two logically distinct ways. We could say, first, that x loves y but not z, when both have S, because y has the additional property "makes x happy" that z does not have. In this case, x loves y exclusively when (i) x loves y in virtue of T, that is, "makes x happy" (or both S and T), (ii) only y has T (or both S and T), and (iii) having T (or both S and T) is necessary for x to love anyone at all. The logically central feature of this version of the D-S solution is that y is construed as having a valuable property that z lacks. In the second way of understanding the D-S solution, no mention must be made of y's having a property T that makes y unique. Between encountering y, who has S, and encountering z, who also has S, x undergoes various changes in having had his desires satisfied. Hence, x's encountering y, who has S, and later encountering z who has S is not a repetition of the "same situation," and there is no expectation that S in z should have the same effect on x. (If I have a headache and take an aspirin, I have no reason to take another qualitatively indistinguishable aspirin; and if I do take it, the aspirin will not have any effect.) Both y and z have the relevant first-order properties in virtue of which x loves y, but once these properties in y have had time to do their work on x, by satisfying x's desires and making x happy, there is no room for those properties in z to be effective. Love in this case is still erosic, since x's love for y is partially subject-centric and partially object-centric (1.3).

The D-S solution claims that y's satisfying x's desires or fulfilling x's needs is an additional reason that x has for loving y (or is alone sufficient); that unless x's desires and needs are satisfied by a beloved, x will not love anyone; and that x exclusively loves y because y in particular has the ability to satisfy x's desires (perhaps this is what it means for y to "match" x's nature). Consider an analogy. Suppose that x needs an automobile or desires to own one. X shops around, looking for automobiles having an S suitable to x's needs, and from among the candidates x makes a selection. The fact that at a later time x encounters an automobile that also possesses S, even S to a higher degree, has no effect on x; x's desires have already been satisfied, and are still being satisfied, by the automobile x has purchased. Even though this later-encountered auto could have satisfied x's desires and might have been purchased had x encountered it first, no unsatisfied desires remain in x that S in this auto can satisfy; x has changed, and a new appearance of S has no effect. If we replace "automobile" with "beloved," what results is the D-S solution to Gellner's paradox. X need not discount S in z, refuse to treat love-reasons as general, or imagine that S makes his beloved unique. One virtue of the D-S solution, therefore, is that it makes x's exclusive love for y look perfectly rational. Further, the D-S model of love can explain why x finds certain first-order properties valuable: y's properties that x values are those that enable y to fulfill x's needs.

2. IMPLICATIONS OF THE MODEL

The D-S solution, however, does not succeed in showing that erosic love will be, or even tends to be, exclusive. Suppose that our automobile consumer has strong needs for the advantages and comforts provided by automobiles. Then, even though the consumer cannot afford another auto, she might feel tempted to make a second purchase. In cases of extremely strong and diverse needs and desires, the consumer might buy a second car (one having the S of the original, or one having T), even if doing so means postponing the payment of other debts. The D-S model does not, therefore, rule out x's loving both y and z. If x's desires that are satisfiable by persons who have S are powerful, x might require a double dose of S and love two people who have it. Or if x's desires are diverse, S in y will satisfy some of them while T in z will satisfy others. Thus, the D-S model countenances the popular justification (or excuse) appealed to by nonexclusive lovers: "No one person can completely satisfy all my needs." (Exclusive lovers must be those having comparatively weak and few desires, or needs that are easy to fulfill.) If x's desires are so powerful as to make x insatiable, there will be no limit on the number of people x might love. In loving nonexclusively, x may be acting rationally insofar as x applies his love-reasons perfectly generally, yet x may also be deviously calculating how many loves he can maintain at once without a net decrease in desire-satisfaction. Or suppose that x's specific need—one that can be satisfied only by a large number of people—is the need to be loved (see 8.3). This nonexclusive lover is driven by this one need; the S that y and z and all the others have in common is simply the ability and willingness to provide x with the love x needs.

To the extent that the nonexclusive lover is conceptualized by the D-S model as someone who is strongly needful or difficult to satisfy, the model provides a too-narrow and unflattering picture of the multiple lover. The consumer might buy three autos mostly because she is wealthy; the limit placed on the number purchased may be a function of the consumer's capacity to buy and have less to do with the satisfaction of urgent needs. By analogy, the multiple lover may be someone having a large capacity to love others. (Consider the mother and wife, or the husband and father, who manages to love nonexclusively.) But there is no room in the D-S model for the multiple lover whose relationships are due to generosity and not to her needs being satisfied. This generous multiple lover does not necessarily love nonexclusively because doing so satisfies desires or needs she has—as if she were loving nonexclusively just because her capacity to love demands satisfaction or an outlet. Nor do we have to view the generous multiple lover as loving agapically. The consumer who buys several automobiles does not buy every auto available, and she selects the ones she does buy on the basis of their particular properties. This consumer buys several automobiles not because she needs them but because she likes or admires them for their characteristics. By analogy, a multiple erosic lover need not select beloveds purely on the basis of the satisfaction of desires and needs. It is not logically incompatible with the eros tradition to say that x needs y because x loves y, rather than x loves y because x needs y, as long as x's loving y is grounded in other properties of y.

The D-S model has similar problems with the constancy of love. First, the typical consumer attitude toward a purchased item is that eventually the item, worn out or broken, will have to be replaced. Therefore, unless the D-S model draws the analogy only between selecting a beloved and purchasing a durable good like a house, the model entails that the lover's attitude at the very start of the love relationship is that the love will not endure. The lover has no intention that their love be constant; the lover might even intend that the relationship *not* be constant. Second, x's desires might change, in which case x will no longer love y—unless y is fortunate enough (or x is fortunate enough?) to be able to satisfy x's new desires. Or y may change in such a way that the new properties y has no longer satisfy x's desires. Hence, the constancy of love is secured by the D-S model only under fairly restrictive conditions: either x and y remain the same (x's desires do not change, and y is always able to satisfy them) or x and y change in tandem (x's desires change, but y can accommodate). In the D-S model, whether x will love anyone at all depends on x's meeting someone who can satisfy x's desires. Even if that does not make love chancy, the fact that x and y must remain the same or change in tandem makes love chancy by making its constancy chancy.

There is a third reason that love will be inconstant in the D-S model. Earlier I said that once x meets y who has S and has his desires satisfied, noticing S in z will have no effect on x, in the same way that the consumer's encountering another auto with S, after having purchased one, will not have an effect on him. But that was too quick. (The second aspirin may have no effect on my headache, but it may damage my stomach.) The consumer might not have a reason to buy the second auto, but it can still have an effect on him: longing or regret. Similarly, x's meeting z, whose properties promise to satisfy x's desires more fully than y's, will cause x at least to feel regret, and because beloveds are in some ways easier to replace than large-investment consumer goods, x's regret may motivate him to abandon y and seek z as a beloved. (See Woody Allen's "Manhattan.") Finally, many consumers who purchase an item because they believe it will prove satisfying discover later that it does not satisfy them as expected; the item is not what the consumer imagined he wanted. It is stored in the attic, suffering no better a fate than the y that x no longer loves for the same reason.

This type of inconstancy is entailed, in particular, by Plato's account of eros in the *Symposium,* although Plato does not view it as a problem. At the lower levels of the ladder of love, the Platonic lover discovers that he is not genuinely satisfied by the love objects available at those levels (beautiful bodies, even beautiful minds). Unsatisfied by these imperfect beauties that he thought would be satisfying, his love for them wanes, and he begins to seek true satisfaction at the highest level of the Ascent where he can possess Beauty and Goodness themselves.[1] Similarly, Augustine (see 1.6) discovered that he could not be satisfied with the worldly items he believed he wanted and that only God could make him happy; this is what he had been seeking all along, unbeknownst to him.[2] But only accounts of love incorporating a Grand Vision (movement toward God or the Forms, for example) see it as a *good* thing that earthly loves are short-lived because unsatisfying. If we dispense with the highest level of Plato's Ascent, inconstancy in personal love, due to discovering that one is not satisfied by that which one hoped would be satisfying, is not a blessing but a curse. The D-S model gives us no reason to think that inconstancy of this sort will be unlikely. And the D-S model does not include any device like Plato's Forms or Augustine's God as a rationale that could make this consequence at least palatable even if not the redemption of the model. Now, the D-S model could embrace a Grand Vision to serve this purpose: assume, with Luther, a doctrine of original sin according to which human nature is selfish or corrupt.[3] Then necessarily humans must love D-S style and will always be disappointed in their loves, since the corruption infects both lover and beloved. In fact, presupposing the doctrine of psychological egoism would accomplish the same thing for the D-S model. But the eros tradition need not assert this thesis.

Because love may not be by its nature or conceptually either exclusive or constant, the fact that the D-S model does not secure the exclusivity and constancy of love is no powerful strike against it. As an account of personal love, however, the D-S model still leaves much to be desired; it seems not to have a firm grasp on why loves that are not exclusive or not constant (or *are* exclusive or constant) are the way they are. And it seems plainly false that the beloved's possessing specifically those properties that satisfy x's desires is necessary for x to love y or to select y as a beloved. X might find y's properties valuable not because x's needs are satisfied by them but because x enjoys these properties or wants to share in them. If I want to share in y's P, hoping it will rub off on me, I might be attracted to y because P can make me a better person. This does not mean that my ultimate goal is to satisfy a desire for self-improvement, for I might want to improve myself for the sake of others or because it is my duty. Reading Plato from a perfectionist perspective, we might even say that "the higher form of *eros* is . . . love of the 'better' self, the self that strives to complete itself through the highest values."[4] Or x's admiration for y's properties—even admiration for y in virtue of those properties—might be more significant than the ability of these properties to satisfy x's desires.[5] If x admires and loves y for having S, x's admiration need not "really" be satisfying some desires of x, nor must x be judged irrational if x assesses S as admirable rather than as need-fulfilling.

3. GIVING IN ORDER TO GET

Russell Vannoy is quite candid about understanding love—especially what he calls "erotic love"—in consumer terms. He writes:

> The owner of a new . . . car devotes endless hours to polishing it or . . . keeping it in working condition. He does these things not out of any devotion to the car but only because [of] the thrill and ego-fulfillment. . . . When the car begins to require sacrifices that outweigh the benefits it gives, he trades it in. He has "given" but only in order to "get". . . . This example of the car applies perfectly to lovers as well: They give in order to get and if they think they aren't getting as much as or, hopefully, more than they are giving, they trade the once-loved in on a new model.[6]

As a description of how people think and behave as lovers, what Vannoy says is at least partly false. Some x's remain with their y's, even continue to love them, even though x would admit that x is getting less than x is giving. And not every x hopes to get more from y than x gives to y; some x's find such transactions psychologically burdensome or morally objectionable. (Do not say that x is getting as much as x gives, since part of what x is getting is the satisfaction of x's desire not to get more than x gives.) But the problems with Vannoy's D-S account go much deeper. His "perfect" analogy ignores a crucial difference between x's having a "give in order to get" attitude toward an automobile (an inanimate object) and x's having that attitude toward a person. The automobile cannot wonder about the motives of the owner who polishes and repairs it. But the human objects of x's attention may wonder about the attitude that x has toward them and their relationships: y may think to herself, "x is giving in order to get, and if he thinks he isn't getting as much as or, hopefully, more than he is giving, he will trade me in, the once-beloved, for a new woman."

If x's attitude toward y is "give to get," but y does not know that this is x's attitude, then x's attitude may have no effect on y. If x's attitude toward an automobile, which cannot be aware of x's attitude, is "give to get," x might treat the car identically (polishing and repairing it) to the way x would treat it if x did not have that attitude. Similarly, if y does not know that x's attitude is "give to get," then x's attitude may have no effect on y's experience of their relationship; x's treatment of y may appear impeccable to y. As long as x is getting as much desire-satisfaction as x hopes for, y may never have a clue that x loves y *because* y satisfies x's desires and needs. X's giving to y may even strengthen y's love for x as long as y does not know why x is giving. Perhaps that y, unlike the auto, could know about x's "give to get" attitude means that x will not always act and speak as spontaneously as he otherwise would. And perhaps, eventually, changes in x's treatment of y will provide y with clues about x's attitude, for love on the D-S model is prone to be inconstant. But at a given time y may have no reason to suspect anything. Nevertheless, even though x may be treating y superlatively, something is wrong in this scenario. Y does not know certain facts about x's love for y: namely, what motivates x to give and why x loves y. Knowledge of the ground and nature of x's love is being deliberately withheld from y by x, or y has made no attempt to figure out x's attachment to her. A love in which this knowledge is absent is hardly an ideal erosic love (see **8.4** and **8.6**).

Suppose, instead, that y does know that x's attitude toward y is "give to get." If x loves y because y satisfies x's desires, and y knows this, yet y does not have the same attitude toward x, the x-y relationship may be unstable. They clash not only in how their respective loves are grounded but also in their fundamental attitudes toward the other person. A precondition for reciprocal love might be that x and y agree, and know they agree, about such fundamental things (11.5). Nevertheless, in the present scenario y's knowledge that x disagrees in this specific way is bound to upset y, who sees herself, through x's eyes, as a consumer good. X may be giving to y superlatively, yet the whole meaning of x's giving has changed once y knows that x's acts are motivated by x's "give to get" attitude. Indeed, even though the actions of x that constitute this superlative treatment are behaviorally no different from those in the previous scenario, they are different acts when y knows their motive, insofar as y's description of them must now include reference to x's motivation. Furthermore, if x's attitude is not merely "give to get," but "hopefully" to get more than he gives, y's recognition of this attitude must repulse her, for x's attitude entails that x *hopes* that y the beloved will get *less* than y gives. (Is such an attitude even compatible with x's claim to love y?)

Vannoy writes about y, the beloved, that she "faces a fatal contradiction: she wants to be chosen for her own intrinsic worth as a person and not just as a means of satisfying her lover's needs."[7] Vannoy's subsequent remarks suggest that there are two ways of understanding the beloved's contradiction. First, she wants to be chosen and loved "for her own intrinsic worth as a person." In addition, she "wants to be selected for her . . . qualities. . . . [H]er pride dictates that she merit love by having those qualities that win the heart of another." Now, this problem—can x love y *both* "as a person" *and* in virtue of y's attractive properties?—is a general one for the eros tradition (see chap. 13) and seems not especially relevant to y's worry about x's "give to get" attitude toward her. Vannoy forces the beloved into having a more specific version of this purported contradiction by implicitly assuming that if x loves y for y's attractive or meritorious properties, then x loves y because y satisfies x's needs and desires. It surely looks contradictory for y to want both to be loved by x "as a person" and to be loved by x just for her value in being able to satisfy x's desires. But this contradiction does not entail that y must abandon the desire to be loved for her attractiveness, where that is not exhausted by her ability to satisfy x's desires.

In the second reading of the contradiction, the beloved must abandon her wish to be loved "as a person." For in merely wanting to be loved in this way the beloved is already involved (for Vannoy) in a contradiction; she wants something that she logically cannot have. A person, says Vannoy, is only his properties: "One cannot separate pure 'personhood' from" a person's properties. Since there is no transcendental or metaphysical self, wanting to be loved "as a person" rather than for one's properties is incoherent. Now, all this may be true (see 13.7 and 13.8), yet it seems irrelevant to y's worry about x's attitude. Again Vannoy forces the beloved into the more specific contradiction of wanting "to be chosen . . . as a person and not just as a means of satisfying her lover's needs." This is a contradiction if wanting to be loved as a person could only mean wanting to be loved for one's properties (since a person is her properties), and if being loved for one's properties (*pace* Vannoy) is necessarily to be loved in virtue of satisfying the other's desires. But, again, any hint of contradiction can be eliminated simply by denying that when x loves y for her attractive S, x does so precisely for the desire-satisfaction provided by S.

Vannoy's advice to this contradiction-prone beloved is clear, as is his advice to the beloved dismayed by her lover's "give to get" attitude. This is human nature and the reality of love. Further, do not have any illusions about your own motives in loving. If you love x, it is not "as a person" in some esoteric sense; you love him for his ability to satisfy your needs and for his properties that enable him to do so. If x's giving to you induces your love in return, it is only because you too have a "give to get" attitude. But Vannoy's advice is sound only if properties have value simply because they satisfy desires —or if psychological egoism is true. But the eros tradition is not compelled to make either of these assumptions.

In the D-S model, then, the ideal case of love would have to be one in which x and y love each other for the same D-S reason, have the same "give to get" attitude toward the other, and openly acknowledge these facts. "I'm glad that you are getting what you need from me," says x, "because that allows me to get what I need from you." And if y can say the same thing with equal glee, what could anyone complain about? Maybe a few little things. X is hoping to get more from y than y gets from x and hoping, therefore, that y gets less from x than y gives to x. Y knows this about x. But y has the same attitude; and x knows that about y. Where is the stability in the x-y relationship? That x wants y to get less than y gives, and y wants y to get more than y gives, injects tension, even a battle, into their relationship that may override the stabilizing influence of their agreement on the nature of love. It also leads to frustration, for x and y cannot both succeed in getting more than they give. Perhaps, however, they settle for equality; but can they trust each other to do so? If the D-S model has difficulty securing love between two D-S persons, it will have difficulty securing trust: x will be troubled continually by the thought that y is satisfying x's desires only because x has satisfied y's desires (and vice versa).[8]

Why not suppose that x and y could be happier if the other is satisfying one's desires not for that reason alone or primarily, but for one's own sake? John Stuart Mill told us in his autobiography that seeking happiness directly may be counterproductive; happiness may come most easily to those not seeking it. Having one's desires and needs satisfied is very likely necessary for happiness or for love, but deliberately pursuing satisfaction by forming relationships on a "give to get" basis might not be the way to achieve genuine happiness or fulfilling love. At the very least, the tension in the relationship between two D-S lovers suggests that this is, after all, not the ideal case of D-S love. A genuine D-S lover would want his desires satisfied by a person who is not similarly motivated; the fullest satisfaction of x's desires is achieved when x is loved by an altruistic y (or one not bent on maximizing her own desire-satisfaction), not another genuine D-S lover. If the ideal relationship for a D-S lover requires a beloved who does not love in D-S fashion, the D-S model does not provide a general account of love. If there are going to be any truly satisfied D-S lovers, the model must allow the existence of lovers who love in some other manner.[9]

There is one more point to be made. Vannoy assumes that (1) x loves y because y satisfies x's needs and desires and that (2) x has a "give to get" attitude, even hoping to get more than he gives. But the second assumption might be false even if the first is true. If x's desires are satisfied by y, why should x care if x is giving more than x is getting? Suppose x's desires are weaker or more easily satisfied than y's; in this relationship, both x's and y's desires are fully satisfied even though x is giving more than x gets. So x has no cause for complaint. The point is that the D-S model need not embrace the second assumption. At the same time, however, assumption (1), as I have argued, is too strong. X's being happy with y, in virtue of having his desires satisfied, might very well be only one necessary condition for x to continue to love y, without it being true that the satisfaction of his desires exhausts his reasons for loving y.

4. A NORMATIVE CONCEPT

While comparing Plato's account of love, that is, "the desire . . . to possess what is beautiful," and Aristotle's definition, "love is wishing good things for someone for that person's sake," Donald Levy raises some objections to the latter. For Levy, there are "clear examples of love" that are "negligent, selfish, confused,"—that is, that do not conform to Aristotle's definition.[10] His examples include "the love of children and parents for one another . . . 'smothering' mothers, murderously jealous husbands."[11] If these are cases of love, then it is false, contra Aristotle, that "a necessary condition of one's loving a person at all [is] that one seeks what is good for the other for the other's sake." Levy's contention is not that a lover always seeks what is best for himself or that whenever a lover seeks the good of another he does so ultimately for his own sake. Levy is not, that is, defending the D-S model of love. What I have argued is that the D-S model is too extreme; it does not countenance any cases of loving someone independently of his ability to satisfy desires. Levy's point is that Aristotle's definition is too extreme in the opposite direction; it does not countenance, for example, any cases of love in which D-S motives predominate.

Levy also contends that on Aristotle's definition it would be "impossible to distinguish between a person's loving well, and that person being a genuine instance of a lover." Crude D-S lovers (jealous husbands, selfish children) are, for Levy, not wonderful lovers, but they are lovers nonetheless. In Aristotle's account, they are not lovers, because they do not seek the good of the other for the other's sake. But how does this mean that Aristotle conflates "loving" and "loving well"? The idea is that if Aristotle's view implies that nasty lovers are not lovers, it has no power to judge any *lover* to be deficient. But we know that Aristotle does judge use-lovers inferior (10.5). Still, Levy proposes that in contrast to Plato's account, Aristotle's is "a definition not of what love is, but of what love ought . . . to be."

It seems to me that Levy, not Aristotle, is confused. Levy draws a conceptual distinction between a descriptive definition of love that tells us what love is and a normative definition that tells us what love ought to be. But then Aristotle's definition of love conflates "loving" and "loving well" only if it is both descriptive and normative. Aristotle's definition, if descriptive, says nothing about "loving well"; if normative, it says nothing about "genuine instances" of love. Aristotle did not conflate "loving" and "loving well" unless he meant his definition to be both descriptive and normative, and Levy has given us no reason to suppose he did. Note that if the point of Levy's counterexamples (the jealous husband and the others) were to show that not every case of love involves seeking the good of y for y's sake, then Levy would be disputing Aristotle's definition understood descriptively; but if the point of the counterexamples were to show that not every case of love is normatively praiseworthy, then Levy would be confirming Aristotle's definition understood normatively.

As a matter of fact, it would not be terribly implausible to read Aristotle's definition as both descriptive and normative. Consider, again, the distinction between "a definition . . . of what love is" and a definition "of what love ought . . . to be." How should the "is" be taken? In one sense, a definition of what love "is" will be straightforwardly empirical: we examine various emotional phenomena that we would preanalytically call love and then construct a definition from their most common characteristics. Neither Plato nor Aristotle defines love in this manner, so it cannot be what Levy means by "a definition of what love is." (His counterexamples, however, suggest otherwise; why else would he include the murderously jealous husband as a lover?) The main problem with this methodology is that it lacks critical power; we would be stuck with claiming that love is simply whatever most people believe is love. A more sophisticated methodology would go beyond these common observable characteristics and postulate theoretical entities that explain what people are "really" doing, or trying to do, in these emotional phenomena. This is Diotima's procedure in arriving at a definition of eros while instructing the young Socrates. Hence, this is probably what Levy means by "a definition of what love is," since Plato, in Levy's view, is telling us what love "is" rather than prescribing what love ought to be. The more sophisticated procedure also begins by selecting, from among all the cases preanalytically judged to be love, only those outstanding exemplars of love that could serve as a solid foundation for the theory. There might be little, if any, difference between a theoretico-empirical definition of love, on the one hand, and a conceptual analysis of "love" or a philosophical account of the nature of love, on the other.[12] Because they both float relatively free of preanalytic judgments, a theoretico-empirical and a conceptual account of love will entail that phenomena preanalytically taken as cases of love are not, after all, cases of love. What they have in common—the power to reject the presumption that a case of love is what it purports to be—shows that the distinction between "is" and "ought" definitions of love is questionable; insofar as an account of love is constructed on the basis of cases segregated as being the "best" examples, the resulting descriptive definition will also be evaluative.

Aristotle fathomed how bizarre the D-S model of love is, how strange it is to picture love as a species of consumer behavior; his definition of love is a protest both against considering the D-S lover to be a lover and against seeing him as one who loves well. In *The Art of Loving,* Erich Fromm lodged a similar complaint, while exploring the analogy between love and sexual practices in the capitalist West, on the one hand, and consumer behavior and the operation of the free market, on the other. Some of Fromm's ideas about love in the West imply that he believes that the philosophical and popular tendency to conceive of love in terms of the properties of the beloved is a "reflection" of the material conditions of Western society. As a thesis about the genesis and maintenance of the eros tradition within systems of ideas, Fromm's belief is implausible; for the notion that love is property-based thrived in pre- and noncapitalistic societies. Nevertheless, his thesis makes more sense if applied to one particular theory in the eros tradition—the D-S model of love. As a mere straightforward empirical description of contemporary love, the D-S account, with its flavor of consumerism, has some truth to it. And as a "theory" mirroring directly the practices of a consumerist society, the D-S model will look plausible.

But a philosopher, Aristotle implies, should not rest content with mere description, a redundant theory. In philosophizing about love, we would like to get at the very concept of love, a concept partially independent of practices and their vicissitudes; a concept that tells us what love is, even if most of us act according to, say, the D-S model; a concept that presents us with a picture of the ideal lover, even if such lovers are rare; a concept that is normative, showing us what we can and should become in love and as lovers. In all these ways, the D-S model of love is not an inspiration but an excuse to continue loving in the same humdrum fashion in which we conclude deals and (if we can) deceptively violate the terms of our contracts. Surely the eros tradition has done, and can do, better than this.

5. THE ROLES OF DESIRE IN LOVE

If the D-S model were to embrace psychological egoism, it would become metaphilosophically strange. It would begin by assuming a general philosophical view of human nature (namely, that everything we do is geared toward the satisfaction of desire) and then apply this thesis to love. But the standard counterexample to the general philosophical thesis has always been love or other acts of benevolence. The D-S model of love then has to force love into that mold in order to show that love is not, after all, a counterexample. As I suggested earlier, the D-S account would be more interesting if it claimed only to be analyzing select cases of erosic love rather than all cases; there are easily identifiable cases of D-S love, but not all love fits this pattern. Even so, the D-S model puts more emphasis than deserved on the satisfaction of desire as a ground of love, and it leads us away from more important questions in the philosophy of love: What *are* the desires involved in love, and what roles do these desires play?

Consider the central desire of Aristotle's *philia:* x's desire that y's well-being be secured for y's sake. Can philia, or something like it, be incorporated into the D-S model of love? Suppose that x does not have the ordinary desires that most of us have, or has them very weakly, or does not consider the satisfaction of these desires very important. Instead, x has one desire that is his most powerful: the desire to benefit another person. Earlier we generated a worst-case scenario of D-S love by assuming that x's most powerful desire was to be loved. Can we not, then, generate a best-case scenario of D-S love by assuming that x's most powerful desire is to benefit another person? Y will be x's beloved, then, if with respect to y x is able to satisfy x's desire to benefit someone. This version of the D-S model has interesting implications. As x secures the well-being of x's beloved y, the satisfaction of x's desire necessarily involves the satisfaction of y; this is a far cry from the "give to get" attitude of Vannoy's crude D-S lover. Furthermore, there is now room for a non-derogatory account of the generous multiple lover. Finally, this account explains the existence of some unreciprocated love: if x's most powerful desire is the desire to benefit another person, this desire might be satisfied even when the beloved does not return the love.

However, if x's main desire is to benefit anyone at all, there are many persons who could be x's beloved; the property "is willing and able to allow x to satisfy this desire" is widely shared. Thus, the ability to satisfy this desire is not a ground of love that distinguishes one from other potential beloveds. If y wonders, "Why is x benefiting me in particular?" y might not come up with any reasonable answer. What this analysis misses is that usually when x loves y, x wants to benefit y in particular, and that if x does not love y, there is less reason to think (unless we construct elaborate stories) that x would be especially concerned for y's well-being. If x loves y, then perhaps x will be motivated, as a result of x's love for y, to benefit y. In this case x's desire to benefit y is conceptualized as a causal consequence of love. Because it is difficult to make sense of the claim that x loves y when x does not care one whit about the happiness, prosperity, flourishing, and desire-satisfaction of y (see 12.1), the connection between x's love for y and x's wanting to benefit y might be even tighter: x's wanting to benefit y may be either a logically necessary condition for, or partially constitutive of, x's loving y. But it is implausible to think that x loves y because x wants to benefit y in particular, or because y allows x to satisfy x's desire to benefit y.

We must therefore distinguish among three possible roles for desire in love: as preceding and grounding love, as constituting love, and as resulting from love. (1) Before loving anyone, x might have, say, sexual desires that are satisfiable by a person having P. X may love y because y satisfies these desires in virtue of having P. In this case, y's having P, or y's satisfying x's desires, is the cause of or reason for x's love; certain of x's desires precede both x's evaluation of y as lovable and x's love for y. (2) Or x might have a desire that is love itself. If we claim that love is the desire to merge with another person, we would be postulating this kind of role for desire in love. Another example: love is the desire to benefit the beloved. Or love may be in part constituted by various desires, without being identical to any one desire.[13] (3) Finally, in loving y, x may come to have certain desires as a result of this emotion. The desire to benefit the beloved is an example; this desire may not be partially definitive of what it is to love, but a contingent, and very likely, result of x's emotion. Another possible causal effect of love is the desire to spend time with the beloved or to engage in joint activities. In these latter cases it is difficult to decide whether the desire is necessary for love and therefore partially constitutive (that is, in its absence there is no love at all), is only a likely consequence of x's loving y, or is a consequence in "ideal" cases of love.

These distinctions will help us evaluate Jenefer Robinson's account of love. The central case of love she discusses is x's loving a y who objectively is not a very lovable person: y is "ugly, morally despicable, and . . . boring."[14] Yet x "may love [y] because he is friendless, lonely, and has so many failings." Robinson is not asserting that personal love is agapic; she is not claiming that x loves y disregarding his faults. Rather, these faults, which make y unlovable for others, are precisely the things about y that make him lovable for x. She explains:

> The judgmental element of my love ([y] is lovable because he is friendless, alone, unattractive, despicable, etc.) is not the *ground* of my love; it is rather the *consequence* of my pre-existing desires. I have a desire to regenerate and rejuvenate [y], and hence I evaluate as lovable a man whom perhaps nobody else so evaluates: my desires directly determine my conception of my beloved. For the same reason they also determine whom I pick out as a lover in the first place: looking for a lonely and worthless man to cherish, I naturally warm to [y].[15]

Robinson accounts for this case of love by appealing to a D-S model: x loves y because y has properties S, these properties enable y to satisfy x's antecedent desires, and x evaluates S as attractive or valuable (and hence y as lovable) because S will satisfy x's desires. This thesis does not contradict the eros view that x loves y because x believes y has meritorious P and that this love then causes or is constituted by various desires in x toward y. In this picture desires play two roles. Some of x's desires (those existing antecedently) yield the evaluation that y is lovable: if x has a desire to do some rejuvenating, then of course someone who requires rejuvenation will appear eminently lovable. Then as a result of x's love, x will have certain other desires toward y.

Thus, it is curious that Robinson contrasts—as if they were incompatible—x's judging y lovable as the ground of x's love, and x's judging y lovable as the consequence of x's preexisting desires. (Robinson claims the first is false, the second true.) Suppose that Robinson were contrasting (1) x loves y because x finds y lovable in virtue of S, and (2) x finds y lovable in virtue of S because x loves y. This is a genuine *Euthyphro* dilemma, and (with the qualifications given in 1.3) the two claims are incompatible. If this were the contrast Robinson had in mind, her denying that x's evaluation of y as lovable is the ground of x's love (that is, her rejection of option [1]), in favor of x's evaluation of y as lovable being the consequence of x's love, would be tantamount to asserting that love is an agapic, not an erosic, phenomenon. Robinson's contrast is not, however, *Euthyphronic;* to claim, as she does, that x evaluates y as lovable in light of the fact that y's properties can satisfy x's preexisting desires is not to claim that x evaluates S favorably because x already loves y. Therefore, x's evaluation of y as lovable being a consequence of x's preexisting desires does not rule out x's evaluation of y as lovable being the ground of x's love. Indeed, since x's evaluation of y as lovable is the consequence of x's preexisting desires, it is wrong for Robinson to assert that x's evaluation of y is not the ground of x's love. If x's evaluation of y as lovable is the consequence of x's preexisting desires, we have every reason to assert (as the D-S model does) that the evaluation is the ground of love.

That Robinson seriously embraces the D-S model can be seen by examining what she says (in effect) in response to Gellner's paradox: "Emotional reactions are not generalizable. Because my conception of [y] is governed by my desires with respect to [y], it does not follow that I will have the same conception of anybody who has [y's] properties. I love [y] because he is friendless and alone and has many failings, but I do not love everybody who has these properties: my desires . . . are satisfied by . . . [y]."[16] But it does not follow from the D-S model that love is exclusive or that love-reasons are not generalizable. Perhaps y and only y can satisfy x's desires; but it is also possible that x's desires require the contribution of both y and z—it depends on the diversity and intensity of x's desires. If x's desire to rejuvenate lost souls is powerful, x will have good reason—and the *same* reason—to love both y and z: they require rejuvenation. Robinson continues: "Moreover, far from loving everyone with a certain set of properties, I rather find lovable in my beloved properties I would find intolerable in anyone else."[17] But his phenomenon is easily handled within the eros tradition; x loves y for having S, so x may very well evaluate the otherwise obnoxious P as attractive in y just because x loves y. One of the desires resulting from love, that is, may be the desire to see the beloved's obnoxious properties in the best possible light. "At the heart of love," she writes, "are not evaluations based on properties of the beloved, but desires directed toward a beloved individual: it is our desires which dictate what properties we find lovable and not vice-versa." This claim, however, conflates two distinct possible, and not incompatible, roles for desires in love: as the antecedent conditions by which certain properties are judged attractive, and as constituents or consequences of the emotion itself. But even if x's preexisting desires might play a role in love, we have already considered reasons why placing too much emphasis on these desires is wrong. The eros tradition is not forced to concede that the only properties x finds valuable in a beloved are properties that will satisfy x's preexisting desires; nor is it forced to concede that x can love y only because y, in virtue of possessing these properties, satisfies x's desires.

CHAPTER 7 *Hate, Love, and Rationality*

We should not love God because of his heaven and earth: we should love heaven and earth because they are God's.

—Max Scheler, *Ressentiment*

Eros loosens the limbs and damages the mind.

—Hesiod, *Theogony*

1. THE EROSIC EMOTIONS

Some of the questions I have raised about love can be asked about other emotions. Looking at these other phenomena is not merely interesting for its own sake but essential for understanding love. If it were possible, we should also examine at least hate, fear, anger, pride, gratitude, respect, admiration, indignation, envy, grief, pity, and resentment. These emotions and attitudes are typically either reason-dependent or property-based, or both; that is, they are erosic in structure. Are they also by nature constant, exclusive, or reciprocal? No. For an emotion to be fear or anger, it need not be constantly experienced or be reciprocated or be exclusively directed at one person or thing. But, on the other hand, one who claims to admire everyone does not know what admiration is and probably does not experience it at all. In addition, we do doubt the authenticity of some emotions if they disappear quickly. Grief that lasts two minutes is not even superficial grief; it is not grief at all. Ludwig Wittgenstein claimed that "genuine duration" was a common feature of the emotions, including love.[1] Hence, "love is not a feeling. Love is put to the test, pain not. One does not say: 'That was not true pain or it would not have gone off so quickly'."[2] In general, however, the emotions I mentioned are typically both erosic and not, conceptually, perfectly constant or exclusive. Why should anyone want to understand love differently, as either structurally agapic or as necessarily constant and exclusive? It is often claimed that love is an anomalous emotion, but we shall find plenty of reason to dispute that.

107

2. HATE AT FIRST SIGHT

Suppose x encounters y, and xAy develops when x notices S in y. Some time later, x encounters a person z who also has S and either does or does not experience A toward z. Can we construct an argument, like Gellner's, to show that A is not hate? The argument for the first horn would be: the "very recurrence" of A toward another person shows that it was not hate. Or the repetition of A so soon shows that A is not hate. Or the encounter between x and y was too brief for A to be hate (x could not know anything significant about y). The argument for the second horn would be: the fact that x does not experience A toward z, even though z has S, shows that the connection between S in y and x's experience of A is not "tight" enough for the emotion to count as hate.

Second-horn solutions, proposed to solve the dilemma when applied to love, attempt to reconcile love's exclusivity and reason-dependence. When these solutions are applied to hate they are clearly inadequate. To say that hate is by nature an E-type emotion seems wrong; only some haters refuse to apply their hate-reasons to similar cases. If x hates y for being S, yet does not hate z who is relevantly indistinguishable, the judgment that x (or the hate) is irrational seems correct. There is not much sense in claiming that x hates y but not z, when both have S, just because x met y before z; no mediating factor could make this comprehensible. Similarly, the D-S model cannot explain why x hates y but not z. Are we to believe that hating y fully satisfies x's desires? To invoke the uniqueness of the behated also fails: x may hate various people in virtue of their different properties, even if those properties make each of the behateds unique; further, the S's in virtue of which we hate are too widely distributed. To say that x hates y because of their unpleasant shared history may accurately describe some marriages; but it is just as plausible to suppose that the x-y shared history has been unpleasant because x and y hate each other. And note that Aristophanes' myth is altogether unhelpful in understanding hate. "A match made in heaven" is said about lovers, not about haters.

What follows from the observation that some second-horn solutions to the paradox, when applied to love, are at least initially plausible, yet do not make sense when applied to hate? I think it points out nothing more than a difference in our attitudes toward love and hate. Second-horn solutions to the hate dilemma are strange simply because the dilemma should obviously be solved by rejecting its first horn; hate is not exclusive. Hence, the impulse some people have to take exclusivity as axiomatic of love may be exactly why they see second-horn solutions to the love dilemma as reasonable. Of course, we cannot establish the first horn of the hate dilemma. To say that x's emotion toward y is not hate because it is repeated toward z (at all or "too soon") is as odd as saying that if x laughs at z's joke after laughing at y's, x was not truly amused by y. To say that x cannot hate y after one encounter because x could not know enough about y is as odd as saying that x cannot fear a ferocious dog at first sight since x does not know that dog in its rich individuality. One might argue, then, that since the first horn is more readily established for love (for example, x's claim to love anyone, when x "loves" y, z, and w at the same time, is very doubtful), hate and love are essentially different. Nevertheless, I resist the conclusion. The failure of second-horn solutions to resolve the hate dilemma, as well as the impossibility of establishing its first horn, should lead us to suspect that second-horn solutions to the love dilemma are *ad hoc* patch jobs and that the first horn of the love dilemma is, after all, indefensible (see chap. 9).

The impulse to conceive of love as exclusive and constant, and the absence of that impulse regarding hate, are probably due to the respective typical or hoped-for effects of love and hate, or the purported benefits of exclusive and constant love. Love brings people together and intertwines their lives happily, while hate keeps them apart and causes mostly misery. But desiring or fearing that love and hate have these effects (or recognizing that they do) should not lead us to suppose that exclusivity and constancy are axiomatic of love. If the fact that hate has nasty effects is irrelevant to the issue of whether hate is axiomatically exclusive or constant, then the fact that love has its own typical, desired effects is similarly irrelevant. The impulse to conceive of love but not hate as exclusive or constant may be, of course, a disguised moral demand. Love is valuable when constant and exclusive, causing behaviors (except in cases of obsessive attachments or extreme jealousy) that are morally praiseworthy and beneficial not only for lover and beloved but also for their immediate acquaintances and even strangers. Nothing but disaster usually results when a hatred is forever nurtured or when someone focuses all his hate on one person. Phaedrus' catalogue of the heroic deeds performed by lovers cannot be matched by a list of heroic deeds performed by haters; love and courage are a natural pair in a way hate and courage are not. But none of these differences warrants the conclusion that love and hate are axiomatically different.

3. EXPLANATIONS AND JUSTIFICATIONS

Suppose we grant that love is generally a "positive" or "good" emotion that brings happiness to lover and beloved and has beneficial effects on other people; and that hate is a "negative" or "bad" emotion that creates misery for the hater, the behated, and other people. Then love never has to be justified or explained; its occurrence is welcome no matter what causes it and even if it has no rational or any ground at all. But hate requires justification; it is an unwelcome occurrence we would rather do without, and the hater must show that its damaging effects on our quality of life are justified. Or perhaps people have a need to be loved and a need to love, whereas they do not have a need to either hate or to be hated. Then love requires no justification or explanation: since its existence is needed, it is welcome, and that which is welcome can come as it pleases. But hate, which is not needed in our lives, we can plainly do without; hence we demand justifications when it interrupts the smooth flow of social intercourse. What is supposed to follow is that love need not be construed erosically, while hate is best construed as an erosic emotion. For the heart of the eros tradition is that love is grounded in the lover's perception of the beloved's value and that, therefore, love does not resist, indeed it invites, explanation; and that the selection by the lover of a beloved not only allows but requires justification—given the large number of potential beloveds having valuable properties. The agape tradition places no such restrictions on love and is therefore a better way to understand an emotion for which complaint is silly or pointless if it occurs unpredictably or mysteriously.

This argument, however, does not compel us to distinguish between love and hate by analyzing the former agapically and the latter erosically. First, from the fact that y has a need to be loved it does not follow that y will not care why x loves her. If y has specifically a neurotic need to be loved, then y might not select lovers erosically. For most people, however, love is an important but not pressing need, so other interests (for example, maintaining self-respect) will lead them to accept love or to give it with discrimination (see 8.3). Love may not be welcome if it requires the loss of other goods, including its own rationality. Surely the behated has a right to either an explanation or a justification for why she in particular is the object of the emotion: "What did I do? What is it about me that annoys you?" But merely because love is welcome, these same questions are not ruled out. Even though I am pleased to be loved, I can still reflect on whether I should be pleased: "What did I do to deserve this special treatment? Why me instead of z?" The lover, too, may not be bent on blindly satisfying his need to love, concerned that he be able to justify satisfying it here rather than there, or at all.

Second, even if something's requiring a justification depends on whether it is "good" or "bad," whether it requires an explanation has nothing to do with its being welcome or unwelcome. Rather, things unexpected or out of the ordinary require explanation when they occur; things that are commonplace do not. Ordinarily, my breathing does not call for an explanation; were I suddenly to stop breathing, the physicians would search for an explanatory cause. If so, whether love is less a candidate for explanation than hate depends on their relative frequencies, not on their moral value. Suppose that humans by their psychological nature have a tendency to love and a tendency not to hate. Then love would require no explanation, but hate would, because love is expected and hate is out of the ordinary. I have no idea how to compare the frequencies of love and hate; nor do I know whether their actual frequencies are higher than their expected frequencies. If most people experience hate more often than love, then love, not hate, needs explanation. Indeed, love often comes as a surprise and is therefore exactly the emotion calling for an explanation.

Third, because hate is unwelcome, we demand a justification from the hater (so the argument goes)—but why? Presumably, the point of demanding a justification is to make sure that any particular occurrence of hate is necessary. Since hate is "bad," we want to minimize gratuitous, indefensible hatreds, and we try to do this by demanding justifications. Those who have no good reason to hate will thereby be deterred, at least from acting on their hate. Similarly, we can try to minimize hate by treating it as an explainable phenomenon; by knowing how it arises, we can control the conditions in which it flourishes. But, then, it does not follow from the fact that love is "good" that explanations are out of place. For if love is welcome, we would like to increase its frequency. That project requires that we treat love as explainable, in order to discover and promote the conditions in which it flourishes. I find little reason to agree with the poetic sentiment that explaining or justifying love kills it[3] (see 8.6).

Fourth, when we demand from x an explanation or justification for why she hates y, we expect to hear what properties or actions of y warrant x's hate for y; we want a true story about the grounding of x's hate in something about y. Hence, our practice of demanding justifications for hate presupposes that hate is an erosic phenomenon. But the fact that we are not always called upon to justify or explain either our loves or our selection of a beloved does not mean that love is not erosic. We usually know why we hate someone; thus we can usually satisfy the demand for a justification. (Note that we demand a justification from x for her hating y when *we* cannot see her reason; we also ask x, who loves an apparently unlovable y, what x sees in y that we cannot.) But frequently being unable to provide clear reasons for our loves does not mean that the request for an explanation is ill-conceived. The inability to provide clear reasons could mean that in reflecting upon the grounds of our love we are psychologically unable or unwilling to probe more systematically and deeply. Perhaps when exposed these reasons turn out to be superficial and embarrassing; perhaps they reveal something about our characters that we would rather not face. Maybe, then, we do not ask for justifications of love as a matter of etiquette, not because love has no reasons. Surely, if love were agapic, seeking explanations might be pointless; we might be tempted to think, therefore, that love is an agapic phenomenon *because* we do not seek explanations. But the fact that we are not always prepared to ask for or provide explanations of our loves does not entail that there are none—in particular, that there are no explanations in terms of the attractive properties of the beloved.

4. IRRATIONAL LOVE

Evidence that love is similar to hatred is provided by the ways in which both emotions can be unreasonable or irrational or otherwise deviate from their typical or ideal patterns. First, they may involve irrational desires. Hate and love may be irrational by proxy insofar as they generate desires to do things that are irrational; for example, acts such as killing the behated if one is convinced one will be caught and executed, or totally abandoning a promising career in order to marry one's beloved, are irrational (although we might excuse what seems plainly stupid to us, because some hates are understandably uncontrollable and some loves are a blessing). If these desires are conceived, instead, as constitutive of the emotions (that is, wanting to harm the behated and wanting to be with the beloved are parts of the emotion), then this irrationality is built into, and not merely contingently tied to, the emotion. Or suppose that certain desires lead x to love y and thereby ground x's love. Then x's love will be irrational if these desires are: for example, x loves y because y mistreats x and satisfies needs of x to be abused. When x hates himself, we usually call it irrational or pathological. But even though reflexive love (xLx) is often said to be many things—selfish, antisocial, vain, healthy, natural—we do not ordinarily call it irrational. This difference between love and hate is attributable to our evaluating love as "good" and hate as "bad": no one in his right mind would want to harm himself. But this is why the x who loves an abusive y, because y abuses x, must be considered irrational.

Second, x's hating or loving y because x believes that y has P, when that belief is arrived at irrationally, will be irrational by proxy. If we are not careful about gathering evidence for our beliefs, or if we base our beliefs on insufficient or dubious evidence, or if we are the victims (even willing victims) of unconscious processes that determine our beliefs independently of the evidence (projection, self-deception, wish fulfillment), our beliefs will be irrational and tend to be false. When hate is irrational in this way—x hates y recklessly believing that y has P—it is also condemnable morally. (I argue in 12.9 that this moral evaluation also applies to love.) Note that this irrationality is not due exactly to x's believing falsely that y has P. If x believes falsely that y has P, on the basis of very weak evidence or independently of evidence, the irrationality of the emotion derives not from the falsity of the belief but from the way the belief arose. Suppose, on the one hand, that x believes falsely that y has P, yet x has excellent evidence for that belief. The fact that x's belief is false gives us no reason to criticize the rationality of the emotion. Now suppose, on the other hand, that x believes truly that y has P, yet x has weak evidence for that belief or arrived at it independently of the evidence. The fact that x's belief is (coincidentally) true does not prevent us from judging that the belief-formation and thereby x's love or hate are irrational. (Consider a related issue: What about x's believing that y has P *because* x loves or hates y? Does this manner of belief formation imply that the belief is irrational? If x's emotion causes x to attribute only a subjective property to y, then the process is not irrational, if only because attributions of subjective properties are never mistakes. But if the emotion leads x to attribute [truly or falsely] an objective property to y, this is irrational; for whether y has such a property is independent of x's emotion. In these cases, x's emotion might be irrational by proxy, not because the emotion results from an irrational belief but because it causes one.)

Third, love and hate may be irrational when xLy or xHy because y has P, yet "having P" is somehow not adequately connected with the emotion. If xLy or xHy because y has P, yet later x no longer loves or hates y even though y still has P, the fact that y's P has not maintained x's emotion does not indicate that x is irrational; x simply no longer considers P either a merit or dismerit. But suppose xHy because y has P, yet at roughly the same time x does not hate z who is relevantly indistinguishable from y: E-type hate, in which hate-reasons are not generalizable, is as irrational as E-type love. More interesting is the phenomenon of x's still hating y even after y has changed and no longer has P (or after x's false belief that y has P has been corrected); here the reason x had earlier for hating y no longer exists, yet the emotion does not dissipate. (Consider fear that persists long after the dangerous dog has been killed.) Ordinarily, the x who hates even though his reason for hating is gone (the "O-hater") is judged irrational and is also often morally condemned. Yet the "O-lover," who loves even though her reason for loving is gone (x loved y for having P and still loves y after y has lost P), is often praised for exhibiting constant devotion. But if love and hate are erosic phenomena, the cases should be analyzed symmetrically. The impulse to conceive of love axiomatically as constant or to evaluate love as good may prevent us from seeing the O-lover as irrational. But why do we condemn the O-hater and praise the O-lover, unless both emotions are erosic phenomena? Condemning the O-hater makes sense if hate is property-based, because we expect the hate to dissipate when its ground is gone. And when we praise the O-lover, we show that we expected the (property-based) love to dissipate and are pleased or surprised that it did not.

In some cases we may be able to explain the constancy of x's love for y, when y no longer has P, by assuming that other properties of y, newly developed by y or discovered by x, maintain x's love (see chap. 10). Such an explanation is awkward for the O-hater. Indeed, love's being property-based and good leads us to think that x's O-love can and should be understood in terms of y's other properties. The premise that hate is property-based and bad leads us to a different conclusion: to judge O-haters as irrational and immoral and not to suppose that O-hate is explainable by other properties of y. Perhaps, however, x continues to love y, even though y has lost P, because x's love has risen to the level of loving "the person." X's O-hate for y may be similarly explained: it has been expanded from merely hating y for P, or hating P itself, to hating y "the whole person" or hating y "as a person" (see chap. 13). If we praise the lover who ascends to the level of loving the person, despite the fact that the beloved's properties have changed and no longer ground that love, we should not criticize as irrational the (immoral) O-hater who has developed, even nurtured, an emotion toward y "the person." We might prefer the alternative: O-love that loves "the person" is as irrational as O-hate that hates "the person." This seems better than the Christian solution, in which love is construed agapically and hate erosically: we should love "the person," not his or her properties, yet we should hate the sin (the property), not the sinner (the person).[4]

Fourth, hate and love may be irrational if they are grounded in inappropriate properties of their object. Suppose that x hates y because y puts on a sock, then a shoe, then the other sock, and finally the other shoe (rather than sock-sock-shoe-shoe).[5] We might say that when x has an emotion toward y for having such a wildly inappropriate P, x's emotion is not even hate; hate is possible only for some P's, not any P at all. It makes more sense, however, to say that x could hate y for this foot-dressing order, there being no limit on the properties a person might find annoying enough to evoke hate, but then to add that hating for wildly inappropriate properties is irrational. If x hates y only because y hates x, this agapic hate is as nonideal or as irrational as x's loving y only because y loves x (see 1.2). Indeed, part of the rationality of hate is understanding that not all P's are appropriate. Consider another example: x hates y for having a property that y has no control over or is not responsible for having, instead of, say, for a trait y deliberately nurtured. It is not implausible that x's hate is irrational because there is no point in hating y for what y could not avoid. (This is not equivalent to saying that there is no point in hating y for

P when there is no possibility P will vanish. Y's having no control over P does not mean that no one does: the hater can get rid of P by killing y. In a sense, the desires caused by or constitutive of hate aim at exactly that: wanting to hurt y is a way of wanting to rid the world of P. By analogy: when x loves y for P, x desires to benefit y so that this valuable property remains in the world.[6])

Similar questions arise about love (see 10.4–10.6; 12.9). Suppose that x loves y because y can spell "occurred." We might say that x's emotion could not be love, since this P is wildly inappropriate; "genuine" love, for conceptual reasons, is based only on "important" properties. Claiming that x's emotion could not be love when it is a response to a wildly inappropriate property sounds more plausible than claiming that x's emotion could not be hate if based on such a property. But this difference is artificial, reflecting only the fact that we usually treat love more soberly and seriously than hate. Consider other weird, possibly love-grounding properties: y is a dreadful bore, y has money, y enjoys torturing flies, y has long legs, y showers infrequently. Even if it is conceptually possible for x to love y for one of these bizarre P's, x's love is still somehow defective: x's love is superficial (or x is superficial), or x's love is irrational because finding *that* P valuable is irrational. Robert Brown is wrong, I think, in asserting that "we can only fear what we take to be dangerous to us in some respect, and we can only love what we take to be . . . worthwhile in some respect. To love what we took to be completely worthless would be like fearing what we thought was completely harmless."[7] Brown is right to point out the analogy between love and fear as erosic phenomena, but his thesis, that an emotion is not love or fear if based on (what looks like) a conceptually inappropriate property, is too strong. In both cases it is more plausible to say that these are irrational cases of the emotions, not that they are not these emotions at all. What emotion other than fear *could* it be when x claims to experience fear while admitting the object is harmless? After all, in agape x loves an object that x might consider completely worthless. Agape may be irrational love, or the agape tradition may entail an odd view of personal love, but agape is still a kind of love. To claim that "we can only love what we take to be . . . worthwhile" is to *define* love in such a way that the erosic view is automatically true, and doing that is a mistake.

Fifth (and most obviously, in light of sect. 3), we often suspect that something is fishy with x's hate for y, and we judge it irrational, when x does not understand and cannot explain why x hates y. Indeed, it should be clear to x himself that if x has no idea at all why he hates y, something is wrong with his emotion—and if it is not clear to x, that too is irrational. Yet some people would not criticize the lover for not being able to explain why she loves y or for her not considering it strange that she is not able to account for her love. But, I have been arguing, to treat love and hate differently in this regard is incorrect. Similarly, love and hate may be irrational when the lover or hater has false and poorly grounded beliefs about the nature of these emotions. Suppose that x believes "you always hurt the one you love" and conducts the love relationship accordingly; or suppose the beloved y believes that x does not love her unless x occasionally beats her. There is reason to judge these lovers irrational, if their beliefs about love are not well founded. What if x somehow believes that the sort of love we typically have for a person can be directed without change to an inappropriate object of such love? Imagine wooing a sheep with flowers and wine, and getting jealous when someone else shows affection for, and sexual attention toward, that sheep.[8] Or suppose that x believes without much reflection that love is axiomatically exclusive (that is, that if xAy and xAz, then A ≠ L). Love might be irrational at this metalevel.

Sixth, love and hate may be irrational when the emotion is radically disconnected from its object—not merely when x has latched onto some bizarre property, or when x has an unwarranted belief about y's properties, but when the emotion has nothing at all to do with y's properties. Suppose that we ask x why he hates y, and x is unable to answer the question with "because y is P." Now, we might suspect that x is lying (not wanting to reveal how silly his hate is) or deceiving himself; that is, we would tend to say that x's hate *is* grounded in some P of y's, and x is irrational because he is not aware of his reason for hating. But suppose that x's hate does not, after all, originate from any consciously or unconsciously perceived P that y has. I think we would readily judge this hate irrational, even though some people would not judge x's love for y irrational if it were not in any way grounded in y's properties. The explanation for this difference is familiar: since love is "good," we do not care how it arises and refuse to judge it critically even though it exists in a manner that would lead us to condemn other emotions if they existed that way. Consider the O-hater, who hated y for having P, yet continues to hate y after y no longer has P, and does so *now* for no P at all. What has happened is that x's hate has changed from an erosic hate to an agapic hate. The same is true of the x who hated y because x believed falsely that y had P, yet continues to hate y when the belief is corrected. In both cases, the coherence of x's hate has degenerated. Yet some people would not be disturbed if x's love continued in analogous situations, having changed from an erosic to an agapic phenomenon.

The points are that (a) when hate is agapic, it is morally condemned and judged irrational; (b) we are told to hate, if at all, erosically, in order to be able to justify the emotion; and (c) if the agape tradition were used to characterize hate, the account would be implausible: hate is typically an erosic emotion. Yet some people balk at treating love symmetrically, finding nothing wrong with conceiving of personal love agapically, as neither property-based nor reason-dependent. To argue that hate is erosic and love is agapic, on the grounds that hate is "bad" and love is "good," is unconvincing; I cannot see how these evaluations have any relevance for the question of the structure of these emotions. The evaluations explain only why we would like to believe love and hate are, respectively, agapic and erosic phenomena. But love, too, can look strange when it is agapic. Suppose, as in Walter Davison's "Ode,"[9] that x loves y exclusively, constantly, and unrequitedly; in fact, x continues to love y even though y hates x, not only resisting x's attempts to benefit y but also being downright nasty to x. X's love is pathological if any case of love is; when x exclaims, "Tears, sighs, prayers fail, but true love lasteth forever," he earns pity, not admiration.[10] This love might very well be property-based—x loves y here because x believes y is uniquely perfect—yet its obsessive constancy and attempts at benevolence in the face of nonreciprocation and hatred make it look agapic. For in some ways Davison is describing Jesus, who loved humans constantly even though he was despised and tortured by them. When personal love takes on the features usually attributed to agapic love, it (like hate) can appear bizarre. And if this happens to our perception of personal love when it is property-based, should it not happen more dramatically when x's love is not property-based?

5. LOVE AS AN ANOMALOUS EMOTION

I wish to discuss in some detail three contributions to the philosophical literature on the emotions. Doing so is necessary to fine-tune and confirm my conclusions from section 4.

A) In an essay by D. W. Hamlyn, I find the view that even though both hate and love are typically erosic phenomena, agapic hate is irrational but agapic personal love is not. Consider how Hamlyn analyzes the emotions. He begins by arguing that for the emotions in general, in order "to *have* [the emotion] . . . one has either to have a certain sort of belief about [the] object or to see it in the corresponding way."[11] For example, Hamlyn claims that if x does not at least believe that y is dangerous or perceive y as dangerous, then x's emotion toward y cannot logically *be* fear (p. 8). Similarly, x for logical reasons cannot "take pride" in or "feel pride" about something unless x believes that x had something "to do with" it or some responsibility for it (pp. 8–9). In this view, some cases of fear and pride will be irrational in virtue of the irrationality of the beliefs conceptually required for having the emotion. X's fear of paper towels is irrational if x's belief that paper towels are dangerous is unwarranted; x's emotion is still fear, however, since x does believe they are dangerous.

But why agree with Hamlyn that if x does not believe A to be dangerous, x's emotion cannot *be* fear, or that if x acknowledges that x had "nothing to do with" B, x's emotion cannot be pride? That is, why not say of such cases that x has the emotion and that it (or x) is irrational in yet another sense? As far as I can tell, Hamlyn provides no argument; we are supposed to intuit that if x does not believe that x is in some way responsible for B, "then whatever he feels about the object it is not pride" (p. 9). Suppose, however, that x reports having an inner experience of what x would always call fear, that x says the emotion is directed at A, but x also says that he finds A cuddly. The first point to make is that we are not forced to claim that at some level of consciousness (or unconsciousness), or that in some esoteric sense of "belief" this x does in fact have the characteristic belief that A is dangerous. The second point is that Hamlyn cannot sidestep this case by saying that he is concerned with emotions and not (mere) feelings, for too often he speaks of having an emotion *as* having a feeling (for example, pp. 8–9, 15). The final point is that after claiming that in this case x's emotion is not fear, Hamlyn does not proceed to tell us what he should tell us: If the emotion is not fear (or pride), what emotion is it? To say only "*whatever* he feels . . . it is not [fear]" leaves a lacuna in his analysis. Not being told what this phenomenon is, we cannot even judge whether it is a typical or atypical case of "it." (Free-floating anxiety is not exactly fear without its characteristic belief.) For these reasons I find it equally plausible that x's emotion is still fear, but irrational in a more radical way.

Hamlyn wonders about "the extent to which [his analysis] applies to love and hate" (p. 9), and asks "if one does love X, what beliefs must one have about X, and how must one see or regard X if it is really to be love?" (p. 11). If x's emotion toward A cannot be fear unless x believes A is dangerous, then can we also say that x's emotion toward y cannot be love unless x believes . . . about y, filling in the ellipsis with "a certain sort of belief" about y? Hamlyn answers no, providing (what I take to be) two separate arguments. First, it is logically possible for x to love y "full-stop": x loves y "without there being anything that the love is for" (p. 12). The idea is that if x can love y but not *for* anything, then x can love y but not for having certain properties. If so, x can love y without believing that y has any (specific) properties. Thus, there is no "certain *sort* of belief" that x must have about y if x loves y. Hamlyn's first argument, I think, amounts to this: x can love y without having any reasons for the love (p. 16), so x need not have any particular beliefs about y that are presupposed by having reasons. The argument, then, really asserts that reason-independent love is logically possible, that some cases of x's loving y could be agapic cases of personal love.[12]

Second, Hamlyn argues that the ellipsis cannot even be filled in with x's very general belief that y is lovable or attractive, as if we were to set up (*pace* Robert Brown) this analogy to specify the logically characteristic belief of love: x fears A only if x believes A is dangerous, and x loves y only if x believes y is lovable. Hamlyn's reason for rejecting the latter is that x's loving y is "not incompatible with" x's not respecting y, x's finding y "distasteful," or x's "recognizing in [y] a whole series of bad qualities which are not overridden by good qualities" (p. 13). Again, Hamlyn's thesis is conceptual; he does not defend this claim by mentioning actual cases of x's loving y when x believes y is worthless—he claims only that such love is not logically impossible. Hence, there is no "particular belief that [x] *must* have about [y]," "no particular kind of belief *about* [y]," in order for x to have the emotion love toward y (pp. 13, 14). If x need not believe anything in particular about y (and not even that y is lovable), x need not believe that y has wonderful properties; and, of course, x need not love y in virtue of properties about which x has no beliefs. Hamlyn's second argument, like the first, merely asserts that personal love can be agapic.

Hence for love, at least, Hamlyn thinks he has shown that this emotion can "exist without any intimate connections between these feelings and any beliefs on the part of the person concerned of the sort that certainly seem requisite for many emotions" (p. 15). In effect, Hamlyn is claiming that for most emotions (for example, fear and pride) the erosic account is logically true, but personal love is an exception or anomaly, conceptually permitting agapic cases. Thus, x logically cannot fear A if x does not believe A is dangerous, but x can love y regardless of x's beliefs (or, x can love y "full-stop," without reasons).[13] But suppose that we take the alternative account of fear seriously: x *can* fear A even if x does not believe A is dangerous, which is to say that x can fear A without having any "particular kind of belief about" A. Of course, we tack on that x's fear of A is irrational, that its irrationality is due to its being in this case agapic, and that fear is typically or ideally erosic. If so, Hamlyn has not succeeded in showing that personal love is anomalous: fear and pride are erosic emotions, not logically but only typically, in the same way that love is typically but not logically erosic (because agapic personal love is logically possible). But now the question arises, if agapic fear is irrational, then is not agapic personal love irrational? When Hamlyn says that reason-independent love is "a logical possibility and even a human possibility in the sense that it is intelligible in human beings . . . as an isolated phenomenon" (p. 16), the implication is that Hamlyn countenances both agapic and erosic cases of personal love, but that the erosic cases are typical. But why not also say that agapic cases are not only atypical but also irrational?

To approach this question, we began by noting that for Hamlyn hate is to be understood conceptually in the same way as love. This means that hate can be "full-stop": x can hate y but not *for* anything about y; hate can be reason-independent (agapic hate is logically possible). It also means that hate, like love, is an anomalous emotion, for in contrast to most emotions, no particular belief is required for x's emotion toward y to be hate. When x hates y, x need not believe y is obnoxious or that y has done something to x to warrant being hated, nor must x consider y's hateable properties to outweigh y's merits. But hate "full-stop" is irrational; when x hates y for no reason or in the absence of believing y has some nasty P, x's emotion is too radically divorced from its object. Hamlyn agrees: "When this happens as an isolated phenomenon in human beings we tend . . . to set it down as a mere quirk. When it happens quite generally and in an extreme way . . . we tend to reach for the category of the psychopath; for it is part of the psychology of such a person that such emotional attitudes . . . are unrelated to any range of appropriate objects. . . . Hence while hatred of something without reason . . . is possible in a human being . . . where it manifests itself frequently the word 'inhuman' . . . comes to mind" (pp. 16–17).[14]

Hamlyn should be prepared to say similar things about love "full-stop," but he vacillates: "Love without reason [is] little more than irritating, if that. Even this need not be so; the case of someone being dragged down to some ill fate by someone else's infatuation is not *that* uncommon. Nevertheless, it is reasonable to expect hatred to have . . . more obvious bad consequences than love. . . . Correspondingly, it is perhaps more difficult to think of a love as being inhuman than so to think of hatred; even so I do not think that the idea can be ruled out as senseless" (pp. 17–18). Hamlyn cannot quite make up his mind whether love "full-stop" is irrational or pathological. But since he is not sure, and since his only reason for resisting that conclusion is the unhappy argument that love is "good" and hate is "bad," should not the demands of consistency—after all, *his* thesis is that love and hate are structurally the same—push him over the fence? Indeed, Hamlyn claims that a person loved "full-stop" has "the right to demand more" (p. 16), that is, to demand reasons for the love. Exactly this requirement, however, applies to hate, and when it is violated "irrational" is the correct assessment. After all, Hamlyn does say that "love and hate can be considered rational when their objects have certain appropriate qualities" (p. 20), which is to say that the rationality of love and hate is a function of the beliefs they involve. Hence, love and hate should be considered irrational when these beliefs are absent. Hamlyn, however, goes in a different direction: "If such qualities do not exist in their objects love and hate are not necessarily and for that reason to be considered irrational, even if they are, so to speak, non-rational." This is a fudge. If love and hate are nonrational when appropriate qualities or beliefs are absent, both emotions are nonrational even when the qualities and beliefs are present. Hamlyn should not refrain from calling some cases of love and hate irrational if he wants to call other cases rational.

Even as Hamlyn is willing to condemn agapic hate as pathological, yet goes soft on agapic personal love, he readily admits that the agapic versions of these emotions are largely isolated cases (p. 16). "Human love and hate could not universally be" agapic (p. 20), and therefore typically both love and hate are erosic emotions in which the lover's or the hater's believing that y has P plays a central role. Apart from his claim that other emotions (for example, fear and pride) are conceptually erosic and do not admit of agapic cases, I do not disagree with Hamlyn. The first view of personal love, derived from the eros tradition, does not claim that it is a logical truth that x loves y only if x believes that y has P. Rather, it claims that love typically or ideally has that structure. Hence, to show that agapic personal love is possible deals no blow to the eros tradition.

B) George Pitcher has argued that because emotions are not merely feelings but involve beliefs, particular tokens of the emotions generally can be judged reasonable or unreasonable. Using fear as an example, Pitcher lists five types of "unreasonable" emotion: (1) x fears y because x believes B about y, but x's belief is false and "unreasonable" (in this case, says Pitcher, the belief would be a good reason to fear y were it true); (2) x fears y, yet x "acknowledges that there is no danger" (Pitcher calls this "irrational" fear, thereby disagreeing with Hamlyn's claim that x's emotion in this case is not even fear); (3) x fears y because x believes B about y, but this belief provides a very bad reason for fear ("superstitious" fear, as when x sees a black cat); (4) x's fear is directed at an unsuitable or inappropriate object ("neurotic" fear, as in fear of a coffee cup); and (5) x's fear may be disproportionate to its cause. Hate and anger also admit of being judged "unreasonable" and "irrational."[15] But Pitcher thinks love is anomalous:

> If Paul loves Suzy, there seems to be no clear sense in which his love might be called reasonable or unreasonable, rational or irrational. . . . A love can be unsuitable, dangerous, unfortunate, disastrous, unhealthy, a blessing, . . . but not . . . reasonable or unreasonable. To be sure, if a person loves an object that is wildly odd—if he loves, say, his cat (*i.e.* loves it as one person . . . loves another) or his mother's shoes—then his love is "sick" or psychotic, and might therefore be called irrational; but within the vast range of cases . . . the distinction seems not to apply at all. This strikes one at first as odd, for . . . hatreds can certainly be unreasonable, and very likely reasonable as well. (p. 341)

This passage is surprising, since three of Pitcher's types of unreasonable emotion apply directly to love (in addition to type [4], which he admits does apply): (1) x loves y because x believes that y has P, but this belief is false and unreasonable; (2) x loves y, yet acknowledges that y is eminently unattractive and unlovable; and (3) x loves y because y was born on a cusp. (On [5]—x's love for y is disproportionate to its reasons or causes—see 13.10.) Why does Pitcher deny, then, that love can be unreasonable or irrational? He does try to account for (what he takes to be) the fact that the distinction between "reasonable" and "unreasonable" does not apply to love.

Pitcher begins by noting that when x loves y, x wants to spend his time with y, wants y to be healthy and happy, and so on; his argument turns on investigating why x has these wants. "The man in love wants . . . to be with his beloved . . . simply because he enjoys her company" (p. 341). This sounds tautologous, but that is precisely what Pitcher is driving at: "There is no reason for it, he just wants to be with her." Yet if we ask x why x wants to be with y, x "could specify which of [y's] qualities makes being with her a pleasure." Does this not imply that x's wants are based on beliefs about y and hence can be judged reasonable or unreasonable? No, for Pitcher continues: "Such a reply obviously does not give the whole story, nor even the heart of it: it is an answer which a person might give in public when he does not wish to reveal his deeper feelings." *That* is strange; Pitcher claims that in public x explains his desire to be with y by mentioning y's properties, in order to shield his "deeper feelings." But *these,* he has just told us, are (deeply?) tautologous: x wants to be with y because x enjoys her company. "For him, the only really honest answer, finally, is either no answer—*e.g.* 'Because I just do'—or one which merely rules out other possible reasons that there might be, but does not itself give a reason— for example, 'Because I love her'" (p. 342). But, for Pitcher, this is not something different: to say "because I love her" is to say "in effect, that in the final analysis there just is no reason, and that he simply *does* want to be with her all the time." No wonder x does not say this in public; not to shield his feelings, but to avoid looking silly.

There are two problems in Pitcher's view. First, he has not made it clear why x's having only a tautologous (or no) reason for wanting to be with his beloved implies that love cannot be qualified as reasonable or unreasonable. Second, while claiming that if x loves y, then x wants to spend his time with y, Pitcher never tells us whether this want is constitutive of love or its causal effect. If x's wants, including the desire to be with y, are constitutive of x's love for y, then of course "because I love her" is no explanation of or reason for x's wants. In this case, x's having no reason for these wants is equivalent to x's having no reason for loving y. We could just as well ask x not why x wants to be with y but why x loves y—and, for Pitcher, the answer would be equally unrevealing: "Because I just do." Now we can understand why x's having no reason for wanting to be with y might imply that love is neither reasonable nor unreasonable: love is reason-independent and, hence, we should call it "areasonable," if anything. But this argument is unconvincing, even on Pitcher's view. For there is no difference between x's fearing A when x admits that A is not dangerous (which Pitcher calls "irrational"; see his type [2], above) and x's loving y without having any reasons. X's fearing A when x admits that A is not dangerous is a case of x's fearing something with no reason. "Why do you fear A?" "Because I just do."

Suppose, instead, that x's wants are causal effects of x's loving y. In this case, x's explaining his desire to be with y by saying "because I love her" makes perfect sense; causes do explain their effects, and thus, contrary to Pitcher, x may offer this coherent reason for his wants. But now we should ask why x loves y. Pitcher seems to think that x's answer is "because I do," that love is reason-independent and hence cannot be criticized for involving beliefs that might be unreasonable.[16] Since love is reason-independent, the examples of unreasonable love I provided above fail because all attribute love-grounding beliefs to x. For Pitcher, "a person's love of another, like his preference for chocolate over vanilla ice cream, cannot be adjudged reasonable or unreasonable[,] because it includes evaluations for which . . . there can be, within wide limits, neither standards of criticism nor justifying reasons" (p. 342). "Why do you prefer pistachio?" "Because I just do. I could tell you that it tastes the best, and if you ask why, I'll just repeat: because it does." X's loving y is to be understood in the same way. Pitcher's view would not be disturbing were it not for the fact that, unlike Hamlyn's love "full-stop," Pitcher's reason-independent love is not the odd case of personal love but typical. It is probably false, however, that x's public answer ("because y has P") would differ greatly from the answer x gives y in private; and as Hamlyn says, y would have the right to demand more than "because I just do." (See 8.3.) If Pitcher thinks x's preference for y is logically equivalent to x's preference for pistachio, he underestimates (the honesty of?) both lover and beloved. More to the point, the fact that x provides no better an answer than "because I do" does not entail that there is no better answer. X's not providing a reason for loving y might mean that x's love is not reason-dependent, but it could also mean that x's love is irrational insofar as x is cut off from his reasons.

There is a deeper flaw in Pitcher's position. Suppose it were true that we have preferences for beloveds as subjective as our preferences for ice cream flavors. What follows? It seems to me that the subjectivity of our evaluations of persons is consistent with claiming that typically x loves y only if x believes y to be attractive; the subjectivity of evaluations only means that what x and z find attractive might differ or that there are few limits to what lovers will find attractive in beloveds. It does not follow from the subjectivity of evaluations that love involves no particular *sort* of belief or no beliefs at all, and hence it does not follow that love is not reason-dependent.[17] The subjectivity of evaluations does not entail, then, that love cannot be judged unreasonable or irrational; we could still examine the beliefs surrounding those evaluations in order to see if they are well founded. If x finds crudity attractive—which evaluation alone cannot be called a mistake—still x might be mistaken in believing that y is crude; perhaps y is only pretending to be crude. Further, we might judge that x's preference for gasoline-flavored ice cream is bizarre enough to be irrational and make the same judgment about an x who loves y because y abuses x. Thus Pitcher has not succeeded in showing that love is anomalous in never being unreasonable. When he writes, "Most other emotions—including hate—differ from love in this respect. . . . [X hates y] normally, because [y] has what [x] deems to be a despicable character" (p. 342), Pitcher misses the implication of "deems." If hate requires only that x *deem* y to be despicable, external standards of criticism are lacking also for hate, which puts it into the same Pitcher-boat as love. Hence, Pitcher must conclude either that love can be unreasonable despite subjective evaluations (because hate can be) or that hate is not properly judged "unreasonable." But surely if x hates y because y wears green socks on Tuesdays, x's hate is irrational even though there is no doubt that x finds this trait despicable in x's subjective world. The subjectivity of evaluations in hate, then, is no bar to calling it irrational; indeed, it may be exactly why we *can* call it irrational.

C) Gabriele Taylor's discussion of love is faithful to our by now familiar pattern: after first analyzing the emotions generally by outlining some necessary conditions, she proceeds to ask whether love is anomalous. One condition is that "if x feels the emotion, and if y is the object, then x will believe y to have a specific property or set of properties."[18] This condition states that x must believe that y has or is φ, where φ is the emotion-defining property (what Taylor dubs the emotion's "determinable quality") and x's belief that y has φ is the characteristic belief of the emotion. (φ for fear is "dangerous," for gratitude "has done me a good turn.") Second, if x has the emotion, then x believes that y has φ *because* x believes that y has or is ψ, where ψ are the emotion's "determinate qualities." (X believes the bear is dangerous because x believes it has sharp claws and is hungry.) What immediately interests Taylor are the questions: What limits can be placed on the ψ properties; in what sense can the emotions, given this analysis, be judged rational or irrational, justified or unjustified; and how well does love fit into this picture?

Taylor suggests that φ will place limits on ψ. Since x believes that y has φ because x believes that y has ψ, the determinate properties ψ must be able to "explain why x believes *y*" to have φ (p. 148). We thus have the following restrictions: a property P can be ψ, or included in it, only if x's believing that y has P explains x's believing y to have φ. As Taylor concedes, this is not much of a restriction, and ψ will vary widely according to person, situation, and time. Still, we can now see that there are two ways (at least) in which the emotions can go wrong; if x's belief that y has ψ is irrational (for example, x's belief that the bear has sharp claws and is hungry is ill-founded), or if x's belief that y has φ because y has ψ is irrational (for example, x believes the bear is dangerous *because* it is cuddly), then x's emotion is both irrational and unjustified (p. 149).

Turning to love: Does love have a φ as do the other emotions? Can restrictions be put on love's ψ? And can love be judged rational or justified in the same way? Taylor argues that love has no φ and hence (agreeing with Hamlyn and Pitcher) that love has no characteristic belief. Not even "lovable" and "attractive" qualify, for "there seems to be no contradiction in saying that *x* loves *y* although he does not believe *y* to be lovable in the accepted sense, as there is a contradiction in saying that *x* fears *y* and yet does not believe *y* to be dangerous" (p. 152). The argument is weak. First, it might not be contradictory to say that x fears y, yet does not believe y is dangerous; this might just be another type of irrational fear. Second, the argument equivocates; x's loving y, yet not believing y lovable "in the accepted sense," should be compared with x's fearing y, yet not believing y dangerous "in the accepted sense" (or the clause should be omitted throughout). Surely, there is no contradiction in saying that x fears y while not believing that y is dangerous according to common notions of "dangerous," and consistency would require Taylor to conclude that fear, like love, has no φ (a conclusion she would not want to embrace). Third, that there is no contradiction in saying that x loves y, yet does not believe y lovable "in the accepted sense," is entirely consistent with all lovers finding their beloveds "lovable" (that is, to have φ), while the ψ in virtue of which lovers believe their beloved to have φ varies tremendously. I think Taylor wrongly supposes that the subjectivity of our evaluations of a person as being φ ("lovable" or "attractive") demonstrates that x's believing y to have φ is not characteristic of love.

As if anticipating these criticisms, Taylor writes: "If all that can be said is that if *x* loves *y* he finds *y* lovable, then although this may tell us something about *x* and his tastes, it can tell us nothing whatever about what [ψ] qualities to look for in *y*" (pp. 152–153). Hence, "lovable" (love's purported φ) "cannot be used to put constraints upon the ψ qualities which *x* may believe *y* to have" (p. 153). The argument seems to be: love has no φ, such as "lovable," because (1) any candidate φ for love "tells us" nothing about the ψ's that x believes y to have and hence cannot place any limit on ψ; and (2) it is a feature of those emotions that do have a φ, that this φ does place limits on ψ. But there are three things wrong in this argument.

First, Taylor did not assert earlier that a φ's being able to place limits on ψ was a necessary condition for having an emotion (but only that x believes y to have φ because x believes y to have ψ). Nor does she ever argue for claim (2); indeed, (2) is untenable (as I show below). Second, if our knowing that x finds y lovable (to have φ) "tells us nothing" about y's ψ-properties (and that is why love has no φ), then fear, too, has no φ (contrary to Taylor's analysis of this emotion). For from the mere fact that we know that x finds y dangerous (to have fear's purported φ), we similarly have no idea (but only a fair guess) of the ψ in virtue of which x finds y to be φ. Third, for Taylor the relationship between φ and ψ is not one in which φ places limits on ψ by allowing us to deduce particular ψ's from φ. It is the other way around (as she said earlier): φ places limits on ψ in the sense that the ψ-properties "explain why *x* believes *y*" to have φ. But if x's belief that y has sharp claws can explain why x finds y dangerous, then x's belief that y has a gentle, sarcastic, self-ironical wit can explain why x finds y lovable.

Having concluded that love has no φ, and thus no φ which could put limits on ψ (that is, that love is anomalous), Taylor turns to the question: does this entail that love cannot be judged rational or irrational, or justified or unjustified? Her strategy is to uncover some other way in which love's ψ-properties can be limited—since love *does* have ψ-properties: "It seems true and even trivial that very often at least if *x* loves *y* then he does so in virtue of . . . determinate qualities . . . he believes *y* to have" (p. 153). This "other" way may provide a handle on love's rationality. Taylor's strategy is commendable; for even if *she* has not shown that love has no necessary φ, that claim is probably true anyway. If love has no φ and therefore no logically characteristic belief, this means only that personal love is not necessarily or conceptually an erosic emotion; it does not mean that personal love is not typically, normally, or ideally erosic, for personal love still involves ψ-properties.

Before we proceed to Taylor's "other" way, let us see what happens to love's rationality given Taylor's analysis of the emotions. X's loving y would be irrational if (a) x's belief that y has ψ is ill-founded (x believes without any evidence that y is kind) or (b) x's belief that y has φ *because* y has ψ is irrational (x finds y lovable because y has some strange or silly P). Clause (b), of course, gives us pause; what P's can we fill in for x's finding y lovable because y has P to be irrational? The fact that listing the particular ψ's of irrational fear is vastly easier than listing the corresponding P's for love or hate (a reflection of the role of subjective evaluations in the latter) might lead us to think that love could never be irrational in sense (b) and hence is not vulnerable to the "fuller" irrationality of other emotions. There are three points to make, however. First, if love is never irrational in sense (b), that should not make us overlook the frequent irrationality of love in sense (a), an irrationality that is possible even if love has no ϕ. Second, if there are no cases of sense (b) irrationality for love, it does not follow that love violates Taylor's condition that ψ be able to explain why x believes y to be ϕ, that is, lovable. Indeed, if x's believing that y is lovable because y has P could be true and rational for any P at all then every love-ψ is capable of explaining why x believes y to have ϕ.[19] Finally, it is likely false that love is never irrational in sense (b); consider, again, x's believing y lovable because y mistreats x.

Taylor's "other" way to place limits on love's ψ resorts to the wants or desires involved in love (here Taylor disagrees with Pitcher, who claims that x's love-wants are reason-independent). "If . . . we can find a set of wants which are typically involved in the case where x loves y then this will put a constraint upon the beliefs concerning particular qualities in virtue of which x can love y" (p. 153; note "typically"). At first we might suspect that Taylor is going to offer a desire-satisfaction account of ψ: the ψ's that x finds valuable in y are those that satisfy x's antecedent desires; hence antecedent desires place a limit, for each x, on ψ (see Robinson, 6.5). Or we might wonder whether Taylor succumbs to Pitcher's problem, that of failing to distinguish between wants as constitutive of love and wants as causal effects. But Taylor clearly does not embrace the D-S model, and I think she can sidestep the constitutive-causal effect distinction. If x loves y, says Taylor, x wants to be with y and wants to benefit y (and so on). "Such wants allow us to impose constraints on x's beliefs in that only those [beliefs about y's ψ] are now relevant which can explain his wants" (p. 154). Now, if these wants are constitutive of love, then ψ is constrained in the sense that x's belief that y has ψ must be able to explain why x loves y. If, instead, the wants are the causal effects of x's love, then the explanation of x's wants is directly that x loves y but indirectly that x believes y to have ψ, since the latter belief can be taken to explain why x loves y. Taylor avoids Pitcher's problem simply because she claims that love typically is reason-dependent, grounded in x's belief that y has ψ. (Note that if Taylor is right that ψ can explain x's wants, or x's love, then there is reason to think that ψ can also explain why x believes y is "lovable," that is, has ϕ, at least in typical cases of love.)

Again, however, this way to place limits on ψ is not very powerful. Hunting around for some constraint on why x loves y or wants to be with y, about all that Taylor finds is this: "Presumably . . . there are some descriptions of x's belief which x himself cannot subscribe to, as for example 'y is such a *deadly* bore'" (p. 154). It seems contradictory to say that x wants to be with y because y is a deadly bore; so limits can be placed on ψ by referring to x's wants. But I wonder. In this case we might still say that x finds y's boring chatter humorous or comforting. Yet something seems wrong with this love that is grounded in an inappropriate property or is so bizarre as to be irrational. At any rate, Taylor herself cannot say that x could not love or want to be with y because y is a bore; after all, she claims that x need not even believe that his beloved y is "lovable."

Nevertheless, focusing on wants allows Taylor to propose two interesting ways in which love can be irrational in virtue of its desires (see sect. 4). First, x's love is rational only if x's wants have "a real possibility" of being satisfied (p. 157); we can add, I think: and only if x's belief that x's wants have "a real possibility" of being satisfied is well founded. Hence, if x wants to be with y, yet x realizes that this want has no chance to be fulfilled, x's love is irrational. If x's love includes or causes the desire for reciprocity, and x knows that y will never love x, x's continued love is irrational—or if x recklessly believes that y will eventually love x. Second, x's love for y is irrational if it involves wants that *can* be satisfied, it would be irrational for x to satisfy these wants (say, their satisfaction conflicts with wants that x considers to be more important), and x proceeds to love y, or to satisfy these wants, anyway (see n. 31). Taylor recognizes, however, that "we tend to think of love as such a good . . . that it may be better to have loved irrationally than not to have loved at all" (p. 161). Thus: how ridiculous, but how wonderful. As Taylor points out, this explains "the difficulty we have in moving from the irrational to the unjustified" for love. We clearly have no such difficulty making that move for hate (that "bad" emotion). But that love is "good" does not mean that "unjustified" is always out of line.[20]

6. A *EUTHYPHRO* PROBLEM

Just as we can ask whether (1) x loves y because x finds P in y to be valuable or attractive or (2) x finds P in y valuable or attractive because x loves y, we can ask whether x hates y because y has an annoying P or x finds P annoying because x hates y. Remember that x's loving (hating) y for having P is erosic; that x's finding P in y to be attractive (repulsive) because x loves (hates) y is erosic only if x loves (hates) y because y has some other Q; and that x's finding P in y to be attractive (repulsive) because x loves (hates) y, period, is agapic. Indeed, we can ask about any emotion E (for example, fear, anger, admiration) whether x has E toward y because x believes y has P, or x believes y has P because x is experiencing E toward y. For all these emotions, including hate, the connecting order maintained by the eros tradition between x's perception, belief, or evaluation of y, and x's emotion toward y, seems correct. Either the emotion conceptually requires that it depend on the judgment ("x believes y is a great chess player merely because x admires y" is incoherent); or the emotion typically exhibits the erosic order (x might believe that y is a great chess player merely because x admires y, but it infrequently happens that way); or the emotion is condemned if it exhibits the agapic order (if x believes that y is a great chess player merely because x admires y, x is irrational). Whatever emotion we consider, the agapic order is strange in some way. The fact that anyone would think that the agapic order applies typically to love as an anomalous emotion does not show that the structure of love differs from the structure of other emotions; it shows only that our attitudes about love are different.

The sort of contrast we find between the erosic and the agapic order is common in philosophy. Consider the *Euthyphro* dilemma (9d–11c): (3) *A* is the right act because *A* has been commanded by God or (4) *A* has been commanded by God because *A* is right. This is analogous to our love dilemma: (1) = (4) and (2) = (3). If we insist on the reason-dependence and explicability of love, we opt for the erosic order, (1), which asserts an independent origin for love; this is analogous to opting for (4) in the *Euthyphro* dilemma, which asserts an independent standard of rightness.[21] Harry Frankfurt has discussed a dilemma similar to our love dilemma: (5) we might care about something because it is important to us or (6) something might be important to us because we care about it. The erosic order is captured by (5): the importance of what we care about is grounded independently of our caring about it, and its importance explains our caring about it. The agapic order is expressed by (6): something is important to us only because we care about it, and no explanation is offered for our caring about it. Frankfurt defends (6) by appealing to the value of *caring* itself; by analogy, this is to defend (2) by appealing to the value of love itself, which is welcome no matter what.[22] But if the value is in the caring itself, and the care exists independently of and prior to the object's importance, how could we rationally decide to care about "lah" rather than "dah," or explain that decision? Frankfurt writes:

> Even when the justification for caring about something rests upon the importance of caring itself . . . the choice of object is not irrelevant or arbitrary. . . . What makes it more suitable . . . for a person to make one object rather than another important to himself? It seems that it must be the fact that it is *possible* for him to care about the one and not about the other. . . . When a person makes something important to himself . . . the situation resembles an instance of divine *agape*. . . . The person does not care about the object because its worthiness commands that he do so. On the [contrary], the worthiness of the activity of caring commands that he choose an object he will be able to care about.[23]

Annette Baier responds to Frankfurt by arguing that his selection principle lacks critical power.[24] It cannot distinguish between x's caring about and thereby making Nazism important, just because x is able to care about Nazism, and x's making the protection of the environment important, by caring about it, just because x is able to care about environmental protection. Baier's point, I take it, is that (6) is morally defective. Despite the value of caring itself, and even though x is able to care about something, certain things should not be cared about—because they independently have no value. Further, Frankfurt's answer does not silence the objection that the agapic order is irrational. How does the *possibility* of my selecting lah make that selection either "suitable" (his word) or rational?[25] To say that x selects lah rather than dah to care about (or to bestow value on), because x is able to care about lah but is unable to care about dah, does not place enough limit on the choice to prevent its being arbitrary and hence irrational. And suppose we ask: Why is x able to care about lah but not dah? The only answer that avoids irrationality is that x does or can find antecedent value in lah but not in dah. Perhaps this is why Frankfurt also says that x might select lah rather than dah because x is able "to care about the one in a way which is more important to him than the way in which it is possible for him to care about the other." Importance underlies caring after all.

Nevertheless, the agapic order between love and the lover's evaluation of the beloved is commonly held. Robert Kraut says that "someone's love for a specific person is not 'based upon' the belief that the person has superb qualities; if anything, it is the other way around."[26] Kraut offers no argument for his view, except to defend it by observation: "Walter might judge Sandra to be the most marvelous person in the world, and these judgments might evoke feelings. But it seems to work precisely the other way around. The amorous feelings often come first; the favorable judgments . . . are already 'guided' by—that is, are a consequence of—the emotional responses."[27] Kraut does not explain the qualification "often" or explore its implications. If love can therefore exhibit either the erosic or the agapic order, should he not wonder which one is rational? W. MacLagan also claims that "x loves y because y has valuable P" gets things backwards; he cites Bradley's *Aphorisms:* "We may approve of what we love, but we cannot love because we approve. Approbation is for the type, for what is common and therefore uninteresting."[28] The implicit argument here against (1) and in favor of (2) is that the erosic order is incompatible with the exclusivity of love. (Bradley should have said, "We cannot love exclusively because we approve." He did not, I suspect, because he takes love to be axiomatically exclusive.) If x loves y because x approves of y, then x will have reason to love z of whom x also approves; approbation is for properties shared by many people. Note that Bradley has solved (or rejected)

Gellner's paradox: love is exclusive exactly because it is not property-based, but rather an agapic phenomenon. Now, perhaps in the eros tradition exclusivity is hard to come by, but Bradley's argument is incomplete: it does not follow from (2) that love is typically or necessarily exclusive. Nor is it clear that (2) is even compatible with exclusivity (see 9.9).

John Brentlinger has argued that there may be "no general answer" to the question whether the eros or agape tradition provides the correct account of personal love. Brentlinger begins by noting that eros "proceeds from" value and agape "creates" value.[29] Brentlinger suggests that the distinction between eros and agape derives from a logically prior philosophical difference between conceiving of values as objective (values exist independently of the lover's attitudes and beliefs and hence are the kind of thing love could "proceed" from) and conceiving values as "relative" or subjective (values exist in virtue of the lover's attitudes and hence are the kind of thing that love could "create"). If so, he argues, we can decide between eros and agape by deciding one of the great issues in metaethics: Are values objective or subjective (p. 126)? As I argued earlier (1.3), however, the distinction between objective and subjective values does not correspond to the difference between loving erosically and loving agapically; in the eros tradition, x might love y quite because x subjectively evaluates y as beautiful. Brentlinger acknowledges this point and proposes that deciding between eros and agape boils down, instead, to deciding whether x's believing y to have value leads x to love y, or x's loving y leads x to believe y has value. At this point Brentlinger throws up his hands and declares that the problem is unsolvable: "*Neither* concept is by itself sufficient to explain all cases of love. Rather, some lovers and loves will be cases of *eros* and some of *agape*. . . . [B]oth have existed and . . . both are possible" (p. 127). There is "no general answer" to the question of which type of love is "preferable."

But Brentlinger sells short his own account. He says that in the case of eros x loves y because "the beloved is thought to be valuable," while in the case of agape "the value-making condition is love itself, which does not in turn exist for a reason that the lover can offer." This supports the claim that erosic personal love is "preferable" to agapic. We must understand Brentlinger as saying that the agapic lover cannot offer a reason for loving because her love is neither property-based nor reason-dependent; otherwise, she is just an erosic lover who lacks self-awareness. If so, erosic love is "preferable" because it conforms to a standard of rationality, one that insists that in personal love we can and should have some idea why we select a particular person as a beloved. For Brentlinger to say there is "no general answer" to the question of whether erosic or agapic personal love is preferable is as unconvincing as saying there is "no general answer" to the question of whether erosic hate is preferable to agapic. (See 8.3 for another argument for the superiority of erosic love.) Brentlinger does note that for proponents of agape, "it is *better* to love without a reason, than with a reason" (p. 117), but he does not examine the credentials of arguments that might be used to defend this normative thesis. For example, reason-free love is better than reason-based love because only the former is constant. But why think that constancy is a virtue for either lover or beloved; why think constancy is required for love to be what it claims to be; and, most important, why think that reason-independent love, or the lover's inability to offer reasons, secures any more constancy than reason-based love? (See 8.8 and 10.7.)

7. LOVING THE UNLOVABLE

Sappho's lines, "There are those who say an array of horsemen, and others of marching men, and others of ships, is the most beautiful thing on the dark earth. But I say it is whatever one loves,"[30] can be understood in several ways. First, she might mean that love has the highest value and is more important than other things (for example, military and commercial success). In this reading, Sappho is at the beginning of a women's love tradition, one scoffed at in Byron's *Don Juan* (I, 194) and currently advanced in the moral psychology of Carol Gilligan. But how can it be denied that love was also supremely important for (the male) Plato? Second, Sappho may be asserting that the Greek eros view of love is correct, but that which makes the beloved attractive for the typical Greek man (for example, military prowess) is not what makes the beloved attractive for women; men's eros involves shallow evaluations of beloveds. In this reading, Sappho might be insisting on the non-utilitarian value of women in the face of a culture that found no value in women (other than domestic). Again Sappho can be put at the beginning of a women's love tradition, one that emphasizes genuinely meritorious properties, not men's silly ones. Yet Plato, again, was no proponent of vulgar eros.

Finally, Sappho might be advancing the agapic order between love and the lover's evaluation of the beloved, hence making a radical break with Greek eros. To say that "the most beautiful thing is whatever one loves" is similar to saying that if x loves y, x thereby sees y as beautiful. In this case, Sappho begins a (women's) love tradition that incorporates the agapic order rather than the erosic order. But there is no other hint in the poem that Helen finds her lover attractive *because* she loves him.[31] At any rate, men's love today is commonly conceived of as erosic, and women's love as agapic. Men love on the basis of physical beauty (or other dumb properties), they love egocentrically or even selfishly (demanding, like the worst D-S lover, the continual satisfaction of their desires), and they are notoriously inconstant and nonexclusive. Women, by contrast, are said to love unconditionally or despite the nasty properties of those they choose to care about, they value love for its own sake rather than instrumentally, they give more than they take or get, and their love tends to be constant and exclusive. Not only are these generalizations false, but they also amount to a criticism of women. For if women exhibit the agapic order between love and evaluation, then women lovers are irrational. Would anyone seriously suggest that men, rational creatures that they are, hate erosically, while women, branded ever since Aristotle as having a lesser share of reason, hate agapically?

The question of whether Sappho is proposing a different conception of attractive properties or asserting that the beloved's properties are irrelevant because the love comes first has even been asked about Jesus' love. Thomas Gould suggests that in the New Testament "there is . . . a startling new emphasis on the value of that which anyone would have thought to be *without* value," among which Gould includes the retarded, criminals, prostitutes, lepers.[32] Gould does not mean that Jesus loved these people because they had the same positive inherent value as anyone else. "In actual fact," says Gould, "Christ . . . ask[s] us to turn the values of society upside down—to take even brilliance, deep learning, style, and the achievement of happiness in society as signs not of success but of the very reverse." We are to love not regardless of merit and not despite clear dismerit, but in accordance with a topsy-turvy idea of merit: "Love only those whom you cannot love, Christ seems to say."[33] The command might be expressed: love that which is unlovable, or love that which you are not able (contra Frankfurt) to care about. The prostitute, the criminal, the leper are to be loved because they do have the property appropriate to love; they have the determinable property "unlovable in the worldly sense of 'lovable'."

If interpreting Jesus this way is a stretch, Kierkegaard's agape is a better illustration: "The task is not: to find—the lovable object; but the task is: to find the object already given or chosen—lovable."[34] We ask, as we asked Frankfurt, What objects are we to choose and then find lovable? "True love is precisely [to find] the unlovable object to be lovable," answers Kierkegaard (p. 343). In contrast to "that simple wise man of ancient times," Socrates, who said that to love is to desire the beautiful and joked about loving the ugly, Kierkegaard announces that we ought to love "the ugly" (p. 342). Kierkegaard, unlike Robinson (6.5), does not mean that x should love y in virtue of y's ugliness if that property arouses x. Rather, we are to love those who are unlovable in the worldly sense of "lovable" exactly because they are unlovable in this sense, not because they turn out to be lovable in our subjective perception of them.

Claiming that we should love the unlovable, however, is paradoxical. If the prostitute and the criminal (in contrast to, for Kierkegaard, one's friends, kin, and beautiful beloveds) are unlovable, then those with "brilliance, deep learning, style, and the achievement of happiness in society" (Gould's list) are equally unlovable, if not more unlovable, because these properties are "not signs of success but of the very reverse." The worldly successful—not the worldly unsuccessful— are the truly unlovable simply because they are lovable in the worldly sense. The prostitute is worldly unsuccessful, hence in the worldly sense unlovable, and therefore in the Christian sense perfectly lovable. But the brilliant stock investor, because she is worldly successful, hence in the worldly sense lovable, is for that reason cut off from being lovable in the Christian sense and so is genuinely unsuccessful and genuinely unlovable. Are we to say now that because she is genuinely, even Christianly, unlovable she is Christianly *lovable*? Another, similar, paradox arises in Kierkegaard. There is no point, for Kierkegaard, in recommending or commanding that we love the beautiful, our kin, the worldly lovable, the successful; our natural inclinations suffice in generating love for these fine objects. But we must be commanded to love the worldly unlovable, because our inclinations shrink from loving the ugly; we must overcome our inclinations in order to fulfill our duty to love the unlovable.[35] But if there are grounds for thinking that natural passions or inclinations will lead us to love the beautiful and the worldly successful and to spurn the ugly, there are equal grounds for thinking that our natural reaction to the worldly successful will be envy, not attraction or love, and our reaction to the ugly will be pity and benevolence. Thus overcoming our natural inclinations means mustering love for the worldly lovable and successful; and there is no reason to command us to love the ugly, for our natural share of pity suffices to generate that love. Of course, these tangles are avoided by Kierkegaard, who in spite of his flashy talk of loving the unlovable is merely saying that genuine love is neighbor love, which encompasses love for both the successful and the unsuccessful.[36] Kierkegaard's doctrine is no different from the standard reading of Jesus: love all, regardless of their merit and defects, because stripped of our worldly appendages we are the same.

8. DISTINGUISHING LOVE FROM HATE

The fact that we can even entertain the notion of loving the unlovable is consistent with two claims discussed earlier: (1) the lover need not have any particular kind of belief about the beloved (that is, love has no characteristic belief and no determinable property φ) and (2) love is not necessarily an erosic phenomenon (that is, personal love may be typically or ideally erosic, but not conceptually so). Analogous claims about hate are also defensible. "Despicable" is about as adequate a candidate for the determinable property of hate as "lovable" is for that of love. There is nothing contradictory (as Hamlyn said) in the idea of hating "full-stop," and (as Hamlyn might have said) x can hate y even if x respects y and finds y perfectly tasteful. (This hate is queer, but that is the point.) It follows that hating the attractive, hating the lovable, and hating the unhateable make sense. Rather than respond with hate or anger, x might love the y who abuses x; if that is loving a despicable y, then hating an attractive y is possible: x might hate y simply because y is benevolent toward x. Our natural reaction to the worldly successful might be envy rather than love. Our response to a beautiful, witty, friendly, educated person is not always love; sometimes these properties produce hate (in addition to or instead of envy or resentment). When x hates y in virtue of y's attractive properties, this is not necessarily because in x's subjective world these properties are unattractive; x might very well admit that they are attractive. Even though x often hates y because y has done something harmful to x, sometimes x hates y because y has done something to benefit x. Loving behavior might generate not return love or even gratitude, but annoyance.

The fact that x may either love or hate y in virtue of y's attractive properties might illuminate a disturbing phenomenon: x's emotion toward y occasionally shifts back and forth between love and hate. Indeed, Hamlyn relies on the phenomenon of love's changing into hate to argue that these emotions are not "determined" by beliefs: "Love may turn easily into hate without any beliefs changing . . . and without the change being due to any newly acquired beliefs."[37] But if this happens to x's emotion, the category to invoke is "irrational." Further, even though x might either love or hate y in virtue of the same attractive P, it does not follow that whether x is experiencing love or hate at a specific time is no function of x's beliefs. Notice that Hamlyn mentions only the case of love's changing into hate. When we consider the case in which x initially experiences hate toward y, and later comes to love y, we have to assume that x's beliefs about y have at least partially changed; if not, the emotional switch is inexplicable and irrational. But if the switch from hate to love depends on a change in x's beliefs about y, then in the case in which x initially loves y and later comes to hate y, the explanation must be that x's beliefs about y have changed. But what about the hard case in which x's emotion toward y vacillates between love and hate? One reason for x's love changing from love to hate could be the realization that y is not going to reciprocate. As long as x believes that y will reciprocate, x loves y; but when x realizes that y could care less, x's emotion turns to hate. X's love vacillates, then, in response to she-loves-me, she-loves-me-not, she-loves-me, and so on. (A Stendhalian beloved manipulates x's beliefs about the possibility of reciprocity. Or should we call this person a Machiavellian beloved?) For an x who does not strongly desire reciprocity, constant love instead of vacillation might be expected; this x perhaps experiences only sadness, not hate, when y remains aloof. Thus, a given x might both love and hate y in virtue of P, yet this does not entail that whichever emotion x experiences is not a function of other beliefs that x has.

What all this leads to is the question of how love and hate are to be differentiated as distinct emotions. The ordinary way of identifying emotions is by referring to their characteristic beliefs. Thus x experiences *fear* when x believes y is dangerous; and x's emotion toward this same y is *gratitude* when x believes instead that y has benefited x. Yet if x can either hate or love y when x believes y has the same attractive P, the ordinary way of identifying the emotions fails. Hamlyn argues that because love and hate do not involve characteristic beliefs, they are "not differentiated by beliefs [but] by factors other than beliefs." (He declines, however, to tell us what these factors are.) On the other hand, perhaps a distinction between love and hate can be made after recognizing, as David Annis does, that x might love y even though x believes that y is nasty, *or* that y is ugly, *or* that y is a deadly bore, yet it does not follow that x will love y believing that y is nasty *and* ugly *and* a bore.[38] Because the erosic emotions are a function of the interplay between attractive and unattractive properties of the object of the emotion, love might be the emotion in which the attractiveness outweighs the unattractiveness of its object, while for hate the relationship is the other way around.

Nevertheless, imagine the worst-case scenario for distinguishing love and hate: (1) neither emotion has a characteristic belief; (2) both emotions can be reason-independent; (3) neither emotion is necessarily caused by a desire, hence no particular antecedent desire distinguishes love and hate; (4) love and hate may be accompanied by identical behaviors toward y (sometimes we do cruel things to our beloveds, and such mistreatment is indistinguishable from the harm done by x to x's behated); and (5) since the behaviors that accompany hate and love can be similar, perhaps there is no firm distinction between that which is responsible for these behaviors: the desires that are either constitutive of or the causal effects of love and hate. (If the desire to spend time with the beloved is either part of love or one typical result of love, that may not distinguish love from a perverse hate in which x relishes opportunities to be with y in order to provoke y.) The conclusion seems inescapable: love and hate can be differentiated only by their phenomenal feels, by how they register in the consciousness of the person experiencing these emotions.[39] This does not mean that love and hate are nothing but a sensation; but it does mean that the person who has the final (or only) say as to whether x loves or hates y is x, for only x has access to what x is feeling. This conclusion is untenable; indeed, it runs counter to most contemporary thought, both philosophical and psychological, about the emotions. How could x ever learn to label x's sensations as love or hate if x has the final say? Surely, love and hate feel different; but that difference must be explained in terms of other features of these emotions.

Robert Brown suggests that "if we are to distinguish love from hate, the former must embody recognizable good will toward the beloved and the latter ill-will toward the victim. A lover who over the long term wished only ill-will toward his consort would be as much a definitional absurdity as a man who, filled with hate for his consort, would wish her only good."[40] Hate with no ill will and only goodwill is not hate at all; love with no goodwill and only ill will is not love. (Or are they pathological or irrational forms of hate and love?) Brown's idea, then, is that love and hate can be distinguished by certain desires that are usually constitutive of or the typical causal effects of these emotions: the desire to benefit or to harm the object of the emotion or the desire that the welfare of the object increase or decrease, respectively. Brown's idea seems to handle adequately the case of the lover who occasionally hurts his beloved; for as long as the pattern of x's desires over the long haul is a string of goodwill desires, x's emotion is love rather than hate or some other emotion altogether. Single acts performed in accordance with passing impulses do not distinguish love from hate. But we must investigate what the "concern" of love amounts to (chap. 12) and ask whether the eros and agape traditions can do justice to it as a feature of personal love. This way to distinguish love and hate—by their typical desires—might be superior to distinguishing them through their structures, that is, by pointing out that in love, but not in hate, x believes that y's attractive properties outweigh y's defects.

CHAPTER 8 *Defending and Refining Erosic Love*

Still it pleads and rankles: 'Why do you love *me*?'
Replies then jammed me dumb; but now I speak,
Singing why each should *not* the other seek—
The octet will be weaker—in the fishful sea.
Your friends I don't like all, and poetry
You less than music stir to, the blue streak
Troubles me you drink: if all these are weak
Objections, they are all, and all I foresee.

—John Berryman, *Sonnets* (24)

1. LOVE WITHOUT ANY SIGHTS

In laying out his paradox, Gellner supposes that when x meets y, x notices that y has attractive properties S, and as a result x has an emotion (perhaps love) toward y; later, x encounters a person z who also has S. But we need not assume that x meets z (see 3.2). Further, we need not even assume that x meets y, for x might draw up a list of properties that x believes his ideal beloved would have. Already x is in Gellner's bind: if love is reason-dependent, x is committed to loving everyone who instantiates these properties. With Gellner, we worried about love at first sight, but now we have something more dramatic to worry about: x's loving y without any sights. If x loves y because x believes that y has S, as the first view of personal love claims, then x should love y when x believes that y has S, no matter how that belief arises. If x is told that a person y who has S lives up the street, the mere description of y should induce x to love y "at a distance." Hence, x should love y independently of and prior to any meeting with y. Thus love cannot be reason-dependent, since that thesis leads to an absurdity.

This objection fails, although it does allow us to discover some interesting things about love. It should first be pointed out that love in response to a description does occur, and its possibility is countenanced by the eros tradition. Lucy Hutchinson wrote in her *Memoirs* that not only did Colonel Hutchinson love her before they met, but also that the colonel felt more comfortable about doing so when he recalled "the story of a gentleman who, on being told of . . . the recent death of a young gentlewoman, had grown 'so in love with her description' that he had fallen 'desperately melancholy'."[1] Aristophanic first-generation persons, if they are separated after fission and have a weak memory, will love the person they know only by description as their other half. Diotima claims that a person loves the Beautiful even though at lower stages of the Ascent the person knows it only by description and has "noticed" only hints of it from imperfect copies in bodies, minds, and institutions. And lovers of God, unless they have direct sensuous experience of Him, could love God only by description: "For we know nothing but that, long ago,/ We learnt to love God whom we cannot know" by acquaintance.[2] The intellectual apprehension of God's perfection (as in Descartes's *Meditations*) is enough to produce erosic love for Him before any meeting that might later occur. Indeed, if we assume a small set of attractive properties and a small population of persons to choose from, love by description would not be unusual.[3] Hence, the objection to the thesis that love is reason-dependent should not be expressed in the following way: in that view love by description must occur, yet it cannot or does not. For it can and does happen. Rather, the objection should be that (1) reason-dependence entails that love by description must occur more frequently than it actually does and (2) love by description is a flawed love. If so, the eros tradition does not provide an accurate account of typical or ideal personal love.

We might be tempted to respond by saying that x's noticing P in y, and therefore x's meeting y, is crucial, because before noticing P in y, x has no idea that P would induce x's love. X might suspect that beauty would be love-inducing, but x does not yet know whether blondeness or tawniness will arouse x. Or noticing P in y might be x's first experience of that property, in which case an earlier description of a person having P could not have induced love in x. But this consideration only forces a modification of the objection: for those many x's who have experienced love and have learned that certain properties induce love, a description of a person who has these properties should evoke love. The x who draws up a list of properties or has a mental picture of an ideal beloved, therefore, does not get off the hook. In Gellner's scenario, after x notices S in y and on that basis loves y, x cannot claim to have no idea that for x S induces love, and at this stage a mere description of the similar z should result in x's loving z.

It often happens that when x hears a description of a wonderful person y who has S, x wants to meet y and feels a twinge of excitement. But normally x will not yet love y. At the very least, x will not love y until x has met y and can make sure that y has no defects that offset y's having S. (Recall, in *Pride and*

Prejudice, Elizabeth's eagerly anticipating a meeting with Darcy after hearing the scouting reports, followed by her disappointment upon noticing, falsely, that his character was defective.) This response to the objection is consistent with love's being reason-dependent, since love in that view is a function of the interplay between y's attractive and unattractive properties. Suppose the objection claims now that if the description presented to x includes not only S but also y's defects (or the fact that y has none), then x should love y in advance of any meeting. But how likely is it that x will believe by hearsay that y's defects do not outweigh y's merits, or that x will believe that x is being presented with a complete list of y's defects? (Friends of y will minimize y's faults.) The point is that the thesis of reason-dependence alone does not entail that x will love y; in addition it must be assumed, which is implausible, that x will believe, on the basis of someone's description, that y has an agreeable combination of properties. This response to the objection applies to descriptions of not only y's defects but also y's merits. Even if x will love anyone having S, x's being presented with a description of a person y who has S does not mean x will love y prior to any meeting, because x's hearing or reading the description does not entail that x believes that y has S. The reason-dependence of love does not make love by description an expected course of events, because seeing, rather than hearing, is believing: in most cases, x himself must perceive S in y in order to believe that y does have S or that the description is accurate. In order to verify or refute the description, x must meet y.

Now we can see why "it is irrational for someone to love—or even to claim to love—a person known only by description."[4] Love by description is irrational because relying on a description is not the most reliable epistemic procedure for forming beliefs. Indeed, that someone can provide a description of y presupposes that another, superior, epistemic procedure is available to x: at some stage in its construction, the description depended on someone's direct acquaintance with y. Hence, x's loving y by description is irrational when x's belief that y has S has not been arrived at by a superior epistemic procedure to which x has access. But this also implies that love by description is not necessarily irrational. There may be cases in which a description is known to be accurate or in which the formation of beliefs on the basis of a description is the most or only reliable epistemic procedure available. In these cases, the fact that reason-dependence makes love by description possible may be a virtue, not a flaw, of that thesis.

For example, is a person's loving God possible and rational? If the only way to know God's properties is by intellectual apprehension and not by acquaintance, then loving God is possible; it is not irrational simply because it is love by description. If loving God is irrational, it is irrational for a different reason: one may have arrived at the belief in God through an unreliable epistemic procedure. What about x's loving the fictional character y? Here direct acquaintance with y is ruled out, so knowledge of y's properties can be obtained only by a description of y (say, in a novel). Hence x's loving a fictional y is not irrational simply because it is based on a description. If it is irrational, the reason is that it should be clear to x that y does not exist. Further, in some cases of personal love descriptions might play an unobjectionable role. Consider a man in prison who loves a woman, whom he has never met, on the basis of what he believes about her from the letters she has sent him for several years. This case is interesting because it muddies the distinction between knowing y by description and knowing y by acquaintance. Does knowing about y only through y's letters count as knowledge by (self-) description, or does it count as x's meeting y? Indeed, in ordinary scenarios when x meets y face-to-face, much of what x discovers about y is based on y's description of herself. It would be irrational for x to believe automatically these face-to-face descriptions; he must verify them by repeated encounters with y. Hence, we have turned the objection on its head.

That descriptions may play a role in love, then, is no strike against the erosic account of love. In this regard, there is no difference in principle between love and other emotions that are reason-dependent. I have never met Sigmund Freud, but I admire him because I have read good things about him (and believe some of them, since reading is the only reliable epistemic procedure available to me) and because I find his writings fascinating. I can hate someone (Adolf Hitler) if I am told something especially abhorrent about him, and this hate is rational if I have grounds for believing the description. If I am told that a friend has died, I will feel grief without actually being there. If I fear pit bulls and am told that one lives next door, I will not immediately break out in a sweat if I realize that I am in no danger at home. Then again, I might experience fear without making the dog's acquaintance, but I would be judged acutely afraid of such animals rather than irrational. Thus, the fact that erosic emotions permit E-by-description, or E-toward-y independently of any encounter with y, is no cause for alarm. And if there is nothing objectionable with well-grounded respect, admiration, hate, or fear by description, there is nothing wrong with well-grounded love by description. The only difference among the erosic emotions may be that for some (love, for example), but not others, belief by description is rarely well grounded. By the way, the second view of personal love is equally vulnerable to the objection that it permits love prior to any meeting with its object. Since in agapic personal love the attractive and unattractive properties of the object have nothing to do with love's basis, there is apparently nothing to *prevent* x from loving a person whom x has never met.

2. THE INDESCRIBABLE BELOVED

Kierkegaard wrote, "Is it not obvious that the person who is really in love would never dream of wanting to prove it by . . . reasons. . . . Anyone who does it is not in love. . . . [H]e is so stupid that he merely informs against himself as not being in love."[5] This objection to conceiving of love erosically, as reason-dependent, is psychological. Its logical version has been provided by Robert Burch: "If you love someone, you cannot say, 'I love her because . . . ,' referring to *anything*. . . . If you can correctly give any reason for that tender attitude you have toward her, then that attitude you have is not love but something else, be it admiration, respect, pity, selfish interest, or what not."[6] If so, personal love is necessarily an agapic phenomenon.[7] Burch's claim is not that x might have, at some level of consciousness, erosic reasons for loving y but need not be "in touch" with them. Rather, x could not, conceptually, have any erosic reasons for x's love, no matter how meticulously introspective x is. Is this thesis defensible?

Paul Gilbert claims that "when I like something I can often tell you what is likeable in it" and that its being "likeable must depend on common human desires and satisfactions"; but these features of liking do not hold for loving: (1) when x loves y, x cannot say what is lovable about y, and (2) what x finds lovable in y does not depend on what is common among persons.[8] The argument here seems to proceed from (2) to (1). Because x finds y lovable as a particular rather than as an instantiation of general properties, x is unable to say why x finds y lovable—x's inability is not psychological but metaphysical. Gilbert even expresses his thesis much the way Burch does: "What makes [x's] response one of [loving y] . . . involves [x's] being unable adequately to describe what is [lovable in y]." The central claim here is that because x loves y the particular, or as a particular and not as an instantiation of attractive properties, x logically cannot provide erosic reasons for her love.

But why agree that x's loving y as a particular implies that x cannot say in erosic terms why x finds y lovable? "The ideal basis of [x's] love," says Robert Ehman, is "the unique concrete personality of [x's] beloved," which "even the lover cannot fully reveal." Ehman connects this inability to the exclusivity of love: "In the measure that a person's love . . . focuses on a single person to the exclusion of others, he will feel that the basis . . . goes beyond all repeatable properties that the person shares with others. For this reason, he will not be satisfied with attempts to provide reasons for his love. . . . He will tend to claim that his love is based on nothing less than the unique personality . . . of the beloved."[9] But the fact that y is unique is no logical bar to x's loving y in virtue of properties that x can fully describe (see 3.7). If one wants to argue that x's inability to provide erosic reasons for love is metaphysical or logical rather than psychological, one must affirm either that x's loving y as a particular means that x does not even love y as a unique instantiation of properties or that what grounds x's love is something about y that "goes beyond all repeatable properties." What is this sense of "particular"? If x loves y as a particular, the idea seems to be, x is logically unable to provide erosic reasons because x loves y in virtue of y's being y or because y has the property "is y." As John Hardwig says, "I love you because you are you."[10] The ground of x's love is y's "y-ness," something not reducible to general properties. (Note how similar this is to the claim that x loves y for P-in-y [3.3].)

Confronting a horse, I can describe its component features, pointing out those I like; confronting a patch of yellow, all I can say is that it is yellow and I enjoy it because it is yellow. Similarly, x's inability to describe y is due to y's being not a composite but a unified whole, like a patch of yellow (or the taste of Pitcher's pistachio ice cream? See 7.5.B). Confronted with y, x confronts only y-ness, and this logically prevents x from providing erosic reasons for x's love. In our ordinary experience, however, persons are complex compounds of various elements and, thereby, composed of describable properties. So the claim must not be that persons are metaphysical particulars, but that there is something about love such that qua object of love a person appears before us as a particular. As the object of x's love, y takes on the ontological status of a particular from x's perspective, even though from the viewpoint of others y remains a complex of properties. Roland Barthes describes this phenomenology: "The amorous subject perceives the other as a Whole . . . and, at the same time, this Whole seems to him to involve a remainder, which he cannot express. . . . [The] Whole cannot be inventoried without being diminished. . . . [A]bout it I shall never know anything; my language will always fumble, stammer in order to attempt to express it, but I can never produce anything but a blank word, an empty vocable."[11] Consistently, Barthes claims that personal love is not erosic: "So I accede, fitfully, to a language without adjectives. I love the other, not according to his (accountable) qualities, but according to his existence. . . . What I liquidate in this movement is the very category of merit: just as the mystic makes himself indifferent to sanctity (which would still be an attribute)."[12] Max Scheler offers a similar argument: we cannot give erosic reasons for our love, "the beloved is reason enough," because "love seizes on the individual kernel of value of the beloved, and this kernel can never be completely captured in any set of universal judgments."[13]

I have frequently heard it asserted that when x loves y, the beloved y becomes in x's world an ontological particular (and hence indescribable), but I have not found any rigorous defense of this thesis. It is one thing to claim that the second view of personal love or the agape tradition is internally consistent, in holding both that the beloved is perceived as a particular and that love is not reason-dependent. But if reason-independence is taken to follow from the "fact" that x loves y for y's y-ness, we have a right to demand that more be said on behalf of the premise. After all, if x loves y because y has the property "is y" or because y possesses the kernel of value describable only as "y-ness," we will wonder about the comprehensibility of love. Yet for one defender of the agape tradition, this implication is taken in stride. Robert Johann writes that "since [love] cherishes in us what is most incommunicable, it is mysterious. . . . The deeper the love, the less it has to say in its own defense. Its sincerity can almost be measured by its speechlessness."[14] Really? Ordinarily we do not judge a love sincere *because* it cannot be explained, and we are suspicious of a lover who says "I have no idea why I love you." Johann continues by comparing agapic and erosic personal love, which "has no difficulty in finding words to justify itself."[15] Johann interprets erosic love as satisfying needs: if x loves y because y is beautiful, y satisfies x's passion; if x loves y because y is virtuous, y teaches x goodness. Thus Johann's argument is not that love is never reason-dependent but that reason-dependent loves are inferior. In describing his alternative reason-independent love, Johann writes: "What about the love that is tongue-tied? . . . Why do I love you? because you are—*you*. That is the best it can do. It is indefensible." At this point Johann almost proudly proclaims, "To the extent that it can list no reasons for its own existence, is it irrational." We should say the same thing about Pitcher's "Because I just do."

3. LOVE AND SELF-RESPECT

In their love relationships people tend either to assume explicitly that love is reason-dependent or to act as if they believed this thesis were true. Ordinary people, of course, do not say "y's having S is both necessary and sufficient for my loving y"; but their not verbalizing the thesis is no evidence that they do not believe or act according to it. The closest that people get to acknowledging that love is reason-dependent is when they ask "Why do you love me?" and expect the answer "because you are or have S"—a perfectly coherent question and an equally coherent answer.[16] It is true, of course, that some beloveds ask "Why do you love me?" and do not mean it literally; as a sentence in a natural language, the question can be used for various purposes. The question may indirectly accuse the lover of not really loving the beloved or may disguise a request for reassurance. It may be asked teasingly by a beloved whose lover writes about love or sarcastically by an unsatisfied beloved who wants to embarrass her lover, and to be rid of him, by prompting him to admit that his love has no foundation. And *"Why?"* (do you love me) may be a perverse response to a lover's declaring "I love you." But the question is very often meant literally and seeks a direct answer. The lover and beloved want to understand their love rationally; to make sure the other is loving for good reasons rather than out of despair or obligation; to find out whether the lover values in the beloved those qualities the beloved himself values; to inquire about the depth of the lover's self-reflection about the ground of her love; to discover what about himself has elicited this powerful (perhaps welcome, perhaps unwelcome) response.

Thus, there are moral and prudential reasons for asking "Why do you love me?" and expecting or giving a serious answer. A shrug of the shoulders, the nonverbal equivalent of "I haven't the foggiest idea," falls as flat as the Aristophanic "because we were made for each other." Agapic answers are equally unsatisfying: "Because you are *you*" (Montaigne and Johann) and "because of your kernel of value" (Scheler) are perceived by the beloved as thoughtless and silly answers. They ignore the beloved's request for an accounting of her valuable qualities that elicit love, or they demonstrate a failure of self-knowledge or candor on the part of the lover. "Why do you hate me?" (one could substitute: respect, envy, fear, and so on) is an equally sensical question and also demands an answer of the form "because you are or have S." A response such as "I haven't the foggiest idea" or "because you are you" does not entail that the hate is feigned, not genuine, or some other emotion. But neither response satisfies the behated, and neither response should satisfy the hater.

Ordinarily we prefer and want to be loved erosically, in virtue of properties that we are proud to possess or that both lover and beloved find valuable. When Michelangelo wrote, "If I love in thee, beloved, only what thou lovest most, do not be angry; for so one spirit is enamoured of another" (*Sonnet* 55), he did not need to apologize. We are not satisfied if, as beloveds, we cannot believe that we have admirable qualities that elicit love or if, as lovers, we cannot think that something valuable about our beloveds makes them especially worthy of love and makes our selection of them comprehensible. The reason for this concerns self-respect. Lovers are not able to think well of themselves if a strong need to be loved or to avoid solitude leads them to settle for anyone. Beloveds cannot respect themselves if they believe that they have no properties capable of eliciting love, that they are loved as a charity case or from a sense of duty, or that they are loved simply because the lover's self-respect is so low that he can envision a relationship only with a person whom he regards as unattractive.[17] Beloveds want to hear that they are loved because the lover finds them attractive (the erosic order), not that the lover finds them attractive only because the lover loves them (the agapic order), which also leaves the beloved befuddled as to why she is loved at all. The point is not exactly Pascal's: "Women like to perceive fastidiousness in men, and this is . . . the most vulnerable point whereby to gain them: we are pleased to see that a thousand others are contemned and that we alone are esteemed."[18] Some beloveds may prefer being loved erosically because it allows them to lord it over competitors who have not been selected. But to defend the preference for being loved erosically in terms of self-respect is not to defend it on the grounds that erosic love enables us to be victorious in contests. For the mere fact that y has been chosen by x over a thousand others will not support y's self-respect if x has selected y only as the best of a bad crop.

Being esteemed because all others are contemned is hardly comforting; it does not show y that x has a genuine regard for y's attributes. When Sartre says, in contrast to Pascal, that "the [beloved] is irritated and feels himself cheapened when he thinks that the [lover] has chosen him *from among others*," he is right if he means that x surveys the field and, after culling the misfits, selects y by elimination ("this choice must not be relative and contingent").[19] But we should not denigrate the contribution to our self-respect made by the lover's selecting us in virtue of our valuable properties, even if that selection means, coincidentally, that we are chosen "from among others." We feel cheapened, to the contrary, when we are loved out of desperation, insecurity or obligation, or because "you are *you*," not when we are loved in virtue of our admirable properties. "A love that does not discriminate," said Freud, "forfeit[s] a part of its own value, by doing an injustice to its object."[20]

The fact that personal love is ordinarily believed to be reason-dependent explains why people have difficulty comprehending or accepting the unconditionality of Christian neighbor-love. Being loved regardless of merit is similar to being the object of indiscriminate sexual desire, which contributes little to one's self-respect. People do not take fondly to being told that they are neighbor-loved unconditionally, with indifference to their merit, especially when they were hoping to be the recipient of a different kind of love, one elicited by their valuable properties. Of course, we may react unfavorably to x's profession of neighbor-love because we do not believe x is really offering such a love or because the words leave us void of concrete expectations. (There is nothing easier than the child of God telling us we are loved or saying "I love you," when we will be on the plane in ten minutes.) Certainly, the unconditional neighbor-lover can answer "Why do you love me?" with "because I am commanded to" or "because I love everyone, and you are one of everyone," but these answers make no contribution to our self-respect. And they are odd if the question was "Why do you love *me?*" Wanting to be loved with discrimination, we resent being loved altogether nonexclusively; everyone receives this unconditional neighbor-love, and "such an enormous inflation of love can only lower its value."[21]

The fact that personal love is recognized to be ordinarily reason-dependent also helps explain why people are forever urged to love their mates unconditionally. The urging implicitly acknowledges this harsh reality, otherwise it would be pointless.[22] But complaints about property-based love are not altogether ridiculous. One can easily see in erosic love a devil's temptation, an invitation to search continually for better properties in other beloveds. Or erosic love may be doomed from the start, because all beloveds have defects that eventually take their toll. Kurt Vonnegut, Jr., worries about what will happen to human love when, as technology advances, people become useless and thereby unlovable—because love is presently property-based. (Of course, if our defects are extensive, or we are otherwise lacking in merit, that future is already upon us.) Vonnegut's solution is that we should be ready to progress from property-based to nonproperty-based love, to develop the ability to love humans simply because they are human.[23] And many bemoan the dreary fact that in our culture men love women for their beauty and women love men for their power and money, two property-based loves that often end in disaster.[24] Note that when women insist on being loved for their minds rather than (or in addition to) their bodies, they do not thereby demand nonproperty-based love. They want to be appreciated for properties that their lovers tend to overlook or deprecate, to be loved for having a variety of valuable properties; the demand is for Pausanias' heavenly eros, or at least for a mixture of the heavenly and the vulgar.

There is plenty of evidence, then, that love is commonly recognized to be property-based. And it is not surprising that the abundance of nonideal property-based love is often regretted. We often do not love in virtue of our beloved's significant, rather than trivial, properties; our loves are often based on artificial preferences; and sometimes we find ourselves loving merely to fulfill needs or because our beloved is useful to us. But these facts show that we can at least conceive of a satisfactory or ideal property-based love, one in which we admire a beloved in virtue of her fine qualities without necessarily (or only) wanting something from her, in which a response to her merits is a confirmation of her value and "uplifts" her self-respect. Such a love could occur in a culture that encourages significant human qualities to blossom fully and allows people to develop autonomous preferences. Our goal need not be, contra Vonnegut, to be able to give and receive nondiscriminating love.

If, for reasons of self-respect, we prefer erosic personal love, perhaps for other more important reasons we prefer the agapic variety. "Unconditional love corresponds to one of the deepest longings . . . of every human being," says Fromm.[25] "To be loved because of one's merit . . . always leaves doubt . . . a fear that love could disappear. Furthermore, [such] love easily leaves a bitter feeling that . . . one is loved *only* because one pleases." Perhaps some people do long for unconditional, nonproperty-based love because they believe that erosic personal love is irreparably inconstant. But agapic personal love does not obviously guarantee any more constancy than erosic love (see 10.7). Further, if a person who loves erosically can be self-deceived or under a delusion about the presence of valuable properties in a beloved, so too can the one who claims to love agapically: x may believe falsely that the beloved's merits do not ground x's love or that the beloved's defects do not continually threaten to destroy x's love. Perhaps this is why Willard Gaylin, after pointing out that "to many, *receiving* love effortlessly, as a child—undeserved love, unearned love—is the glorious ideal," says that *providing* such love is an "often painful and arduous experience" (yet more "nourishing" and "profound" than receiving it).[26] These considerations hardly instill confidence that agapic personal love is more secure. Indeed, when Michael Balint declares that "this primary tendency, I shall be loved always, everywhere, in every way, my whole body, my whole being—without any criticism, without the slightest effort on my part—is the final aim of all erotic striving,"[27] I wonder how there could be any love at all. Who could reliably provide such love? Who could, then, realistically hope to get it? Who has the arrogance to expect such love? Who would not be repulsed by this infantile creature? Just as there would not be much love if most people were crude erosic D-S lovers (see 6.3), there would likewise not be much love if most people desired to be loved unconditionally ("without the slightest effort on my part"). Two Balint-humans do not form a viable relationship: both demand total care and acceptance, neither makes any effort.

It makes psychological sense, however, that people might want both kinds of personal love. I do not mean that x wants to love y erosically while being loved by y agapically (although this is possible in any event), as if x's human relationship with y mimicked a relationship x could have with God. (This case is analogous to the loving pair composed of an egoist and an altruist.) Rather, I mean that x might want to receive both erosic and agapic love from the same person y. As Aryeh Kosman puts it, "We want our lovers at once to accept us as we are and to admire us for what we are."[28] If being accepted "as we are" (and "as we may become") can be construed only as the unconditionality of agapic personal love, and if people want to be loved both "as they are" and for their attractive properties, then their desires are contradictory. This does not mean that it is impossible to desire being the recipient of both erosic and agapic personal love (or to desire both the self-respect of erosic love and the purported security of agapic), only that it is unlikely that both desires can be satisfied at the same time.

4. LOVE AND WILL

Suppose that we do want to be loved erosically, for our merit, and agapically, regardless of our merit. Then if we make certain metaphysical assumptions, we can derive another paradox. If erosic personal love is altogether causally determined (x is causally determined to find some P's attractive but not others; or x's love for y is a perceptual-causal response to y, like the fright experienced at seeing a spider on one's trousers), then x does not love y freely. And if agapic personal love is not causally determined exactly because it is not a response to the properties of the beloved, then x's unconditional love for y can be seen as perfectly free. If so, y's wanting to be loved both erosically and agapically amounts to y's wanting to be loved both unfreely and freely. Or we can state the paradox conversely, as Sartre does: "The man who wants to be loved does not desire the enslavement of the beloved. He is not bent on becoming the object of passion which flows forth mechanically. He does not want to possess an automaton. . . . On the other hand, the lover cannot be satisfied with that superior form of freedom which is a free and voluntary engagement. . . . Who would be satisfied with the words, 'I love you because I have freely engaged myself to you and because I do not wish to go back on my word'."[29] Since we do not want to be loved either deterministically or freely, we want to be loved neither erosically nor agapically.

The questions suggested by this paradox are important. Should it bother us that erosic personal love is causally determined, if or when it is? This may be a reason for preferring agapic personal love. Is erosic love not even love because it is determined; and, therefore, does only agapic personal love deserve the name? We can approach these questions by first considering this one: Does the fact that x is caused to experience a complex of beliefs, feelings, and desires that we would ordinarily call love mean that x does not love y? I cannot see that it does. The fact that x is caused to experience a complex of beliefs, feelings, and desires we would ordinarily call hate (respect, pity) does not mean the emotion is bogus. Indeed, perhaps the fact that x's emotion is causally determined by y is crucial, since that anchors the emotion in its object.

It might be argued that love could not be causally determined, because were that true the notion of a love potion—a drug that causes x to love y— becomes (as it should not) credible. If love is a causally determined state, then a love potion is possible, since an elixir would simply bring about this generic state through some other mechanism. But, goes the objection, either a love potion is an impossibility *or* no state we would ordinarily call love is really love if brought about by a potion.

It is not obvious, however, that a love potion is impossible. Suppose that x is causally determined, by x's perception or belief that y has P, to feel love for y, to want to be in y's presence, and to desire to benefit y. Nothing inherent to this state rules out its being produced by a potion. A hallucinogenic potion could cause x to perceive or believe that y has P, and a tranquilizing potion could cause x to feel fondly toward and desire to benefit y. On what grounds, then, can it be asserted that a potion is impossible? Perhaps: a love potion is impossible because the beliefs involved in love are more complicated than I have made them out to be; for example, "My feelings are of . . . love if I believe that the feelings are caused by my belief that I am now in love."[30] If this is right, a love potion is possible only if an elixir can induce not merely the ordinary beliefs, feelings, and desires of love, but also x's belief that x loves y and x's belief that x's feelings are caused by x's belief that x loves y. Yet these conditions seem satisfiable. If the potion can cause the ordinary beliefs, feelings, and desires of love, there is little reason to deny that it can also elicit x's belief that x loves y. And if beliefs are causally produced phenomena, there is no reason in principle to deny that a potion could make x believe the involuted "my feelings are caused by my belief that I love y." The most we can conclude is that a love potion (like love-by-description) is unlikely, not that it is impossible.

Rather than deny the possibility of a potion that causally produces a state indistinguishable from love, the objection should claim that a potion-induced state is not genuine love precisely because it is potion-induced. It is not obvious, however, that a love state induced by a potion could not be genuine love. Suppose that y is ugly, boring, a moral monster, and heaps abuse upon x. Yet x, under the influence of a potion, believes y to be beautiful, intelligent, and warmhearted, and x thereby desires to be in the presence of and to benefit y. There is no difference between this case, in which x is caused by a potion to love as a saint a person everyone else knows is a monster, and any other case of love in which x is radically mistaken through various processes (for example, wish fulfillment, self-deception, y's deliberate deception) about y's character. Of course, these cases are not ideal, since they involve false and irrational beliefs, but nonideal does not mean bogus. The intentionality of the emotions allows them to be genuine even though caused by odd processes, and love is no exception. Even "substitution" arguments against reason-dependence (see 2.5) assume that x could love z for five years, all the while believing that z was y.

Whether this belief is caused by a potion, by z's brilliant deception, or by x's self-delusions makes no difference.

Clearly, something is wrong with being loved as the result of an elixir. At least for reasons of self-respect, we do not want to be loved this way; it does not follow, however, that we object altogether to being loved as the result of a causal process. There are potion causes and there are other kinds of causes, and a potion cause simply happens to be the wrong sort of cause. We want our lover to have true and rational beliefs about us; further, we want our lover to be genuinely, not artificially, aroused by our properties. These desiderata are satisfiable even if love is a causal phenomenon, but are not satisfied by a potion. We want love to proceed naturally from our lover in response to our properties that mesh with his or her preferences and values. And this process is natural even though, if not because, it is a causal process. If x loves y by some natural causal process in which y's properties mesh with x's inclinations and values, and if this process works efficiently and smoothly, then to both x and y this love might seem, phenomenally, to be free. The very naturalness of the process imbues a causal phenomenon with the quality of freedom, when the love arises from the meshing of x's own values and y's properties. What a love potion removes from this process is precisely the relevance of x's *own* values and x's natural response to y. Thus, in one respect not wanting to be loved on account of a potion is similar to not wanting to be loved with neighbor-love. If neighbor-love is merely the causal effect of God's grace working through the lover (*pace* Nygren's Luther), then we are not being loved *by* that person. The problem is not that this neighbor-love and potion-love are causal loves but that the causes go beyond the lover, are not inherent to the lover, and supersede the causation that would have proceeded from the lover's own nature.

Furthermore, our earlier assumption—that erosic love is fully determined, but agapic love is free—is implausible. The concept of "unconditional, nonproperty-based love" does not entail that such a love is not causally determined; it entails that x's love for y is not a response to y's attractive properties, which rules out only one type of cause. If erosic personal love is causally determined (that is, the cause is partially the subject's nature in virtue of which he responds to certain properties), then because agapic personal love proceeds from lover to beloved without being triggered by the object (that is, entirely as a result of the subject's nature), there is equal reason to think of agapic love as caused. Of course, agapic personal love might proceed genuinely, rather than artificially, from the lover's own nature, as can erosic love. In any event, there is also logical room within erosic love for the operation of the lover's will. Since we often cannot just *decide* whether or not to believe something, our beliefs are partially causally determined—in particular, beliefs about the properties of the beloved. Even so, we can decide to look for additional evidence relevant to our beliefs about y, and this decision may affect the course of our love. Further, x's preference for beloveds who have P might be causally determined, yet x can decide to change himself in such a way that P is no longer important for him—or x can decide to remain the way he is. (Someone who decides to forsake meat, becoming a vegetarian, can train herself to lose her preference for steak and to find her new menu delicious.) The lover x can reflect on the causes of her love for y and subsequently can consciously accept or reject these causes, in order to grant or deny them the status of reasons, by acceding to or overcoming them. (Note the difference between the person who wants to be an agapic lover, and so discovers the reasons for or causes of her love in order to end up having none, and an erosic lover who discovers the reasons or causes in order to improve them. This ambiguity can be found in Descartes's letter to Chanut; see 2.2.)

If, when x and y investigate the grounds of x's love for y, they find that x's preferences are apelike and unreflective, that knowledge might threaten their love, as it should. For to the extent that x's preferences are not at least partially autonomously chosen, x's love is a lesser love and might not deserve to persist. A mark of being a "deep" rather than a "superficial" lover—in a non-metaphysical, nonarchaeological sense—is the willingness to investigate the origin and quality of one's preferences,[31] and then to modify them accordingly; complacency in such matters is a moral fault. Thus, Jerome Neu is not altogether correct in saying that "love is not a matter of will, it cannot be given on demand,"[32] if he means that the will never plays a role in the style of one's love or in the decision whom to love. Of course if a person y whom x does not find attractive wants x's love, x cannot on demand love y. But x, after reflecting on what properties elicit x's love, or even prevent it, can bring it about in some cases that x responds to the properties y does have. And x's loving y after doing so will satisfy y in a way in which x's loving y after y slips x a potion will not.[33]

Consider, finally, Robert Brown's claim: "With respect to love, [x and y] are patients, not actors, and as patients they do not have reasons for being acted upon."[34] The argument implicit here is that love cannot be reason-dependent, because love does not involve freedom (lovers are the patients of determining causes) and causally determined love could not involve reasons. What is wrong with the argument is the assumed connection between love's being determined and (therefore) love's not being reason-dependent. For if we can be determined to have beliefs, we can be determined to have reasons, since beliefs are integral to reasons. And if we can be determined to have reasons, we can be determined to have reasons to love. Hence, we can be determined to love on the basis of reasons, in which case love's being determined is not incompatible with its being reason-dependent. Further, if we can reflect on that which determines our love and then embrace or reject these causes as our reasons, then as lovers we are not mere "patients." The lesson to be learned is that what makes a difference is not the distinction between causally determined and free love, but the distinctions (1) between reason-dependent love (which can be free or determined, or a mixture) and reason-independent love (which can also be free or determined) and (2) between processes that are causally natural in virtue of stemming from the lover's own values and autonomously formed preferences, and processes that are artificial, in which the lover's own nature is irrelevant (which distinction also applies to both erosic and agapic personal love). Indeed, the reason we do not want to be loved in virtue of an artificial process is also the reason we want others to be attracted to us at least in part for our significant, rather than our silly, properties. In ideal erosic love, we expect an uplifting interaction between the nature of the lover and the nature of the beloved, between what is best about both.

5. EX POST FACTO REASONS

The fact that we can reflect on the causes of our loves and embrace them as our reasons (or refuse them the status of reasons) means that some cases of erosic love are primarily property-based and only secondarily reason-dependent, since the reasons for love in these cases exist only in retrospect. But if reasons for love can be given only (or usually) ex post facto, is it correct to speak of love as a fully reason-dependent emotion? Perhaps it might still be argued that love is an anomalous emotion: it is neither reason-dependent nor *not* reason-dependent, but something in between.

Roger Scruton claims that love is reason-dependent, but love-reasons are not generalizable (see 3.1): "Although there is, no doubt, some feature of James which is a reason (perhaps even *the* reason) why I love him, I am not obliged to love William as well, just because he shares that feature."[35] Like resentment, which is fully "reason-based" (Scruton's term) in the sense that "if I resent you it is *on account of* some feature" you possess (p. 97), love is also reason-based since, as Scruton said, some feature of James may be *the* reason James is loved. And since the question "Why do you feel that?" is asked perfectly coherently about attitudes that are reason-based (p. 99), love again is reason-based. Thus, the main issue Scruton deals with is how love can be reason-based in these two senses yet take a particular as its object. We have previously seen his solution: "My love of Beethoven's Violin Concerto may coexist with aversion towards every other work of music, without for that reason being inconsistent with itself. Aesthetic interest is nevertheless reason-based. There has to be *something* that could be . . . pointed to in answer to the question 'Why are you interested in that?' " (p. 98). Love-reasons, like aesthetic reasons, are not general. Note that Scruton is not arguing that love is not reason-based because love-reasons are not general. And note that Scruton denies the thesis we examined in section 2—that because the object of love is a particular, the beloved is not describable in general terms and therefore love is not reason-based.[36]

In contrast to attitudes that are reason-based, some are what Scruton calls "reason-free": the existence of these attitudes "does not depend upon the subject's *having* reasons" (p. 97). Because reason-free attitudes lack an intentional structure, Scruton's example (not curiously) is a dog's wanting to sniff another dog, for which the dog can have no reasons. (A dog can neither formulate a reason nor reflect on the causes of its want.) Are any human attitudes reason-free? Scruton mentions only that "people sniff each other similarly" and that "I may just want something, for no reason (although perhaps not a saucer of mud)." For Scruton, love is not a reason-free attitude; he countenances no such thing as agapic personal love. Yet, despite the fact that love has two characteristics of reason-based emotions, Scruton is reluctant to say that love is fully reason-based. Instead, love is a member of a third category of attitudes—those that are "reason-involving." Scruton does not mean that some cases of love are fully reason-based while others are reason-free. Rather, love is a reason-involving attitude that exhibits a distinct kind of relationship to reasons.

Reason-involving attitudes seem to have three significant features. First, "a truly reason-based attitude—like resentment—is liable to *refutation,* by a demonstration that the object does not possess the feature for which he is resented" (p. 97). Love, then, is reason-involving because it "is liable to suffer reversals when its reasons are destroyed . . . [and] to be undermined, . . . but not exactly to be refuted." Second, "the more one has to *look* for the reason—the more one has to 'discover why' . . . one loves a person . . . —the more we should speak of love, not as reason-based, but as reason-involving" (p. 99). Hence, for a truly reason-based attitude like resentment, one does not have to discover one's reasons or give them only ex post facto. And third, "it is unclear . . . that love *is* really based in the reasons that are offered for it" (p. 97). Scruton is miserly with details, but I think he means that a gap exists between the actual reasons why x loves y and the reasons x offers for loving y, a gap that does not exist for truly reason-based attitudes. Love, then, is anomalous; Scruton gives no other example of a reason-involving attitude.

Scruton has not clearly distinguished reason-based from reason-involving emotions; nor has he argued convincingly that even though love has two characteristics of reason-based emotions (y's having P may be *the* reason x loves y; "Why do you love y?" is a coherent question), love is only reason-involving. Consider, to start, the claim that reason-based attitudes can be "refuted," while reason-involving attitudes can be "reversed" and "undermined." Scruton's point could not be that a reason-involving attitude is "jeopardized by . . . new knowledge" (p. 110), but a reason-based attitude will survive when new knowledge corrects the subject's beliefs about the object; for we expect truly reason-based attitudes to die when the subject realizes that the object lacks the property in virtue of which the attitude arose. For Scruton's distinction to make sense, he must mean that a reason-based attitude is both "refuted" and "reversed" when its reason is destroyed, while reason-involving attitudes are only "reversed." But what does it mean for an attitude to be refuted and for an attitude to be reversed but not refuted? Scruton never explains, but there are three possibilities.

1. A reason-based attitude is refutable if showing its subject that the object does not have the property in question kills the attitude, while a reason-involving attitude only tends to be killed by that revelation. Refutable, then, means "really reversible" in contrast to "not necessarily reversible, but tending that way." Or, the distinction between reason-based and reason-involving is between "strongly" and "weakly" reversible. It is unlikely that this is what Scruton means. After all, not even fully reason-based emotions like resentment are refutable in this sense; some cases persist even though x plainly sees that y really does not have P, or has it no longer.

2. If x's emotion toward y continues even though x realizes that y does not have P, but its continuation would not be judged odd, then the emotion is reason-involving; but if the continuation of the emotion implies that something has gone wrong, the emotion is reason-based. One candidate for this oddness is "irrational." Hence, even though love (as reason-involving) tends to be reversed when its supporting beliefs are shown to be false, it may continue without x's being accused of irrationality. By contrast, a reason-based attitude like resentment is judged irrational if it persists in similar circumstances. To put it another way, a reason-based attitude is refutable in the sense that a demonstration that its object does not have the relevant property either kills the emotion or shows the emotion to be irrational if it persists..A reason-involving attitude is not refutable, but only reversible, in the sense that in the same situation the emotion may or may not persist, and its persistence is not a fault.

This criterion will not work, however, for two reasons. First, it is not necessarily a mistake to judge irrational a love that persists when its grounding beliefs are destroyed (see 7.4); hence, if this criterion does analytically separate the reason-based from the reason-involving, love can be reason-based. Second, the criterion does not distinguish reason-based from reason-involving attitudes, but restates the distinction between reason-based and reason-free attitudes (and the category of reason-involving attitudes drops out). An emotion that persists when its reason is gone is at that stage reason-free. If some loves persist, yet others end, when their grounding beliefs are shown to be false, that means that some loves are or become reason-free (agapic) and others are reason-based (erosic), not that love is "reason-involving."

3. Finally, reason-based emotions may be refutable in the sense that they are unjustified when they persist despite a corrected belief about the object; they can be evaluated as being justified or unjustified, while reason-involving emotions are not vulnerable to this evaluation. This criterion, too, will not work. Because love can be evaluated as justified or unjustified (see 7.3 and 7.5), love would turn out to be reason-based. Scruton provides no argument that love is not open to this assessment. Further, cases of the emotions can be evaluated as justified or unjustified precisely in virtue of their rationality; hence criterion (3) is not essentially different from (2). An unjustified emotion, which persists even though its subject sees that its object does not have the relevant property, is likely reason-free; hence by this criterion an unjustified reason-based attitude is a reason-free attitude, and "reason-involving" does not denote a distinct territory.

What about the other differences between reason-based and reason-involving attitudes? Scruton's suggestion that love is only reason-involving because the reasons offered by x for x's love may not be x's genuine reasons will not support the distinction. The fact that x may unintentionally offer a bogus reason for x's love does not distinguish love from resentment; epistemological and psychological mishaps are, of course, possible for reason-based emotions. Finally, consider this difference between reason-based and reason-involving attitudes: "The more one has to *look* for the reason . . . the more we should speak of [an attitude] not as reason-based, but as reason-involving." This does not mark a genuine difference between the two categories, since standard reason-based attitudes will in some cases turn out to be merely reason-involving. Even in resentment, Scruton's "truly" reason-based emotion, x may have to search for the exact reason why x resents y. If we "have" to hunt for reasons because they are not immediately apparent, that shows only that we sometimes do not know ourselves, not that there is a distinct category of "reason-involving" attitudes. But another claim Scruton makes is relevant here. "Love," he writes, "is reason-hungry, searching always for a foundation in its object" (p. 233). Love's being "reason-hungry" may be how we should understand its being reason-involving: "There seems to be a definite tendency within love to find a *basis* in its object. . . . [L]ove *seeks* to base itself in reasons" (p. 97). Now, there is a difference between x's hunting for a reason because x *has* to hunt (since the reason is temporarily hidden) and x's hunting because x *wants* to hunt (because x "seeks to base" x's love in reasons); these two criteria for "reason-involving" are not equivalent. But love's being reason-hungry (the latter criterion) is not even a claim about the structure of love. For if love were reason-free, it could still be reason-hungry (but futilely); and if it were reason-based, it could be reason-hungry (successfully). So if "reason-involving" means "reason-hungry," the concept does not pick out a distinct type of attitude. Surely cases of resentment can be reason-hungry and hence would by this test be merely reason-involving (which it is not). And why is love reason-hungry? Or why is the lover reason-hungry? For the same reason resentment or the resenter is reason-hungry: they seek to demonstrate that their reason-based attitudes are rational and justified.[37]

Suppose something in all this distinguishes love from standard reason-based emotions. The point would have to be that, because we either *need* to find reasons for love (since they are not immediately apparent) or *want* to find reasons (in order to feel and to convince others, including the beloved, that our love is rational), providing these reasons is ex post facto, and therefore love is not fully reason-based. Since the offering of love-reasons occurs only retroactively, love is not fully reason-based in the sense that love-reasons play no role in the prior selection of y rather than z as a beloved, but only explain that selection afterwards. Even so, would love be wildly different from standard reason-based emotions? X might not be searching for someone to hate and does not select y as an object, yet hate is a reason-based emotion even if its reasons are provided ex post facto. Further, if "reason-based" is taken to mean that the emotion's reasons must already exist and influence the selection of an object, many cases of love will qualify as reason-based. As recognized by the argument against the claim that love is reason-based, which relied on the absurdity of loving by description (sect. 1), x may very well carry around reasons with him, waiting for an opportunity to apply them to an appropriate object.

6. DESTROYING LOVE

The first view of personal love claims that we can know the reasons for or causes of our loves, and that ideally we should know them. But perhaps seeking the causes of, or reasons for, one's love undermines the love itself. The objection is not that if one seeks and then successfully provides a reason, one no longer loves *just because* one has provided a reason (sect. 2), but that what is discovered reacts on the love and destroys it. If love is a reason-hungry beggar, it had better come up empty-handed. Hence, the first view of personal love must be wrong in claiming that ideally we should discover why we love. It might be true that "only barbarians are not curious about where they come from, how they came to be where they are, [and] where they appear to be going,"[38] but when it comes to love, barbarians are the lucky ones.

Before we discuss the objection, note that the question "Why do you love me?" has answers at three different levels. At the lowest level, the erosic answer has this form: x loves y because (x believes that) y has valuable S. At the second level, we seek to explain why x evaluates S in y to be valuable, so that x's preference for S can be seen to be either an autonomous feature of x's nature or an artificial and uncritical aspect of x's personality. Let us call these two levels of explanation the local level. The third or global level is the territory of "deep causes"; a global explanation purports to tell us what is really (or ultimately) going on in the dance of love. Aristophanes' myth is one example; others are familiar enough: evolutionary and sociobiological theories and the various versions of psychoanalytic theory. Even religious doctrines provide deep explanations of human love, replacing (or supplementing) evolutionary and psychological accounts with their own particular theories about the meaning or *telos* of love.

The objection can now be extracted from something written by Bernard Williams:

> It is one aspiration, that social and ethical relations should not essentially rest on ignorance and misunderstandings of what they are, and quite another that all the beliefs and principles involved in them should be explicitly stated. That these are two different things is obvious with personal relations, where to hope that they do not rest on deceit and error is merely decent, but to think that their basis can be made totally explicit is idiocy.[39]

There is an ambiguity here. About "social and ethical relations" Williams contrasts the idea that it is undesirable that they rest on false beliefs (and hence that it is desirable that they rest only on true beliefs) with the idea that all the true underlying beliefs "should be explicitly stated." Does Williams mean that not all the underlying beliefs and principles can be known, and hence not all can be stated? Or does he mean that all the true beliefs underlying social relations can be consciously known and acknowledged, and hence *could* be stated, but should not be stated? Or, finally, does he mean that if they are stated, they should be stated implicitly (hinted at) rather than stated explicitly?

The ambiguity is carried over to "personal relations," where Williams contrasts the idea that it is undesirable (indecent?) that they rest on false beliefs (and hence desirable that they rest on true beliefs) with the "idiotic" idea that the basis of the personal relation "can be made totally explicit." Does this mean that the basis of the personal relation is unknowable and for that reason cannot be stated explicitly? Or that it can be known but is in some way not statable, at least not explicitly? What Williams probably wants to say is that personal relations should not rest on false beliefs (something is wrong when x loves y because x falsely believes that y has P); but that to expect x to give a complete answer to the question "Why do you love y?" is to ask, unreasonably, too much of x. We may ask "Why do you love y?" in order to ascertain that x holds no false beliefs about y; x passes the test as long as she says only true things about y. But there is no requirement that x be able to state everything she knows about y, about x, about love, and about the world that is relevant in explaining why she loves y.

But is it really an idiotic ideal that x and y be able to make "totally explicit" the ground of their love? Perhaps, if the full answer includes a global explanation of a kind that is bound to undermine their love. Who, genuinely believing that in seeking a love partner one is really seeking a mother- or father-substitute, or a return to infantile bliss, could view himself and his love experiences with respect? Who, genuinely believing that in seeking a mate one is only a Schopenhauerian being, living and acting for the species or following a pattern dictated by a Life Force, could think of herself as other than merely another minor mechanism? Who, genuinely believing with the sociobiologists that, in accordance with genetic imperatives established long ago (even if the leash between genes and behavior is long and loose), men are instinctively drawn to women for their youth and beauty and women are instinctively drawn to men with wealth and power, could look at heterosexual love with anything but cynicism and horror? Both we and love are better off, it seems, if we remain ignorant of global explanations, especially the frightening ones concocted by professional academics. If I were a male black widow spider, I would not want to know in advance (because knowing would ruin my enjoyment) that my female would reach her own climax as she sunk her fangs into me and began to devour my paralyzed body. On the other hand, some people have no trouble believing religious global explanations; these tend to be wholesome, uplifting, comforting. Love is supported more by our thinking that it is part of the plan of a benevolent, personal deity, or the contribution of Man to His perpetual creation,[40] or a duty to a transcendental purpose than by thinking that our feelings and actions are the result of blind, impersonal evolutionary forces.

The conclusion should not be that we are better off believing only those global explanations that sweeten our loves and replacing a logic of truth-value with a logic of love-value. For why not, then, also jettison truth-value at the local level as well, if doing so supports our loves? At any rate, I surely have not proven that some global explanations definitely undermine love while others tend not to do so. Were I convinced that sociobiological or religious deep explanations were true, that conviction, I suspect, would ruin love for me. But others might love, and be loved, comforted by a Schopenhauerian or a sociobiological explanation, in the way some are comforted by the religious.[41] The important factor seems to be not which global explanation one buys but whether persons who love each other have bought the same one (see 11.5). If it is difficult to imagine a stable love relationship between a person x who explains x's love for y sociobiologically and a person y who explains y's love for x (and x's love for y!) in Roman Catholic terms, it should not be difficult to imagine a stable love between persons both of whom explain their relationship psychoanalytically (same school). So the objection that we should not seek full (that is, global) explanations, because doing so undermines love, has not borne much fruit. Of course, if people should ideally not be mistaken about the local explanations of their loves, then neither should they be mistaken about global ones. The saving grace is that global explanations, being the least verifiable notions ever to enter the human mind, are not the sort of thing one can believe *mistakenly*. (If their epistemological status changes, beliefs about deep causes that turn out to be false will condemn any love grounded on them.) We can know what grounds our loves at the local level, but we cannot know, and hence cannot be mistaken about, the deepest level of causation. Several things follow: (1) replacing truth-value with love-value for global explanations may be rational (although still wrong for local explanations); (2) a full explanation of x's love for y will *not* include the global level but only verifiable statements at the local level; and (3) Williams is right that demanding a full explanation—*if* that includes the global level—is idiocy. If it is rational to believe some global explanation or another, it must be rational to refuse to believe any global explanation and to deny that claims about deep causes have any relevance for our loves.

However, Williams might mean that it is idiotic to think that a full local explanation "can be made totally explicit." Perhaps, that is, trying to provide a full local explanation undermines love. Although Annette Baier agrees that it is a "normative" requirement of "reason" that the existence of a love "not depend on ignorance of its own nature and history,"[42] she worries about the extent to which we should seek explanations:

> If . . . we confronted all the facts . . . relevant to our emotional attitudes, we would have to consider all those . . . persons we might have loved instead of the

ones we do love, all the facts about the possibilities foreclosed by the actual history of our past loves. How many actual carings would survive this . . . total unselective flood of knowledge is unclear. I surmise that if one . . . were confronted with full knowledge . . . one would go mad and be incapable of any sustained attachment.

Thus it is one thing, and unacceptable, to love in ignorance, when removing the false beliefs would jeopardize love (as it *should*), and another thing, and acceptable, to love in the absence of a full explanation, when overcoming this lack would jeopardize love (as probably it should not be allowed to do). Nevertheless, the distinction seems slight: the ability of a love to withstand a confrontation with its full explanation may be exactly what it is for a love not to be based on ignorance of its own past. Further, it is not clear that a confrontation with its past will destroy a love that is not based on false beliefs, nor that x's carrying out this investigation about x's love for y (and later for z, and so on) will ruin x's capacity to love anyone. Baier's surmise that investigating the history of our loves will destroy our capacity to care is, I think, derived from an unrealistic idea of what a full explanation involves. It does not mean (which would be Williams-idiotic) that we must know all "the possibilities foreclosed" by our actual choices. It involves only (1) x's ability to state explicitly the true and rationally formed beliefs about y's character in virtue of which x loves y and (2) x and y's understanding how x came to have the preferences and values mentioned in x's reasons. Given this reasonable notion of a full local explanation, many loves will survive a confrontation with their past, and those unable to withstand this knowledge do not deserve to survive.

But Baier's conclusion is qualified: she is less worried about a full investigation's destroying x's particular love for y than she is about the investigation's destroying x's ability to love anyone at all; hence, we should object to an investigation's undermining the particular love x has for y only when in doing so it also tends to undermine x's capacity to care in general. In that sense, truth-value may take a back seat to love-value. "Where the new knowledge has the effect of destroying any carings, rather than [only] altering the object or the style of caring, then cognitive therapy is no therapy, but itself a disease," says Baier. But it must be possible, then, for knowledge of the full local explanation, in my sense, to destroy x's particular love for y (by leading x to change the object of x's caring), and for this destruction to be desirable ("a love which cannot survive a confrontation with its own past is an unworthy love"), without this process of discovery making x totally incapable of loving anyone else. Seeking an ideal erosic answer to "Why do you love me?" need not be idiotic or drive us crazy.

7. REASONS NOT TO LOVE

Capellanus' Eighth Rule for lovers states, "No one should be deprived of love without the very best of reasons"; one of these "best" reasons is the beloved's sudden loss of property.[43] In addition to considering reasons for withdrawing love, as Capellanus does, we could consider reasons for not loving in the first place: x was attracted to y before their first meal together, but at this time x noticed y removing the sliced almonds from the cheese Danish (to avoid eating them), or x watched in silent horror as y picked the onions, peppers, and mushrooms out of the spaghetti sauce that x had spent an hour making. Perhaps these defects would not give x reason to call off an engagement, but they might prevent x from developing a stronger attachment to y. Of these examples we might say: x's reason for not loving y is a silly reason; the property x finds annoying enough to prevent x's love should not have that power. Of course, it is difficult to distinguish defects that should count as a reason against love from defects that should not matter, just as it is difficult to distinguish attractive properties that should count as a reason for love from those that should not. But at least we can say: if x can reflect on x's preferences for properties that x evaluates as valuable, and investigate to what extent these are x's autonomous preferences and hence part of x's own nature, then x can also investigate to what extent x's finding certain properties unattractive—that is, which operate negatively on x's capacity to love people who have them—is an artificial or uncritical component of x's nature.

Another issue is suggested by Capellanus' rule. We often want truthful, nonrationalizing, nonevasive reasons (rather than lame excuses) for why we are no longer loved or are not loved in the first place. We do not like hearing "because I just don't feel the same," which begs the question. (Note: that answer is like Pitcher's "because I just *do*.") Nor do we accept "because I just don't feel that way toward you," since we are sure (having been in the other's position ourselves with respect to people we could not love) that there is something about our properties, which either by their absence offer the person no reason to love us, or by their presence prevent the person from loving us. Erosic personal love is property-based or reason-dependent in both ways: attractive properties are causes of or reasons for love, while defects are causes or reasons operating against love. Our belief that erosic reasons can be given to explain why love does not arise to begin with complements our belief that "Why do you love me?" has an erosic answer.

Perhaps, however, love is asymmetrical in that there can be reasons against, but not reasons for, love. This would be a significant sense in which love is not fully reason-dependent, since it becomes senseless for us to want to be loved for our attractive properties. Berryman's sonnet (see epigraph) would have us believe that there are only reasons against love. But the implication is that "Why do you love me?" would have only very strange answers: "Because you have no defects that prevent me from loving you" or "because the defects I see don't amount to a hill of beans." The answer is queer because it does not tell us why the lover is drawn to *us*; in fact, either statement could be made by someone not drawn to us at all.

The claim that there can be only reasons against love has apparently been advanced by Bernard Mayo: "The difference between moral and personal relations can be illustrated by a felicitous remark of [Henri de Montherlant] on the difference between loving and liking: 'We like someone *because* . . . we love someone *although*. . . .' 'Because' introduces a clause mentioning a reason for whatever is asserted in the main clause; 'although' introduces a reason against what is asserted in the main clause."[44] I said "apparently" because Mayo argues that love is not even reason-dependent in this truncated sense. Even though "I love y, although y has defect D" implies that y's having D is a reason against my loving y, the very fact (also implied by the sentence) that I do love y shows that this reason against my love "must, to avoid a contradiction, be inadequate or inconclusive." I tend not to approve of people who have D, applying this reason generally (as I should), yet this reason for not loving y does not prevent my love. Indeed, Mayo claims, I may even disapprove of y because y has D, yet love y anyway. It follows, he says, that "love is a personal relation which has *nothing* to do with reasons."[45]

Mayo's conclusion is a non sequitur. From the fact that I disapprove of y because y has D yet still love y, nothing follows about the reason-dependence of my love. Mayo argues that this fact shows that neither reasons for nor reasons against are involved in love. But the fact is surely consistent with an erosic explanation for my loving y: I love y even though y has a property that ordinarily leads me to disapprove of and not love people, because y has attractive properties that ground my love for y and outweigh or make me discount D. The locution "I love y, although y has D" has another meaning overlooked by Mayo: not only does it assert that I love y, and not only does it imply that my reason against loving y is "inadequate," but it also suggests that I have *good* reasons for loving y that outweigh my disapproval of y. "I want item A, although I realize A has this disadvantage" implies that I am prepared to state the advantages A does have, which explain why I want it despite its bad qualities. Why, then, is "I love y, although y has D" not a contradiction (as Mayo correctly claims)? Either because reasons have nothing to do with love or because reasons have everything to do with love.

8. CONDITIONAL UNCONDITIONALITY

Earlier I examined the argument that love could not be reason-dependent because the beloved is a particular and hence not describable in general terms, in which case reasons for loving that mention the beloved's properties are conceptually unavailable.[46] There is another argument against reason-dependence that turns on the beloved's indescribability, the major premise of which, however, is that love is unconditional. Now, the sense of "unconditional" crucial to the argument is not: x loves y unconditionally if x loves y regardless of y's properties. In that sense of "unconditional," reason-independence follows automatically, since "unconditional" is synonymous with the central thesis of the second view of personal love.

Susan Mendus asserts that "if I now claim to be committed to my husband I precisely cannot give an exhaustive account of the characteristics he possesses in virtue of which I have that commitment to him."[47] Since x cannot give this exhaustive account, love cannot be reason-dependent if that requires x to be able to explain x's love in terms of y's properties. Mendus concludes that although y's properties "make more intelligible" x's loving y, they do not explain x's loving y but only why x finds y "lovable." Further, because y's properties do not explain x's love, Mendus is able to flirt with the agapic causal order between x's love for y and x's evaluations of y (to be expected, if love is not reason-dependent). Much rides, then, on Mendus' assertion that if x is now committed to y, x "cannot give an exhaustive account" of the properties in virtue of which x loves y. Mendus' explicit argument is that "if I could do so" (that is, if she could give that exhaustive account), then "there would be a real question as to why I am not prepared to show the same commitment to another person who shares those characteristics." This argument is our old friend—the purported incompatibility of exclusivity and reason-dependence. But Mendus hints at a more interesting argument. Note that Mendus uses the expressions "x loves y" and "x is now committed to y" interchangeably (pp. 246–247); at least, "x is now committed to y" is part of the meaning of "x loves y." Thus, her argument is that if x loves y, then x is now committed to y, and in virtue of this present commitment, x cannot give an exhaustive list of y's properties that ground x's love. It is more precisely the fact that love involves a *commitment,* for Mendus, not the fact that love involves an *exclusive* commitment, that implies love is not reason-dependent.

Mendus is not arguing that if love entails a commitment, then love is *constant,* and if love is constant, then it exists through all changes in the beloved and hence is unconditional. For this sense of "unconditional" is just the sense that automatically means that love is reason-independent. Mendus' notion of commitment is more subtle. In particular, she does not claim that love is constant in one standard sense: "We need not . . . go so far as to say that 'love is not love which alters when it alteration finds', but only that love is not love which allows in advance that it will so alter" (p. 250). The intention to love constantly, not constancy itself, is a mark of love: "I am not now prepared to admit that my love for my husband, my commitment to him, would disappear were he revealed to be a cheat and a liar" (p. 246); "I promise to love . . . and in so doing I cannot now envisage anything happening such as would make me give up that [love or] commitment" (p. 247). Mendus' point is not that if x loves y, then x promises to love y no matter what y may become; x is not predicting x's future attitudes toward y but only claiming to have certain intentions *now* about x's future with y. Since x's commitment means that x has "a present intention to do something permanently" but not "a permanent intention," x's commitment does not entail that x will always love y. Rather, if x loves y, then x has the intention *now* that the love will persist, and the fact that the love might not persist would not necessarily mean either that the present love is not genuine or that the earlier intention was fraudulent. Thus, Mendus distinguishes between (a) x's loving y now and intending to love y despite changes in y, yet x's discovering later that "she has lost her commitment (perhaps on account of changes in her husband's character)" and (b) "the person who [now] promises to love . . . only on condition that there be no such changes in character" (p. 246). Case (b) involves no commitment (no "weak" unconditionality in Mendus' sense) in the first place, while case (a) involves an unconditional commitment, but one the lover has found she cannot sustain.

How does this mean love is not reason-dependent? The idea seems to be this. Any lover realizes that the relationship's future is partially out of her hands; both x and y will change in unforeseeable ways. This does not mean that x plans in advance to withdraw love if changes occur; quite the contrary. But x will not necessarily love later the y who has changed. Then again, it could turn out that x will later love that changed person (with the same love, not with a numerically new love). At least, at the beginning x intends to love y even if y were to change in unforeseeable ways. As a result, x intends to love a person under a description that x in advance has no firm handle on. But loving a person under a description that is unavailable (since it exists only in the future) is not to love under a description at all: the future beloved that x now intends to love is undescribable. Robert Brown has advanced a similar argument:

> To love a particular person is . . . to commit oneself to an open-ended relationship. It is . . . not merely to love the present person or to love that person as one who has a specific history. It is also to be *prepared* to love the person in the future despite—or because of—the many changes that may take place in the character . . . of the beloved. Since the details of such a commitment cannot be specified in advance, the complete . . . character of the relationship between the lover and the object of love cannot, at any given time, be specified. . . . Similarly, the object of love cannot, at a particular time, be identical with a specifiable complex of qualities. The complex is essentially incomplete, and hence so is the object of love. . . . [I]n loving someone . . . we . . . cherish . . . the incompletely specifiable beloved. . . . [W]hile the relationship is in progress, and we are committed to its continuance, we cannot know what qualities we shall discover in the beloved.[48]

In one sense, Brown's argument is just Mendus': if x loves y now, x is prepared now to love y in the future, even though y might have different properties. But x cannot in advance describe what y will be like; hence x is prepared to love an undescribable y. But Brown's point might be stronger. The person that one loves now *includes* the person one intends to love later; the object of love now is not merely the present person but the present-and-future person. Hence the object of love is undescribable even now because it is in part the undescribable future beloved. X's love for y now, therefore, cannot be reason-dependent.

But we do, with justification, love conditionally in the sense rejected by Mendus and Brown. Mendus claims that if x loves y, then x intends now to love y even if y turns out to be a cheat and a liar. Brown claims that if x loves y, then x is now prepared to love y despite (unstated) changes in y. Brown's claim in particular is incredible. Surely when x declares love for y, x is not giving y carte blanche to change in every unforeseeable way. And Mendus' example handles only a relatively easy case of a possible change in y. Even if x is prepared now to love y should y become, or reveal himself to be, a cheat and liar, x need not be prepared now to love y should y become violently abusive or sexually promiscuous, or should y run away to Paris or undergo a dramatic metanoia. No one expects anyone to be prepared in advance to love someone who later becomes or is revealed to be a monster, and so it is implausible to claim that such an intention follows from "x loves y" or from the nature of love. Indeed, if we deny, as Mendus does, that strong unconditionality is a necessary feature of love (that is, if we deny that x loves y only if x in fact continues to love y no matter how y has changed), then we must also deny Mendus' weak unconditionality—because it cannot be required to intend to do what no one is required to do.

Furthermore, if x's realism about the unpredictability of relationships is why x is expected to make only a weak rather than a strong unconditional commitment (an intention, not a prediction), then that realism is precisely why we do not expect x to make even a weak unconditional commitment. Even if x never says explicitly to y (or to himself), "I will not be able to love y if later y becomes or is revealed to be an utter monster," this does not mean that x's love for y is not at that time conditional on y's not becoming a monster. Mendus writes, "When I promise to love . . . I do not mutter under my breath, 'So long as you never become a member of the Conservative Party'" (p. 244); but if she is to be rational, she had better mutter "as long as you do not become an alcoholic, crazy wife-beater." Perhaps x never thinks the unthinkable—that y may become a monster—but this too does not mean that x now intends to love y should y become a monster. X knows at some level and in advance that if y turns out to be a monster (in x's subjective sense of "monster"),[49] x will probably no longer love y. Mendus' claim rings true only when x is romantically obsessed with y, believing that nothing y might do would destroy x's love or that y will always remain perfect and unchanged. This might be an accurate psychological description of some lovers, but it is not a conceptual truth about love.

The argument, then, does not establish that the beloved, as an evolving object of love, is sufficiently indescribable to rule out reason-dependence. When the lover thinks the idea attributed to her by Mendus or Brown ("I intend to love you even if"), the lover only means "I am now convinced, based on my knowledge of the present you, that your good properties will likely outweigh whatever defects I eventually find." Hence, the "intention" and "preparedness" of love are explicable in terms of love's being reason-dependent. And x *does* have a description of the future beloved that the lover now knows will determine the course of love: x will likely be able to love y as long as y does not become a monster, as long as y's valuable properties continue to provide reasons for love more powerful than any possible future reasons not to love. Call this feature of erosic love its "conditional unconditionality." This is the reason-dependent commitment x makes to y when declaring love; this concept characterizes x's thought: "I intend to love you as long as you do not become D—as I fully expect and hope you won't." The commitment is conditional because it does, contra Mendus, contain an escape clause; it is unconditional (weakly) in that the lover in advance believes that the escape clause will not be invoked, that the beloved's good properties will likely outweigh the bad found later. It is the realist's way of saying "I will love you no matter what." It is also less pompous and pretentious than the agapic lover's saying "I love you pledging myself to you no matter what defects arise in your character, and knowing that since you are human you will sin and err." This agapic forgiveness in advance for "inevitable" faults[50] is an insult to the beloved; the lover has more faith in his commitment than he has in the beloved's ability to maintain a good character.

CHAPTER 9

Exclusivity

> Whatever compass of mind one may have, he is capable of only one great
> passion.
>
> —Pascal, "Discourse on the Passion of Love"

> Eager to conserve his resources, . . . Balzac would generally practice coitus
> reservatus with his mistresses. But once, carried away by the ardor of his
> sexual partner, he allowed himself to reach orgasm, only to comment
> afterwards, ruefully, "Well, there goes another book!"
>
> —Peter Gay, *The Tender Passion*

1. TWO NOTIONS OF EXCLUSIVITY

Gellner's paradox turns on the thesis that love "can only have one object"[1] or that the "very recurrence" of x's attitude toward another person entails that it is not love. But the expression "love is exclusive" is ambiguous; in particular, it is insensitive to time.[2] The expression, then, can be analyzed in two distinct ways. In what follows, I treat the claim "love is exclusive" in this way: the claim presupposes a definition of "exclusive" and it asserts that genuine love satisfies the conditions stated in the definition. Thus, each analysis of "love is exclusive" implies that if an occurrence of an emotion does not satisfy the definition, that emotion is not love.

"Love is exclusive" can mean that love is *timelessly* exclusive or "for all times"; the very recurrence of an emotion or attitude toward a second person at any time entails that it is not love.[3] This is exclusivity in its strictest sense; love is an emotion that a person can experience only once in a lifetime and toward only one person. Hence, in this sense of exclusivity, (i) after xLy begins, x can love no one other than y, and (ii) before xLy begins, x could not have loved anyone else. Note that this is not merely a psychological thesis about the state of mind of the lover, but a claim about the nature or logic of love. Timeless exclusivity has two variants, timeless constant exclusivity and timeless non-constant exclusivity: the former adds that once xLy begins, x will always love y,[4] while the latter does not add this condition.[5] Both notions of timeless exclusivity thus entail that (iii) one's first beloved is one's only beloved and (iv) if that beloved dies, x will not love anyone else. But timeless nonconstant exclusivity allows discontinuities in xLy: x may love y at time t_1, not love y at t_2, yet love y again at t_3, as long as the gaps are not filled in with xLz.[6]

"Love is exclusive" can also mean that love is *timed* exclusive, or exclusive "at one time." If an attitude is directed at two people at the same time, it cannot be love; having two objects at the same time is the "very recurrence" ruled out by the exclusivity of love.[7] Timed exclusivity allows (but does not require) serial and bracketed multiple loves: x loves y and only y at t_1, yet x may love z and only z at some other time t_2. Whereas the doctrine that love is timelessly exclusive prohibits multiple loves altogether, the doctrine that love is timed exclusive prohibits only multiple loves that overlap in time or are cotemporaneous.[8] Thus, someone who asserts that love is exclusive might mean either that x can love only one person *period* or that x can love only one person at a time; and someone who denies that love is exclusive might mean either that multiple loves occurring at different times are possible, or even that multiple overlapping loves are possible ("timeless nonexclusivity"). Serial and bracketed loves can be conceived of as either exclusive or nonexclusive, depending on which doctrine is assumed to be true.

If love is timelessly exclusive, it is indeed an anomalous emotion. Were this analysis taken as an empirical claim about what we ordinarily call love, it would be false; as a conceptual claim, it implies that the world has known very little personal love. One virtue of the timed exclusivity analysis is that it implies that if xLy at t_1 and y dies or runs away, then xLz can be true at the later t_2; the doctrine does not entail that x's first beloved is x's only beloved. Timed exclusivity also avoids the other extreme: it conceptually allows x to love y and z at different stages of x's life without giving x conceptual carte blanche to love w, y, z, and their siblings all at the same time. But the doctrine of timed exclusivity gets caught in the middle, attacked by both defenders of strict exclusivity and proponents of nonexclusivity. In principle timed exclusivity places no limit on the number of loves x can have, as long as they are temporally discrete. This is not exclusivity at all, claim both the purists and the nonexclusivists. Is there not a point at which the sheer number of serial loves (even if bracketed) implies that not all these instances are love? We might try to put a theoretical limit on the number of loves by requiring that (a) some amount of time elapse between brackets (set a minimum length to loveless gaps) or that (b) any bracketed love last some minimum amount of time. But filling in the details of (a) seems arbitrary and futile. Route (b) implies that the fuzziness of the idea of timed exclusivity is to be patched up by the idea of constancy—but that concept is no less fuzzy.[9] Alternatively, defenders of the doctrine of timed exclusivity might insist that what matters, in deciding whether x loves, is the quality of x's emotion, not the number or duration of its instances. But timed exclusivity then gives way to nonexclusivity, because that view claims that what matters is quality, not the triviality that x's love for y overlaps with x's love for z. The purists, however, step in: *that* is not trivial; if you want the quality of genuine love, it must be timelessly exclusive.

Gellner never says whether he means love can have only one object in the sense of timeless or timed exclusivity, but he seems to presuppose the stronger definition. In rejecting the "primacy of encounter" solution to his paradox (4.1), Gellner claims that an E-type lover x cannot admit, for logical reasons, that x would have loved z rather than y had x met z before y. But the doctrine of timed exclusivity permits x to admit that x had loved an earlier z. Further, x as an E-type lover cannot admit, while x loves y for having S, that x might love another person z having S who comes along later. The E-type lover, then, is a timelessly exclusive lover, or at least believes that love is timelessly exclusive. However, only the weaker definition of exclusivity is needed to generate Gellner's paradox: it is sufficient, to establish Gellner's first horn, to demonstrate that if x loves y at t, then x can love no one else at t. The incompatibility of timed exclusivity and reason-dependence, then, is the point of Gellner's dilemma. Suppose that xLy at t_1 on the basis of y's having S, then xLz at t_2 on the basis of z's having S, but xLy ends before xLz begins. This scenario is permitted by timed exclusivity. But it is incompatible with reason-dependence, for if xLz in virtue of S, yet xLy has ended even though y still has S, then x's emotion is not tied closely enough to S.[10] If both y and z have S and love is reason-dependent, then xLy should continue at t_2 while xLz. This situation is ruled out by timed exclusivity; only the possibility of overlapping or cotemporaneous loves (nonexclusivity) is consistent with reason-dependence.

2. DIFFICULTIES IN MULTIPLE LOVES

Niklas Luhmann writes that "one of the most obvious hallmarks of the semantics of love (in contrast to . . . friendship) is its *exclusivity,* in that it is generally regarded—and there is broad consensus on this point—that one can only love one person at any one time. It is additionally sometimes claimed that this can only happen once in a lifetime."[11] This thesis is remarkable. Luhmann also claims, perhaps to support it, that whoever defends nonexclusivity "must write a whole book about it. . . . The assertion of exclusivity, in contrast, requires only one sentence. This unequal distribution of the onus of the argument illustrates more than do the arguments themselves what was, despite all proofs, nevertheless plausible."[12] The idea seems to be that if there is a broad consensus that love is timed exclusive, then exclusivity need not be defended, and that the minority bears the burden of showing that love is not in any sense exclusive. Further, he implies, even if "proofs" of nonexclusivity are logically rigorous, they are likely to be discounted because their conclusion contradicts a firm, if not incorrigible, belief. But I am aware of many writers who defend some doctrine of exclusivity; by Luhmann's logic, this suggests that there never has been a broad consensus that love is exclusive. Asserting that love is not exclusive is easy, since human experience bears out the claim immediately; to argue that despite these experiences "true" love is (or, weaker, ought to be) exclusive therefore requires a whole book. But Luhmann's logic is too simple. The fact that there are many writers who defend the view that love is by its nature exclusive might mean that even if there *is* a genuine consensus that love is, or tends to be, exclusive (almost equally borne out by human experience), the belief is nevertheless held insecurely. The arguments quiet these doubts by showing that decent reasons can be adduced for what many of us believe. The arguments defending exclusivity can be understood, then, not as an attempt to make us take seriously a minority belief but (in accordance with Mill's recommendation in *On Liberty*) to prevent a living truth from degenerating into a dead dogma.

In this and the next few sections I look at various arguments designed to show that love is (or is not) exclusive. Let us begin with a fairly common observation, Robert Brown's claim that "a relationship of affectionate care . . . is limited in its number of participants by the limitations imposed by the requirements of interest, attention, committal, and intimacy. Because we cannot be equally interested in, attentive to, committed to, and intimate with, a large number of people, we cannot enter into relationships of equally affectionate care with them. To have close and affectionate relationships with a few people ensures not having such relations with any larger number."[13] There are material, economic, temporal, and psychological constraints on our ability to love.[14] Notice that love is not, in this view, exclusive solely by *its* nature, but in large measure in virtue of its surrounding environment. Yet it might be asserted that these pragmatic considerations are powerful enough that our loves must be timelessly or timed exclusive in order to be genuine. No one, of course, argues that practical constraints place powerful limits on the number of people we can admire, respect, or hate. Thus we would have to claim that the nature of the attention and concern in love requires it to be exclusive in some sense; since attention and concern are features of love but not of the other erosic emotions, it follows that only love is expected to be exclusive.

A different sort of defense is advanced by Robert Ehman: "Although [the lover] might put two or more persons ahead of all others, he cannot put two persons absolutely first in his life; and this is what love demands. . . .

When the lover admits that his beloved is merely one of several whom he counts as equal, he takes back his claim to love her."[15] Whereas for Brown the attention and concern involved in love imply that love cannot be extended equally to *too* many people (and hence that there are pragmatic obstacles to loving nonexclusively), for Ehman this attention and concern logically can have only one person as their object. The lover might be able to extend superlative attention and concern to two people, but he had better not—on pain of negating his claim to love anyone. (Ehman's view, by the way, has a strange implication: if x has a personal love for y, his wife, then she must be "absolutely first" in his life—but, then, what about his love and concern for their children? Do they come "second" in his life? See 12.8.)

In contrast to Ehman, W. Newton-Smith claims that "there is *nothing* in the concept of love that rules out" x's loving y and z at the same time, and that exclusivity "cannot be presented as a fact about the nature or essence of love."[16] Newton-Smith's opponent is Karl Jaspers, who claimed that "he only does love at all who loves one specific person" (*Philosophie*). Newton-Smith suggests that this is a "normative" claim disguised as a conceptual truth, a "legislative" decision, or merely "an *ad hoc* rule." In arguing that love is not exclusive, Newton-Smith begins by acknowledging what Brown asserted— that the nonexclusive lover "is apt to find himself spread a little thin if he attempts to provide the sort of concern, interest, commitment and so on which we take love to involve." This may be seen as an admission that defending nonexclusivity will require some work; for if love does involve concern and commitment, the right conclusion might be that this thin-spreading is incompatible with these features of love. Newton-Smith's rejoinder is: "That it will be difficult to bring it off," that is, for x to love y and z at the same time, "does not show it is in principle impossible." But Newton-Smith's rejoinder at best only *legislates* that x can, in principle, provide enough concern (and so forth) to both y and z. Newton-Smith must do more than this. He must offer some account of the kind or amount of concern that is involved in love and then argue that, given this kind or amount, when x attempts to provide concern to both y and z, x will not be spread so thin that x ends up loving neither. That account would explain, surely much better than the mere assertion that "difficult" does not entail "impossible," why nothing in the concept or nature of love rules out overlapping loves.

The way Newton-Smith continues this discussion confirms the weakness of his argument. "Difficulties [in x's bringing it off] are most apt to arise if the set-up is not mutual all round": when x loves both y and z, and y and z do not love (perhaps even hate) each other. In this case, Newton-Smith worries that x's loving y will distress z, and x's loving z will distress y; x's causing them both distress may be incompatible with x's loving them, since in causing distress x cannot "really be concerned for both." His answer to this quandary is amazingly simple: "Probably all that is required for [x] to be thought of as loving both [y] and [z] is that he [is] distressed at their distress." But this is as legislative and as ad hoc a claim about love as one could hope to find. To say that in causing y and z distress x is *adequately* concerned for them as long as their distress distresses x, is to appeal to an implausible notion of concern. Why not say, instead, that if x is genuinely concerned for y and z, x will desire to remove the cause of their distress? As if realizing his answer may not do the trick, Newton-Smith ultimately handles this case by abandoning argument: "To show that love is not so exclusive as to rule out multiple love relationships we need only imagine a set-up that is mutual all round," that is, x loves y and z, y loves x and z, and z loves x and y. (In this fully mutual situation, no distress arises to bring into doubt x's love for y and z.) This "argument" begs the question. If, in order to demonstrate that love is not necessarily exclusive, all we need to do is to imagine a love-triangle in which xLy, xLz, yLx, yLz, zLx, and zLy, then all we need to do in order to show that *x* can bring off loving both y and z is to imagine that two other persons, y and z, *are* able to bring it off. But whether anyone can is the issue.

Further, Newton-Smith's ability to "imagine" this arrangement no more establishes nonexclusivity than Jaspers' inability to imagine it would establish exclusivity. Yet Newton-Smith pretends otherwise: "Consider [that is, *imagine*] that all factors involved in loving, excepting any reference to numbers, are satisfied to a high degree by the pair of persons A and B, and by the pair, C and D. What grounds could one have for retracting a description of these cases as cases of love when it is discovered that [A and C] are the same person?" Newton-Smith then claims that "the only grounds" would be "*ad hoc.*" But this argument begs the question against those who claim that the kind or amount of concern required by love is incompatible with overlapping loves. Were Jaspers to imagine that A is loving B with *that* large amount or special kind of concern and that C is loving D similarly, then Jaspers could not "discover" that A and C are the same person. There are "no grounds" for retracting the description only if we already assume that love's concern can be spread around without becoming too thin to count as love.

Since Newton-Smith claims that the difficulty of x's loving y and z at the same time does not mean it is impossible for x to do so, he seems committed to claiming that even the difficulty of loving three people at the same time does not rule out the possibility that some x might be able to do so. And so on, for any number of overlapping beloveds. But then what could Newton-Smith say about "someone who declared with complete equanimity that within a very short space of time he had indulged in a series of intimate associations with a large number of people . . . and yet that he loved them all"?[17] Newton-Smith's position seems powerless to rule out this x as a genuine lover. "Consider," we might say to Newton-Smith, "that A loves B, C loves D, E loves F, and G loves H. By your logic, the discovery that A = C = E = G should not make you retract your description of all these cases as love." To rule out this extravagantly multiple lover, Newton-Smith must claim that at some point the amount or kind of concern involved in love cannot be multiply-satisfied (at that point, the concern will be too thin); at some point "difficult" is too difficult and becomes "impossible." Newton-Smith would then be providing the account, which we asked for earlier, of the amount or kind of concern involved in love. And then Newton-Smith would have to explain why a difficulty becomes an impossibility for *n* beloveds but not for any number less than *n*, in particular *n*-1. If there is some *n* close to 2 for which "difficult" implies "impossible," it becomes suspicious to claim that *nothing* in the concept of love rules out x's loving y and z at the same time.

Thus, it makes sense that, whereas Newton-Smith recognizes that practical difficulties prevent many of us from loving more than one person at a time but still concludes that love is not exclusive, Brown relies on similar difficulties to argue that love is or tends to be exclusive, implying that there is some limit on multiple loves inexpressible given the philosophical technique of Newton-Smith's argument. An alternative approach would invoke various features of love in order to pick up Newton-Smith's slack, not to argue with him that love is conceptually not exclusive but in effect to argue against him. This approach would provide reasons for thinking that love is or tends to be exclusive even though there might be the odd lover to whom this does not apply and who is the counterexample on which Newton-Smith's style of argument relies heavily. My point is not that Newton-Smith's view is false or that writers who defend a doctrine of exclusivity have done a good job of it. To the contrary, if it is unclear that the concern involved in love can be spread around to several beloveds without self-destructing, it is equally unclear that this concern *cannot* be spread around without becoming too thin. Further, I find it surprising that few people argue that loving exclusively is beset with practical difficulties that tend to make love nonexclusive (Newton-Smith would welcome that argument) or that the difficulty of loving only one person does not mean it is impossible.

3. THE LOVER'S SELF-CONCEPT

An intriguing argument for a doctrine of exclusivity rests upon the psychological claim that x's self-concept, or x's sense of who and what x is, is formed in and by the significant attachments in x's life. In particular, in a love relationship x's self-concept is influenced by the mutual accommodation that occurs between x and y, by x's seeing the world as y sees it, by what x thinks y thinks about x, by x's making herself a person that x thinks y can respect, by the minute details of x's daily interaction with y that shape what x is and how x perceives himself. Thus "it is unsurprising to find one confused, even incoherent when his closest social relationships cease. When persons who form the core of one's social sphere disappear from that sphere, one's own sense of . . . identity becomes seriously threatened."[18] And it is thus understandable that when one's beloved dies or leaves, one experiences trauma (worse than a tooth extraction); the props that supported one's self-concept are gone, and the sense of who and what one is floats free.

If this account of the formation and maintenance of a unified self-concept is plausible, there are pressures that militate against overlapping loves. Consider a person who stabilizes her self-concept in a loving relationship: "Previously uninterested politically, she now identifies herself as a liberal. Previously alternating between dimly articulate religious positions, she now declares herself an agnostic. Previously confused . . . about her sexual emotions, she now understands herself as an unabashed hedonist."[19] (Alter the details if you wish: x had been divided about dropping gum wrappers on the street, but as a result of his relationship with y he becomes an unabashed litterer.) This person, "having 'found herself' as a liberal, an agnostic and a 'sexually healthy' person, *ipso facto* liquidates the possibilities of becoming," or defining herself as, "an anarchist, a Catholic or a Lesbian."[20] But this will not be the case if she then enters another intense relationship at the same time: her religious, political, and sexual self-definitions are thrown into doubt. She becomes confused as to who and what she is, even if (which is more likely) her doubts revolve around thoughts, feelings, and attitudes more subtle and less dramatic than these. If x's self-concept is built in x's relationship with y, then x's relating with z in the same loving way will induce in x another self-concept. If y and z are different enough, the self-concept that x derives from y will differ from the one derived from z. The nonexclusive lover winds up having two self-concepts, and that state of affairs is psychologically stressful and too difficult to withstand on a continuing basis. The nonexclusive lover is courting existential disaster; she is not sure of who and what she is, since she is at once so many things. This might imply that the only persons capable of maintaining overlapping loves are those who do not care about having, or can function while having, multiple self-concepts.

But if a love relationship builds one's self-concept, it also partially destroys the self-concept one had prior to the relationship. This has two implications. First, some people may resist love relationships because they want to retain their comfortable self-concept, or they do not want to replace a known with an unforeseeable self-concept, or they fear that a change in self-concept means a loss of themselves. This confirms the argument that considerations of self-concept promote exclusivity, since the x who builds a self-concept in a relationship with y has these additional reasons not to endanger that self-concept by embarking on a relationship with z. (Indeed, the argument becomes a defense of timeless exclusivity.) Second, however, there is the implication that x may desire overlapping loves, not because x perversely wants multiple self-concepts but because nonexclusivity allows x to maintain the self-concept that x had prior to both relationships.[21] Because x's attention, interaction, and concern are divided, neither relationship can modify x's cherished self-concept in a way x would see as destructive. Thus, considerations of x's self-concept do not necessarily tell in favor of exclusivity; they can, instead, tell in favor of nonexclusivity. However, the x who wants to maintain x's self-concept against significant challenges will have to form relatively less intense or intimate attachments. Yet, can these multiple relationships, in which x intentionally avoids a depth or intimacy that would significantly affect x's self-concept, be called love relationships? We have arrived at a tangle similar to our problem with concern: what amount or kind of intimacy is required by love? Does this amount or kind of intimacy permit spreading without becoming too thin, or does its being extended to y and z at the same time mean that x loves neither person?

There is one more reason that this argument fails. Prior to x's loving y, x had attachments to parents, co-workers, and friends, all of whom contributed to x's self-concept. Before x loves y, then, x will already have multiple self-concepts; this is simply a fact of life and not normally an existential disaster. Further, while x is loving y and building that self-concept, x normally will have some close friends, and these friendships will generate at least partially different self-concepts in x; yet x will not avoid loving y while being friends with z merely because doing both creates multiple self-concepts in x. Indeed, the value of a separate friendship may lie in helping x to maintain the independence and individuality required for x to make x's *own* contribution to the self-concept being formed in the love relationship. Otherwise, x is in danger of being swallowed up by y, of having x's self-concept determined entirely by y.

4. JOINT INTERESTS

"Love," wrote Hegel, "is indignant if part of the individual is severed and held back,"[22] thereby explaining why love is exclusive: when x attempts to love y and z at the same time, x must hold back something from each beloved, and so x ends up loving neither. If love means sharing one's whole self with another, nothing is left to share with someone else; an intense or intimate relationship therefore requires at least serial, bracketed exclusivity. I think the best defenses of a doctrine of exclusivity rely on some version of this thesis, even though Hegel's elaboration is unconvincing. Sounding like Aristophanes, he says: "What in the first instance is most the individual's own is united into the whole in the lover's touch and contact; consciousness of a separate self disappears, and all distinction between the lovers is annulled."[23] Hegel's idea, that there is no love if part of the lover is withheld, can be developed without the literal union of two selves.

J. F. M. Hunter argues that love is exclusive by appealing to the "joint interest" that love involves.[24] "When we profess love, we can be expected to give ungrudgingly, and to treat the loved one's interests as if they were our own. . . . [Love involves] the wish to unite one's interests with those of another person." This concern feature of love is "logically connected" with the lover's "readiness to unite oneself to one person, to the exclusion of others," in the following way. Love is marked by a coalescing of the lovers' previously separate interests into one indivisible joint interest; my interests become your interests and your interests become my interests. This coalescing of interests is a union, not an exchange, because if my interests are both yours and mine, and your interests are both yours and mine, then our interests are identical. This union of interests is not only a union of needs but also a union of the capabilities to satisfy those needs. This union explains why love is exclusive: "It is, if not impossible, at least uncommonly difficult to be related to two people at the same time in such a way that the joint interest is primary. . . . It is often wrongly treated as a psychological question whether it is possible to be in love with two people at the same time. . . . It is not, however, a psychological question, but a question of whether one's interests can be united simultaneously with two other people; and the peculiar difficulty of it is that my time, my affection, my productivity, however selflessly I am prepared to give them, are not, if I am in love, entirely mine to give. They belong jointly to me and another person."

Hunter's way of making the point is unfortunate. It sounds as if he is defending exclusivity not conceptually but as a moral obligation. If what is x's "belongs" to y, and hence "what is offered" by x to a potential second beloved z "is not entirely at [x's] discretion to give," then not loving y exclusively is theft. That x's affection "belongs" to y does not entail that x *cannot* give it away elsewhere, but only that x *ought not* to. Hunter, however, thinks that exclusivity is required neither morally nor psychologically, but conceptually. If x desires to join x's interests with y's, then x is conceptually prevented from loving z, since x cannot also desire to join those same interests elsewhere; the first desire contradicts the second. One might respond here that there is no contradiction: x can still desire both things, just as x can desire both to live with y and to live with z; what is ruled out is x's satisfying both desires. On behalf of Hunter, we might say that x cannot genuinely desire both to join x's interests with y's and to join them with z's. Or we might say that x can desire both, but add that this nonexclusive love is irrational; in loving both y and z, x must entertain contradictory desires, one of which must remain unsatisfied. But neither rebuttal would please Hunter; the first makes exclusivity a psychological question, and the second abandons the conceptual necessity of exclusivity. What Hunter must have in mind is that love involves not merely the desire to join interests but the actual joining of interests. In loving y, x has already joined x's interests with y's, and hence x is logically prevented from loving z at the same time; even if x desires to join x's interests with z's, x has no interests left over that x could join with z's. X's interests per se no longer exist to be joined with z's because they have been incorporated into the x-y joint interest, and a joint interest is not the sort of thing that can be divided and shared with another person. Thus, Hunter's saying that nonexclusive love is "if not impossible, at least uncommonly difficult" is, in his own view, at best misleading and at worst false. If exclusivity is not simply a psychological feature of love but follows from "joint interests," then multiple loves are logically impossible, not merely difficult.

We thus have an account of love according to which x's loving y means giving himself totally to y, thereby ruling out overlapping loves. Were x to give part of himself to a second person z, that would mean that x had dissolved the x-y joint interest, and so no longer loved y. Or if x maintains the x-y joint interest, then nothing exists for x to give that could count as x's loving z. We might wonder, though, about two little things. First, Hunter's argument relies on the reciprocity of love in deriving its exclusivity. Analyzing love as the actual joining of interests builds reciprocity into the meaning of love and awkwardly makes nonreciprocal love a logical impossibility. (If love involves only the *desire* to join interests, then reciprocity is not assumed; but in this case, as we have seen, love is not necessarily exclusive.) Second, the claim that a complete joining of interests is required for love seems too strong; surely it will be difficult to establish that love requires the total surrender of oneself to another implied by the complete joining of interests. What we want is an argument based on less contentious and vulnerable considerations. But Hunter's style of argument is right on target.

5. INTIMACY AND EXCLUSIVITY

The principles underlying Hegel's suggestion that love involves sharing can be rendered formally and abstractly by the following two "conditions of sharing": (1) x shares *all* of x's A with whomever x loves, and (2) x shares x's A *only* with those whom x loves (where "A" ranges over things that x has and can share with others). Note that neither condition is stated in such a way that the exclusivity of love follows from either condition alone. The first condition of sharing allows that x might be able to share x's A with a number of people, all these beneficiaries simultaneously getting all the A that x has to offer—it all depends on what "A" refers to. The second condition of sharing similarly allows x to share A with an indefinite number of people, this set of objects being restricted only by the condition that they have in common being loved by x. Further, when stated abstractly the two conditions of sharing not even taken together imply that love is exclusive. The point is that the two conditions define neutrally what love's sharing involves, so as not to beg any questions about exclusivity. Whether love is exclusive, then, will depend on precisely what "A" refers to, a matter for argument. Further, the two conditions of sharing provide a way of looking at the *intimacy* of love. For example, if A are x's interests and capabilities, A may be the sort of thing x is willing to share only with beloveds and the sort of thing x can share with only one other person, in which case x's love will be exclusive. At the same time, x's sharing all x's interests with y and only y might be what the intimacy of their relationship amounts to.

Charles Fried has proposed that the intimacy of love "is the sharing of information about one's actions, beliefs or emotions, which one does not share with all."[25] In Fried's view, A is information about x; per condition (2) x restricts the sharing of this information to x's beloveds. In addition, it might be claimed that x shares all information about x with x's beloved; love involves "absolute openness" about one's beliefs and feelings, according to Jerome Neu. Neu also claims that "exclusivity is essential to the nature of [a loving] relationship."[26] If we combine Fried's claim with Neu's, not only can we fashion an interesting defense of exclusivity, but we also get a distinctive account of the intimacy of love. The lovers are "absolutely" open with each other, sharing their thoughts, beliefs, feelings and, especially, all the details of their past and the current events of their lives. They reveal to each other facts and feelings that are delicate, touchy, embarrassing, shameful, vulnerable to criticism, or that they consider so personal as to constitute the core (the deep self?) of their identities.[27] Being psychologically close to another person, or forming a psychologically sound union; being able to show concern for the other, fulfilling her needs, in light of a complete understanding of her character; being able to interact spontaneously, with a sense of being accepted in a context of mutual trust—all these concomitants of the absolute sharing of information are central features of a loving relationship.

On the basis of the first condition, there is already some argument that love is exclusive. If x loves y, x must be completely open with y about x's life; then if x also loves z, the first condition similarly requires that x be absolutely open with z about the same things. For this A (information), there is no logical bar to x's sharing all of it with more than one person. So x will be sharing with y and z the same set of x's delicacies, and in doing so x must share with z the delicacies of the x-y relationship, and with y the delicacies of the x-z relationship. It would be morally wrong, however, for x to reveal to z the details of x's life with y, which necessarily includes revealing details about y.[28] Or it would be psychologically difficult for x to reveal to more than one person at a time x's delicacies, for x to reveal to z the delicacies of x's relationship with y, or for y and z to listen to x's description of x's other relationship. Thus, the first condition—that x be absolutely open with whomever x loves—does not conceptually rule out overlapping loves; it implies only that nonexclusivity is morally objectionable or in practice difficult. In order to obtain a conceptual conclusion about exclusivity, we need to invoke also the second condition.

To complete the argument we must claim that love requires that what is shared within the relationship is not per force shared elsewhere, not as a matter of morality or psychology, but as a matter of the logic of intimate sharing. In a loving relationship, y does not simply open up to x but opens up to an extent that y would not open up to others whom y does *not* love or otherwise would not choose to open up to. Thus the second condition implies that in opening up to x, y is *not automatically* opening up to other people via x or on account of x's dealings with third parties. Part of the reason is that delicacies lose the status of being delicacies if they are spread around indiscriminately. And part of the reason is that by sharing delicacies selectively we signal to their recipient that he or she is special to us: y shows x that y's attitude toward x is or may become love by conveying that this bit of information has been reserved just for x.[29] Note that the second condition also does not conceptually rule out multiple loves. But the two conditions together do. For if x has loving relationships with both y and z, then x and y are completely open with each other and x and z are completely open with each other; x therefore shares the details of the x-y relationship with z (as per the first condition). But then y, who in opening up to x *as* x's beloved (as per the first condition) is automatically opening up to z, who is not y's beloved or someone y wants to open up to—which violates the second condition. Or if x and y completely open up to each other as beloveds, and x abides by the second condition (information about y is restricted to y's beloveds), then were x to form a loving relationship also with z, x could not share details with z of the x-y relationship—which violates the first condition.

The argument we teased from Fried and Neu has problems similar to Hunter's. First, it assumes that love is conceptually reciprocal (and so concludes that love is conceptually exclusive) or that the specific love between x and y is reciprocal (and so concludes that when a love is reciprocal, it turns out to be exclusive). Of course, x's revealing delicacies to y one-sidedly is no more a mark of love than is x's confessing to a priest. But that the sharing of information is a feature of reciprocal love does not entail that there is no such thing as nonreciprocated love. Second, if the assumption that love requires a total union of interests is weak, the assumption that love requires absolute openness is also weak. The boundaries of individuality, and the need for the opportunity for x to make x's own contribution to the formation of x's self-concept, imply that both parties would benefit from a less-than-absolute openness. Neu agrees, although he resists saying so explicitly: "One might want to test the exclusivity of absolute intimacy [by] same-sex friendships that remain different and apart from the intimacy of lovers who are otherwise absolutely open and share everything. . . . [The friendship] need not destroy the relationship. . . . [A] friendship which is not shared [may] strengthen a relationship that depends on everything being shared. This paradoxical strengthening would come about because a need that might otherwise go unmet gets satisfied outside the relationship it might otherwise disrupt."[30] But if the value of the friendship is that x shares things with a friend that x does not share with x's beloved, then it is incorrect for Neu to say that the x-y relationship "depends on everything being shared." Since x's friendship helps the relationship, the latter does not depend on absolute openness.

Jeffrey Reiman has objected to conceiving of the intimacy of love as the mutual sharing of information that is not shared with others.[31] A position like Fried's, claims Reiman, attains the conclusion that "love *logically* implies exclusiveness" only because it practices "the high art of ideology: the rendering of aspects of our present possessive market-oriented world into the eternal forms of logical necessity" (p. 33). In Reiman's view, the argument embodies a "market conception of personal intimacy" because "if the value—indeed, the very reality—of my intimate relation with you lies in your sharing with me what you don't share with others, then if you do share it with another, what I have is literally decreased in value and adulterated in substance" and because "the reality of my intimacy with you is constituted not simply by the quality and intensity of what we share, but by its unavailability to others—in other words, by its scarcity" (p. 32). If the intimacy of love is the sharing of information that is not shared with others, then the value to the relationship of the shared information derives from its artificial scarcity—it has primarily exchange-value, not use-value. Reiman protests: *this* is not why shared information has value in love, nor does this sense of intimacy capture what is intimate about love.

For Reiman, "what constitutes intimacy is not merely the sharing of otherwise withheld information, but the context of caring which makes the sharing of personal information significant" (p. 33). There might not be anything to disagree with here, if Reiman means only that x's already loving y (that is, caring about y) is itself part of the reason that the sharing of information is valuable. But Reiman means something special by "context of caring": "The kind of caring I have in mind is not easily put into words, and so I shall claim no more than to offer an approximation. Necessary to an intimate relationship such as . . . love is a reciprocal desire to share present and future intense and important experiences together, not merely to swap information" (p. 33). Reiman means that the *caring* involved in love is literally the (reciprocal) desiring to share present and future experiences. Because intimacy is "the context of caring which makes the sharing of personal information significant," by substitution of equals he derives "in the context of a reciprocal desire to share present and future intense . . . experiences, the revealing of personal information takes on significance" (p. 34). Reiman must implicitly be distinguishing concern from care. It is just as well that he does, for to claim that concern for someone's welfare is a reciprocal phenomenon is farfetched: x might care about and take care of the needs of y—that is, be concerned and show concern for y—without reciprocity.

To avoid confusion, let us state Reiman's thesis this way: love involves the desire to share intense and important experiences; the intimacy of love is, or results from, the satisfaction of the desire for shared experiences; and the sharing of information has value because it contributes to the satisfaction of that desire. Hence, "the more one knows about the other, the more one is able to understand how the other experiences things, what they mean to him, how they feel to him. . . . [T]he more each knows about the other, the more they are able to really share an intense experience instead of merely having an intense experience alongside one another" (p. 34). That makes sense; absolute openness with another person maximizes the possibility of genuinely sharing experiences with her. This confirms the claim that the first condition of sharing, when "A" refers to information, applies to love. Of course, Reiman is objecting to the second condition of sharing, not the first, because the second condition makes sharing valuable simply because the sharing is restricted. I do not see, however, why we cannot have it both ways: the sharing of (all) information is valuable because openness contributes to the sharing of experiences, and the sharing of (restricted) information is valuable because its imposed scarcity is a sign that the beloved is special for us.

Reiman's account of intimacy, I will proceed to argue, itself implies that love tends to be exclusive; it is also vulnerable to the very objections he raised against Fried's view. In claiming that love involves the desire to share present and future intense experiences, is not Reiman aggrandizing our current concept of love as a timeless truth and hence practicing the high art of ideology? For example, Reiman's emphasis on "experiences," rather than on behavior that shows concern for the welfare of one's beloved, might reflect a bit of our contemporary narcissism. The important question, however, is about Reiman's concept of intimacy, that is, the sharing of intense experiences: does not *this* sharing have to be parceled out restrictively, and is not part of the value of a shared intense experience the fact that it is deliberately not shared with others? We can agree with Reiman that x's sharing information only with y does not constitute a robust intimacy between them, if they go no further. We can agree that selective sharing of information is important because it permits x and y to share intense experiences, and that this sort of sharing constitutes a robust intimacy. But this robustness is in jeopardy unless the sharing of experiences is restricted. Suppose x shares with y, whom x claims to love, a number of intense experiences, but x also shares these experiences separately with z (say, x and y visit Paris, and a month later x does the same thing with z). It would be insensitive to tell y that y merely has a market orientation toward relationships were y to complain that x's repeating this experience with z "adulterated" and "literally decreased in value" y's shared experiences with x. The sharing of experiences, that is, is governed by the second condition: x's restricting this sharing of intense experiences to y is essential not only for x's showing y that qua beloved y is special, but also for x's acknowledging that these shared experiences are important. Not only intimacy as the sharing of information yields exclusivity; intimacy as the sharing of intense experiences equally yields exclusivity (under the questionable assumption of reciprocity).

Reiman attempts to rebut the charge that his view smells of the market: "On [my] view . . . the unsavory market notion of intimacy is avoided. Since the content of intimacy is caring, rather than the revealing of information . . . , there is no necessary limit to the number of persons one can be intimate with, no logical necessity that . . . love be exclusive. The limits rather lie in the limits of our capacity to care deeply for others" (p. 35). Reiman is confused. First, the mere fact that an account of love does (or does not) make love exclusive does not correspond with whether it reflects the market. Thus, if it were true that on his account of intimacy love is not conceptually exclusive, that would not mean he has avoided a "market notion." Rather, whether an account of love smells of the market turns (as Reiman said) on whether the shared item is parceled out selectively to create scarcity. On this score Reiman's account, if I am right, does no better than Fried's. Second, if we read this passage using Reiman's technical sense of "caring" as the reciprocal desire to share intense experiences, it says that love is not logically exclusive because there is no necessary limit on the number of people with whom one can share intense experiences without destroying intimacy. But this is not to provide an argument for thinking that robust intimacy in his sense is not exclusive; it is merely to make an assertion as empty as Newton-Smith's "nothing in the nature of love rules out multiple loves." But should we read this passage in accordance with Reiman's technical sense of "caring"? If we do, then to say that the numerical limits on intimacy depend on "the limits of our capacity to care *deeply* for others" is to say that the numerical limits on intimacy are a function of the depth of the reciprocal desire to share intense experiences. But this claim surely implies that love at least tends to be exclusive. If we interpret "care" in this passage more naturally as "be concerned for the welfare of" (I suspect Reiman is trading on our doing so), then the passage claims that love is not exclusive *because* the limits on love are only our limits to be deeply concerned for others. But this is just Newton-Smith's weak argument.

I do not think that Reiman's notion of intimacy is wrong; quite the contrary. The intimacy of sharing intense experiences is a thick intimacy, whereas the intimacy of sharing delicate information is thin. Consider loves that are serially exclusive. During the first bracket, x shares x's delicacies with y; during the second, x shares x's delicacies with z; during the third, x shares them with w, and so on. Similarly, x consecutively hears y's, z's, then w's delicacies. Won't x eventually see the sharing of x's delicacies as a routine exercise having little value? And won't x be bored by hearing the other's delicacies and see her revealing them as a mechanical routine she is going through for the nth time as well? If so, shared-information intimacy is psychologically compatible with only timeless exclusivity, a style of love that prevents this progressive decrease in the value of sharing delicacies. There is, in fact, another reason for thinking that shared-information intimacy favors timeless exclusivity. Suppose that x has loved y for a long time and that y dies. This x, given the first condition of sharing, must share with a later would-be beloved z the details of x's relationship with y, but x may painfully feel that doing so betrays y or y's memory. The point is that the two conditions of sharing, when applied to delicacies, may entail that conceptually love is timelessly exclusive. If x and y share delicacies at t_1, and then x at a later time t_2 loves z with whom x shares delicacies, the first condition requires x to share with z at t_2 the delicacies of the x-y relationship at t_1, which includes delicacies about y. But this violates the second condition, since at t_1 y had been revealing information to x that is shared by x with z, whom y does not love and has not chosen to open up to. Perhaps x can love this later z only if x literally forgets everything known about y.

Reiman's view, that intimacy is marked by the sharing of intense experiences, is not as vulnerable to the objection that this intimacy progressively decreases in value with time or repetition. If x is a serial, bracketed, exclusive lover, x will not likely find the sharing of intense experiences more and more routine, probably because having intense experiences is closer than revealing or sharing information to what it means to live a life. If the x-y intimacy is only their sharing information, their intimacy is thin because sooner or later they will run out of delicacies to share. (Indeed, this may be a reason to think that shared-information intimacy is psychologically more compatible with nonexclusivity than with exclusivity.) An intimacy of shared experiences, by contrast, is thick because running out of intense experiences to share, with a little luck, is not something x and y have to fear (and note that these experiences then provide the material for sharing thoughts). But what if both x and y are couch potatoes who year after year share the same televised experiences together? Does this count for them as their *intense* shared experience, or is this case a counterexample to Reiman's thesis? Nevertheless, there is at least one exception to the superiority of shared-experience intimacy: the limiting case in which the two types of intimacy merge. Sharing intense experiences will become routine for x if x believes (perhaps because x's first revelation of delicacies to another person was an intense experience) that sharing personal information is precisely the intense experience lovers share. Some loves are no more intimate than mutual psychoanalysis.

6. EXCLUSIVE TRIADS

In Books Eight and Nine of *Nicomachean Ethics,* Aristotle had much to say about philia, including a few curious but interesting things about its exclusivity. "To be friends with many people, in the sense of perfect friendship, is impossible, just as it is impossible to be in love with many people at the same time. For love is like an extreme," he argues, "and an extreme tends to be unique" (1158a10–12).[32] The numerical limit on friendship, according to Aristotle, depends on the type of friendship. The limit on friendships based on usefulness or pleasantness, in which x and y are friends only as long as they are useful or pleasant to each other, is the number that x can "accommodate" with x's own stock of usefulness and pleasantness. How many useful and pleasant friends can one have without friendship becoming counterproductive or without additional friends becoming, by their diminishing marginal utility, valueless? "More friends than are sufficient for one's own life are superfluous and are an obstacle to the good life, so that there is no need of them" (1170b25). The limit on this type of friendship is not determined by the availability of useful or pleasant persons; they abound (but see 1158a13). Regarding perfect friendship, however, in which x and y are friends not in virtue of use or pleasure but in virtue of their moral virtue, the limit is set quite differently. Because "such men are few," perfect friendship is "rare" (1156b25); "we must be content if we find even a few friends of this kind" (1171a19–20).

Assuming that persons of virtuous character can be found, is there some optimal number of genuine friends one should have? "As regards morally good men, should we have as many in number as possible as our friends? Or is there some limit to the number of friendly relations a person can have, just as there is a limit on the size of a city-state?" (1170b30). The analogy Aristotle uses in posing the question hints at his answer. If x and y are friends, x and y desire to live together; indeed, "living together is the surest indication of friendship" (1171a2; see also 1158a8–10). If x is friends with both y and z, then x will desire to live with y and to live with z; but this seems as contradictory as x's wanting to join interests with both y and z. The solution is that if x and y are friends and x and z are friends, then x *must* spend x's days with both y and z; and this is possible only if y and z are also friends and therefore wish to spend their days together: "One's friends should also be the friends of one another" (1171a4). The trio x, y, and z will be the best of friends and live in the same house—a little city-state of the virtuous (free, white, male person). Aristotle concludes: "The right course is . . . not to seek to have as many friends as possible, but as many as are sufficient for living together" (1171a9). Aristotle's "but" is inaccurate; given his reasoning, the number that can live together is exactly the number of friends it is possible to have.

Aristotle's idea—that x can be friends with both y and z if y and z are also friends—can be applied to love. Indeed, Hunter argues that there *is* one situation in which x can love both y and z, and join interests with the interests of both y and z, without generating a contradiction that destroys x's love: when y and z also love each other. "One of a pair of persons in love cannot unilaterally profess love to a third person without cancelling the existing relationship . . . ; but it is possible for a [loving] relationship between three . . . people to come into being, in which each person is happy to share and be shared with each of the others."[33] This three-way love relationship, constituted by the x-y-z joint interest, is made logically possible by the specific way in which Hunter defends the thesis that love is conceptually exclusive. (This is an *argument* that love triads are possible, which is more interesting than Newton-Smith's saying that "nothing in the concept of love rules out" a triad and his simply asking us to imagine that x, y, and z have pulled it off.) Hunter's full conclusion, then, is that love is necessarily two-way exclusive or three-way exclusive or *n*-way exclusive. In all cases, love is exclusive in the sense that x logically cannot offer his interests to some party who is not willing to share everything with x's beloved(s) or whom x's beloved(s) will not accept. Thus, the "difficulty" about multiple loves Hunter has in mind (see sect. 4) is not the psychological difficulty of x's loving both y and z when y and z are not on good terms or even hate each other, but rather the obstacles that might prevent all three of them from successfully joining their interests. For Newton-Smith, love is *not* exclusive because the three-way case is "in principle" possible; for Hunter, love *is* exclusive because even the three-way case manifests the joint-interest exclusivity of love.

Hunter's conclusion also follows from the shared-information view of intimacy. If x and y love each other, then x is conceptually prevented from unilaterally loving a third party z. But x can love both y and z as long as y, too, loves z; in this case, x, y, and z can be absolutely open with each other without violating the second condition of sharing. But this love triad is logically possible precisely in virtue of that feature of love that otherwise makes it two-way exclusive; and the x-y-z triad is exclusive in the sense that no single member can form an outside loving attachment without destroying (by violating the second condition's restriction on the sharing of delicacies) the loves that already exist. Even Reiman's account of intimacy has this implication. If x loves y, x cannot unilaterally love z, since that implies that x shares the same intense experiences separately with y and with z; but x can love both y and z as long as y and z love each other and all three persons share intense experiences together.

On the other side is Montaigne, who wrote as if he were challenging Aristotle: "He who supposes that of two men I love one just as much as the other, and that they love each other and me just as much as I love them, multiplies into a fraternity the most singular and unified of all things."[34] But why does Montaigne think that "perfect friendship . . . is indivisible"? He gives a Hegelian reason: "Each one gives himself so wholly to his friend that he has nothing else to distribute elsewhere."[35] If we read this literally, Montaigne claims that the item "A" referred to by the two conditions of sharing is the person himself; it is true that I cannot divide myself in order to love two people. But if I give myself "wholly" to my beloved, so that I have nothing left to distribute elsewhere, I also have nothing left for myself. What is wrong here is exactly what is wrong with insisting on absolute openness; the lover drops out of the picture. If we take Montaigne's claim less Aristophanically, the argument makes sense if what x shares with y (A) is something less than x himself and something that logically cannot be shared with more than one person. Information can be totally shared with many people, so Montaigne's point does not work against that view. But he might score against Hunter. When x and y expand their love to include z, some of x's capabilities are diverted from y to z and some of y's capabilities are diverted from x to z. Each party is giving only half of his or her capabilities to the other two parties. True, each party receives two halves and gives two halves, exactly the situation when x and y love only each other. But x is not satisfying the first condition of sharing toward any person.

The possibility of a triad may seem to solve Gellner's paradox by reconciling exclusivity and the reason-dependence of love: x can love both y and z in virtue of their having S, as long as y and z also love each other. But of course this solution is inadequate. Exclusivity and reason-dependence are reconciled only for a small number of cases. Further, x might meet a fourth person w who also has S; by reason-dependence x is expected to love w as well, thus violating the exclusivity of the triad—unless, by a miracle, y, z, and w all love each other. Finally, it is not clear that Gellner would call triads "exclusive," even when everyone loves everyone else. Triads are exclusive only in the special sense that one party cannot unilaterally form, at the same time, a loving attachment outside the triad. But given our earlier definitions (sect. 1), any party in a triad is loving nonexclusively, for he or she is engaged in multiple, overlapping loves.

7. EROSIC EXCLUSIVITY

We have considered five arguments defending the thesis that love is at least serially exclusive: (1) if x cares deeply about the welfare of y, x can love only y; (2) if x wants a stable, unified self-concept, x must love only y; (3) if x joins x's interests and capabilities with y's, x can love only y; (4) if x and y have a shared-information intimate relationship, x and y can love only each other; and (5) if x and y desire to share intense experiences, x and y can love only each other. The good news is that these arguments do not take exclusivity as axiomatic of love; they argue for a doctrine of exclusivity on the basis of other features of love. Thus, Newton-Smith's bald assertion that "nothing" in the concept of love means it is exclusive was hasty. Love is a rich concept or a rich phenomenon, and this richness allows someone with enough imagination to defend the logical necessity of exclusivity. We should not be disappointed if these arguments get the weaker conclusion that conceptually love tends to be, rather than is, exclusive; or the conclusion that only psychological or practical factors tend to make love exclusive.

But there is bad news as well. All the arguments (except the one based on concern) take reciprocity as axiomatic of love or apply only to loves that are reciprocal. These arguments, then, are too narrow; they are powerless to explain the exclusive attachment in which x adores y and only y, yet y does or will not reciprocate. Further, each argument (except the second) appeals to what it treats as a logically prior feature of love: concern, the joining of interests, sharing information, sharing experiences. Thus, the conclusion that love is exclusive will be only as firm as the claim that the particular feature from which exclusivity is derived is a necessary feature of love. Except for the claim that concern for the welfare of the beloved is essential to love, these presuppositions are not easy to defend. One can assert, without being unreasonable, that even though love usually involves the joining of interests and the sharing of information and experiences, these features are not logically required. (There is something, after all, in Newton-Smith's complaints.) Perhaps these features look like logical requirements only because we are theorizing about love from our own little slice of time and space; we enshrine into the nature of love ingredients that we are merely accustomed to having in love or even those that we wish were always part of our loves. (There is something, after all, in Reiman's complaints.) And the arguments, including the one based on concern, assume that the particular feature of love from which exclusivity is derived is present to an extreme degree: total concern with the other's welfare, absolute openness, complete sharing of capabilities, and so on. Defined in such extreme terms, it is implausible that these features are logically required for love. That some concern, some openness, and some joint interests are logically required for love seems right, but then the conclusion that love is logically exclusive is unattainable. If one still wants to insist that the openness of love is absolute or that true lovers desire to share every experience, the following alternative recommends itself: couples who have achieved exclusivity are exactly those couples who *as a result* come to be absolutely open with each other or share all their experiences. The exclusivity of their love explains the extreme sharing or openness, not vice versa.

Some cases of love, we have reason to think, are either serially or timelessly exclusive; other loves, we have equal reason to think, are not exclusive. No single explanation will tell us why the loves that are exclusive, are exclusive. Some loves are exclusive because the partners completely satisfy each other's desires; some are exclusive because one believes the other to be unique; some are exclusive because the partners believe exclusivity is morally proper and train themselves not to experience love toward anyone else; some are exclusive because the lovers, having shared their deepest thoughts and most intense experiences, have no desire, opportunity, or power to love someone else; some lovers learn that their self-concept is too painfully damaged by loving nonexclusively. Similarly, no single explanation will tell us why the nonexclusive loves are not exclusive or why loves that had been exclusive are no longer exclusive. Some loves are not exclusive because the lovers cannot or do not satisfy each other's desires; some are not exclusive because one person is capable of showing deep concern for more than one person; some loves are not exclusive because the sharing of personal information or intense experiences with one person does not reduce the value of sharing these things with someone else; and some lovers find that persons other than their beloved have properties, either the same or different, that they find valuable or attractive.

This state of affairs has implications for the problem of reconciling the reason-dependence and exclusivity of love. Since love is not necessarily exclusive, one might say there is nothing to reconcile; the eros tradition does not, therefore, lead us into contradiction. Indeed, in implying that we should not expect love to be exclusive, the eros tradition is confirmed by this state of affairs. But Gellner's paradox is not completely solved by rejecting the claim that love is conceptually exclusive. Some cases of love are in fact exclusive, and in these cases the tension between exclusivity and reason-dependence remains. Perhaps we can appeal to the (perceived) uniqueness of the beloved, the D-S model, and so forth; but no one solution will handle all these cases (the eros tradition is an inner tube patched up in several places), and there is no guarantee that all exclusive loves will be covered by one solution or another (the inner tube still leaks). Perhaps this means only that exclusive loves are agapic, not reason-dependent, or that exclusive lovers are irrational E-typers. Further, the exclusivity of love, for many people, is either what they would like to have or what they consider the ideal. Of course, we cannot always get what we want and ideals are not always attainable. Nevertheless, the eros tradition implies that it is foolish, even irrational, for people to desire exclusivity or to consider exclusivity an ideal. In light of these problems, should we jettison the first view of personal love in favor of the second?

8. THE DESIRE FOR EXCLUSIVITY

In his poem "September 1, 1939," W. H. Auden offered this dismal prognosis:

> For the error bred in the bone
> Of each woman and each man
> Craves what it cannot have,
> Not universal love
> But to be loved alone.

We desire to be loved exclusively; we insist that our lovers love us and no one else; we are not happy receiving a love (from God or His ministers) that is extended to persons in addition to ourselves. "The distinctive joy of being loved," says Robert Ehman, "is that of finding oneself singled out as a unique individual for special evaluation."[36] That is not quite right. Being singled out is not the only joy of love and likely not the most significant one; compare the joy of sharing intense experiences. And the joy of being singled out is not restricted to love; winning a contest or competition provides the same joy. Nevertheless, we do desire to be loved exclusively, at least because we believe that the other joys of love, and love itself, are put in jeopardy when we are not loved exclusively. Auden is therefore right, I think, in claiming that we hope ("crave") to be loved exclusively. What is curious and almost contradictory in his gloomy prognosis is that this desire is "bred in the bone" (natural by our psychology or biology), yet is unsatisfiable. It is a strange Nature that plants a desire in us but fails to arrange for its satisfaction (unless in Nature's, or God's, or Freud's great plan the frustration of this particular desire, or of some desire or other, plays a central role in the achievement of other things).

Other than believing that love and its joys are jeopardized by nonexclusivity, what reason might one have for desiring to be loved exclusively? The security of love is only one consideration, and the constancy of love is hardly guaranteed by exclusivity, even if exclusivity makes constancy more likely. Herbert Spencer proposed an answer that is especially pertinent to our theoretical concerns: "To be preferred above all the world, and that by one admired beyond all others, is to have the love of approbation gratified in a degree passing every previous experience. . . . Further, the allied emotion of self-esteem comes into play."[37] To be preferred before all others by exactly that person whom we prefer before all others is a stroke of good luck (and may make us feel that we have found our literal other half). Being preferred before all others by someone whom we do not prefer above all others is less satisfying and exciting. Why is this? Consider being admired by a person whom you do not admire at all. That person's admiration counts little toward your self-respect; indeed, realizing that you are admired by a person whom you do not admire may reduce your self-respect. Similarly, being preferred by one whom you do not at least admire will not support your self-respect; and being preferred, wanted, desired, and admired by someone toward whom you feel at least some of these things to a certain degree is good for your self-respect. I do not mean that being loved exclusively by one whom we love exclusively is necessary for self-respect, although this arrangement may easily maximize it. I do mean that being loved exclusively (being preferred before all others) by a person for whom we have some positive regard is desirable because it can make a significant contribution to our self-respect.

But if self-respect is an important reason for wanting to be loved exclusively, our theoretical dilemma—the incompatibility of reason-dependence and exclusivity—is pressed upon us even more urgently. The considerations I appealed to (self-respect) in explaining why we want to be loved in virtue of our prized properties (8.3) are precisely the considerations I have appealed to in explaining why we want to be loved exclusively. Thus, if we want to be loved both erosically to support our self-respect *and* exclusively to support our self-respect, yet reason-dependence and exclusivity are incompatible, we cannot in general satisfy both desires. We may have to (i) sacrifice being loved exclusively if we want to be loved erosically or (ii) settle for being loved regardless of our merit if we want to be loved exclusively. Both options have the same motivation: to snatch some self-respect out of the fire. We now have a way of understanding Auden's claim that our desire to be loved exclusively must remain unsatisfied: if it were true that personal love was logically erosic or that humans, psychologically, could love only on the basis of the object's merit, then the second option is senseless. ("Only God, my dear,/ Could love you for yourself alone/ And not your yellow hair.")[38] But we need not claim that personal love is necessarily erosic (which is false) in order to show the inferiority of the second option.

The most glaring weakness of option (ii) is the assumption that agapic personal love is guaranteed to be exclusive or at least will tend to be exclusive more often, or more reliably, than erosic personal love. This assumption will be scrutinized below. There is possibly another problem with option (ii). In abandoning the desire to be loved erosically, the person who wants instead to be loved exclusively must accept being loved irrationally. (See 7.4 and 7.5 for the argument that reason-independent love is irrational.) That realization alone may be a blow to her self-respect that is not offset by the contribution to her self-respect made by being loved exclusively. But the point is more general: the attempt to gain support for one's self-respect by being loved exclusively may be doomed from the very start, if it means abandoning being loved erosically. In not being loved erosically yet being loved exclusively, the power of being loved exclusively to support self-respect may be undermined. If one realizes that one is not being loved in virtue of one's prized attributes, how could being loved exclusively make one feel special? If one's properties have nothing to do with the fact that one has been selected to be loved exclusively, then one will have doubts that there is any reason at all to feel special. One might think that one is being treated as special by the lover for no reason that actually does make one special. The existence of the self-respect gained from being loved exclusively, then, may depend either on the self-respect that is gained from being loved erosically or on the fact that one is loved erosically. On the other hand, in those cases of love in which x loves y both exclusively and erosically—x believes that y is unique, or x has all her desires satisfied by y—y may receive a double-dose of self-respect. Whether y's self-respect doubly benefits in these situations will depend on what y thinks of the explanation for x's loving y both exclusively and erosically. If x believes that y is unique, and this belief is not mildly false (which may be excusable) but grossly false, fueled by x's inability to separate fact from fantasy, then y has little reason to dance for joy. Or if x loves y exclusively and erosically because y satisfies all x's desires, and y knows this, y may not welcome the fact that x's love is instrumental.

Regardless, the advice of the eros tradition is plain: desiring to be loved both exclusively and erosically is an uncomfortable mix; hold on to the latter and do not take too seriously the desire, "bred in the bone," for exclusivity. This does not mean abandon all hope for exclusivity, all ye who love erosically; but ye should not be surprised if exclusivity, as Auden warns, proves to be elusive. Of course, people have desired and will continue to desire to be loved both exclusively and erosically, because of (I suspect) the widespread belief that everyone is unique—a notion that, with qualification, reconciles exclusivity and reason-dependence. There is another reason: the belief that there is one right person in the world for each of us, someone who has exactly that set of properties we need, want, and passionately hope for in our beloved. Since this person is perfect, and perfection (as scholastic philosophers said about God) is contrary to multiplicity, we love this creature exclusively (timelessly). The heroine of Doris Lessing's "How I Finally Lost My Heart"[39] once believed that "one must search for an A, or a B, or a C or a D with a certain combination of desirable or sympathetic qualities so that one may click, or spontaneously combust" with that person. This search for the person with the right properties is "the [second] most important business in life" (after making money). Therefore, "even when we are . . . being very serious indeed with one person we still have an eighth of an eye cocked in case some stranger unexpectedly encountered might turn out to be even more serious. We are . . . in the right to taste, test, sip and sample a thousand people on our way to the *real* one." This looks deceptively like nonexclusive loving, or at best serial exclusivity. It is not an accident of psychology, but rather the inherent logic of this philosophy that the heroine also believes retrospectively that earlier loves, though serious at the time, were never as serious as her current love, indeed were not really loves at all: she believes that love is timelessly exclusive, and hence one's first (real) love is one's only love.[40] Searching for and finding the person with the right properties, putting off union with y because a better z might be around the corner, forming a union with y yet holding back a part of oneself because z might turn up—these frenetic erosic maneuvers assume exclusivity. Why keep an eye cocked unless one desires exclusivity? Otherwise, one might as well join with them all. Our heroine, however, is not just a neurotic about whom the rest of us can say, "there but for the grace of eros go I." Whether our loves are serial and bracketed or nonexclusively overlapping, we either perceive or rationalize our current love as the best of the lot. Their very existence may depend on our "bestowing" on our current love relationship the value of being superior, even if we remember quite clearly wonderful earlier relationships.

9. AGAPIC EXCLUSIVITY

Rejecting erosic personal love in order to achieve the contribution to self-respect that comes with exclusivity assumes that agapic personal love is more reliably exclusive. But if personal love is neither property-based nor reason-dependent (or when it lacks that structure), is exclusivity to be expected? In order to assess the ability of the agape tradition to provide a plausible theory of personal love, we must first discuss agape itself.

God's agape for humans and human neighbor-love for humans (insofar as neighbor-love copies God's exemplar) are extended toward humans universally; all humans are equally the objects of these loves. Why are these loves object-universal? One answer is that every human has the same property, P, in virtue of which he or she is an object of love: "being a human being." P is not conceived of as a meritorious property, for otherwise agape and neighbor-love would be universal erosic loves. Rather, humans have no value in themselves; being loved by God, they thereby become valuable. By analogy, being neighbor-loved by humans, humans become valuable. Or one might say: treating all humans as having equal value is the prime act of neighbor-love. Since P is not meritorious, x's neighbor-love for y because y has P is not erosic love. P serves not as the basis of neighbor-love but as an indicator of the *scope* of neighbor-love. In the case of God's agape, God loves because that is God's nature; in the case of humans, x neighbor-loves y because x obeys the commandment to love all those having P (including himself).

Alternative interpretations of neighbor-love seem unavoidably to make it a universal erosic love (but not a vulgar or selective erosic love). The property P that all humans have, "being a human being," is meritorious in the sense that it represents the fact that a human is a creation of God (and therefore has value) or contains, or is, a piece of God. Then this meritorious P both indicates the scope of, and is the basis for, neighbor-love. Or "being a human being" may be meritorious in that every human has objective value as the result of being loved by God. God of course does not love humans in virtue of their merit; instead, in loving humans God bestows value on them. It is this bestowed value that makes each human a worthy object of neighbor-love, and neighbor-love becomes a universal eros. Neighbor-love can even be understood secularly in Kantian terms.[41] Every human has value, and the same value, in virtue of being an autonomous, rational being. Every person is and must be regarded as an end-in-himself and as possessing inherent value. In virtue of this value, every human is an object of "respect-love."

Is it odd to conceive of neighbor-love as a universal eros? On the one hand, yes. Diotima's insistence that exclusivity in an erosic lover is a fault—he or she can and should recognize the beauty in all bodies and minds (*Symposium* 210a4ff.)—then seems scarcely different from the response of neighbor-love to the inherent value of every human. In this form neighbor-love would also seem barely different from cases of sexual love in which the lover's standards of an acceptable sexual partner are such as to include all members of one or the other sex, or all members of all sexes.[42] Thus when Karol Wojtyla rebukes a Philo for avowing "I love you madly, Laura, and all those like you!" (this is not love, says Wojtyla),[43] we might find it strange, in principle, that Wojtyla does not rebuke the neighbor-lover for loving me and all those like me. But on the other hand, this conception of neighbor-love is not odd. Even in the universal eros interpretations of neighbor-love, a person is "valued as, or in that he is, a person qua human existent and not because he is such-and-such a kind of person distinguishing him from others." Humans are loved in virtue of their "generic" endowment, not in virtue of "idiosyncratic qualities and attainments."[44] Hence a distinction can be made between the neighbor-love that focuses on the generic value a person has qua person, and erosic loves that focus on the particular attractive properties people have by nature, nurture, or social convention. The structures of the two loves are the same, but they place their own characteristic restriction on the type of property involved in love. Further, in neighbor-love there is "no exclusiveness, no partiality, no elitism,"[45] while erosic love in principle allows for preferentiality. That is, neighbor-love is logically nonexclusive, while erosic love can focus on idiosyncratic attractive properties and thereby exclude many persons from the role of beloved. Indeed, for Kierkegaard what is wrong with "erotic love" is precisely that it is preferential and exclusive, although the variety of eros he has in mind is the romanticism described above by Doris Lessing.[46]

If we want to keep agape and eros structurally distinct, we should favor the interpretation of neighbor-love according to which it is not a universal eros. This is especially important if the agape tradition is to be used to fashion an analytically distinct view of personal love. Further, an agapic account of personal love probably could not yield exclusivity if neighbor-love is construed as a universal eros. Thus, we should interpret the agapic P as indicating only the scope of neighbor-love and emphasize that neighbor-love is, or results in, the creation of value. Then the agape tradition delivers a distinctive view of personal love, in claiming that personal love is neither property-based nor reason-dependent, and permits two arguments that agapic personal love is exclusive.

First, if x's loving y for having attractive properties S implies that x's love is not expected to be exclusive, then x's not loving y in virtue of y's properties implies that x's love should be exclusive. That is, if x erosically loves y, then the appearance of S in another person will tend to induce x to love nonexclusively; but if love is not reason-dependent, the appearance of the same S in another person should not have any effect. Thus, if love is agapic in structure, there is no reason to think that it will not be exclusive. This argument, of course, will not do the trick. From the fact that x's loving y erosically means that x is not expected to love y exclusively, it does not follow that x's not loving y erosically means that x will love y exclusively. If x loves y not because of y's attractive properties but for some other reason, whether x is expected to love y exclusively will depend on what other reason x has for loving y, if any. Suppose the explanation of x's agapically loving y is the same as the explanation of God's loving humans: it is x's nature to love. Then x's agapic personal love for y is due altogether to something about x and nothing about y. But what is it about x's nature that should make us expect x to love y exclusively? Surely it is un-illuminating to say that x loves y exclusively because it is x's nature to love exclusively. For all we know, x by nature may be capable of loving nonex-clusively. Or suppose x has no grounds at all for loving y but has just *decided* to love y; then cannot x just decide to love z as well? Since x's selection of a beloved is not based on y's attractive properties, we have no firm handle on exactly how x selected that (or any) beloved and hence have no way to tell whether x will be an exclusive lover.[47] Indeed, since x's agapic personal love is not prevented by unattractive properties, everyone is a candidate for x's love, and so agapic personal love may be less exclusive than erosic, in which a person's having certain defects will eliminate him from the ranks of potential beloveds. Agape itself is nondiscriminatory; no wonder that infusing agape into personal love will not necessarily make it exclusive.

The second argument is this: in agapic personal love, x does not respond to y's value but creates value in y or makes y valuable. Then x's agapic personal love for y will be exclusive either if there are strong limits on the ability to create value in others or if the concept "creating value" implies exclusivity. But this argument also fails. If none of the arguments we already considered for a doctrine of exclusivity is successful, then it is unlikely that a person's ability to create value in others is limited to one recipient. If x is not logically barred from sharing interests, capabilities, information, and experiences with more than one person, it is futile to defend the thesis that x can, conceptually, bestow value on only one person. If the thesis is that for practical and psychological reasons it will be difficult for x to create value in more than one person, we still need a fairly clear account of what the creation of value amounts to and of what obstacles might prevent x's creating value in more than one person. In light of the fact that for neighbor-love itself there are not supposed to be any serious obstacles to loving nonexclusively (we are told neighbor-love may be "difficult" but are reminded that with determination we can pull it off), it is unlikely that the agape tradition has the power to show that personal love will be exclusive. Further, an x who loves y erosically can also create value in y (in addition to responding to y's prior value) as a result of loving y. So if agapic personal love does attain exclusivity precisely through x's creation of value in y, erosic personal love will equally attain exclusivity. Actually, however, that love involves the creation of value provides little reason to think that either agapic or erosic love will be exclusive.

We have exhausted almost all the resources of the agape tradition: we appealed to the fact that neither God's agape nor neighbor-love is reason-dependent; to God's agape as flowing from God's nature; and to the fact that God's agape and neighbor-love create value in their objects. There is one feature of neighbor-love that we have not yet examined. Remember that "being a human being" indicates the scope of neighbor-love but not its basis. Why, then, does x neighbor-love y and all the others who come within x's field of vision? Because x obeys the Commandment to Love. This suggests one more defense of the claim that agapic personal love is exclusive: exclusivity is a moral obligation, required not by the logic or psychology of love but by the ethics of love or more general ethical considerations. There are, in fact, arguments that defend the moral value of exclusive love. And perhaps they are good arguments. But notice that such arguments presuppose that love is not by its nature or by human psychology exclusive; otherwise the moral demand to love exclusively would be incoherent. Hence these arguments admit that not merely in virtue of its structure can agapic personal love be expected to be more reliably exclusive than erosic.

10. LOVING PROPERTIES

Suppose that x loves y because y has S, and x also loves z because z has S. "There are individuals," says Ortega y Gasset, "who in the course of their lives love several women; but with clear persistency each one is a repetition of a single . . . type."[48] In a sense, this x who loves both y and z for having S *is* an exclusive lover, never straying from a specific type: "This [is a] kind of masked fidelity, in which . . . a single . . . woman is loved under the guise of many women." Freudian love for a mother-substitute is a faithful love in this sense, and even the agapic neighbor-lover loves a "type," since his beloveds have a common characteristic. Speaking literally, however, if x loves both y and z for having S, x is not an exclusive lover (as long as x does not believe y and z are the same person). Further, if S elicits x's emotion toward both y and z, and hence x's emotion is directed at two tokens of the same type, perhaps x does not *love* y and z at all. A thesis about what it means to "love the person" can replace a thesis about exclusivity in defending the first horn of Gellner's paradox: if xAy for S and xAz for S, then x's attitude is not love, not because love "can have only one object" but because no attitude directed at tokens of a type can be love.

When x loves both y and z for having S, x might not love *them* because x might, instead, be loving S itself. What appears to be the basis of x's love for y and z (namely, S) is actually the object of x's love. This might even be true when x exclusively "loves" y for having S. However, x's love might involve x's loving y (the object) for having S (the basis) as well as x's loving S. Thus, S is both the basis of x's love for y and one of the two objects that x loves. (Is this x a nonexclusive lover because x loves y and S cotemporaneously?) Even in this complex case one might argue that in loving y for having S, x's love never attains the level of "love for the person" and, therefore, that x's attitude toward y is not genuine love. We shall return to this issue (chaps. 10 and 13).

Robert Brown claims that if we love the properties of a person, it is difficult to explain why "we love a particular person who possesses them rather than making us confine ourselves to loving those in whomever they are found."[49] Thus, not only does x's loving y because y has S conflict with exclusivity, but also x's loving S itself conflicts with exclusivity: if x loves S, and if both y and z have S, then x is expected to love both y and z. But this conclusion is not quite correct. If x does love S as it exists in y and also loves S in z, then since x loves only S, and neither y nor z, we cannot accuse x of engaging in nonexclusive personal loves. Since x loves only S, x's attitude toward y is not recurring toward z because x has no attitude toward y to begin with. The lover of properties, even when the properties she loves exist in many people and she loves all these instances, is not a multiple personal lover.

Indeed, the lover of properties might be an exclusive lover: if x loves *only* the one property P, wherever it occurs, x is loving P exclusively.[50] Ordinarily, however, x will be attracted to several properties, loving both P and Q at the same time. Further, a property is a thing, and there are, ordinarily, many nonpersonal or inanimate things we love. So loving properties could be exclusive, although given the variety of items we find attractive or valuable it does not usually turn out that way. But imagine that Scruton's Beethoven Violin Concerto lover, who loves no other music, is so obsessed with it that she loves nothing else in the world. Or consider the intense passion of some patriots and other monomaniacs. We need not, however, look for oddballs to see that a lover of properties may be exclusively devoted to one property. For Plato (or Diotima) the only thing the true lover loves is beauty, or The Beautiful as manifested imperfectly in humans and things. If loving beauty means that we never attain love for persons, that is for Plato no strike against us. If we want love to be constant and exclusive, we must put aside personal love in favor of the superior search for Beauty, just as some lovers of God do.

11. SEXUAL EXCLUSIVITY

If personal love includes an element of sexual desire, either conceptually or by human psychology, then love will tend to be exclusive to the extent that sexual desire is exclusive. In *The Passions of the Soul,* Descartes wrote: "Although we [men?] see many persons of the opposite sex, yet we do not desire many at one time. . . . But when we observe something in one of them which is more attractive than anything we observe at that moment in others, this determines our soul to feel towards that one alone all the inclination which nature gives it to pursue the good which it represents as the greatest we could possess."[51] Sexual desire, in this view, is at least serially exclusive by its nature ("at that moment"). Descartes, of course, is not alone in holding this view. "Eros makes a man really want, not a woman, but one particular woman . . . in some mysterious but quite indisputable fashion," says C. S. Lewis.[52] But for Descartes the phenomenon is not mysterious; it is explainable in terms of "nature," which has "implanted certain impressions in the brain." Today, Descartes's explanation is reoffered by some sociobiologists, who try to provide an evolutionary account of serial sexual exclusivity—mostly in women but also, in some theories of the pair-bond, in men.[53]

For other thinkers, sexuality is an indiscriminate instinct, but it can be brought to focus on one object by personal love, which is a nonnatural controlling device: "instinct tends to amplify indefinitely the number of objects which satisfy it," says Ortega, "whereas love tends toward exclusivism"; hence, "nothing immunizes a male against other sexual attractions so well as amorous enthusiasm for a *certain* woman."[54] This optimism about the power of love to make exclusive a sexual drive that is not by its own nature exclusive has been, through the ages, the brunt of cynical humor. In the twentieth century there is the wit of James Thurber: "I am in love, . . . but just the same I don't like the way I looked at Miriam last night. . . . And if she *is* my darling . . . what caused me to take such a long, critical look at the girl in the red-and-brown scarf this morning when I was breakfasting in the Brevoort?"[55]

The argument suggested by the Cartesian picture of sexuality is that personal love is exclusive because sexual desire is exclusive. Assume that x loves both y and z at the same time; then x will sexually desire both y and z; but this cannot happen because sexual desire is felt as exclusive. Hence, our initial assumption, that x loves nonexclusively, must be false. The cynics, of course, deny that sexual desire is exclusive and even assert that it tends not to be exclusive; so, if personal love includes sexual desire, then we should not expect love to be exclusive. Alternatively, we might say that even if x's loving y does not rule out x's sexually desiring both y and z, x's loving y conceptually (or psychologically) rules out x's acting on x's desire for z. Hence, x's claim to love y is not defeated by x's merely desiring z but by x's actually engaging in sexual activity with z. This argument turns the tables; it argues that sexual *activity* is exclusive, given the nature of love. It might even be seen as a version of the intimacy arguments considered earlier: if x loves y, x will restrict x's sexual activity to y, since x's engaging in sexual activity with z negates the intimacy of the x-y love.

In the Judeo-Christian tradition, believers are enjoined to love and worship God and to have no other objects of devotion before Him; to love Him with all their heart, soul, and mind (Matt. 4:10, 22:37–39). Loving God exclusively, preferentially, and fervently is how one loves God well; or loving God that way is either a moral or religious duty.[56] Similarly, the claim that personal love is exclusive may be an evaluation of the quality of love or a moral pronouncement (recall Newton-Smith on Jaspers). One argument that love ought to be exclusive assumes that love necessarily includes a sexual element: the immorality of multiple sexual relations is transferred to multiple loves (in the same way that some have transferred the phenomenal exclusivity of sexual desire to love). The argument rests on there being something morally wrong with multiple, overlapping sexual relations independently of the fact that the person who engages in them might also love someone; otherwise the wrongness of multiple sexual relations could not explain why multiple loves are morally wrong. That is, the argument must be distinguished from the argument that because personal love involves a mutual promise of sexual fidelity, sexual relations outside the love are morally wrong. In this case, the moral obligation to love exclusively does not follow from the immorality of multiple sexual relations, but the immorality of the latter follows from a contingent fact about some love relationships—that they include promises—not from a truth about the logic or psychology of love.

But if personal love does not necessarily include sexual desire as a component, or if multiple sexual relations are not always morally wrong, why would anyone claim that x ought to love y and no one else? If love is a good thing, does not morality imply that x ought to love nonexclusively? The common reply to this thought is that perhaps ideally x ought to love nonexclusively; in a perfect world x would be able to do so, but in the real world there are practical limits on x's time, energy, and capacity to show concern. But these practical considerations are not morally neutral. To argue that the cost to x in terms of x's resources properly places a limit on what can be expected of x as a lover is to enter the moral debate, not to sidestep it. The argument would have to explain why the value of love does not imply that x ought to make a greater effort or rearrange priorities in order to maximize the extent of x's love and concern. (Many *do* argue that some x's ought to make a greater effort in showing concern to y, when y is their only beloved.[57] So urging people to make greater efforts to show concern is not a wild idea.) Of course, x cannot be expected to show loving concern to so many people that x's own welfare is jeopardized (see 12.4). But this observation is not very satisfying: there is a lot of room between x's being niggardly with x's concern (that is, loving only when doing so is consistent with x's own good) and x's extending concern as widely as possible without obliterating x. But the point remains; loving exclusively might be in practice the easiest course, yet to defend exclusivity morally by invoking its ease is to travel the road of reactionary complacency, not the road of revolutionary transformation. Kierkegaard, I think, would here for once agree with me. (See 12.8, 12.9, and 13.10.)

CHAPTER 10 *Constancy*

The foreverness of real love is . . . why even unrequited love is a source of joy. The human soul craves for the eternal of which, apart from certain rare mysteries of religion, only love and art can give a glimpse.

—Iris Murdoch, *The Black Prince*

Love lives in the moment. . . . There is only the moment. The now. . . . Love is now!

—Leo Buscaglia, *Love*

1. A NEW PARADOX

Suppose that x has an emotion at t_1 toward y in virtue of y's S, but at a later time t_2 y no longer has S. As in Gellner's paradox, there are two exhaustive, mutually exclusive possibilities: either x's emotion toward y continues or it ends. Both possibilities imply that x's emotion is not love: (A) if x's emotion toward y continues when y no longer has S, x's emotion is not love because x's emotion at t_2 is not "tightly connected" to y via y's properties; or (B) if x's emotion toward y ends at t_2, it had not been love because love is constant. This new paradox assumes that love never ends ("Love's not Time's fool") or at least does not end merely because its object has changed: "Love is not love which alters when it alteration finds."[1] Thus, the new paradox is a vehicle for expressing the prima facie incompatibility of reason-dependence and constancy. Love might be reason-dependent and not constant, as in the lower stages of Plato's Ascent, and love might be reason-independent and constant, as in agape ("Love never fails").[2] But can personal love be both constant and reason-dependent?

Gellner's view that love is an E-type emotion does not solve this paradox. An E-type lover fails to respond to another person who has S, which says nothing about x's emotion when y loses S. But analyzing love as an E-type emotion is relevant to a different situation in which constancy is an issue. In this other sort of case, x's emotion perishes even though y still has S. Note the similarity between (i) x's loving y at t_1 in virtue of S, but x's not loving z at t_1 even though z has S (because x is an E-type lover) and (ii) x's loving y at t_1 in virtue of S, but x's not loving y at t_2 even though y still has S. In case (i), x's love-reasons are not object-general, while in (ii) x's love-reasons are not time-general. If x as an E-type lover has no trouble refusing to apply x's reason ("has S") to another person z satisfying that description, such an x should also have no trouble refusing to reapply this reason to y, who still has S, at a later time. The irrationality of E-type lover is therefore more extensive than we originally thought.

The uniqueness solution to Gellner's paradox can be modified to solve our new paradox. Recall that x can love y exclusively if x loves y for S, only y has S, and an object's having S is necessary for x to love anyone. X's love for y will be both constant and exclusive if the conditions hold not only at t_1 but always. Hence, rigidity of character is sufficient for constant erosic love: y always has S, and x always responds to S. If y changes, constancy is jeopardized, unless (perhaps in response to y's love) x alters x's preferences. The problem of orchestrating simultaneous changes that match arises also in the desire-satisfaction model. X will love y constantly only if the unchanging y always satisfies x's rigid, unchanging desires; or if y's ability to satisfy x's desires changes to keep pace with x's changing needs; or if x changes x's needs so they are satisfiable by y's evolving abilities. But if these scenarios are possible, then contrary to claim (A) of the new paradox, x's emotion can be love if it continues when y no longer has S, as long as it has a new erosic basis. Hence, it is not true that erosic love can be constant only when grounded in enduring rather than transitory properties (that is, love would not alter because it would have no alteration to find). Love's being grounded in enduring properties may be sufficient for the constancy of erosic love, but it is not necessary. And note that invoking y's enduring properties as the basis of x's love does not solve the new paradox, but only sidesteps it by denying the change in y that the paradox assumes. This move is identical to "solving" Gellner's paradox by postulating that x never meets the z who also has S, and it fails for the same reason: we can always ask x, "What if, even though it will not happen, y *does* lose S?"

We can see, then, that there are three kinds of constant lover. Constant lover C_1 loves y at t_1 because y has S and still loves y at t_2 because y still has S; this erosic love is constant because y rigidly has S and C_1 rigidly responds to S. Constant lover C_2 loves y at t_1 because y has S and loves y at t_2 because y has T; this erosic love is constant because the partners change in tandem. Constant lover C_3 loves y at t_1 and t_2, despite the fact that y has changed, his love never being based on y's properties; this is Shakespeare's reason-independent (agapic) constancy. C_1 and C_2 can be compared with two kinds of nonexclusive lover. Multiple lover M_1 loves y and z because both have S; M_1 is an erosic lover who rigidly responds to S. Multiple lover M_2 loves y because y has

S and loves z because z has T; M_2 is an erosic lover who responds flexibly to various attractive properties. I see little difference between constant lover C_1 and multiple lover M_1: the facts that M_1 loves nonexclusively and C_1 loves constantly are due to precisely the same thing, that the subject of love responds to the same S. And there is little difference between C_2 and M_2: the facts that M_2 loves nonexclusively and C_2 loves constantly are due to precisely the same thing, that the subject of love can respond to different properties. Hence that which makes constancy possible also makes nonexclusivity possible; whether x is a flexible or rigid constant lover, x's loving y constantly shows that x would not be inconsistent in loving nonexclusively. This intuitively odd relationship between exclusivity and constancy is found not only in erosic love. Compare constant lover C_3 with a third type of multiple lover, M_3, who loves y and z (and countless others) not in virtue of their attractive properties but wholly in virtue of M_3's nature. There is little difference between C_3 and M_3. The facts that C_3 loves constantly and M_3 loves nonexclusively are due to precisely the same thing, that in both cases the love is reason-independent; that which allows C_3 to love constantly is that which allows M_3 to love nonexclusively.

Notice that the case in which y once (at t_1) in fact had S and loses it (at t_2), where x's beliefs about y's properties are always correct, and the case in which y never had S, but x believed falsely (at t_1) that y had S and now (at t_2) recognizes correctly that y does not have S, are structurally equivalent. So suppose that x loves y at t_1, believing that y has S, and that at t_2 x discovers that y did not and does not have S; as in our new paradox, either x continues to love y or x's love ends. (Or x discovers that y has a defect that x has been overlooking. For example, x comes to see that y is, after all, indistinguishable from an order of smelts; see 1.3.) About this case W. Newton-Smith claims that "if [x] would feel as strongly about [y] should he come to see that she does not possess the properties in question, he does in fact . . . love her. He has simply been radically mistaken about her."[3] Thus, Newton-Smith denies the first-horn claim, (A). He also accepts the second-horn claim, (B): if x would not feel the same toward y "if he came to realize his mistake, . . . he never loved anyone at all." Whether x loves y is easily settled, for Newton-Smith, by determining if x still loves y when x discovers the mistake: x's emotion is love if and only if it persists when x finds out what y is really like.

This thesis is implausible at least in those cases in which x believes falsely that y is a saint and later discovers that y is, or has become, a monster (8.8). Further, this view implies that x's going through a process normatively required by the standards of rationality—making sure x's emotion is not based on false beliefs (8.6)—could result in x's "discovering" retroactively that x never loved y. But x's eventual realization that x's emotion is badly grounded, and hence its coming to an end (as it should), does not necessarily mean that x had never loved y. We would not reach that conclusion about hate or other emotions. Finally, Newton-Smith does not pause to ask *"who* was responsible for x's false belief?" If x falsely believes that y has S because y deliberately deceived x into believing that y had S, there is surely less reason to think that x's emotion, when it ends upon the discovery, had never been love.

Suppose that because y has S, x has an emotion toward y at t_1, which is apparently hate, and that at t_2 y no longer has S. If x's emotion ends at t_2, we do not conclude that x did not hate y; indeed, a mark of rational hate is that it does perish at t_2. The same holds for admiration and resentment. Furthermore, if y no longer has S at t_2, yet x's emotion continues, we do not immediately conclude that x's emotion is not hate. Instead we conclude that x's emotion probably switched from erosic to agapic hate (and is now irrational) or that x has found something else to hate about y. So we are not compelled to say that if x's emotion continues when y no longer has S, x's emotion is not or had never been love. Perhaps x's love has switched from being erosic to agapic (x has become a C_3 lover), or x's emotion is grounded in different properties of y (x is a C_2 lover). Here, then, is the dispute between the two views of personal love: from an erosic perspective, if x's love continues when y no longer has the S that induced x's love, x's love is rational and ideal only if it is now based on something else about y; from an agapic perspective, that x's love continues unconditionally when y no longer has S is exactly what is expected for genuine love.

2. VARIETIES OF CONSTANCY

When we were analyzing the concept of exclusivity, we had a choice between a restrictive notion (x timelessly loves only y) and a fuzzy notion (serial, bracketed) that left open the number of beloveds x could have and still be a lover. Regarding constancy, the choice is between a restrictive notion (x will always love y) and a fuzzy notion that leaves open the length of time x's emotion must last in order to be love. The fuzzy notion of exclusivity got caught in the middle between proponents of the doctrine of strict exclusivity and proponents of nonexclusivity, both claiming that serial, bracketed exclusivity was not exclusivity at all; the fuzzy notion of constancy has similar troubles.

The doctrine of *strict constancy* claims that "love is constant" means that love lasts forever or, less poetically, that if x begins to love y at t_1, x will love y at all times after t_1; thus, if x's emotion toward y ever ends, it had never been love. This implies that x will love y after y dies (for all eternity), if we take it literally.

Our ordinary beliefs about the constancy of love, however, do not require, though they do allow, that x loves y after y dies. And to say that x loves y after y dies might entail that a disembodied soul is the object of x's love. The mere analysis of love's constancy, however, should not commit us to the thesis that disembodied souls exist and that they can be loved (these claims should be defended some other way). William Lyons claims that "love would normally be thought to be about present objects though it does seem that one might still love someone knowing that they are dead and while not believing in any form of afterlife. And . . . it seems implausible to claim that the person . . . is just reliving a past love . . . or that one is loving a person . . . in one's thoughts or imagination."[4] But if all these latter possibilities are ruled out, what is it to love a dead person? Perhaps the right move here is to deny that x *can* love y after y dies. If a necessary condition of x's loving y is that x desires to benefit y, then x cannot love the dead y, if the dead cannot be benefited. X's loving the dead y, then, is (for example) really only x's longing for y. Of course, x might believe that x can benefit the dead (through prayer, and so on), but in this case x believes that y still exists—as a disembodied soul. Similarly, if a necessary condition of x's loving y is that x wants to be in y's presence, then if y is alive x simply hops on the subway; but if y is dead, either x cannot love y or x must believe y exists as a disembodied soul and so desires to be with y eventually in the afterworld.

Let us take the doctrine of strict constancy as claiming, instead, that if x loves y at t_1, then x loves y at all times after t_1, as long as both x and y are alive— "until death do us part"—and that if x's emotion ends before y dies, it had never been love.[5] Even this is not precise enough: no one expects x to love y if *x* is alive but irreversibly comatose; the point of this analysis, however, is that if x loves y, then x's emotion continues if *y,* instead, is irreversibly comatose. (Note that the analysis is not merely a psychological claim—if x loves y, x's state of mind is such that x always loves y, as long as y is alive—but a thesis about the logic or nature of love.) Kierkegaard rejects this modified doctrine of strict constancy, claiming that y's death is an excellent test of the genuineness of x's love; after y's death, x can no longer get anything from y, so the continuation of x's love shows that x's attitude toward y was not instrumental.[6] Regarding love for an inanimate thing, Robert Brown says something similar: "The test of genuine love [is] that the love continues after all possible use of the object merely as a means . . . ceases."[7] (Is not the object's being of no use guaranteed only when, *pace* Kierkegaard, it no longer exists?) We should infer, then, that if x's love persists when y does not reciprocate (Kierkegaard: cannot reciprocate, because dead), this is also an excellent sign that x's love is genuine, for here, too, x's love does not depend on x's getting something from y. Although there is wisdom in these suggestions, they do not disturb the ordinary belief that the constancy of love does not require loving the dead. There must be ways to determine whether x loves y that do not depend on y's dying or not reciprocating (the quality of x's concern for y or the depth of x's intimacy with y), since we do believe some x's when they claim to love a y who is alive and reciprocates x's love.

The doctrine of strict constancy can be employed either critically or defensively. The critical use is suggested by Shakespeare (and Karol Wojtyla; see below): if x's emotion toward y ends, it had never been love—despite x's protests to the contrary. The doctrine thus connotes a negative evaluation; something was wrong with x's emotion such that it did not measure up to genuine love. But the doctrine of strict constancy can also be used defensively: if x's emotion ends, then it had not been love—which relieves x of the burden of having had to do those things that are expected of lovers. And if x's emotion ends, x is now free to pursue genuine love once again, a love that might very well be strictly constant. The escape clause of strict constancy thereby makes it easier to embrace the doctrine of timeless exclusivity. For x's loving only y and later loving only z does not violate the conditions of timeless exclusivity as long as (by the doctrine of strict constancy) the termination of x's love for y means that x had never loved y. In this way, z becomes x's first and only beloved.

Strict constancy is most often associated with the second view of personal love, although the reason-independence of agapic personal love does not entail that love will be strictly constant (as I explain later). But strict constancy is theoretically compatible with the first view; erosic personal love can be strictly constant if x and y are rigid in their preferences and properties or if they are continuously flexible. Kierkegaard would object to my saying in one breath that both agapic and erosic personal love can be strictly constant; he distinguishes "love is constant" when it is said about neighbor-love and when it is said about romantic eros. To say of neighbor-love (or agape) that it is strictly constant is to say that it "never fails . . . it abides." For Kierkegaard, the constancy of neighbor-love is understood psychologically as adherence to duty, whereas romantic eros is constant, if at all, in virtue of psychological inclination alone. But the plain fact is that romantic eros does not last. We need to protect ourselves from that knowledge, because we want it to last, because we think love *should* last. In our confusion about the different kinds of love we mistake a pretender for the real thing and end up expecting strict constancy where it is inappropriate. So we conveniently invoke the escape clause: any case of romantic love that does not last was not love to begin with; we are then free to look for our first and real love all over again.[8] Of course, Kierkegaard is right that romantic eros is not a constant love. It does not follow, however, that wanting personal love to last forever is senseless; nor is it a shuffle to claim that some of the personal loves that buckle under the strain had been love, while others had dissipated long before the strain.

The fuzzy analysis of "love is constant," the doctrine of *indefinite constancy,* does not require that x love y forever, yet claims that an emotion must last some length of time for it to count as love. In this view, love is like grief and resentment. It makes no sense to suppose that one experiences only momentary flashes of these emotions (unlike pain or a bolt of blind rage); their enduring for an indefinite amount of time is logically necessary for having them at all.[9] The favored analysis of constancy seems to be indefinite constancy, as the favored analysis of exclusivity seemed to be serial, bracketed exclusivity. At least, strict constancy must give way to a less restrictive analysis, as timeless exclusivity had to give way to a weaker notion. The trick is to say something more precise than simply that love must last some length of time to be love, otherwise the doctrine of indefinite constancy gets caught in the embarrassing middle between the claim that love is strictly constant (which does not see indefinite constancy as constancy at all) and the claim that love admits of *no* time constraints (for example, Leo Buscaglia's claim, reminiscent of the metaphysics of Baba Ram Dass, that "love lives in the moment"; see epigraph).[10] For to claim that love must last some vague length of time is not to put *any* time constraint on love.

The doctrine of strict constancy requires one more refinement. If x's loving y means that x will love y at least until y dies, then x's loving y also means that x will love y at least as long as y remains y. X's loving y until y dies and x's loving y as long as y remains y are equivalent under the assumption that y's identity as y is only a matter of bodily integrity: the later person y is the person whose body is the causal descendent of the numerically distinct body of the earlier y. Strict constancy, as I define it, requires x to love this bodily identified y for as long as y exists; in particular, y's undergoing dramatic personality changes does not count as y's no longer being y and therefore does not count as y's no longer existing ("dying"). The major thrust of the doctrine of strict constancy is that if x's emotion is love, it will continue toward this changed y. If we make a different assumption about the beloved's identity, however, a more specific version of the doctrine of indefinite constancy emerges: if x loves y at t_1, then x loves y at all times after t_1, as long as y remains morally and psychologically y. This analysis of constancy does not require x to love y if y has undergone a change in identity and has become z, where z's body is causally continuous with y's, yet z's character, morally or psychologically, is quite different. That is, if x's emotion toward y ends when y becomes z, its termination does not put into doubt that x's emotion earlier had been love. If x no longer loves y when y becomes z, x's love is gone only because its object is gone, not because there is some fault in x's emotion. Indeed, were x to love this brand-new z that y has become, merely because x had loved y, we may doubt that x had loved y at all, since who y was is seen to have had little to do with x's emotion. But if x loves this z who is qualitatively different from y because z is attractive to x independently of z's bodily continuity with y, x may be accused of loving nonexclusively (x's loves for y and z are separate loves), but x cannot be accused of failing to love y constantly.

This version of indefinite constancy (*identity constancy*) does not take "forever" literally (as does strict constancy) and means "indefinite" seriously: actuarial tables can inform x what the "forever" of strict constancy likely amounts to, but no statistics predict how long people retain their moral and psychological identities. But in one respect identity constancy is indistinguishable from strict constancy: on both views, x's love must persist as long as y exists, and if x's love for y ends when y no longer exists, this is not a failure of love's constancy but the absence of an object to love. To keep identity constancy and strict constancy distinct, we must assume that they presuppose different notions of personal identity, in which case their consequences will be different. For example, if x no longer loves y because the ordinarily hedonistic y has become celibate, the doctrine of strict constancy implies that this cessation constitutes a failure of x's love to be constant and puts into doubt x's claim to have loved y; identity constancy implies that the cessation of x's love is not a failure of constancy but the absence of an object to love, since y's celibacy represents a radical break with y's character. The difficult question faced by the doctrine of identity constancy, but avoided by strict constancy, is this: when does a change in y count merely as either an internal, smooth development of y's enduring moral-psychological identity or a trivial change having no relation to y's identity, and when does a change in y count as a development beyond y's character, significant enough to constitute the appearance of z on the scene? For this reason, this analysis provides only a fuzzy notion of constancy. The difficulty—or the ease?—of answering this question even allows some lovers to extract an excuse from identity constancy's escape clause, as recognized by John Donne ("Woman's Constancy"):

> Now thou hast lov'd me one whole day,
> To morrow when thou leav'st, what wilt thou say?
> Wilt thou then Antedate some new made vow?
>   Or say that now
> We are not just those persons, which we were?

On the bright side, identity constancy makes room for both rigidity (sameness of identity) and flexibility (changes within that identity) in the course of love.

Another version of indefinite constancy maintains that the lover must have an appropriate intention or desire regarding constancy. The thesis is not exactly that beliefs about the constancy of love play a role in love: believing, and acting on the belief, that a love will persist helps it to persist; whereas believing that the love will not persist can be a self-fulfilling prophecy. Rather, the doctrine of *intention constancy* claims that x's loving y at t_1 is compatible with x's not loving y at t_2, as long as at all times t at which x does love y, x intends the love to continue (indefinitely) beyond t—which might include t_2. Hence, a conceptual requirement for x's emotion toward y to be love is that x does not intend that x's emotion continue only for a specific length of time or that x intends the emotion to continue indefinitely. Annette Baier, for example, claims that "one must in *some* way intend the love to continue, for it to be love at all." J. M. Stafford agrees: "The will to make the attachment a lasting one is a necessary condition of love." We might defend this analysis by arguing, with Michael Bayles, that the "concern and trust [of love] would be seriously weakened or destroyed by setting a time limit" in advance[11] or that intending to love only for as long as certain conditions are met negates the commitment involved in love.[12] One must not deliberately refuse to make certain kinds of plans with the beloved, which plans imply that the love relationship will last indefinitely; one must not make plans that definitely imply a specific limit on the length of one's love. The point is not that x's refusing to envisage a future with y is bound to be seen by y as callousness and to drive y away. Rather, the intention to love constantly is supposed to follow from the nature of love or from other necessary features of love.

The doctrine of intention constancy might claim, of course, that the intention conceptually required by love is that the love continue forever. But this will not do. If love is not required to be strictly constant, it makes little sense to think that intending it to be strictly constant is required. If it is claimed that love requires only the intention that it lasts indefinitely, this problem is avoided. But the doctrine of intention constancy gets caught in the middle. From the perspective of strict constancy, the intention that love continue indefinitely is incompatible with love. For to intend to love only indefinitely is in effect to announce at the very beginning, "you can't count on me in the very long run." And from the perspective of the other side, genuine lovers need not have even these weaker intentions. "Nothing in the concept of love," it might be claimed, entails that the lover must intend it to continue indefinitely. Two lovers x and y might show concern for each other, share intense experiences with each other, and so forth, and yet never breathe a word or think a thought about their future. They live in the now. Or they might even intend, by mutual arrangement, that their relationship last only the year they have available to be together, recognizing in advance that their love will slowly die after that period is over.

In order to make the doctrine of indefinite constancy less vague, I wish to lay out another way to distinguish, analytically, among strict constancy, indefinite constancy, and the doctrine that love admits of no time constraints at all. Let us say that an R_1 reason for the end of love is a reason that strongly brings into doubt that the love earlier had been genuine; an R_1 reason might even negate the emotion's claim to have been love. And let us say that an R_2 reason for the end of love does not call into question the claim that the emotion earlier had been love. The doctrine of strict constancy, then, is logically equivalent to the thesis that the set of R_2 reasons is empty (or that there are only R_1 reasons for the end of love). Since for this doctrine love must last forever, it makes no difference why love ends, if it does; all reasons for the end of love challenge the claim that love had earlier existed. This is not quite precise enough; of course our modified doctrine of strict constancy allows that if x's emotion ends because x is dead or y is dead, that does not mean it had never been love. So the doctrine of strict constancy holds that there are no R_2 reasons *other* than these. (Notice that these trivial R_2 reasons apply to all our analyses of constancy.)

Similarly, the doctrine that love has no time constraints at all is logically equivalent to the thesis that the set of R_1 reasons is empty (or that there are only R_2 reasons for the end of love). Since there are no time constraints on love, its genuineness is never put into doubt if it ends, regardless of the reason. The doctrine of indefinite constancy, then, can be understood more technically and precisely as the thesis that both R_1 reasons and R_2 reasons (beyond the trivial R_2 reasons) exist, rather than as the vague claim that love must last "some" length of time to be love. The point is that questions about the constancy of love are hereby changed from worries about its duration per se to worries about *why* it ends. Note that the doctrine of identity constancy also admits both R_1 and R_2 reasons. If x's love ends because y has become z, that is no defect in x's love (but this is only a trivial R_2 reason); but if x's love ends while y has remained y, it puts itself into doubt (this is an R_1 reason).

I think it is plausible to reinterpret Shakespeare as saying not that love is strictly constant but that love does not end whimsically or capriciously; that some reasons for the end of love, but not others, call into question its earlier reality. "Love is not love which alters when it alteration finds" does not exclude love's altering for other reasons. It only states one sufficient condition for x's emotion not to be love. Furthermore, when later in *Sonnet* 116 Shakespeare says that love "bears it out even to the edge of doom," he did not write that love bears it out to doom itself. If the lover has to bear it out only to the edge of doom, Shakespeare thinks there are some R_2 reasons: if x's continuing to love y means that x would have to cross over the edge into doom, then x's love may end at that point without calling itself into question. Unless Shakespeare means that the beloved's death is the edge of doom—but the beloved's death, or the lover's death, would seem to be doom, not its edge. And saying that love "bears it out" to the edge of doom does not sound like saying "until death do you part" but rather sounds like a reminder that the course of love is difficult. Shakespeare is claiming that genuine lovers bear the difficulties ("tempests") to the edge of doom but not to doom itself, not if continuing to love means the death of the lover or the annihilation of his identity. Hence, "Love's not Time's fool" cuts both ways. On the one hand it does assert that love is constant, but it also asserts that love does not foolishly persist so long that it takes the lover to doom.

The reluctance to claim that love must last to doom is found even in a writer who insists that personal love is not erosic. Karol Wojtyla says that love "is put to the test most severely when the sensual and emotional reactions . . . grow weaker, and sexual values . . . lose their effect. Nothing then remains except the value of the person."[13] Wojtyla does not mean that the only severe test of love comes when sexual excitement declines, for on the very next page (as we shall see) he proposes another severe test. But it is clear that, for Wojtyla, a love that ends when sexual desire ends is not genuine love.[14] Hence he admits R_1 reasons. Does he also admit R_2 reasons? Since agape "endures all things" (1 Cor. 13:7), and Wojtyla's personal love is agapic, he should not. Consider, however, this passage:

> We love the person complete with his or her virtues and faults, and up to a point independently of those virtues and in spite of those faults. The strength of such a love emerges most clearly when the beloved . . . stumbles, when his or her weaknesses or even sins come into the open. One who truly loves does not then withdraw his love, but loves all the more, loves in full consciousness of the other's shortcomings and faults. . . . For the person as such never loses its essential value. The emotion which attaches itself to the values of the person remains loyal.[15]

On the one hand, the beloved y has the generic value of the person "as such" that never changes or diminishes.[16] Always having this value, y should always be loved by x, whose "emotion . . . remains loyal." This lover is a rigid C_1 lover, loving in virtue of the unchanging essential value of the person, even when y sins. Indeed, this is the test of x's love—its enduring when y sins, thereby showing itself to be attached to the value of the person as such. On the other hand, Wojtyla is not comfortable requiring x to love y despite *any* of y's sins, that is, beyond the edge of doom. For, as he says at the beginning, love must endure only "up to a point . . . in spite of those faults." Here he admits the possibility of R_2 reasons. But he fails to fill in the details and thereby gives the impression that no R_2 reasons exist.[17]

If Wojtyla embraces the doctrine of strict constancy, which variety of strict constancy he presupposes is not clear; his position on x's loving and marrying z, if x's spouse y dies, is complicated.[18] On the one hand, it is "justifiable" and "permitted" for x to marry a second time, since "marriage is strictly a feature of man's physical and terrestrial existence, so that it is naturally dissolved by the death of one of the spouses." Yet he also says that not to marry again is "altogether praiseworthy." The reasons are that not marrying again "emphasizes more fully the reality of the union with the person now deceased" but, more important, that not marrying again recognizes that "the value of the person . . . is not transient, and spiritual union can and should continue even when physical union is at an end." This makes sense; if y's essential value is spiritual, it never diminishes. The love that endures despite y's sins, and which attaches to the beloved's essential value, is a love that endures despite the death of y's body. Wojtyla concludes his discussion: "In the Gospels, and especially in the Epistle of St. Paul, we find widowhood and strict monogamy praised." This is quite appropriate; after all, Paul gave us this similar gem: "It is well for a man not to touch a woman. But because of the temptation to immorality, each man should have his own wife and each woman her own husband. . . . To the unmarried and widows I say that it is well for them to remain single as I do. But if they cannot exercise self-control, they should marry. For it is better to marry than to be aflame with passion" (1 Cor. 7:1–9).[19]

3. DEFENDING A DOCTRINE OF CONSTANCY

Some version of the doctrine of indefinite constancy must be right. Strict constancy, in not admitting any R_2 reasons, entails that x's love must bear it out through everything on pain of never having been love, which is implausible; and the doctrine that love has no time constraints, in not allowing any R_1 reasons, entails that x's emotion need not bear it out through anything in order to be love, which is equally implausible. Since both R_1 and R_2 reasons exist, love must be indefinitely constant in the technical sense. For example: if x's love ends because y satisfies none of x's needs, that looks like an R_2 reason; if it ends merely because y fails to satisfy one tiny need of x's, that is an R_1 reason. Or compare x's emotion ending because x discovers that y is incorrigibly deceitful with its ending because y forgets to turn out the lights. Hence, the doctrine of indefinite constancy wins by default. But are there any positive reasons to think that love is indefinitely constant?

Note that we cannot easily sidestep this conclusion—that the doctrine of indefinite constancy must be right—by suggesting that the two rejected doctrines are talking about a different kind of love or are analyzing a different concept of love. We might be tempted to say that the doctrine that love has no time constraints would be true if love were only a *feeling,* for regarding the ending of feelings there might not be any R_1 reasons. Alternatively, if love is conceived of as much more than a feeling, whatever else it includes (say, concern for the welfare of the beloved) might be that in virtue of which it is strictly constant. Although there is some merit in this diagnosis, I do not find it convincing, for at least the reasons that (1) it is no contradiction to claim that even if love is more than a feeling, love still is not bound by any time constraints and (2) one could claim (as do some romantics) that the love that is strictly constant is indeed primarily a feeling that does last forever.

The arguments that attempted to establish that love is exclusive (chap. 9) might have implications for its constancy. One argument went: overlapping loves face powerful obstacles, both pragmatic and psychological. This argument was countered by Newton-Smith's "difficult does not imply impossible." In contrast, however, there is no point in arguing that loving unconstantly faces practical and psychological difficulties. Rather, loving constantly faces obstacles ("tempests") in the way that loving nonexclusively faces obstacles. Hence, if our loves succumb to difficulties, they will tend to be at least serially exclusive and literally indefinitely constant. As a matter of fact, many loves are exactly what this "theory of difficulties" entails that love will be (and remember that the doctrine of timed exclusivity must deny strict constancy; see chap. 9, n. 9). We seem to think that we should try to overcome the obstacles to loving constantly, but we should not try to overcome the obstacles to loving nonexclusively. A case can be made, however, that if we should try to overcome the obstacles to constancy, we should also try to overcome those to multiple love: we should replace the common pattern of serially exclusive, indefinitely constant love with a pattern of constant, cotemporaneous loves. If love is such a valuable thing, we should bring more of it into existence; loving nonexclusively and constantly does exactly that.

The argument for exclusivity based on the idea that multiple loves threaten the lover's stable and unified self-concept might also support the claim that love is constant:[20] the stability of x's self-concept requires stability in x's relationship with y that is responsible for x's self-concept. But this argument has a curious implication. The longer the x-y love lasts, the more x's self-concept is wrapped up in x's life with y; hence, the longer their love lasts, the less prone x will be to love nonexclusively and the more traumatic it will be for x if y dies or withdraws. But this means that the longer the x-y love lasts, the longer after *that* their love will last, since x's self-concept has become quite dependent on the love. A long period of constancy in the x-y love generates further constancy. Conversely, the shorter the x-y love has lasted, the easier it is to end; the shorter the time that it has lasted, the less of a threat its ending is to anyone's self-concept. All we can conclude from considerations of self-concept, then, is this: love is literally indefinitely constant. Once the love has endured, it will tend to endure; but nothing about the formation of self-concept implies that it will endure in the first place. If the early love is not working out well, self-concept formation will neither prevent it from ending nor help it progress to the stage at which constancy is self-reinforcing.

Hunter's view—that when x and y love each other, they join their interests and capabilities—does not entail that their love will be constant. What is ruled out is x's unilaterally partitioning x's interests between two beloveds, y and z; but x is not conceptually prevented from withdrawing totally from the x-y joint interest and forming the x-z joint interest. Further, if it is claimed that once the interests of x and y are joined, they logically cannot be separated at a later time, Hunter's view would entail that love is both timelessly exclusive and strictly constant: one's first love is one's only love. Fried's argument—that the intimacy of love is constituted by a sharing of information that is not shared outside the relationship—might imply that love is constant. If x and y's sharing information at t_1 means that neither x nor y can love someone else at t_1, then x (and y) may be conceptually prevented from loving someone else at t_2, since satisfying the conditions of sharing at t_2 would violate the conditions of sharing at t_1. If so, love must be timelessly exclusive: x and y either love only each other constantly (or discontinuously), or after loving each other, they love no one else. Reiman's view—that love includes the desire to share "present and future" intense experiences—entails that love is at least "intention constant." X's having the desire to share intense experiences *now* with y does not involve any constancy, but x's having the desire to share experiences with y in the future means that x envisages their love existing at a later time. But Reiman's view that x has a desire for both "present and future" experiences with y begs the question; those who think that love has no time constraints would be right to demand an argument that the intimacy of love, or love itself, includes not only the desire to share experiences now but also a desire to do so in the future. Second, this intention constancy is hardly robust. X's having the desire *now* to share experiences with y in the future provides no reason for thinking that x's present desire to share experiences with y will itself continue. Yet, it seems strange to say that if x loves y, x desires to share only one intense experience with y.

Robert Brown suggests another argument when he writes, "Love . . . is directed . . . at benefiting the beloved. To do this the lover must try to satisfy the needs and wishes, present and future, of the beloved."[21] Perhaps an argument that love is conceptually constant can be fashioned from the claim that if x loves y, then one of x's central desires, if not the central desire of love, is to enhance y's welfare. Brown's way of making the point—x desires to enhance y's welfare "present and future"—may seem illicitly to smuggle constancy into love in the way that Reiman's view, that x desires to share "present and future" experiences with y, begs the question. But perhaps someone who is concerned for another's welfare cannot, on pain of contradiction, be only briefly or momentarily concerned. If x does something now to enhance y's well-being, the effect of x's action is not limited to now; an enhancement of y's well-being is an enhancement, ceteris paribus, of y's well-being into an indefinite future. X's knowing that benefiting y now will carry into the future implies that being concerned for another's welfare is a forward-looking attitude. Still, there is a difference between (1) x's desiring now that y be better off in the future and (2) x's desiring in the future that y be better off. If love includes desire (1), that does not entail it includes desire (2)—or at least whether love does include desire (2) is precisely the issue under discussion.

A connection among love, concern, and constancy is asserted by Newton-Smith: "Being genuinely concerned . . . seems to involve a willingness on my part to extend that concern . . . to the person [I love] even if I have been mistaken about that person with regard to some feature of her that led to the concern, and even if that person ceases to have those features that led me to be concerned."[22] To claim that x's concern, if genuine, will persist in this situation is to say that concern is reason-independent. Thus, if x is "timelessly" concerned for y, x's love will be strictly constant. But, as we saw earlier (sect. 1) Newton-Smith's view entails that if x discovers that y is really a monster, and x as a result is no longer concerned for y's welfare, x's concern was not "genuine." This is implausible. Nor is it convincing to say that if x's love and concern are genuine, x will still desire to benefit this monster y, yet will not *act* on that desire. It is true, however, that when we worry about the constancy of love, we are in part worried about the constancy of concern. We want love to be constant not because we value constancy per se, but because (in part) we want the concern of love to be constant. The question, What are the R_1 reasons that imply, if love ends, that it had never been love, and what are the R_2 reasons that allow, if love ends, that it had been love all along? is not far from the question: When does the end of concern mean that the concern is bogus, and when does the end of concern not bring into doubt its earlier reality? (Answer: when x refuses to benefit y when y accidentally annoys x; when y becomes a monster.) There are both R_1 and R_2 reasons for the failure of concern, just as there are both R_1 and R_2 reasons for the end of love, if concern is a feature of love. Thus love is only indefinitely constant, and the concern feature of love might be called "conditional altruism."[23]

In one of her songs Carole King asks Donne's question: "Will you still love me tomorrow?"[24] Proponents of strict constancy answer "yes"; if x loves y today, then of course x will love y tomorrow. That answer is not satisfying, for King instead has to worry whether x's emotion today is love. Proponents of indefinite constancy answer "maybe." But if King worries whether x's emotion today is love, apparently she cannot know this until x's emotion ends and she finds out whether it ends for an R_1 or R_2 reason. Proponents of the view that love has no time constraints answer her question with silence or the counter-question, "Why would you think of asking that?" Perhaps King has the consolation of being able to believe that x at least loves her today, since this view admits no R_1 reasons. But suppose that King really wants to know during her experience, not afterwards (despite her roundabout question), whether she is loved; in this case Kierkegaard's test (King's death) is a bad joke. No answer framed in terms of the constancy of x's emotion can fully tell her that, for the constancy of an emotion is at most necessary, but not sufficient, for it to be love. If we want to judge now whether an emotion qualifies as love, we should probably focus on the quality of concern that x shows for y, along with other considerations (x's desire to be in y's presence, to share personal information and intense experiences with y). For the quality of x's concern for y can be evaluated at least in part independently of its duration. We can often tell whether x's concern for y is loving concern without waiting to see if x's concern ends and, if it does, whether it ends for an R_1 or R_2 reason. If the quality of x's concern for y during the relationship means that x's emotion is love, then ex post facto judgments about x's emotion are superfluous. Further, if the quality of x's concern during the relationship means that x's emotion is love, that fact overrides the retroactive judgment, based on the emotion's ending, that x's emotion had not been love. The only decent argument we have that love is by its nature at least indefinitely constant is that love includes concern; yet the test of x's love for y is not its constancy or the constancy of its concern, but rather the quality of x's concern while it exists. We therefore have some reason to claim that if x loves y believing that y is beautiful, but x's emotion evaporates when x finally sees y as an order of smelts, x's earlier emotion toward y had been love as long as x was at that time fulfilling what the concern of love demands— whatever *that* happens to be (see chap. 12).

4. LOVE FOR THE PERSON

Suppose that x loves y on the basis of property-set S, which properties are not the properties that constitute y's identity. For example: x loves y for y's blondeness and deep voice, which make no contribution to y's being y; y could turn gray without becoming a different person. It can be argued that if x loves y specifically for S, x does not genuinely love y: x's emotion is grounded in properties extraneous to y and hence never amounts to loving y "the person." In this view, x loves y only if x loves y for y's identity properties, which means that x's emotion must last through all changes in y's nonidentity properties in order to be love. This proposal for what "love for the person" means bears some resemblance to the doctrine of identity constancy: if x loves y at t, then x loves y at all times after t, as long as y has remained morally and psychologically y. However, to say that love is identity constant is not to say anything about the basis of x's love: x might love y for as long as y remains y, without loving y for y's identity properties, if (for example) x is a C_2 constant lover whose emotion variably attaches to y via different nonidentity properties. The proposed analysis of love for the person goes further and claims that x's emotion must be grounded only in y's identity properties to be love. Yet, if x's loving y entails that x loves y for y's identity properties, it follows that x's love will be identity constant. This can be construed as an argument for this version of the doctrine of indefinite constancy.

From the thesis that love for the person (or genuine love) is x's loving y for y's identity properties, it follows not only that (1) if x loves y, x will love y for as long as y remains y, but also that (2) if x loves y, x will love y *only* as long as y remains y. That is, if x's emotion toward y continues even though y has lost the properties that make y who y is, x could not have been loving y in virtue of properties constitutive of y's identity. Thus, on the assumption that x loves y only if x loves y in virtue of identity properties, the persistence of x's emotion shows it had never been love—as asserted by the first-horn claim, (A), in our new dilemma. We have seen how Wojtyla responds to this reasoning. For him, love for the person has the contrary implication: if x loves y the person, x's emotion must persist through all changes in y, even those moral and psychological changes that bring into doubt y's remaining y.

Gregory Vlastos also denies claim (A), but from a secular perspective. For Vlastos, x's loving y "as an individual" entails that x's emotion must continue independently of all "variations in merit":

> Constancy of affection in the face of variations of merit is one of the surest tests of whether or not a parent does love a child. If he feels fond of it only when it performs well, . . . then his feeling for the child can scarcely be called *love*. There are many relations in which one's liking . . . for a person [is] strictly conditional on his measuring up to certain standards. But convincing evidence that the relation is of this type is no evidence that the relation is one . . . of love. It does nothing to show that one has this feeling . . . for an *individual,* rather than for a place-holder of qualities.[25]

Vlastos then claims that this "value attaching to a person's individual existence, over and above his merit" is a person's "individual worth" and is the focus not only of "personal love" but also of justice. Vlastos defines "merit" as "all the kinds of valuable qualities or performances in respect of which persons can be graded";[26] by contrast, the individual worth of persons cannot be graded, because it is possessed equally by everyone. Hence Vlastos' notion of love for someone as an individual is a secular version of Wojtyla's love "for the person as such."

But Vlastos also claims that a "valuable human characteristic" is a merit only if it is "acquired," that is, "represents what its possessor has himself made of his natural endowments and environmental opportunities." Since everyone has individual worth equally, this proviso makes sense; if "individual worth" existed in virtue of what a person has made of herself, it would vary from person to person. There are however, two problems with the proviso. First, in the contrast between the unvarying individual worth that grounds genuine love and the variable merit that is irrelevant to love, the category of innate traits ("natural endowment") gets lost. On the one hand, innate traits are not acquired and hence are like individual worth, which is not acquired by anyone's effort. On the other hand, some innate traits are valuable, as well as variable and gradable, and hence are like merit. The way Vlastos defines merit, then, leaves mysterious the role played by natural endowments in love.

Second, the distinction between innate and acquired properties weakens Vlastos' claim that x loves y as an individual only when y's merit is irrelevant. For the distinction suggests the alternative analysis that x's loving y as an individual is precisely x's loving y in virtue of y's acquired valuable traits rather than y's innate traits. It is the contrast between innate and acquired valuable traits, in this alternative view, that gives meaning to love for the person rather than the contrast between acquired value and ubiquitous individual worth. The idea is that y's acquired valuable traits (as Vlastos says) are those y has by virtue of y's own efforts; acquired valuable traits therefore represent the person that y has made of herself. Vlastos says, "If [y] is valued for some meritorious quality, . . . [y's] individuality does not enter into the valuation. . . . No matter how enviable a package of well-rounded excellence [y] may represent, it would still follow that if [y] is valued only for [y's] merit, [y] is not being valued as an individual."[27] But this seems wrong if y's merits are acquired properties. To value y in virtue of y's acquired traits—those achieved through y's own efforts—is to value y as an individual.

Some of y's innate properties are as attractive and as valuable as y's acquired properties, both in their own right and because they are the foundation upon which y builds acquired traits. Do we then have to legislate that x genuinely loves y only when x loves y for y's acquired valuable properties? It is one thing for x to love y for y's brute intelligence, and another for x to love y for y's intelligence as it has been nurtured by y. But I think there is no need for such legislation. Some valuable innate properties *require* input from their possessors; y's blondeness, musical talent, intelligence, and physique will deteriorate unless y makes an effort to maintain them. Hence, x's loving y for y's innate properties *is* to love y for y's acquired properties, to the extent that x finds y's innate properties attractive because they have been maintained, if not improved, by y's efforts. Note that acquired properties are not more valuable than innate properties merely because they are acquired, as if y's making an effort per se is what gives acquired properties their value. After all, y might have exerted effort to develop a vice, and the fact that effort has been exerted does not make it any less a vice. If acquired properties are more valuable than innate properties, it is because as a result of effort they simply turn out to be better. None of this rules out x's loving y for the attractive property "makes an effort to improve natural endowments." But that consideration is independent of x's loving y for the high quality of the properties acquired through that effort.

Thus there may be something worth paying attention to in this alternative analysis of love for the person.[28] Notice that this view cannot maintain that x loves y only if x's emotion is based on y's identity properties. There is no equivalence between a property's being an acquired (or a maintained innate) property and its being a property that partially constitutes y's identity. A person's innate intelligence, even if maintained and improved by her efforts, is not necessarily partially constitutive of her identity; she may later lose that acquired property and remain the same person. And some innate properties (y's being Caucasian) are properties that cannot be improved or developed and, hence, are forever "brutely" innate, yet are partially constitutive of identity (y cannot cease being Caucasian without ceasing to be y). It is just as well, however, that this analysis of love for the person cannot claim that x loves y for y's identity properties. For the view that in genuine love x loves y for y's identity properties is untenable.

5. LOVING FOR IDENTITY PROPERTIES

Let us begin this story with Aristotle's account of the constancy of philia in *Nicomachean Ethics*. Aristotle distinguishes among friendships based on y's usefulness, those based on pleasure, and those based on y's morally good character (9.6). The first two kinds are inferior, and the third is "the perfect form"—"that between good men who are alike in excellence or virtue" (1156b6). The friendships based on use and pleasure are inferior because one is not loved "for himself" but only because he is useful or pleasant. "Such friendships are easily dissolved. . . . [T]he affection ceases as soon as one partner is no longer pleasant or useful to the other" (1156a16–21), and being useful or pleasant can easily change. Aristotle also claims that a friendship based on pleasure is less inferior than one based on use, since the former has the potential to develop into the perfect form (1157a10–12). "[W]hen it is the useful . . . that is exchanged in a love affair, the partners are less truly friends and their friendship is less durable[,] dissolv[ing] as soon as it ceases to be to their advantage" (1157a12–14; see 1165b1–4).

Aristotle contrasts the "incidental" inferior friendships with the perfect form, in which the friend is "loved for being the kind of person he is" (1156a18–19). His suggestion is that a person's being useful or pleasant is an incidental property, not part of the *kind* of person he is, and perfect friendship is based not on the incidental but on the friend's identity properties. "When friendship is based on character," says Aristotle, "it does last, . . . because it is friendship for its own sake" (1164a12–13). We hope Aristotle's point here is not that perfect friendship is "for its own sake" and endures merely because it is not for the sake of use or pleasure and therefore cannot be undermined by factors that plague inferior friendships. Rather, Aristotle must be saying both that perfect friendship endures because it is grounded on character and that character, or the kind of person one is, endures.[29] After all, his favorite contrast is between the inconstant inferior friendships based on changeable utility and pleasure and the constancy of perfect friendship based on (by implication) unchangeable character. Now, if constant love is defined as x's loving y as long as y remains y, then if x loves y for y's character, x's love will be constant. We saw this earlier. However, what Aristotle adds is strange; it is irrelevant to say that x's love endures *because* y's character endures, for even if y's character were not to endure, x's *love* would not fail to be constant. Hence, if Aristotle presupposes identity constancy (instead of strict constancy) for perfect friendship, he must claim something other than that perfect friendship endures because character endures. Does he? Consider:

> The perfect form of friendship is that between good men who are alike in excellence or virtue. For these friends wish alike for one another's good because they are good men, and they are good *per se*. Those who wish for their friends' good for their friends' sake are friends in the truest sense, since their attitude is determined by what their friends are and not by incidental considerations. Hence their friendship lasts as long as they are good, and goodness or virtue is a thing that lasts. (1156b6–12)

Hence, perfect friendship is based not merely on character but on the beloved's *good* character, and x's love is constant because goodness endures. But this does not solve the problem. Since the goodness that grounds x's love is part of y's character, the endurance of y's virtue and y's identity are tied together: were y to lose y's goodness, y would no longer be the kind of person y had been. There is no difference, then, between x's love being constant because it is based on y's enduring goodness and x's love being constant because it is based on y's enduring character. It is senseless to say that x's love is constant because its basis, y's good character, endures; for if y's good character does not endure, and x's love ends, x's love has not failed to be constant. Its object is gone.

All this assumes that Aristotle holds the doctrine of identity constancy; but what does "constancy" mean for him? Aristotle suggests that inferior friendships have no time requirement at all:

> Surely, there is nothing strange about breaking friendships based on what is useful or pleasant when the partners no longer have the qualities of being useful or pleasant. For they were friends of these qualities . . . and it is only reasonable that the affection should pass with the passing of the qualities. (1165b1–4)

So there are R_2 reasons for the end of inferior friendships; a friendship based on use is dissolved when use runs its course, and its ending does not mean it had never been a friendship (see also 1156a19–20). Are there any R_1 reasons that apply to inferior friendships? It is difficult to imagine a reason for which a use-friendship ends that implies it had never been a friendship—probably because Aristotle is already being generous in calling these relationships "friendship." We cannot say that if xLy for y's usefulness while x is deceiving y into believing that xLy for y's virtue, then the termination of x's affection when y is no longer useful is an R_1 reason for the end of use-friendship; if anything, it is an R_1 reason for the end of perfect friendship. However, what if xLy for being useful in one way while y believes that y is loved for being useful in some other way, and x's love ends when the former usefulness is gone? This might be an R_1 reason for the end of use-friendship, since the relationship lacks the reciprocal awareness of intentions that Aristotle thinks is a necessary feature of even use-friendships.

But what notion of constancy does Aristotle embrace for perfect friendship? There seems to be nothing in the idea of x's wishing y well for y's sake that speaks to the question of constancy. Yet Aristotle comes close to asserting the doctrine of identity constancy. He considers a case in which x loves y for y's goodness, but at some point y is no longer good and has become evil. He asks: "Should the friendship . . . be broken off at once?" He answers: "Probably not in every case, but only when a friend's wickedness has become incurable. But if there is a chance of reforming him, we must come to the aid of his character" (1165b17–19). X is not expected to love an incurably evil y that x *once* loved. "But," Aristotle continues, "no one would regard a person who breaks off such a friendship as acting strangely, because the man who was his friend was not the kind of man [he used to be]: his friend has changed, and since he is unable to save him, he severs his connections with him" (1165b20–22).[30] What existed earlier between x and y had been a perfect friendship, so x's ending the friendship because y is now incurably evil is an R_2 reason. Aristotle also says that if y's character *can* be salvaged, x is a genuine friend only if x bears it out during the salvaging. Hence, the ending of a friendship because y is curably evil is an R_1 reason, raising doubts about x's love. In admitting both R_1 and R_2 reasons for the end of perfect friendship, Aristotle holds the technical version of indefinite constancy that looks very much like identity constancy.

Aristotle's account of the constancy of friendship has one other trouble. He claims that perfect friendship endures because "goodness or virtue is a thing that lasts" (1156b12). Why, then, does Aristotle even consider a case in which the virtuous y becomes not merely morally mediocre but evil? If virtue does last, how can it change into its opposite? Indeed, y's enduring virtue has turned into incurable—that is, enduring—evil.[31] We are left wondering, then, how the beloved's virtuous character explains the constancy of perfect friendship. Aristotle is probably not claiming that virtue endures because it is part of one's character and one's character itself endures. That is a petitio and gets things backwards. Aristotle's belief that virtue lasts may be merely empirical; when he takes a look around, he sees virtue enduring. That permits the odd case in which y turns from a saint to a monster. But usefulness and pleasantness can endure as long as virtue. Aristotle continually implies they do not, but that may be wishful thinking. He should argue that love endures when it is based on the beloved's virtue, but that it endures for some reason other than the endurance of the beloved's virtue: love based on virtue endures longer than love based on use and pleasure, even if use and pleasure can in some cases last longer than virtue, because there is something in the nature of virtue, not present in either use or pleasure, that more powerfully cements the love.[32] But what is it about virtuous character that makes love endure, preventing it from being undermined by tempests? The answer cannot be that tolerating y's defects is easier if x loves y for y's good character rather than for y's usefulness. For, first, x may find y's usefulness so valuable that that quality induces x to tolerate y's defects; and, second, y's defects themselves may be part of y's character and offset the power of the good parts of y's identity to ground x's love. If all loves include periods or moments of pain, then love based only on pleasure might not endure; but this provides no reason to think that loves based on good character will endure these painful occasions.

The idea that x loves y the person when x loves y for y's identity properties is so appealing that it is even employed by Aryeh Kosman to defend Platonic eros. He argues (as do many writers) that Platonic eros, as ordinarily construed, never amounts to love for someone as a person: in erosic love x loves y because y has attractive S, so x is really only loving S and not the person who happens to have S. But Kosman also argues that neighbor-love fares no better: in agapic love x does not love y for y's attractive properties, and x's love is not prevented by y's unattractive properties, so x's love is not a function of what y is like and therefore y is not loved as the individual y is. Hence, whether x loves y erosically or agapically, x does not love y as a person.[33] Kosman, however, wants to improve our understanding of Platonic eros, to show that it does make room for loving y as a person. His solution is that if x loves y because y has Φ, where Φ are y's identity properties, x's love is both erosic and love for y "as a person." X's loving y for Φ still means that x is loving Φ, but since y is constituted by Φ, x's loving Φ is identical to x's loving y: "If I love [y] because of Φ or love the Φ in [y], I should not be said to love something other than [y] if Φ is *what* [y] is. Thus to love [y] for [Φ] is to love [y] for [him]self" (p. 64).

One problem with the view that either genuine love or love for the person is loving in virtue of identity properties, is that it gets caught in a dilemma: either x loves y for *all* y's identity properties Φ, or x loves y for some subset Ψ of Φ; in either case, the view runs into trouble. Suppose that x loves y for all y's identity properties Φ. Then the view reduces to the claim that x loves y because y is y, or x loves y for being y. X loves y simply because y is the person that y is—and this is singularly unilluminating.[34] Everyone is the person he is—hence x would have equal reason for loving everyone else. If y asks x, "Why do you love *me*?" x might try to answer, "because you have Φ, and I find Φ to be especially attractive." But because y is identical to Φ, x has just uttered a number of empty tautologies: "I find you (y) attractive because I find you (Φ) attractive," "I love you (y) because I love you (Φ)," and so on. Such is the cost of conflating the basis and the object of love. Further, if x loves all of Φ, then x turns out to love every defect that is part of y's identity. But it seems false to say that if x loves y, then x does (or should) love everything about y, and equally false that x loves every identity property of y.[35] It is no contradiction for x to say to y, "I love you for your courage and charm, and I even love your courage and charm, but I dislike the way you characteristically become defensive when someone compliments your appearance."

The alternative—that x loves y for a subset of Φ (say, some of the attractive parts of y's identity)—is also inadequate. Suppose that x loves y for the specific subset Ψ of y's identity properties; then if some other subset λ of Φ changes (y loses λ), x's love for y will not end since its basis (Ψ) endures. This result might seem unobjectionable. Yet consider the situation further: x's love is persisting on the basis of the enduring Ψ, but because some other subset λ of Φ is gone, y could no longer be the object of x's love. Y no longer exists as y but has been replaced by a person z with a different moral and psychological identity. The point is that because x's emotion continues after y has become z, this alternative has not provided a coherent account of loving the person y. The fact that x's emotion is attached first to y (via Ψ) and then to z (via Ψ) counts against x's having ever loved y. Further, Kosman's reconciliation of erosic love and love for the person goes down the drain. That argument was: if x loves y for property-set S, then x loves S; but if y is constituted by S, then in loving S x is automatically loving y, since y is S. But the argument succeeds only if S is the full set Φ of y's identity properties. If S is only the subset Ψ, then in loving Ψ x is not loving y, since y is not identical to Ψ.

To claim that if x loves y, then x's love is based on y's essential properties is to condemn too many loves that have no such foundation. No one denies the genuineness of a hatred based on an incidental property. Nor does anyone complain that if x hates y for an incidental property, x is not hating y "the person." Our loves are often grounded in a mixture of essential and incidental properties (George Moore wrote to Maud: "It is sometimes your white hands that I remember, sometimes it is your joyous spirituality that enraptures me"),[36] and it would seem as arbitrary to condemn a love partially based on incidental properties as to praise a love based entirely on essential qualities. Some incidental properties are as attractive and valuable as essential properties and may be appreciated noninstrumentally. (Aristotle is wrong if he equates the incidental and the useful.) The accident of a mole or the shape of a nose (both enduring physical, incidental properties) may make a person irresistible. Indeed, incidental properties that we find unattractive or repulsive may prevent us from loving an otherwise lovable person. We might be tempted to say: the only defect properties that should count against love are those annoying properties that are part of a person's identity; otherwise we would not be *not* loving that person as a person, that is, we would be rejecting her for properties that have nothing to do with who she is. Not even Aristotle, according to Martha Nussbaum, took that heroic route: "Aristotle calmly points out that people who are physically ugly will have a hard time" finding friendship.[37] If Nussbaum is right, it is a funny detail in Aristotle's account that ugliness could be an unobjectionable obstacle to friendship. Ordinarily, ugliness (or its opposite) is not an essential property; yet Aristotle, the champion of the perfect friendship between the virtuous x and the virtuous y, bows to the power of the incidental. Apparently, x's not being able to overlook this incidental defect, which does not detract from y's good character, does not call into question x's own moral virtue.[38] I am not claiming that physical appearance should play this role.[39] But that some incidental properties may unobjectionably play a role in love seems unassailable.

6. TYPES OF PROPERTIES

Ann Landers reminds us that "both males and females lose out when they rule out prospects based on irrelevancies such as fat or skinny, rich or poor. Skinny women sometimes get fat. Rich men lose their money. . . . Kindness, patience, loyalty, integrity, generosity and the ability to communicate are the things that count."[40] But Landers seems to confuse the question of what properties are logically or morally relevant to love with the question of what properties endure and thereby sustain love. Do kindness and patience (and the like) count because, unlike beauty, they do not wither away? Or do they count because they are logically or morally appropriate to this emotion? Landers, however, might be making two distinctions: kindness and patience versus physique, and kindness and patience versus wealth. The first contrast is between mental or personality characteristics and physical qualities, where the implication is that a love based on the latter either is morally inferior or will not endure. The second contrast is between properties that logically can ground love and those that logically cannot. X could love y for y's kindness or physical beauty, but x is conceptually prevented from *loving* y (as opposed to desiring to marry y) in virtue of y's money. Or we might say: love based on kindness or beauty is comprehensible; love based on wealth per se is incomprehensible and irrational, like x's pathologically fearing pens because x believes they are instruments of writing.

The superiority of loving on the basis of mental properties to loving on the basis of physical properties is often defended with four distinct rationales. Mental properties may have a kind of moral or intrinsic value that physical properties lack, in which case a person possessing mental excellences is a superior object of love and a person who loves in virtue of mental excellence is a superior subject of love. Second, mental properties may be more a part of a person's identity than the physical, in which case love based on the mental is superior because it is directed at "the person." Third, mental properties might be more stable than physical properties, in which case loves based on the former are superior because more constant. And fourth, love based on mental properties might more reliably generate concern for the well-being of the beloved than love based on the physical, in which case the former is more reliably what love is or ought to be.[41] Of course, one can take a reductionist line and argue that some of these rationales are the same. For example, mental properties endure just because they are identity properties, or mental properties are more valuable just because they endure. But these claims are implausible. Identity properties are not guaranteed to endure; a mental property's being essential is not why it endures (if it endures). And the mere fact that something endures does not explain its having value. It should not be surprising, however, that these rationales are often combined. If mental properties are essential and enduring, then a love based on them will be constant since both its object and its basis endure, and the love achieves, in one sense, love for the person. If we add the first rationale, that mental properties are more valuable, then x and y can congratulate each other on achieving an ideal.

There are various ways to classify the properties x might find valuable in y; the distinctions between mental and physical, essential and incidental, are not exhaustive. Another distinction is between attractive properties that y has naturally or innately and attractive properties deliberately cultivated by y. There is also a distinction between attractive properties for which y wants to be loved and the properties for which y prefers not to be loved. For example, y might think of herself as being a certain kind of person and thus want to be loved in virtue of the properties constituting this self-concept; y might simply be proud of P and be attracted to the kind of person who prefers P; or y may be tired of always being loved for Q and wants to be loved, for a change, on the basis of P.

The interesting question, I think, is not whether a love based on one sort of property is more likely to be constant than a love based on some other sort, but whether these categories can be used to distinguish between R_1 and R_2 reasons. Does this proposal sound plausible? If x's emotion is based on mental property M and ends because y loses M, x's emotion had been love (this is an R_2 reason); but if x's emotion is based on physical property N and ends because y loses N, x's emotion had not been love (this is an R_1 reason). Or: if x's emotion ends because y loses a property y wants to be loved for, this is an R_2 reason; but if y did not want to be loved for the lost property, which had grounded x's emotion, this is an R_1 reason. It should be clear that these proposals are inadequate. If x has an emotion toward y on the basis of some unspecified physical property, some incidental property, or some property for which y did not want to be loved, and this emotion ends when y loses that property, we cannot in general conclude that x's emotion was not love. What is needed is a broader perspective that distinguishes between R_1 and R_2 reasons, according to which the loss of some physical properties (but not others) counts as an R_1 reason, the loss of some incidental properties (but not others) counts as an R_1 reason, and so forth. Without this integrative theory, it becomes more reasonable to think that there simply is no distinction to be made between R_1

and R_2 reasons, either because every reason is an R_1 reason (strict constancy) or every reason is an R_2 reason (love has no time constraints at all).

There is a deeper point to be made. When someone asserts that x's not loving y after y has lost P does not mean that x had never loved y, he is really asserting that this specific P is a proper (logically, rationally, or morally) ground of love. What is actually being indicated by an identification of R_2 reasons are the conditions in which x's emotion, at the time it existed, would count as love. Thus, if y loses that property, it is no strike against x as a lover that x no longer loves y, since x's emotion had been properly grounded originally. Conversely, when it is asserted that x's not loving y after y has lost P *does* make doubtful that x's emotion earlier had been love, what is really being asserted is that x's emotion had not been grounded by a property appropriate for love. Hence, disputes over what counts as R_1 and R_2 reasons are really disputes over which properties logically, rationally, or morally serve as the basis of love.

This point can be illustrated by examining one more piece of Newton-Smith's position. He claims that (i) "not all properties which [x] sees [y] as possessing can serve as the grounds for loving [y]," but also that (ii) x "must . . . care about [y] for herself [and] must be attracted to [y] on her own account."[42] Hence, for Newton-Smith, the love-grounding properties must be y's identity properties. Properties that "can be grounds of [x's] loving [y]" he calls "intrinsic," while those that "cannot play this role" he calls "extrinsic." His two examples are straightforward. "Suppose [y's] wealth suddenly evaporates. If [x's] interest in [y] should also evaporate, we conclude that . . . the relation had not been one of love" (p. 122). Wealth is neither a possible ground of love nor an intrinsic property of y; x's emotion toward y was not, therefore, x's loving y for herself ("[x] liked [y]-the-wealthy-woman and not [y] *per se*"). Further, y's loss of wealth counts as an R_1 reason, showing that x's emotion had never been love. On the other hand, "suppose . . . [x] claims to love [y] . . . on account of certain features of her personality and character. But one day . . . [y] undergoes a radical personality transformation . . . [and] no longer has those attributes. . . . Here we are not so inclined to revise" our judgment that x had loved y. Personality features are a possible ground of love, are intrinsic properties, and x's loving y for these qualities is to love y for herself. Y's losing these features counts as an R_2 reason (a trivial one, actually), not bringing into doubt the credentials of x's love.[43]

For Newton-Smith, then, both R_1 and R_2 reasons exist for the end of love, and his distinction between them logically presupposes an account of the proper grounding of love. But his neat and reasonable view would be challenged by some of those who claim that love has no time constraints at all and by some of those who embrace the doctrine of strict constancy. These responses show that the debate about R_1 and R_2 reasons is the surface manifestation of a debate that is also about the nature of the person and not only about the proper grounds for love. Some proponents of strict constancy question the claim that x's loving y for herself or per se is x's loving y for her personality features; *both* x's loving y for y's wealth *and* x's loving y for y's personality features are not to love y per se, but only in virtue of y's incidental properties. In fact, all descriptions of y mention only y's incidental properties, and all the properties y *has* are only incidental to what y *is*. The object of love (say, a transcendental self) is something that goes beyond all qualities; because this object is none of its qualities or has none, it cannot be loved for any quality. Because all y's properties are extrinsic, there can be no R_2 reasons but only R_1 reasons, which is to say that either x's emotion persists through all changes in y's properties or it is not love.

On the other side, for example, is Andreas Capellanus, who considers y's loss of wealth to be a quite adequate reason for x's withdrawing love (see 8.7); the implication is that x had loved y earlier, and y's loss of wealth counts as an R_2 reason. Now, if loss of wealth does not count as an R_1 reason, nothing could count as an R_1 reason. Capellanus' view can be generalized into the following version of the doctrine that love has no time requirement. The object of love is constituted by *all* its properties, in the sense that all the properties y has are intrinsic. Since the object is all its properties, it can be loved only for some intrinsic property or another, and any property can be a ground of love. It follows that x's love should not be expected to persist through any change in y, and all reasons for the end of love are R_2 reasons. (No wonder Donne worried about the escape clause of identity constancy.) This position is the mirror image of strict constancy. For the latter, both the object of love and the proper basis of love continuously exist, and love has no erosic foundation in y's properties; for the former, the object and the basis of love are like Heraclitus' river, or his foot. Indeed, the subject of love (the lover) must be viewed in the same way: x is always changing into someone else w, and so x's love cannot end for an R_1 reason.

The possibility that the lover might change into the morally and psychologically different w must also be taken into account more generally. Suppose that x loves y for P, but later x does not love y, who still has P, because x no longer finds P to be a valuable property.[44] Is this an R_1 or an R_2 reason? If x's no longer finding P valuable marks a radical change in x's character, such that x has become w, it is a trivial R_2 reason. If x has remained x, however, whether x's love has ended for an R_1 or R_2 reason depends on other considerations. If P is a proper love-grounding property, then x's emotion had been love, so it must have ended for an R_2 reason. If P is not a proper love-grounding property, then x's emotion all along had not been love, so it must have ended for an R_1 reason. In this case, x's emotion might have ended because x did exactly that which is required by the morality or rationality of love: x discovered that x's emotion was based on P, recognized that P was an improper basis for love, and as a result x overcame his attraction to y.

There is one other interesting thing about Newton-Smith's approach to these issues. Suppose that we were to *begin* by making a distinction between essential and incidental properties; we could then distinguish between R_1 and R_2 reasons by relying on this logically prior account of identity. This natural approach (implicit in Aristotle and Kosman) at first glance seems to be Newton-Smith's. But dividing properties into the essential and the incidental is no easy matter. To say that an essential property is one such that, when a person loses it, the person has not remained the same person, and that an incidental property is one such that, when lost, does not yield a new person, is analytically true. But it is unhelpful, for how can it be applied to concrete cases? Being able to do so presupposes that we already have a test for "y is (or is not) the *same* person." So the project is circular. What Newton-Smith does is to turn this natural approach on its head, using the distinction between R_1 and R_2 reasons to give concrete content to the distinction between the essential and the incidental:

> The classification of features as extrinsic or intrinsic depends on our attitude [*sic*] to inconstancy, given that the feature in question changed. That is, if [x] claims to love [y] . . . because of her being Φ, and if [x's] attitude to [y] would be negatively affected should [y] cease to be Φ (or, should [x] cease to see [y] as being Φ) then, if we count this inconstancy as evidence against the relation's having been one of love, Φ is an extrinsic property of [y]; otherwise Φ is an intrinsic property. (p. 122)

In this analysis, if (i) x has an emotion toward y in virtue of y's having P, (ii) y's losing P is why x's emotion ends, and (iii) x's emotion ending for that reason means that x's emotion had not been love (y's losing P is an R_1 reason), then P is an extrinsic property of y; otherwise it is intrinsic. This is surely a novel approach to distinguishing the essential from the incidental, but notice its cost. In Newton-Smith's approach, we rely on intuitions ("our attitude") about R_1 and R_2 reasons in order to give content to the distinction between essential and incidental properties (or to the distinction between properties that can and those that cannot ground love). We thus have a typical philosophical quandary: Which end of the string should we pull to tighten the knot? Are our intuitions about the intrinsic and the extrinsic more (or less) reliable than our intuitions about R_1 and R_2 reasons? It might be precisely this tangle that lends credibility to the views of those who deny the distinctions both between the essential and the incidental and between R_1 and R_2 reasons—namely, the proponents of the doctrine of strict constancy and those who defend the thesis that love has no time constraints.

7. AGAPIC CONSTANCY

John McTaggart claimed that "if love has once arisen, there is no reason why it ought to cease, because the belief has ceased which was its cause. . . . Admiration . . . ought to yield. But love . . . could have resisted, and ought to have resisted."[45] If there are no reasons why love should end, love cannot be reason-dependent; for erosic personal love ends in response to x's belief that y has become unattractive or that y has lost his attractive properties. But how can reason-independent, agapic personal love endure? Not because of anything about its object. When McTaggart says that love resists changes in its object, he means that the *lover* resists changes in the object. The "permanence" of neighbor-love "involves persistence in the face of obstacles."[46] Of course, it is inadequate to say that neighbor-love will be constant, despite the obstacles, because "difficult does not imply impossible." So, will agapic personal love fare any better than erosic? The *Ethics of the Fathers* thinks so: "All love which depends on a material thing, if the thing passes away the love passes away; but that [love] which does not depend on a material thing will not pass away [but last] for ever."[47] To be more precise, the argument is: erosic love, since it is based on the beloved's attractive properties, will pass away if those properties pass away; but agapic personal love, since it is not grounded in the beloved's qualities, remains unchanged however much the object changes. The argument is a non sequitur. From the fact that agapic personal love is not based on its object's properties and will not end merely because its object changes, it does not follow that it will endure. Agapic personal love will be only as constant as its own basis.[48] True, God's love is unconditional and constant, by virtue of His nature, but this does not mean agapic personal love will endure.

Kierkegaard recognizes that the lover's nature is crucial to the constancy of agapic personal love. "No change . . . can take your neighbour from you, for it is not your neighbour who holds you fast—it is your love which holds your neighbour fast."[49] The lover's nature is called upon by duty to love constantly: "When love has undergone the transformation of the eternal by being made duty, it has won continuity. . . . [O]nly when it is duty to love, only then is love eternally secure."[50] For Kierkegaard, the agapic order between love and evaluation (7.6) holds for both neighbor-love and marital love,[51] so both are subject-centric. Thus Kierkegaard means that the "transformation" of love by duty also occurs in genuine personal love: "Already in the ethical and religious factors [conjugal love] has duty in it, and when this appears before it, it is not as a stranger, a shameless intruder, who nevertheless has such authority that one dare not by virtue of the mysteriousness of love show him the door. No, duty comes as an old friend, an intimate, a confidant, whom the lovers mutually recognize in the deepest secret of their love."[52]

But the addition of "duty" to the reason-independence of agapic personal love could not make any difference: love will be constant only if one's resolution to do one's duty is constant.[53] Erosic love will change in response to changes in the properties of its object, but agapic personal love will vary as the lover varies in her will, determination, or ability to obey a commandment.[54] There is little reason to believe, then, that erosic personal love will be less constant than agapic. But other comparisons are possible. If love's constancy is a matter of keeping a promise or following a duty, then how does agapic personal love achieve love for the person? *X*'s obeying a moral law is not exactly being faithful to *y*. Further, agapic personal love, not being a function of its object's properties, cannot "be acquired, produced, controlled" by its object. Because its source is the lover's nature, "if it is there, it is like a blessing" or a mystery, unelicited by the object; "if it is not there, . . . there is nothing [y] can do to create it."[55] No amount of improvement of the beloved, no amount of *y*'s effort to develop herself for the delight of *x*, can have any effect on the continuity of *x*'s agapic love. But if an erosic love ends when the beloved loses her attractiveness, it can also be maintained by the beloved's efforts to improve herself. This tactic is not guaranteed to succeed, but the beloved can at least feel that she has some power over her fate. And the beloved can understand why *x*'s love has gone, if it has gone; but since *y*'s properties do not ground *x*'s agapic personal love, and *y* lacks input into the course of *x*'s love, *y* has no way to make sense of *x*'s either loving her or not loving her. It is misleading, however, to say that "a love no [erosic] grounds of which can be described . . . will be a source of . . . lacerating insecurity."[56] Agapic personal love is inconstant if the lover's will is unable to pull up his love by its own bootstraps, and whether *x* has the capacity to carry it out may continually worry *y*. But erosic love is plagued by its own substantial insecurity: the *y* who is loved for P worries about losing P, about the existence of other people who have P, about *x*'s continuing appreciation of P, and about why *x* finds P valuable. On this score agapic and erosic personal love are equally bad.

Kierkegaard does not appeal only to love's being a duty; he also changes the relationship from a dyad to a triad: "The love-relationship is a triangular relationship of the lover, the beloved, love—but love is God."[57] The addition of God as the Third cements the relationship: "When a relationship is only between two, one always has the upper hand . . . by being able to break it. . . . But when there are three, one person cannot do this."[58] And the presence of God is required for all types of love, says Kierkegaard: "Through a strange misunderstanding many . . . think they need God's help to love their neighbour, the least lovable object, but, however, that they can get along best by themselves in . . . erotic love and friendship, as if, alas, God's intermingling here were a disturbing and unfortunate factor. But no love . . . may secularly and merely humanly be deprived of the relationship to God."[59] The constancy of love is secured by nonexclusive loving, or in an exclusive triad (9.6).

In the triad x-God-y, however, God "not only becomes the third party . . . but essentially becomes the only beloved object, so that it is not the husband who is the wife's beloved, but it is God."[60] Kierkegaard's making God not only the Third but the *only* object of love seems odd; the rationale for the presence of the Third is no longer that it cements the love of x and y for each other. If the husband and wife "first and foremost belong to God,"[61] the injection of God has a different—quite opposite—rationale. Kierkegaard may be worried that the x-y love is getting along too well, that their happiness prevents them from recognizing their need for God and from loving their neighbor. Erotic love, says Kierkegaard, is the water to the fire that is the love for God and neighbor.[62] Even "the hearty twaddle of family life constitutes the worst danger for Christianity, and not wild lusts, debauchery. . . . They are not so opposed to Christianity as this flat mediocrity, this stuffy reek, this *nearness to each other*."[63] God is required not in order to cement the nearness of x and y, for their nearness threatens to exclude God from their lives. The rationale for injecting God into marriage, then, is that doing so may be the only alternative to getting rid of marriage altogether. Marriage transformed into a triad in which God is the only beloved is superior to a twaddle-marriage without God, and perhaps also to Paul's marriageless state in which x and y devote themselves only to God.[64]

But God's being the cementing Third in the x-y relationship and being the only object of love are compatible, since part of what Kierkegaard means by loving God is loving the neighbor. Then in the x-y relationship, x's loving God amounts to x's loving y with neighbor-love: your "wife shall first and foremost be your neighbour."[65] The injection of neighbor-love into the x-y relationship achieves constancy by protecting x and y from disappointment when they eventually see their defects and faults with perfect clarity, as a result of their "nearness." However, if this is how constancy is achieved by the Third, it is no more powerful than duty; obedience to the commandment to love is still the factor on which constancy depends. Agapic personal love, then, is no more constant than neighbor-love itself. To put it another way: if God is required as the Third to cement x to y, what cements x to the Third?

Kierkegaard hints at another way God as the Third protects the x-y relationship: "When she thanks God for the beloved her love is secured against suffering; by the fact that she thanks God she removes the man she loves just so far from her that she is able to draw breath."[66] Thanking God for love acknowledges God as an essential part of the relationship; and the human spouses joyfully realize they do not have to depend merely on each other.[67] We can secularize this insight: the intimacy ("nearness") of love can stifle autonomy and individuality. A Third is required not only to cement x and y together but also to keep x and y from getting too close. The delicate balance between interdependence and independence is orchestrated by something that situates x and y at exactly the right distance. Hence, a point we made about intimacy—that *total* sharing cannot be required on pain of destroying individuality—applies here: total sharing threatens constancy. Exclusivity and constancy are again opposed; that which tends to make love exclusive, the sharing involved in intimacy, is that which, if taken too far, undermines constancy (that is, love itself). "The rattle of Woody Allen's ironies," says Bernard Williams, "reminds us that, if all that is interesting to lovers is each other, there may not be much of interest."[68] Perhaps this is why Freud said that the two most important things in life are love *and* work. The dyad is unstable, always on the verge of exploding, and it needs a Third (work, friends, separate vacations, hobbies) for stability. The Third need not be inanimate or supernatural. It might be a person: the x-y-z triad could be a Kierkegaardian arrangement that achieves constancy through nonexclusivity.[69] But it is no panacea. The triad of mommy-baby-daddy is no more stable, despite the wishful prepregnancy thinking of x and y, than the barebones x-y dyad.[70] And how could the x-y-z triad overcome the problems of the separate x-y, y-z, and x-z dyads? If we cannot count on God as the Third, since cementing ourselves to Him is no easy trick, there may be no constancy forthcoming from x and y's cementing themselves to z.

The theory of erosic love also makes room for a Third. Indeed, the structural difference between erosic and agapic personal love can be stated in these terms. If x loves y in virtue of y's S, S is the Third that cements x to y in the erosic triad x-S-y. Since y's properties are irrelevant for agapic personal love, something else (determination, God) must be the Third that cements x to y. Further, if God is one object of love in the agapic triad x-God-y, in the erosic triad x-S-y S may be an object of x's love (in addition to y). So if God as the object of love in the agapic triad is called upon to prevent x and y from getting too close to each other, we can construe x's loving S as a way for x to offset the smothering closeness to y by the detachment made possible by x's focusing on S. Hating P in z, rather than z herself, is an advantage; it places a wall between x and z. Detachment is useful in love for its own reason: to help x protect her autonomy.

CHAPTER 11 *Reciprocity*

There is nothing sadder than to serve a master who knows not that we are serving Him, or, if he knows, gives us no sign that he is satisfied. In such a case love must be strong because it stands alone, unsupported by any pleasure.

—St. Francis de Sales, *The Love of God*

I could never tell my love. That this . . . did not immediately produce a pain of which I died is proof of the immense power, that is *ipso facto* the purity, of the love which I felt for this girl. It was enough happiness to love her.

—Iris Murdoch, *The Black Prince*

1. DEFINING RECIPROCITY

Reciprocity is relatively easily defined: x's love for y is reciprocal, or reciprocated, if y also loves x. Of course, we must be more precise: if x loves y only at t_1 and y loves x only at some other time t_2, their love is not reciprocal. Thus, reciprocal love is x's loving y and y's loving x at the same time. Unrequited love is a special type of nonreciprocal love. Nonreciprocal love is the wider category, in which at a given time xLy but not yLx; but a nonreciprocated love may have been reciprocal at an earlier time. Unrequited love is a smaller category, in which xLy but not yLx, and y has never loved x.

If x and y's love is reciprocal, they have the same emotion toward each other. But what does having the *same* emotion mean? Trivially, x and y's love is reciprocal when both emotions are love. Love, however, comes in many varieties: there is erosic and agapic personal love; there is erosic love based on the physical, and erosic based on the mental. Hence, x and y's having the *same* emotion can mean two different things. In "broad" reciprocity, x and y's having the same emotion is their having personal love of *any* kind toward the other. In "narrow" reciprocity, many details of their respective loves are the same. I will use "mutual" to refer to loves that are narrowly reciprocal, reserving "reciprocal" for loves on which there are no restrictions regarding the details of the two emotions. All mutual loves, then, are reciprocal, but not all reciprocal loves are mutual.[1] The thesis that love *is* a reciprocal emotion is the claim that if x has an emotion toward y, and y does not have the same (broadly conceived) emotion toward x, then neither x's nor y's emotion is love: a necessary condition for an emotion to be love is that the object of the emotion has the same emotion toward its subject.[2] The thesis is not that x is not psychologically able to love y if y does not love x, but that in virtue of the concept or nature of love an emotion can be love only when reciprocated. Love is not unilateral; either x and y love each other, or neither x nor y love each other.

This thesis is strange. No other emotions (except Aristotle's philia) are by nature reciprocal: x can unilaterally hate, admire, or resent y. Further, many varieties of love are not reciprocal: (a) God loves all humans, but some humans do not love God; (b) x may love chess, the Beethoven Violin Concerto, or y's properties, and of course chess and y's courage cannot reciprocate; (c) x may love an irreversibly comatose or dead y; (d) a parent may love his or her young child, who does not yet have the ability to love anyone; (e) x may love a cat, and x's love is not bogus just because a cat has a different kind of affective life; and (f) x's neighbor-love for y is love even when y hates x.

The response to this objection can be piecemeal or general. The piecemeal response explains away each counterexample: (a) God's love generates reciprocity, or to love God a human needs only to believe in God; (b) we may like the Beethoven Violin Concerto or find courage attractive, but we cannot love them, because we cannot be concerned about inanimate things for their own sake;[3] (c) x's loving a comatose or dead y is a limiting case of a previously reciprocal love, or this y (like chess) cannot be loved; (d) parental love is another limiting case, since it aims toward reciprocity; further, infants might exhibit a rudimentary love for their parents; (e) either x's emotion for animals is only affection, or animals (like infants) exhibit emotions close enough to love—remember, only the same emotion, broadly conceived, must be returned; and (f) neighbor-love may work like God's love to evoke reciprocity. Clearly, the piecemeal response is not compelling.

The general response is that personal love, in the neutral sense, is an anomalous emotion. Hence, most of the counterexamples are irrelevant to the thesis that personal love conceptually requires reciprocity. But this will not do. Many cases of reciprocal personal love must have been, at least briefly, not reciprocal; it is unlikely that xLy and yLx begin simultaneously. The thesis that personal love is by nature reciprocal, however, prohibits nonsimultaneous beginnings. One might handle the problem of xLy and yLx not starting at the same time this way: *either* x's love, which begins before y's, is not "fully" love until y reciprocates (and y's loving x is not "fully" love unless x already "nonfully" loves y), *or* x's emotion can be love, as long as shortly after it begins y also loves x. The former route rests on a tenuous distinction between x's "not fully" and "fully" loving y; the latter (even if we overlook that "shortly" is vague) blurs the distinction between unrequited love and not yet reciprocal love. The thesis that an emotion must be reciprocal in order to be love seems a nonstarter.

2. DEFENDING THE DOCTRINE OF RECIPROCITY

The thesis that love is by its nature reciprocal seems supportable neither by observation nor by theory; x's finding y attractive enough to love does not entail that y finds x attractive. Yet some writers claim that love is reciprocal. Robert Ehman says, "While reciprocity is not a condition of our desiring a person . . . it is nevertheless a condition of genuine love."[4] Ehman's argument is the same as his argument that "there is in the strict sense no love at first sight." Love requires knowledge of the beloved's character; not only must x have true beliefs about y that are formed rationally (that is, no idealization), but x's knowledge of y must be extensive. Hence, love at first sight never counts as love, since x could not know enough about y (2.2). Similarly, "there is no purely unrequited love." Never having had "the opportunity to share his life with his beloved," x cannot base his emotion on "the qualities of the person that are at once most unique and most permanent." Instead, "the unrequited lover may make a show of loving, but in fact he loves a mere unrealized ideal."[5] The unilateral lover "in the same manner as an insane person . . . give[s] the imaginary an even higher emotional value than the real." I do not find Ehman's argument compelling. Even if x's loving y requires x to know y well, it does not follow that x cannot love y unless y loves x. The knowledge that x must have to love y might be available only if y spends a good deal of time with x, but this condition is satisfiable without y's loving x (say, x and y work together). Further, Ehman's argument entails that "knowing well" is necessarily a reciprocal relation. From (1) x loves y only if x knows y and (2) x knows y only if y loves x, Ehman derives his conclusion that x loves y only if y loves x—and vice versa. But from claims (1) and (2) it also follows that x knows y only if y knows x, which is absurd. (Note that Ehman conflates the unrequited lover who nurtures his love by deliberately feeding it with idealization, and a more ordinary unilateral lover who does not give "the imaginary . . . higher emotional value than the real.")

Karol Wojtyla also claims that personal love "is by its very nature not unilateral but bilateral."[6] Like Ehman, Wojtyla thinks that unrequited love is not "genuine" and psychologically unsound: "onesided" love does not have "the objective fullness which reciprocity would give it. . . . If a love of this kind persists, . . . this is because of some inner obstinacy." Wojtyla's argument is quite different: "Love is not just something *in* [x] and something *in* [y]—for in that case there would properly speaking be two loves—but is something common to them" (p. 84). Love is a (third) thing to which x and y contribute; it is not their separate loves for each other, but "something 'between' two persons, something shared." Further, since two "I"s merge into a single "we," Wojtyla concludes that "we can hardly speak of 'selfishness' in this context." But it is not clear to me why the love "between" x and y is not merely x's loving y and y's loving x. We would not say that when x and y hate each other, there is only one hatred rather than two. And if we find odd the metaphysics that creates one love out of two, we will find odd the corresponding creation of one item, the "we," out of two separable "I"s.

But Wojtyla is not alone in entertaining such thoughts. Consider the view of the secular philosopher Charles Fried:

> Perhaps the central conception of love between persons involves a notion of reciprocity. . . . [R]eciprocity must be formalized . . . in terms of mutual sharing of interests. . . . There is . . . a creation of love, a middle term, which is a new pattern or system of interests which both [persons] share and both value. . . . In this way reciprocal love represents a kind of resolution of the paradoxes of self-interest and altruism.[7]

How does joint interest provide a "kind" of solution to the problem of self-interest in love? Joint interests can be broken—they are not logically welded together (10.3)—and may be broken when it is profitable for either party to do so. This solution is no more illuminating than claiming that selfishness drops out because two "I"s become a single "we." Are we supposed to imagine the literal re-formation of an Aristophanic circle-person? "The pleasure of the lover . . . is not selfish with respect to the loved one," says Kierkegaard, pretending for a second to be Leo Buscaglia. When he continues we are jolted: "But in union they are both absolutely selfish, inasmuch as . . . they constitute one self."[8] Whereas Wojtyla relies on the union to eliminate selfishness from love, for Kierkegaard the union magnifies selfishness. The reciprocal "passionate preference" x and y have for each other "is another form of self-love."[9] If x and y are more than metaphorically united—"the more securely the two I's come together to become one I"[10]—then in loving y, x is just loving himself: "The beloved . . . [is] therefore called, . . . significantly enough, the *other-self*, the *other-I*."

In arguing that love-as-union is selfish, I do not think Kierkegaard has done better than Wojtyla and Fried have in arguing that love-as-union destroys selfishness. What is interesting is the contrast between Wojtyla and Kierkegaard, both of whom invoke Christian considerations to support their views. For Kierkegaard, who takes his cue from agape, love is not by nature reciprocal. Indeed, one test of x's love is whether x's love persists when not reciprocated, for then x can get nothing from y.[11] Neighbor-love is not by nature reciprocal (one turns the other cheek and continues to love); one would never say of neighbor-love, as Wojtyla says of unrequited personal love, that it has "some inner obstinacy." Given the role that agape plays in personal love for Wojtyla, it would appear to be impossible for him to argue that love is by nature reciprocal. If x's love is expected to endure beyond the point of y's sinning, surely x's love must be expected to endure if y no longer loves x. Wojtyla's thesis that love is strictly constant (10.2) seems incompatible with his claims about reciprocity.

However, the doctrine that love is strictly constant is not incompatible with the doctrine that love is reciprocal. I just said that if love is strictly constant, x's love for y will continue even if y no longer loves x; hence y's having the same emotion toward x is not, contrary to the doctrine of reciprocity, a necessary condition for x to love y. But if love is strictly constant, then *ex hypothesi* we have no right to assume that y no longer loves x. According to strict constancy, if x's and y's emotions are really love, neither emotion will end, and equivalently, if x's or y's emotion does end, the emotion had not been love. Hence, x's love is never faced with the test of enduring when y no longer reciprocates; the constancy of love prevents the situation, xLy but not yLx, that would show that strict constancy is incompatible with reciprocity. Equivalently, if y's emotion toward x ends, y's emotion had not been love; but by the doctrine of reciprocity, if y's emotion had not been love, x's emotion, too, had not been love. Thus there had never been any love that might now be persisting even though not reciprocated; there is no love that fails to endure in the face of nonreciprocation. If love is by its nature reciprocal, it is conceptually impossible for x to stop loving y *because* y has stopped loving x.

Wojtyla gives another reason that love is by nature reciprocal, implicitly acknowledging the notion that humans might love God in response to God's love for humans (1.6). When x loves y, x makes a gift of x's self to y. This gift is no five-and-dime trinket but a "surrender of the innermost self"; the "magnitude of the gift" represents the value of the person as such. X's love is reciprocated by y because the "realization of the value of the gift awakens the need to . . . reciprocate in ways which would match its value."[12] Y can match this value only by making a gift to x of y's self, that is, by loving x. Notice three things about this argument. First, it allows (indeed, presupposes) that xLy and yLx occur nonsimultaneously, since yLx is a response to xLy. Second, love generates its own reciprocity unilaterally. If xLy brings about yLx, it could not have been the case that yLx brought about xLy, for yLx occurs after xLy. Hence, x's love for y must come about some other way than by y's loving x. Both loves involve a giving of the self but have different foundations. Third, the argument is both a conceptual and a psychological defense of reciprocity. Conceptually, it asserts that love involves a surrender of the self; psychologically, it asserts that a gift of such magnitude (always) has the power to induce love.

Erich Fromm holds a similar view: "In giving he cannot help bringing something to life in the other person . . . ; in truly giving, he cannot help receiving that which is given back to him. . . . [L]ove is a power which produces love; impotence is the inability to produce love."[13] In support of his thesis, Fromm quotes Karl Marx:

> If we assume *man* to be *man,* and his relation to the world to be a human one, then love can be exchanged only for love, trust for trust, and so on. . . . If you love unrequitedly, i.e. if your love as love does not call forth love in return, if through the *vital expression* of yourself as a loving person you fail to become a *loved person,* then your love is impotent, it is a misfortune.[14]

But Fromm's thesis is partially contradicted by Marx: love that does not induce return love is, for Marx, still love. If my love does not induce love, *I* am "impotent," or my love is impotent in not having the power Fromm thinks all love has. Were Fromm to respond that impotent love is not genuine love, his claim that love begets love becomes tautologous. Fromm's invoking this passage—which mentions "exchanging" love for love—is also ironic. He claims that when x gives to y, x "cannot help receiving that which is given back to him," and Wojtyla claims that when x gives herself to y, y is induced to give back equal value. If so, the idea that what x gives is a *gift* becomes suspicious; this love looks like Aristotle's imperfect friendship, in which use or pleasure is exchanged homogeneously for equal use or pleasure.

The point is not that reciprocal love must reduce to two self-interested exchanges, but that arguing that love is by its nature reciprocal, on the specific grounds that love evokes love, gives us as much reason to believe it as to deny it. Kierkegaard again is relevant: "There is . . . a repayment for love which is homogeneous with love: requited love. And there is still so much good in the majority of men that as a rule they will regard this repayment . . . in the form of . . . requited love, as the most significant, although . . . they will perhaps not admit that it is repayment."[15] Wojtyla and Fromm will protest: "This is not what we meant. In genuine love, x and y give with no thought of receiving; the giving in love is a gift, not a business deal." But the thesis that giving begets giving, if true, undercuts this protest. What would make it clear that x's giving is not motivated by getting is x's *not* being able to count on x's giving having the power to induce y to give back; in that case x can view giving as a gift.

Further, only if y is not overwhelmed into giving back by the power of x's giving, can x feel that y's giving is not merely tit-for-tat. If y's loving x results from x's loving or giving to y, then x's love for y produces y's love for x in much the same way as a potion would produce yLx (8.4). If love begets love, x cannot feel that x is loved in virtue of y's nature autonomously moving y to x.

The psychological component of Wojtyla's argument, that love begets love, is dubious. True, x's loving y may show y what love is and invoke love by setting an example, but not always. And perhaps y cannot love anyone unless y has at some time been loved. But this provides no reason to think x's loving y will evoke y's loving x in particular. Further, x's giving a huge gift to y may evoke only gratitude or, oppositely, resentment. Thus an already existing reciprocal love might be precisely the framework *within* which giving can be welcomed as fitting rather than as threatening. And there are those—Stendhal, Proust, my dentist—who philosophize that x's giving to y is a sure way to prevent y's loving x; y comes to love x only if x withdraws from y. But in a devious way this tactic still involves love's begetting love. If x loves y and wants y to love x, x should hide the fact that x loves y; causally situated between x's loving y and eventually y's loving x is not Wojtyla's gift, but x's not giving. But if love does not always evoke love, neither does playing hard to get always work. The x who wants y's love must figure out in advance (aha! by knowing y) whether showing or hiding x's love will have the desired effect.

3. THE DESIRE FOR RECIPROCITY

Even if personal love is not by its nature reciprocal, perhaps x's loving y entails that x *desires* that x's love be reciprocated. Annette Baier, for example, claims that "to love someone is necessarily . . . to hope for return love."[16] Mark Fisher, however, provides a counterexample: some lovers "do not want [the] happiness" of reciprocal love because they are "self-lacerating."[17] If there is no contradiction in x's genuinely loving y and x's being "self-lacerating," then x's not desiring reciprocity does not entail that x's emotion is not love. And it would seem strange to say that simply because x is "self-lacerating," x cannot love—except if it is a conceptual truth that x can love others only if x loves himself, and "self-laceration" is incompatible with self-love (5.4).

W. Newton-Smith offers another example of a lover who does not desire reciprocity: x loves y, but y is married to z; believing that were y to love x, that would harm y, x does not tell y of his love.[18] There are two ways to interpret this case: (a) x does desire that y reciprocate, or (b) x does not desire that y reciprocate. Interpretation (a) seems natural; x desires that y reciprocate, but x does not act to satisfy that desire. Interpretation (a) is consistent with the claim that xLy entails that x desires that yLx. Interpretation (b), which refutes the claim, seems neither incoherent nor foreign to human psychology; x might simply not desire reciprocity. Some medieval courtly lovers did not expect and hence did not desire reciprocity, precisely because their beloveds were married.

What is surprising is that Newton-Smith argues that love does entail the desire for reciprocity, yet claims that in his example x does not desire reciprocity even though x loves y. He writes that x "would wish [reciprocity] if all things were equal. But given the circumstances as they are, he does not wish it." The point seems to be that x wishes that y were in a position to reciprocate, that the world were different in various ways, but x's desiring that y were in a position to reciprocate is not identical to desiring that y reciprocate. Even if we grant this to Newton-Smith, how does his own example avoid refuting the thesis that love entails a desire for reciprocity? He asserts that we can see that this thesis is a conceptual truth about love by recognizing that any situation in which the lover did not desire reciprocity is bound to be odd in some way. In his example, x does not desire reciprocity only because y's reciprocating would result, atypically, in "an unhappy love." Or if the lover x is a "masochist" bent on "self-abasement," x might not desire reciprocity; this, too, is an odd situation. If every situation in which x loves y but x does not desire reciprocity is odd, then we are entitled (by an indirect sort of argument) to conclude that "loving entails, *ceteris paribus,* the desire for reciprocated love." Thus Newton-Smith argues that "in the absence" of some oddness in the situation, loving does entail a desire for reciprocity, in contrast to Fisher, who relies on these (odd) cases to refute the thesis that love entails a desire for reciprocity. But Newton-Smith is wrong, I think, in claiming that in his own example x does not desire reciprocity. X's desiring that y were in a position to reciprocate— that is, desiring that y could reciprocate—is too close to desiring that y does reciprocate for interpretation (b) to be plausible. In his example, exactly why does x not tell y that x loves y? "Being magnanimous," says Newton-Smith, x does not tell y because x believes harm would befall y. He claims that x is concerned for y's welfare *because* x is morally virtuous. If so, it makes sense to think that x does desire reciprocity and is dissuaded by moral considerations from acting on that desire. But we need not assume with Newton-Smith that x's goodness toward y is due to x's moral virtue or magnanimity. Rather, since x loves y, and love implies concern for the well-being of the beloved, it is x's love itself that provides x with the motivation not to act on the desire for reciprocity.

The point is that right under Newton-Smith's nose was a direct argument that love entails, ceteris paribus, the desire for reciprocity: the concern feature of love may itself imply the desire for reciprocity. We can begin to lay out this argument by looking at another part of Fisher's view. He claims that one might have thought that xLy entails that x desires yLx on the grounds that (1) love by its nature is sexual (it always includes sexual desire), and (2) "sexual love . . . by its very nature involve[s] a desire for reciprocation."[19] Fisher rejects claim (1) by citing parental love and love for "one's sovereign." I will not quibble over this, even though one could respond that personal love, our topic, necessarily includes sexual desire (see Wojtyla; chap. 10, n. 14); but I do not think that personal love must involve sexual desire or be grounded on sexual attractiveness. Instead, I have doubts about Fisher's treatment of claim (2). He asserts that if sexual love involves a desire for reciprocity, "that will surely be because of its nature as sexual, that is, as involving a desire to give and get sexual pleasure." The question now arises, What does sexual desire have, in virtue of which it includes a desire for reciprocity, that love lacks, so that love (in Fisher's view) does not include the desire for reciprocity?

Sexual desire involves *two* desires, a desire to give and a desire to get sexual pleasure. Presumably, the desire for reciprocity derives from the desire to get sexual pleasure from the object of one's sexual desire; for if in sexually desiring y, x desired only to give pleasure, that desire alone does not entail a further desire for reciprocity (Fisher: x might be "self-lacerating"; Newton-Smith: x might be "magnanimous"). Hence, what sexual desire has that love lacks is a desire to get something from the object of one's attention. This is apparently how Fisher reasons in distinguishing sexual desire from love. If so, what he overlooks is that one need not appeal to a desire to get sexual pleasure in order to derive a desire for reciprocity; the desire to give pleasure itself implies, *ceteris paribus,* a desire for reciprocity. If x desires to give y sexual pleasure, x will not be able to satisfy that desire unless y sexually desires x. For example, y normally will not allow x to do those sexual things that y finds pleasurable unless y desires x, or the pleasure that x can give to y will be maximized when y also desires x. If the only or best way x can satisfy x's desire to give y pleasure is by y's reciprocating, x must desire y to reciprocate if x desires to give y pleasure.

Since a desire to give can be sufficient (ceteris paribus) for a desire for reciprocity, in this regard sexual desire has nothing that love lacks that would account for the former but not the latter's including a desire for reciprocity. If x loves y and desires to benefit y, the satisfaction of x's desire to benefit y may be maximized when y loves x and thereby allows herself to be benefited by x. The concern of love, its desire to give to the beloved, implies a desire for reciprocity to the extent that x's ability to carry out whatever is demanded by love's concern is severely hampered if y is not a willing recipient of x's love. This does not mean that x desires reciprocity because x believes that y's loving x per se will make y happy. That may be true for God, as St. Bernard said: "When God loves, he only desires to be loved, knowing that love will render all those who love Him happy."[20] I doubt that we should take "only" literally, as if God's loving humans reduced without remainder to God's desire to be loved. Nor should we think that what holds for God holds for humans. Instead of arrogantly thinking that x is God's gift to y, x is only thinking that x, because x loves y, is a person who is especially concerned for y's welfare, and that y would benefit by being open to and returning x's affection.

If this account of the connection among x's loving y, x's concern for the well-being of y, and x's desiring reciprocity makes sense, we can understand why x's love might be conditional on y's reciprocating and, therefore, why x's concern might be conditional on y's loving x—a sympathetic explanation that does not merely accuse x of tit-for-tat self-interest or of not really being concerned for y. If y does not love x and, as a result, does not give x the opportunity to benefit y, x will be saddled with a desire to give that x knows must remain frustrated. In the name of rationality—abandoning desires that have no hope of success—x benignly abandons her love for y. We have already come across the idea that x's no longer loving y when x realizes that x cannot benefit y does not count as a fault in x's love; this is precisely what Aristotle claims when he points out that x's withdrawing love from y, because y has changed from being good to evil, is neither objectionable nor indicates that x is being selfish. X can do nothing for this y. (See 10.5.)

Be sure not to conflate two arguments. One is that if x's emotion leads x to desire that y love x, x's emotion cannot be love; x's desire for reciprocity betrays x's self-interested attitude. I have rejected this argument. The second is that if x's love is conditional on y's loving x, then x's love is not the real thing, since (again) this conditionality implies that x's attitude is self-interested. One might think that x's loving y cannot mean that x desires reciprocity on the grounds that x's love would then be conditional on y's loving x—but that is a non sequitur: x's desiring reciprocity by itself does not entail that x will not love y if y does not love x. Further, even if x's loving y is conditional on y's loving x, this fact does not necessarily mean that x is self-interested in a way incompatible with love. If the frustration of x's desire to benefit y is too much for x to bear, x cannot always be blamed for abandoning x's love for y and cannot be quickly accused of morally significant self-interest. X's love is in some cases conditional on reciprocity not because x was hoping to get from y but because x was hoping to give to y.

4. CONVOLUTIONS

We can strengthen the connection between x's concern for the welfare of y and x's desire for reciprocity by investigating exactly what the desire for reciprocity *is*. One distinction to be made immediately is between the desire for reciprocity and the desire to be loved. One can desire to be loved by anyone at all (like desiring something—anything—to eat) without loving anyone; and one can desire to be loved by a particular person without loving that person. But the desire for reciprocity, as a matter of logic, can exist only when one already loves somebody; it is the desire to be loved by the particular person one loves. Note that if love is by its nature reciprocal, the desire for reciprocity—the desire to be loved by the person one loves—is conceptually impossible, since one cannot love another unilaterally. What is possible, if love is by its nature reciprocal, is only the desire to be loved, period, or the desire that one's beloved *continue* to love in return. Finally, note that the mere desire to be loved (like the desire for food) need not be selfish even when it is self-interested; if being loved (like having food) is a basic good—say, it is required for self-confidence—then wanting to be loved is not self-interested in any morally offensive sense. But the desire for reciprocity, to be loved by a particular person, may be self-interested in a stronger sense, if it is unlikely that being loved by a specific person is essential for one's well-being.

Suppose that x's loving y entails that x is concerned for y's well-being. If so, the desire for reciprocity can be unpacked to yield a reductio argument that x's loving y cannot entail that x desires reciprocity. Assume that

(i) x loves y, and

(ii) x's loving y entails that x desires that y love x.

Now, if love implies concern for the welfare of the beloved, then were y to love x, y would be concerned for x:

(iii) y's loving x entails that y is concerned for x.

From (i) and (ii) it follows that

(iv) x desires that y love x

and from (iii) and (iv) we derive

(v) x desires that y be concerned for x.

But in desiring to be the object of y's concern—to be benefited by y—x thereby has a self-interested attitude, which is incompatible with assuming that x loves y. It is no help here to point out that under our assumptions y, too, desires reciprocity in order to be benefited by x. For then reciprocal love is the dyadic exchange characteristic of Aristotle's imperfect friendships. The conclusion reached by this reductio argument is not that love does entail the desire for reciprocity and therefore *either* love does not exist (since its concern is always fake) *or* all love is ultimately self-interested. Rather, genuine love is saved by denying that love entails a desire for reciprocity.

There are two problems with this reductio argument. First, from the fact that I desire something, it does not follow that I desire everything about that thing. If I desire to have a cat, and cats have fleas, I am not compelled by logic or psychology to desire fleabites. So if x desires to be loved by y and a component of y's love is y's concern for x, it does not follow that x desires to be the object of y's concern. Second, if I desire to kiss the girl in the blue dress across the dance floor, and the girl in the blue dress is (unknown to me) a guy in drag, it does not follow that I desire to kiss a guy in drag. Similarly, if x desires that y love x it does not follow that x desires to be the object of y's concern, if x does not believe that in loving x, y would be concerned for x. Perhaps the only component of love that x considers important is the desire to share experiences, in which case in desiring that y love x, x primarily desires that y desires to share experiences with x. Further, even if x desires that y love x and x believes that in loving x, y would be concerned for x, it might still be no contradiction to deny that x desires to be the object of y's concern; something's being foreseen does not entail that it is desired.

Of course, these problems may not sufficiently damage the inference from steps (iii) and (iv) to (v). Even if x's desiring A does not entail that x desires everything included in A, x's desiring A might entail desiring something that is central to A. If I desire to have a cat, I may not desire the fleas, but I do desire to have a pet or a companion or a showpiece. Similarly, if x desires that y love x, x desires whatever is central to love, namely y's concern. And if I desire to kiss the girl in the blue dress, not knowing that she is a he, I am likely to be told, "Look here. What you really want to do is to kiss a guy, whether you realize it or not." Similarly, it can be said about x's desire for reciprocity that what x really wants is to be the object of y's concern; whether or not x believes that concern is an element of love, it still is. But we can continue to confound the reductio by *granting* that if x desires to be loved by y, x desires to be the object of y's concern. The reductio turns out to unpack the desire for reciprocity incompletely.

Suppose, then, that love includes a desire for reciprocity. If so, x's loving y entails that x desires that y love x, and y's loving x entails that y desires that x love y. Hence, if x desires that y love x, and y's loving x entails that y desires that x love y, then x desires that y desires that x love y. That is, x's desire for reciprocity includes not only x's desire to be loved by y, but also x's desire that y desires to be loved by x. The part of x's desire for reciprocity that is x's desire to be loved by y entails that x desires to be the recipient of y's concern. But the part that is x's desire that y desires to be loved by x entails that x desires that y desires to be the recipient of x's concern. Thus, x's desire for reciprocity is both x's desire to be benefited by y and x's desire that y desires to be benefited by x.

Now, to show that loving cannot entail the desire for reciprocity, on pain of contradicting x's claim to love y, one needs to show that it follows from x's desire to be benefited by y (to get from y) and from x's desire that y desires to be benefited by x (x's wanting y to want to get from x), that x's concern is objectionably self-interested—that x wants y to want to get from x *because* x wants to get from y. But it does not follow. X's desire to get from y and x's desire that y desires to get from x were derived independently from x's desire for reciprocity. So we are permitted to conclude at most that when x loves y there will be a constant conjunction of x's desire to get from y and x's desire that y desires to get from x. X's unilateral desire for reciprocity is a desire that both x and y give and that both x and y receive. Hence, in answer to the question, Why does x want y to want to be benefited by x?, there are two answers, neither of which is ruled out by the reductio argument. One is that x wants y to want to receive from x because y's wanting to receive from x facilitates x's getting from y. The other answer is that x wants y to want to receive from x because y's wanting to be benefited by x facilitates the satisfaction of x's desire to benefit y. If love entails a desire for reciprocity, that alone does not mean that x is ultimately proposing a self-interested tit-for-tat exchange with y.

5. MUTUALITY

Reciprocal loves are "nonmutual" if they are in various ways disparate. For example: (1) x and y do not love each other with the same intensity; (2) their loves do not have the same causal effects, that is, their loves lead them to have different desires or to place a different emphasis on the same desire (x's love may induce x to want to live with y, while y's love has no such consequence); (3) their loves are not constituted identically, for example, x's love emphasizes concern more than the desire to share experiences, while y's love favors intimacy over concern; (4) one person loves the other exclusively, while the other loves two persons at the same time; and (5) the persons love on the basis of different things (x loves y in virtue of one sort of property, y loves x for a different sort), or one loves erosically while the other loves agapically. How important is mutuality in love?

"Of all the . . . affections of the soul, love is the only one by means of which the creature, though not on equal terms, is able to . . . give back [to God] something resembling what has been given to it," said St. Bernard.[21] God and His creatures can achieve reciprocity, but we might wonder about two things. First, if humans and God are "not on equal terms"—consider the edge God has in power—will their love, despite reciprocity, lose something in quality? In virtue of this power differential humans have reason to fear God, which suggests that their love for God is tainted. But in the Christian universe, God's being perfectly good means that humans need not worry about His power; God never uses it for evil purposes and, unlike humans, is not corruptible by having it. Second, the love that humans return "resembles" the love they receive; humans return to God, as well as they can, something of equal value by surrendering their selves. But if humans love God erosically and God loves humans with His agape, where is the resemblance? God loves humans because that is His nature. Humans love God because, for example, they stand in awe of His perfection. Thus, the reciprocal love between humans and God is not love between equals; indeed, the reciprocal love between humans and God is not mutual *because* God and humans are unequal.

If God's goodness means that the inequality in power between humans and God does not spoil their reciprocal love, that saving grace is unavailable to the personal loves of humans. Various inequalities between x and y—in physical, psychological, or economic power—may reduce the quality of their reciprocal love.[22] It is often claimed that men love erosically and women love agapically; or that both men and women love erosically but men love in virtue of physical beauty, while women love in virtue of prestige, intelligence, and economic success; that men tend to love nonexclusively and with fickle inconstancy, while women tend to love exclusively and with obsessive constancy (see 7.7). Given the complaining that men and women do about love, their relationships, and each other, inequalities outside of love apparently make even reciprocal love unhappy. We might, then, want to understand Aristophanes, who advises us to seek a mate who "matches" our nature (5.5), as telling us to cultivate love with our social and economic equals, since we thereby avoid the unhappiness of nonmutual love.

If reciprocal love, to be successful, requires mutuality, and if there are serious differences between men and women, it seems that only homosexual love could work. Plato and Aristotle assumed that equality outside love was an important factor in determining the quality of love; both concluded that love between two men is better than love between a man and a woman, in part because men are superior to women in rationality and moral virtue. A similar conclusion is reached by some contemporary feminists, who claim that love between two women is better than love between a woman and a man; or even that, whether by biology or by socialization, men are incapable of love.[23] But for philosophers as diverse as Nietzsche, Fromm, and Wojtyla, the differences between men and women do not prevent love, but make it possible, because in virtue of these differences men and women are yin-yang complements.[24] What these writers have in common, which distinguishes them from Plato and Aristotle, is their emphasis on the role of sexuality in love; if one makes that move, the differences between men and women will look like a precondition of love, not what kills it. Of course, sexual desire can take its leave from love; perhaps, then, we should conclude that heterosexual love is primarily threatened by the fact that men and women are not interested in the same things and therefore are not friends[25]—which brings us closer to Aristotle. But the claim that a precondition of love is similarity in the things (the environment, God) the lovers are interested in is only partially right; x and y's love for each other often explains why they become interested in the same things.

The contrast between Plato and Aristotle, on one side, and Fromm, Nietzsche, and Wojtyla, on the other, suggests that although mutuality is in some ways essential for love, in other ways nonmutuality is essential. Recall that the desire-satisfaction model cannot be a general account of love (6.3) because if everyone were a D-S lover there would not be much love; if x is a D-S lover, x does best to seek a mate who is not a D-S lover. Thus love on the D-S model must be nonmutual. Similarly, if everyone were a Balint-lover (8.3) who demanded perfectly unconditional love, no one would exist to provide this selfless love; Balint-love must be nonmutual. But if reciprocal and mutual love between an egocentric x and an egocentric y is impossible, so is love between two altruists. Fromm says that "love is primarily *giving,* not receiving,"[26] but this cannot be right if he means that when anyone genuinely loves, he or she mostly gives and does not receive. X's desire to benefit y cannot be satisfied if y abandons all y's needs and desires in attempting to fulfill x's needs;[27] if both x and y abandon their needs and desires in order to fulfill the needs and desires of the other, both give but there is no one to receive—so there is no giving.[28] The facts that mutually egoistic and mutually altruisic loves are impossible, and that the reciprocal, nonmutual, but stable love of an egoist and an altruist seems objectionable, may underlie the idea that equality outside love is important because it permits equality in giving and getting within a mutual love (which does not mean that both parties give just in order to get). Inequality outside love is not necessarily disruptive if the inequalities balance each other or provide the substance for equal giving and getting. Further, even if love between a permanent egoist and a permanent altruist is morally indecent, love between two persons who both pass back and forth synchronically between the egoist and the altruist role is not horrifying.

There is another way in which reciprocal love can be nonmutual: not merely that x's concern for y is different from y's concern for x, but that x's and y's *beliefs* about the kind of concern involved in love are different. For

Nietzsche, reciprocal heterosexual love is possible not only because of its nonmutuality (the yin-yang complementarity of male dominance and female submission), but also because "man and woman understand something different by the term love,—and it belongs to the conditions of love . . . that the one sex does *not* presuppose . . . the same conception of 'love' . . . in the other sex."[29] Nietzsche suggests that nonmutuality in beliefs about love is essential for at least heterosexual love. It seems to me, however, that disagreements over what love is commonly disrupt the reciprocity of love.[30] Indeed, a mark of troubled love is the frequency of arguments about love itself: "If you loved me, you would blank"; "I do love you, even if I don't blank, and if you loved me you wouldn't insist on my blanking."[31] The scenario often goes like this: "You don't really love me"; "yes I do"; "on *my* definition you don't." Yet the history of love, were it faithfully recorded, would also include: "You do love me, after all"; "I most emphatically do not"; "on *my* definition you do."

Thus, when Alastair Hannay writes, "The suggestion that you could only love another if the other loved you—in whatever way—implies a . . . conditionality that is surely incompatible with a genuine concern for the other,"[32] he conflates two claims. One is that if x's love for y is conditional on y's loving x in *x*'s sense of love, x's love is not genuine; the other is that if x's love for y is conditional on y's loving x in *y*'s sense of love, x's love is not genuine. In the first case, x may want y to love x in x's sense because y does love x, but not in a sense that x countenances; x might only desire that the reciprocal love x and y already have be, in addition, mutual. But x's love for y being conditional on y's loving x mutually does not entail that x's love for y is not genuine. For x's desire might derive from x's belief that if their love does not achieve mutuality, it is doomed. The second case, in which x would not love y unless y loved x in y's (unspecified) sense of love, more clearly illustrates Hannay's point. For here x may be demanding reciprocity itself. In this case, too, there is an ambiguity: Does Hannay mean that if x's love for y depends on y's love for x at least *starting* at some point, then x does not really love y, or that if x's love for y depends on y's love for x *continuing,* then x's emotion is not genuine love?

6. RECIPROCITY AND CONSTANCY

The statement that x's love for y is conditional on y's loving x embodies two quite different claims: the thesis that love is by its nature reciprocal, and the empirical claim that for some particular x, x's love will not exist if y does not love x. Both assert that y's loving x is a necessary condition for x's loving y. But in one case y's loving x is conceptually necessary and pertains to all lovers, while in the other y's loving x is psychologically required and pertains only to some lovers—unless the claim is intended to state a universal psychological truth.[33] Thus, when Ehman claims that "reciprocity [is] a condition of genuine love,"[34] he does not mean that y's loving x is a psychological condition upon which x's love depends but that x for conceptual reasons cannot love y if y does not love x. However, when Hannay writes, "Unrequited love, or parental love which is not . . . returned as such, are familiar phenomena, so no one could reasonably assert that [reciprocity] was necessary for love. Indeed, the suggestion that you could only love another if the other loved you . . . implies a . . . conditionality that is . . . incompatible with genuine concern,"[35] we are not quite sure that he keeps distinct the conceptual and the psychological. His latter claim—if the continuation of xLy depends on yLx, x does not genuinely love y—trades on a psychological fact about x, while his former claim—unreciprocated loves exist and therefore reciprocity cannot be necessary for love—is a conceptual point.

Hannay continues by claiming that "love, even if it can be discriminating, cannot be conditional in the sense that one loves another only on condition of being loved *by* the other," because that conditionality is incompatible with x's being genuinely concerned for y. But, as I have argued, if y's not loving x means that x will not be able to benefit y, the fact that x's love includes this concern for y implies that x's no longer loving y, if y does not reciprocate, does not negate x's earlier love. Further, remember what we often say to the obsessed unrequited lover, who persists in loving y despite the fact that it is, or should be, clear to him that his beloved will never love him. We try to help this person by getting him to abandon his love quite because his beloved will never begin to reciprocate. For the sake of mental health (to prevent his crossing over the edge of doom), we condone abandoning loves in the absence of reciprocity. The general point is that Hannay's view presupposes that if x's emotion is to be genuine love, then not only must x be concerned for y, but x's concern must be unconditionally constant. We have already rejected that assumption as being too strong (8.8 and 10.1).

Questions about reciprocity, then, are closely tied to questions about constancy. If x's love for y ends because y's love for x has *ended* (rather than never starting), is this reason for x's love ending an R_1 or an R_2 reason? That is, if x no longer loves y because y no longer loves x, does this bring into doubt x's love for y, or is it compatible with x's having loved y? What is interesting about the question is that we are wondering what to say about x's emotion given that it is not constant in the face of y's emotion not being constant. Our initial impulse might be to reach a decision about x's emotion independently of whether y's love itself ends for an R_1 or R_2 reason. If so, we might reason this way: x's no longer loving y because y no longer loves x is an R_1 reason for the end of x's love, since love conditional on reciprocity does not deserve the name (Hannay); or this is an R_2 reason if x's love ends because x realizes that x's desire to benefit y can no longer bear fruit. But now take into account *why* y's love for x ended. Suppose that y's love for x ends for an R_1 reason; for example, y was attached to x in virtue of x's wealth and this attachment dissipates when x's fortune evaporates. Here we want to say that if x no longer loves y because y no longer loves x, this is an R_2 reason for the end of x's love. To generalize: if y's love ends for an R_1 reason, x's love ending because y no longer loves x is an R_2 reason. A case can also be made that if y's love ends for an R_2 reason (say, x reveals his abusive and deceitful side), then x's not loving y because y no longer loves x is an R_1 reason. If that conclusion does not strike anyone as plausible, we would have to say that whether y's love for x ends for an R_1 or for an R_2 reason, x's love for y ending because y no longer loves x is always an R_2 reason. In this sense, x's love being conditional on y's love is not a flaw in x's love.

But the case in which y's emotion toward x ends for an R_1 reason, thereby showing that y's emotion had been ill-grounded and was not love, is problematic. When y's emotion ends for that R_1 reason, and x withdraws x's love because y does not love x, y may protest that y did all along love x and that it is only in some philosopher's sense of love that y never loved x. For some R_1 reasons, y will have a hard time convincing anyone that y really did love x. Yet I wonder: How did it happen that before y's emotion ended for that R_1 reason, x believed that y loved x? One explanation is that x was unaware of y's reasons for y's attachment to x, believing falsely that y's emotion was well grounded. The other explanation is that x, knowing accurately y's reasons, believed truly that y loved x according to x's own notion of love. Thus, x agrees with y that the disappearance of y's grounds for loving x counts as an R_2 reason for the end of y's love. What is an R_1 and an R_2 reason may, therefore, have to be relativized to how x and y themselves conceive of love. This is another way the mutuality of beliefs about love plays an important role in love.

7. EROSIC AND AGAPIC RECIPROCITY

Recall that even though y's loving x can be a reason for x's loving y in both the first and second view of personal love, the theory of erosic personal love rules out x's loving y *only* because y loves x, while that is possible within agapic personal love (1.2). But if x loves y primarily for y's properties, and these properties do not disappear just because y does not love or no longer loves x, then erosic personal love should not be especially conditional on reciprocity (which should please Hannay). For the same reason, x's love will persist as long as y has P even if it is clear to x that y will never love x; erosic love is prone to the obsessions of the unrequited lover. Since the theory of agapic personal love permits x to love y solely because y loves x, x's agapic personal love for y is (paradoxically) vulnerable to y's not loving x. No wonder that within agapic theory x is called on to develop the ability to sustain x's love against all sorts of obstacles. And no wonder, given the power of these obstacles to defeat the determination of ordinary mortals, Wojtyla claims that genuine love is strictly constant and by its nature reciprocal. For if love is strictly constant and reciprocal, x's love for y can never be tested by y's failure to love x; by a neat maneuver, the agapic personal lover is protected from the charge of ever loving on the condition that love be returned.[36]

But suppose that erosic love is understood more in Platonic terms, such that y's attractive properties are either the actual object of x's love (rather than y, who merely bears the properties) or both the basis of x's love for y as object and themselves an object of x's love. Properties, being things, cannot love, so there is no question of x's loving P being conditional on x's being loved by P. Why, however, might x desire to be loved by the y who bears P? X's loving P means that x is happy that P exists and wants to preserve it; in being concerned for P, x is concerned for y as the bearer of P; and x can best satisfy x's desire to preserve P if y also loves x (or the valuable properties in x), since preserving P requires the cooperation of the bearer of P. Reciprocal love between two persons when what is loved (in part or altogether) are the other's valuable properties is a dyadic undertaking to preserve and enhance the value that each finds in the other. Indeed, if properties are the object of love, then the odor of self-interest is eliminated from the desire for reciprocity. For x's desire that y love x is not the desire that *x* be the object of y's love or that x be the direct beneficiary of y's concern, since if y loves x for the value *in* x it is that value that is the focus of y's concern. The attitude that x and y have toward each other can be disinterested (not self-interested) and detached when they love each other's properties, in the same way that P as the Third allows detachment (10.7). And neither x nor y can be accused as readily of giving in order to get, because neither is giving to the *other* in the first place; and any getting that x and y experience *they* do not get, but their valuable properties get. The commonly voiced objection to the love for properties—that it is self-interested—therefore falls flat. To be sure, x is concerned not for y but for P and gives not to y but, in effect, to P. But at the same time and for the same reason x does not receive, and does not expect to receive.

One might say that x, in attempting to satisfy x's desire to preserve the P that x finds valuable, is "ultimately" motivated by an objectionable kind of self-interest: x wants to satisfy one of x's desires. Indeed, one might say that x's wanting to satisfy x's desire to benefit y is similarly self-interested and, hence, that x's desire for reciprocity, and x's concern for y, are after all self-interested. But merely wanting to satisfy a desire does not count as being self-interested in any morally suspicious sense. If it did, what could we say about the altruist whose only desire is to help others? That this altruist is logically impossible or only an egoist in disguise? No. The thesis that no self-interest is benign does not seem to follow from the logic of "desire" or "satisfaction," and as a piece of metaphysics it is perhaps coherent but unconvincing. That it makes me happy to have made you happy does not mean that I have made you happy just in order to make me happy. The reason that I am happy when I have made you happy is not that I have satisfied a desire *simpliciter*.

Let us turn, finally, to Plato's theory of eros itself, which includes the Ascent—x's loving y is only x's loving beauty in y, and this love is but one step on the road to x's eventual contemplation of the Ideal Form of Beauty. It is x's clear-sighted failure to find perfection in y (that is, x does not idealize y)[37] that contributes to x's abandoning love for y and progressing to purer instantiations of beauty. Plato's (or Diotima's) eros is basically a trip of one, not a trip of two: if successful, x confronts the nonpersonal Beauty alone, not hand-in-hand with a human beloved. Reciprocal love, then, plays a very small role in this picture; and it does not occur at the highest level of the Ascent, since impersonal Beauty (unlike God) does not love. If x's seeking Beauty is self-interested, then x's earlier attachment to y may very well have been instrumentally self-interested. But there is a curious implication: it is quite *because* x is self-interested that x does not especially desire a reciprocal love with y or to be loved by y. Rather than self-interest yielding the desire for reciprocity, it militates against making too much of reciprocal human love.

CHAPTER 12   *Concern and the Morality of Love*

We need to be exposed to more role models like the Huxtables . . . and fewer like the Bunkers. . . . At the simplest level, we should be able to learn to treat loved ones with as much politeness and kindness as we do strangers.

—D. Byrne and S. Murnen, "Maintaining Loving Relationships"

1. HOOKING HUMBERT

The epigraph cannot be right. If we should treat loved ones as nicely as we treat strangers, then Archie is an adequate role model. Further, it admonishes us to be nicer to our beloveds (as Kierkegaard says, they are "first" our neighbors), as if love did not express itself naturally as concern but as destruction. But anyone who needs to be told to be nice to a beloved is not a lover. What would make more sense is this: the task is to be nicer to those whom we do not love but who love us; we ought to be nice to them despite the resentment we feel at their constant and obnoxious concern for our well-being. This recommendation would have us exhibit the concern of morality, which replaces our missing concern of love, or perhaps it appeals to our self-interest: the unhappiest are not those who pine unrequitedly, but those who are loved but do not love in return.[1] Were we to love the ones who love us, we would out of love's concern be happy to accept their concern. But the ones who love us also have a task: to realize that their concern brings us pain, to renounce their concern for us out of concern for us. They should learn to treat unwilling loved ones with as much indifference as they do strangers.

"I loved you," says Humbert to himself about Lolita. "I was a pentapod monster, but I loved you. I was despicable and brutal, and turpid, and everything, *mais je t'aimais, je t'aimais!* And there were times when I knew how you felt, and it was hell to know it, my little one."[2] We hesitate to agree with Humbert that he loved her. He was enchanted with her, he worshipped her sweet body, but something was missing—his wanting her to flourish. His insensitivity may be compatible with overwhelming sexual desire or with obsessive romantic love. But his emotion seems not to be even a mediocre personal love. Robert Brown claims that "it is not possible for one person to love another and yet *never* have goodwill toward the beloved." This is a conceptual, not a psychological, truth: "A lover who . . . wished *only* ill-will toward his consort would be . . . a definitional absurdity."[3] But this criterion lets Humbert and other monsters off the hook. As insensitive as he was, Humbert was not insensitive to the effect of his insensitivity on his darling; because "it was hell to know" he was harming her, Humbert felt *some* goodwill toward her. Brown also says, however, that the lover "must embody recognizable goodwill toward the beloved," which does exclude Humbert. The fact that stating precisely how much or what kind of concern constitutes the "recognizable goodwill" of love is difficult should not make us settle for the weak criterion "no goodwill at all means no love." If that net will not catch Humbert, it will not catch anyone.

The thesis that concern is a central feature of love is important, if not very controversial. For if love is to be distinguished from hate (7.8), invoking concern for the welfare of the beloved as a necessary condition of love, as a mark of "ideal" love, or as one of love's typical causal consequences seems the way to do it. But what exactly is the concern of personal love?

2. SELF-LOVE

"Self-love" is a queer thing, if we understand it analogously to personal love. Imagine what x's emotion would be toward herself: x prefers spending time with *x* rather than with other people; x looks forward with excitement to sharing intense experiences with *x;* x sexually desires *x* and wants to give *x* sexual pleasure; x reveals to *x* the delicacies of x's life story; x is concerned for the well-being of *x* even at the expense of x. If we replace the italicized x's with "y," what is described is familiar. But having this sort of love for oneself hardly makes logical or psychological sense. "Self-love," then, must refer to something else. If we understand self-love analogously to neighbor-love, there would be nothing logically odd in self-love: x neighbor-loves *x* for the same reason that x neighbor-loves others—that *x* is a human being; x is as unconditionally concerned for the well-being of *x* as for the well-being of others.[4] Or, at the opposite end of the spectrum, self-love may be construed as selfishness: x preferentially favors the well-being of *x* even to the detriment of others. But self-love can also be understood as a composite of various reflexive attitudes: self-respect, self-admiration, self-acceptance.[5] Self-love in this sense is not equivalent to selfishness. That both personal love and neighbor-love involve concern for its object might have suggested that self-love is always a matter of concern—for the self—and, hence, that it is selfishness. Of course, selfishness exists in our world, and this is one sense in which x might be said to love *x*, but it does not exhaust the meaning of self-love.

Self-love in the sense of respect for oneself and confidence about one's talents and powers is not objectionably self-interested at least because there is no question of x's loving *x*, in this sense, in order to get from *x* by giving to *x*. But it might be argued that the desire *for* self-respect is objectionably self-interested. Similarly, if we want to be loved erosically (that is, in virtue of our attractive properties) because being loved that way builds our self-respect (7.3), our attitude is objectionably self-interested. So claims Russell Vannoy:

> Even the most ardent defender of love's unselfishness does not want erotic love to arise out of mere charity or duty. . . . This demand is itself based on self-interest. For one's self-esteem is damaged if one feels one wasn't chosen for one's merits and appealing qualities and was only worthy of love that is given to just anyone. . . . But if one wants to be chosen for one's appealing qualities, one is committed . . . to the selectivity and exclusiveness that reveal the egoism of one's [lover]. For he or she will be chosen on the basis of qualities that appeal to the [lover's] needs and self-interests.[6]

There are two claims here. One is that when x loves y, the properties in virtue of which x loves y are specifically properties that satisfy x's needs; x's love is therefore "egoistic." But note the difference between x's finding a property attractive because it satisfies x's needs, and a property's bringing x pleasure because x finds it attractive. The latter is compatible with x's loving y erosically without finding y's properties primarily useful: x loves y because x admires y's properties that are a joy for x to behold. One could force this case into Vannoy's model by claiming that x's finding a property attractive, independently of its connection with x's needs, is still egoistic because the property brings x pleasure. But finding properties attractive and being pleased by them no more indicate egoism than wanting to preserve a valuable property (see 11.7).

The second claim is that y is an accomplice in x's egoistic love: y wants to be loved for y's attractive properties because that contributes to y's self-respect, and the desire for self-respect is objectionably self-interested. Erosic love, then, is egoistic in the sense that wanting erosic love is wanting to achieve a certain kind of self-love. Wanting to feel good about oneself, however, is not self-interested in any exciting way. Self-respect and self-confidence are *basic* goods; people want these things, no matter what else they may want, because without them life is hardly worth living.[7] What we have to pay attention to, as a genuine threat to the concern of love, is self-interest in some exciting sense. Humbert's claim to love Lolita was negated not by the pleasure he found in contemplating her face or undergarments, but by his willingness to interfere with her "normal" development and flourishing, since that interference was not essential for his own flourishing. Self-interest is objectionable at least when it becomes selfishness.

3. EGOCENTRIC PHILIA?

Perhaps erosic personal love is suspected of being self-interested in an exciting sense because sexual love, romantic love, and especially Plato's eros are easily seen as egocentric. The criticisms of Plato's eros voiced by Anders Nygren (who labeled it "acquisitive") and Gregory Vlastos ("spiritualized" egocentrism) are well known.[8] But Aristotle's philia is also an erosic love: the basis of x's love for y is that y is virtuous. Does this mean that even philia is egocentric?

George Nakhnikian argues that Aristotle's perfect friendship between two virtuous men is egocentric. "When . . . Aristotle speaks of loving individuals for their own sake, he does not mean wishing for their good . . . and acting accordingly, without any expectation or thought of getting something in return from them."[9] This claim is surprising, because Aristotle partially defines perfect friendship as desiring the good of another for that person's sake; perfect friendship excludes the give-to-get attitude that characterizes use and pleasure friendships and that makes them objectionably self-interested. What is wrong with Aristotle's philia, according to Nakhnikian, is that when x wishes the good for y for y's sake, this boils down to "x's wish[ing] for the good . . . of y . . . out of appreciation for y's goodness as a human being." So? Aristotle's philia is egocentric because it is erosically based on y's *goodness*: x and y therefore (according to Nakhnikian) love each other in part because they "have characteristics" that make "them beneficent to the one who loves them." As a correction of Aristotle, Nakhnikian proposes an agapic conception of loving a person for that person's sake: "It involves perfect good will with no thought of expected returns and no requirement that the person loved be a good human being." Nakhnikian is offering only one criterion, not two, despite the conjunction "and." In his view, it is precisely because philia is based on the object's goodness that x could not have "perfect good will" toward y, that is, no exchange attitude. If x is to be concerned for y for y's sake, the single condition that x must satisfy is loving "without having to think that [y] is a good human being." Then x could not be expecting any return.

The way to defend Aristotle is not to say that philia is a personal love, while Nakhnikian is describing neighbor-love, and that no one expects a standard applicable to the latter to apply to the former. For Nakhnikian's claim that concern is never property-based is meant to apply not only to neighbor-love, but also to self-love, parental love, and personal love. Instead, erosic personal love can be defended by pointing out that Nakhnikian confuses questions about the basis of love and concern with questions about the type of concern expressed in love. There is no contradiction in asserting that x loves y on the basis of y's attractive properties, that x is concerned for y as a result of (or as a part of) x's love for y, and that x's concern for y takes the form of x's desiring y's welfare for y's sake, not for x's. What follows from y's attractiveness being the basis of x's desiring y's welfare for y's sake is that x will have this sort of concern either preferentially for y (that is, nonuniversally) or for anyone else who happens to be equally attractive—for example, for all virtuous men with whom x is able to sustain friendship. While contrasting agape to Aristotle's philia, Vlastos writes: "Discerning the possibility of a kind of love which wishes for another's . . . good for that other's sake, Aristotle thought only men could have it and only few men for few. To universalize that kind of love, to extend it to the slave, to impute it to the deity, would have struck him as quite absurd."[10] The purported fault with philia is not that it does not involve concern for the other for the other's sake, but that in being property-based its scope (or the number of objects this concern is extended toward) is severely limited. Thus, philia is unlike God's agape and neighbor-love, which extend the same type of concern universally, that is, "not proportion[ed] . . . to merit."

Similarly, what follows from x's loving y in virtue of y's attractive properties is that x's concern for y for y's sake is conditional on y's maintaining those properties—the basis of love limits the temporal scope of its concern. But the fact that erosic love is not in principle constant is logically distinct from the type of concern x has for y while x is concerned for y. That x loves both y and z for their attractiveness does not mean that x cannot be concerned for both for their sake; that x loved y on the basis of S, and no longer loves y when y loses S, by itself does not mean that x had not been concerned for y for y's sake. Erosic personal love, to be sure, can be selfish: x might promote y's welfare only when doing so does not interfere with x's pursuit of x's welfare or only because x believes that receiving from y is unlikely unless x does so. These serious defects in x's concern for y's welfare do not follow from x's love being erosic. Further, nothing in the concept of nonproperty-based, nonreason-dependent love entails that such love necessarily involves a superior type of concern for the other's welfare. X's having an agapic personal love for y is as compatible with x's promoting y's welfare because doing so contributes to x's welfare, as x's having an erosic personal love for y is compatible with x's being concerned for y for y's sake.

Nakhnikian argues that x's loving y in virtue of y's goodness means that x loves y in virtue of properties that enable y to be "beneficent" to x, and hence

Aristotle's philia fails to achieve concern for y for y's sake. But it puzzles me why Nakhnikian thinks that x's loving y for y's goodness must have that consequence; "x loves y because y is good, and y has properties that can benefit x" simply does not entail "x is concerned for y not for y's sake but for the benefit x can receive from y." There might be an entailment were Nakhnikian to assume psychological or metaphysical egoism; but if that thesis is true it would apply equally to erosic and agapic personal love. Alternatively, Nakhnikian might claim that x's merely knowing that y is good and has the ability to benefit x makes x's concern for y egocentric. But if that is what Nakhnikian has in mind, Nakhnikian's criterion—x must be concerned for y "without having to think that [y] is a good human being"—turns out to be too weak for his own purposes. If merely knowing that y is good undermines the quality of x's concern, then x could be concerned for y for y's sake only when either (1) x is totally ignorant of y's character (a Rawlsian veil-of-ignorance must operate in real life) or (2) x believes or knows that y is not good, or is unattractive, or otherwise has no properties capable of benefiting x. In either case, most acts of concern done out of neighbor-love will fail to achieve what Nakhnikian wants; and in case (2) an object's being humanly unlovable (7.7) becomes a necessary condition for x's being concerned for her for her sake. It is as if we took Kierkegaard's insight—x's still loving y when y is dead proves that x's love is genuine, since x's love cannot be based on y's making a repayment—and twisted it into: x can be concerned for someone for their sake *only* when that person is dead.

4. LOVE AND SACRIFICE

Let us assume with Aristotle, then, that if x loves and is therefore concerned for y, x desires the good for y and acts to promote it.[11] Of course, x must desire y's welfare for y's sake, not for x's sake. For example, when we desire that our beloved "change for the better," we must desire this not because our beloved's deficiency "produces in us . . . malaise, discomfort, hostility, resentment, or fear" but simply because changing is good for our beloved.[12] Our beloved might want to change for the better to alleviate our discomfort, but that cannot be, ceteris paribus, our reason for desiring that our beloved change. Being concerned for another for that person's sake means that we do not desire that person's good as a means to our own good, that we do not give in order to receive, and that we do not desire the other's good only insofar as it is compatible with our own good. Promoting the other's good only when it does not threaten or reduce one's own good is a stinginess that says to the beloved: my good comes first. This is not identical to x's being concerned for y for x's sake, but it is nonetheless not being concerned for y for y's sake: that must mean that x, at least sometimes and to a certain extent, is willing to put y's welfare ahead of x's.

I doubt this claim will be seen as controversial. What is controversial is how much and what sort of sacrifice for the beloved the lover must be willing to undertake in order to *be* a lover. At what expense to x must x, if x is truly concerned for y out of love, pursue y's good? A terribly large area exists between x's being concerned for y only as far as y's good is compatible with x's, and x's being concerned for y to the point of crossing over the edge of doom to doom itself. It may be true, as Phaedrus says (*Symposium* 179b), that "only lovers desire to die for their beloveds," but x's going over the edge of doom on behalf of y is still, from the perspective of the concern of love, supererogatory—and not as supererogatory as doing the same thing for a stranger, from the perspective of the concern of morality. The concern of love implies only that x is sometimes (not always) willing to sacrifice x's good for y's good; hence, x may sometimes favor x's good over the good of y. (At what expense to y? Not if x secures a nonbasic good for x at the cost of y's basic goods.) We do not expect that when x loves y, x in virtue of x's love always favors the good of y; and if the love of x and y is reciprocal, not both x and y can always put the other's good first (2.5). Nor would they expect that from each other. It is possible, after all, that x can desire for x's sake that y change for the better, if y's not doing so is too great a threat to x's good. What is the balance between favoring the good of the other and favoring the good of oneself that is characteristic of love's concern? The unending disputes between lovers over this question (for example, when careers conflict with marriage) suggest that the concepts of love and concern (or our concepts of them) cannot do more than indicate the rough boundaries. The mistake to avoid is thinking that because there must be some balance between the other's good and one's own good, reciprocal love is merely a give-to-get phenomenon. For the fact that x sometimes favors y and sometimes favors x does not imply that x has that attitude or that x is not concerned for y for y's sake.

"Love and friendship," says Charles Fried, "involve the initial respect for the rights of others which morality requires of everyone."[13] Kierkegaard makes the point in a more radical way when he insists that one's spouse is first and foremost one's neighbor, the point being that at the very least lovers must treat each other as any two persons must in accordance with the general principles of morality. But for Fried love "further involve[s] the voluntary . . . relinquishment of something between . . . lover and lover." In virtue of their love for each other x and y give up some of their general moral rights against each other (which is itself permitted by the general principles of morality). Further, the concern of love goes beyond the concern of morality. When x loves y, y is a special, preferential object of x's concern; hence we expect that x will promote y's good at greater expense to x than that required by the concern of morality. What some lovers overlook, unfortunately, is that just because x's love-concern for y goes beyond the concern of morality, y is not free to violate all the general demands of morality toward x. Taking for granted, or misunderstanding the nature of, x's relinquishing some moral rights against y, y ends up hurting the one y loves by violating the demands of morality that x has not relinquished. But because love means going beyond the concern of morality, we also expect x, out of love, to forgive y more readily than if x were motivated only by morality, and this includes x's forgiving y when y violates unrelinquished moral rights. Our concepts, however, yield no more than this rough outline: x must more readily forgive y, but not necessarily to the point of doom.

To say that if x loves y, then x desires the good for y and acts to promote it, is to say not only that x desires to benefit y by x's own hand but also that x is pleased when y's welfare is enhanced by other persons or processes. If x does desire the good for y for y's sake, y's flourishing will bring x pleasure regardless of its cause. (Similarly, when x hates y, x derives great pleasure when someone else damages y, even if x would also be ecstatic to be the one doing the damage.) Construing the concern of love as x's desire that y flourish no matter who brings about y's flourishing may provide a neat distinction between love and sexual desire; in the latter, x desires that y experience sexual pleasure and that x be the precise one who brings it about—x hardly ever thinks that it would be satisfactory for someone else to do it. Does it follow that if x loves y, then x should desire sexual pleasure for y no matter who brings it about, and that x should be happy at this prospect?[14] Not necessarily. X's being hurt by, and complaining about, y's receiving sexual pleasure from someone else does not mean that x fails to desire y's flourishing *simpliciter*; for x might reasonably not believe that y's sexual relations with z are essential to y's good, or y may be asking x to desire y's good at too great a cost to x's good. But this case, and others in which x's beloved y flourishes at the hand of z, are difficult. Instead of entailing that x will always be happy when y's welfare is enhanced by other persons, perhaps the concern of love means only that x's unhappiness should not lead x to interfere with z's benefiting y and that x need not desire to assist every z whose goal is y's welfare. Much depends on whether y's allowing z to benefit y, knowing that this will cause x pain, is y's favoring y's good at too great an expense to x's.

But if x desires to be the one and only person who benefits y (were that possible) and is always upset when some z acts to promote y's welfare, then x's concern seems incompatible with x's desiring the good for y for y's sake. There is a difference, that is, between x's love for y leading x to put y in a special place in x's life, such that the largest part of x's concern is directed at y, and x's love leading x to desire that every bit of y's welfare be due to x. Similarly, even if x's desiring reciprocity from y means that x desires that y be concerned for x, x must not be so self-centered as to desire that every ounce of y's concern be spent on x. But x's desire to be the one who predominantly benefits y need not indicate that x is ultimately egoistic. Alastair Hannay has pointed out that in parental love for a young child "what is in the loved one's interest is that the love be bestowed by this person," that is, the parent.[15] Out of concern and hence not opposed to concern for y, x may desire to be the one who predominantly benefits y, if x's benefiting y is particularly conducive to y's flourishing. One might be respond that if x, as a parent, desires to be the one who benefits y, the child, it is because x plausibly believes that x's benefiting y is best for y; but the x who has a personal love for y cannot claim that just because x loves y, x's benefiting y is best for y. However, it is the parent's loving the child, and not the bare fact of parenthood, that allows the parent to think that he or she is in the best position to benefit the child. (Bare parents who do not love their children cannot be trusted to care for them as well as they could be cared for.) If so, the x who has a personal love for y can similarly defend the desire to be the one who predominantly benefits y, without necessarily bringing into doubt the quality of x's concern or its motivation. This will be especially true when x and y love each other and y thereby desires to be benefited by x in particular.

5. CARTE BLANCHE CONCERN

The problems revolving around the concern of personal love are neatly solvable if concern means taking on the task of leading the beloved to God. "In point of fact," asserts Karol Wojtyla, "to desire 'unlimited' good for another person is really to desire God for that person: He alone is the objective fullness of the good, and only His goodness can fill every man to overflowing. . . . 'I want happiness for you' means 'I want that which makes you happy'— but . . . only people of profound faith tell themselves quite clearly that 'this means God'."[16] Wojtyla apparently means that x's *love*-concern for y, and not some other concern (say, the concern of religious duty), is what requires x to lead y to God. For once, Kierkegaard agrees with the pontiff: "To be loved by another human being . . . is to be helped to love God. . . . As soon as I in a love-relationship do not lead another person to God, this love, even if it were the most blissful and joyous attachment, . . . nevertheless is not true love."[17] X should lead y to God even if y prefers whatever it is on earth that is incompatible with, stops short of, or is irrelevant to loving God—because God is really y's good. At what expense to x should x attempt to lead y to God? X has no reason to spare any expense; besides, in giving up everything x attains everything. X should not even spare the expense of y's coming to hate x for ignoring y's worldly preferences, says Kierkegaard. Should x desire to be the one who leads y to God? Surely, x has reason to believe x can do it better than one who does not have x's profound faith, but x should also seek the assistance of those who are experts.

Wojtyla insists that x's concern must express itself as x's leading y to God in opposition to x's promoting y's welfare specifically in y's sense of y's worldly well-being. Lovers lacking profound faith say, "I want that which makes you happy," but they "leave a blank to be filled in . . . by the beloved." Let us call this thesis—if x loves y, x's concern must take the form of desiring and doing for y what y wants—the carte blanche view. For Kierkegaard, carte blanche holds in only one context:

> A man should love God in unconditional *obedience*. . . . It would be ungodliness if any man dared love . . . another person in this way. . . . If your be- loved . . . asked something of you which out of honest love and in concern you had decided was harmful to him, then you must take responsibility if you express love by complying instead of expressing love by denying the fulfillment of the desire. But God you are to love in unconditional obedience, even if what he demands of you may seem to you to be to your own harm.[18]

Thus, it makes sense that Wojtyla emphasizes x's leading y to God in contrast to x's being concerned for y carte blance; if x is going to do any carte blanching, it had better be toward God. People must "surrender" themselves to God's desires (they must do His will); they must not have this attitude toward mortals.[19]

There are two versions of the carte blanche thesis: (i) x wants for y whatever y wants, and (ii) x wants the good for y in y's sense of what is good for y. These are not equivalent. Y might want a Big Mac, yet readily admit it is not good for y; to stop smoking might be good for y in y's eyes, yet y does not want to. In these cases, x will not be able to show concern for y consistently with both (i) and (ii). Of course, y might want something exactly because it is good for y in y's eyes. And the fact that y wants something means, ceteris paribus, that y's getting it is good for y; the satisfaction of desire is, within limits, a good. In these cases, x can show concern consistently with both versions of carte blanche. But the question remains: Should x pursue this thing for y because y wants it or because it is good for y in y's eyes? Should x maximize the satisfaction of y's desires even when y admits that in y's perfect life y would not have some of those desires, or should x benefit y in y's notion of what is good for y, even though y resists? Note that both versions must be qualified; x cannot be expected to do everything that y wants or is good for y in y's sense, since some of these things are too harmful to x. We already have, therefore, one argument that the second version of carte blanche is superior to the first. For if x's loving y implies that x is willing to sacrifice at least some of x's good for y's sake, it makes more sense to think that this sacrifice is done for what is *good* for y (in y's sense) and not merely for what y *wants*.

Because the two versions of carte blanche are quite distinct, we should not make the mistake of thinking that if one version is true, the other is. For it is difficult to construe version (i) as an account of concern at all. If x loves y, x desires y's good for y's sake and acts accordingly; the core idea is that x is concerned for y, in a way compatible with x's loving y, only if x desires that y flourish, that y develop into the finest specimen of a human being y is capable of being, and that y be happy, content, and self-confident—in a nutshell, as the formula says, x desires the good for y. However, to be concerned for y in version (i) of carte blanche is not exactly to desire the *good* for y. X's desiring for y what y wants amounts to desiring the good for y only under certain conditions (y's desires being satisfied, all things considered, is good for y; or y desires something *because* it is good for y), but even when these conditions hold, x's concern is directed at y's good and only derivatively at what y desires. Because version (i) of carte blanche is not an account of love's concern, conflating it with (ii) only obscures the main issue: if x loves y, should x promote y's good in y's sense of "good" or in x's sense?

To say "x desires whatever y desires" is not the best way to state version (i). This make it sound as if x incorporates into x's psychological life y's desires: if x loves y, and y desires to eat a peach, then x desires to eat a peach merely because y does. No doubt, this sort of thing happens in (and outside) love, but it has nothing to do with love's concern. Thus, version (i) must mean that if y desires a peach, x desires a peach for y—that is, x desires that y's desire for a peach be satisfied. In some cases, x's desiring for y what y desires does amount to x's incorporating y's desire: if y desires that the Democrats win in Utah, then x's desiring for y what y desires entails that x desires that the Democrats win in Utah. The formula that covers both cases is simply that x desires that y's desires be satisfied. This is how version (i) should be stated. But there is a curious thing even about "x desires that y's desires be satisfied." If x and y love each other, then x desires that y's desires be satisfied and y desires that x's desires be satisfied, which might imply that x desires that *x*'s desires be satisfied. Love appears to become egocentric exactly when it is reciprocated. We therefore have another argument that the concern of love requires that x desire the good for y at least in y's sense of "good." For if x desires the good for y and y desires the good for x, it does not follow that x desires the good for x. There is not even a hint that love becomes egocentric simply because or when it is reciprocated.

"My fundamental thought," writes Mark Fisher, "is that to love someone is to desire whatever he desires for the reason that he desires it,"[20] which is version (i) of carte blanche. In a footnote, Fisher immediately contrasts two things: "It may be important to distinguish between *love,* as I have defined it, and *altruism,* defined as desiring something for another because it will be *for his good* as *I* see it—not necessarily what he wants."[21] Fisher seems to realize that version (i) does not embody concern for the beloved, since for him desiring whatever the beloved desires does not count as "altruism." But this is not what Fisher means, for later he explicitly equates versions (i) and (ii) of carte blanche, thereby showing that version (i), for him, does embody concern, although not "altruism" as he defined it: "Suppose that [a transcendental self] has no concept of love. It never does . . . understand what it is to act with a view to securing someone else's good, as conceived by that other person. To desire that someone else have what s/he desires because s/he desires it is not, for such a being, a possible reason for it to act."[22] Further, for Fisher, when x desires what y desires because y desires it, x is concerned for y for y's sake, since x's desire for what y desires does "not directly connect with the lover's own . . . needs, longings, plans, ideals."[23] It is clear, then, that Fisher understands love in terms of version (ii) of carte blanche, which he assumes is the same as (i), and that both embody a kind of concern for the beloved. But even though we have dispensed with version (i), should we agree with Fisher that if x loves y, then x desires the good for y in y's sense rather than in x's sense?

6. GOOD IN WHOSE SENSE?

Suppose that y wants a Big Mac because in y's sense of "good" having a Big Mac is good for y; in y's sense of "good" the pleasure of eating fast food is ranked higher than eating nutritiously. If x, who loves y, rejects y's sense of "good," x is in a predicament: x's choice is between fetching a Big Mac for y, because it is a good thing for y in y's sense, and not fetching it, because it is bad for y in x's sense. "In such a case," says Fisher, "there will be a conflict between viewing what the beloved wants as bad for him and wanting it because he wants it."[24] Now, if Fisher is right that if x loves y, then x's concern for y takes the specific form of version (ii) of carte blanche, then x's predicament must be conceptualized in this way: x's conflict is between x's concern for y, as part of or identical to x's love for y (which love-concern leads x to desire for y what is good for y in y's sense), and x's concern for y that is *independent* of x's love for y, or as Fisher calls it, x's "altruism" (which nonlove-concern leads x to desire that y not have what is bad for y in x's sense). Hence, x's conflict is between the demands of x's love for y and the demands of another system of values that also involves concern for others.

To be sure, it is possible for x to find that a desire required by x's love for y is incompatible with desires that derive from other values x holds. ("I could not love thee, dear, so much, / Lov'd I not Honour more"—Richard Lovelace, "To Lucasta. Going to the Warres.") But to conceptualize x's conflict as necessarily between x's love-concern and x's nonlove-concern for y is implausible. For what is often going on is that x is pulled in two directions by x's love itself; x's love for y leads x to want for y what is good for y in y's sense, at the same time that x's love for y, not some other system of values, leads x not to want for y what x thinks is bad for y. Further, if x, when faced with the decision whether to promote what is good for y in y's sense or to prevent y from having what x thinks is bad for y, opts for the latter, version (ii) of carte blanche entails that x does not love y, since x's love-independent values have overridden the type of concern required by love. X might have made a poor choice, or a wise one, in preventing y from having what x thinks is bad for y, but x's merely selecting that option does not mean x does not love y.[25] I am not arguing that version (ii) contributes nothing to our understanding of love's concern or that x's desiring the good for y in x's sense is definitive of love's concern. Rather, the concern of personal love is an uneasy mixture of x's seeking the good for y in y's sense and x's seeking it in x's sense. After all, by promoting y's good in y's sense, x shows respect for y's values. Further, x's promoting y's good in y's sense contributes to y's autonomy, which is a good for y as part of y's flourishing: not only x's doing things for y but also x's manner of deciding what things to do for y helps y to flourish.

But x's desiring for y what is good for y in x's sense, and pursuing this for y's sake, cannot be a strike against the quality of x's love, as long as x has attempted to discern what is objectively good for y and has embraced that as x's sense. The reason Wojtyla's position is in principle plausible is that underlying his claim that if x loves y, then x helps y to God instead of doing for y what y wants or thinks is good for y, is the idea that in loving y, x desires the good for y, period—that is, whatever happens to be objectively good for y. X's trying to discern what is objectively good for y means that x must try to occupy a detached viewpoint, in part by disregarding x's own preference and wants but also by disregarding y's sense of good when y is not similarly motivated to discern what is objectively good for y. Because while trying to fashion x's sense of what is objectively good for y, x detaches x's perspective from x's own wants, x's seeking the good for y thereby contributes to x's seeking the good for y for y's sake and not for x's. What x is attempting to do is to achieve for y what is truly good for y; hence, when x promotes y's good in x's sense, possibly overriding y's sense, x is not necessarily doing so for trivial reasons, to assert control over y, or because x is insensitive to y's desires. Furthermore, recall that x's loving y implies that x must be willing to sacrifice some of x's good for the benefit of y. But the necessity of this sacrifice can be understood best if it is required to secure what is genuinely or objectively good for y, not merely what y thinks is good for y. And since x is expected to make these sacrifices, surely x should have some say as to what counts as y's good.

Indeed, were y to attempt systematically to discern what is objectively good for y, x would have little reason to promote y's good in x's sense. This does not mean, however, that x would be conforming to version (ii) of carte blanche; x is still motivated to achieve for y what is objectively good for y, but what that is can now be identified by looking seriously at y's sense of what is good for y. In principle, then, there is no conflict between x's doing for y what is good for y in y's sense and x's doing for y what is good for y in x's sense; the conflict is epistemological—whose sense of y's good is a better mark of what is objectively good for y? For that matter, if y does attempt to discern what is objectively good for y, x might very well express concern for y (on the surface, at least) by doing for y precisely what y desires; for under these conditions even what y desires might be a reliable sign of what is objectively good for y. But x's concern is still x's desiring for y what is objectively good for y.

7. IDENTIFYING WITH THE BELOVED

Fisher actually interprets x's conflict differently: it is not between x's desiring something for y and x's not desiring it for y, but between x's viewing something as bad for y, in x's sense, and viewing it as good for y just because it is good for y in y's sense.[26] X's conflict is not in the realm of desire, but is cognitive. "In order to desire what the other desires," says Fisher, "the lover must see the desired objects 'through the eyes of' her beloved, as it were"; the lover "must to some degree come to share his beliefs about it."[27] Thus, because y views as good what is good for y in y's sense, and x (if x loves y) desires for y what y views as good for y, x also views this as good for y. X's predicament is that x is forced by x's love into believing that something that x independently believes is bad for y is also good for y. To get to the heart of Fisher's view, consider the following account of "identification."

We can feel the pain (or pleasure) of another person in two senses. First, we can identify with a person by thinking of her as if she were ourself: we feel the other's pain (or pleasure) because we would be feeling pain (or pleasure) were we to be in the other's situation. To put oneself into someone else's shoes is really, in this manner of feeling the other person's pain, to put the other person in our shoes, to imagine what they are feeling by noticing what *we* would feel. I may be wearing the other's shoes, but the other person's feelings have been assimilated to my feelings: I have made the other wear my hat. Hence, x could feel y's pain in some situation only if x were to feel pain in that situation. Second, we can identify with a person by thinking of ourself as if we were that person. We put ourselves in the other person's situation in two senses: not only do we imagine that we are in the brute circumstances of the other, but we also look at things from the perspective of the other person. We wear the shoes *and* the hat of the other. When x puts x into y's place in this sense, x imagines what y would be feeling, not by invoking what x would feel but by invoking y's beliefs and values. Hence, x could know that y will feel pain in a situation even if x were not independently to feel pain in that situation. The second sense, I take it, describes what happens at least sometimes when x loves y. The first, by contrast, involves an insulation of x from much of what is central to y's personality and seems incompatible with love.

Fisher's insight might be put: if x is concerned for y only in x's sense of y's good, x is overly assimilating y's perspective to x's. This kind of concern may be appropriate for parental love; but if x is always and only concerned for y in this way, x's personal love for y is brought into doubt. X must to a certain extent assimilate x to y by taking on y's sense of what is good for y as x's sense of what is good for y. Indeed, this means that x will at least sometimes take on y's sense of what is good *for x* as part of x's sense of what is good for x. If so, x's being concerned for y in reciprocal love means that x will desire for y a mixture of what is good for y in y's sense and what is good for y in x's sense, since if y also loves x, y will assimilate y to x and at least partially take on x's sense of what is good for y as y's sense of what is good for y. Hence, the conflict x experiences is between x's maintaining x's independent beliefs and the assimilation of x's beliefs to y's beliefs. The tough question x has to face in some situations is whether x should hold fast to x's independent belief that something is bad for y or jettison that belief by taking on y's belief that this thing is actually good for y.

Fisher is right, of course, that x's never assimilating x's viewpoint to y's nullifies x's loving y, but the opposite extreme, x's always assimilating x's viewpoint to y's, is also suspicious. X's always assimilating x's beliefs to y's is an unacceptable criterion of the concern of love, in the same way that x's sacrificing all x's good for the sake of y's good (that is, x's sparing no expense to x) cannot be a requirement of love: x's abandoning x's sense of what is good for x poses a threat to x's own flourishing. Further, x's always assimilating x's beliefs to y's beliefs, including x's views as to what is good for x, means that were y also to love x, y's concern for x would always take the form of doing for x what is good for x in y's sense—which contradicts Fisher's carte blanche. But if x is not expected to assimilate totally to y, why x should assimilate some of x's beliefs to y's (those that have to do with y's sense of what is good for y) but not others is unclear. If x is not required by love to jettison beliefs or values that x considers important to x's identity or integrity, because jettisoning those beliefs is a larger sacrifice of x's good than is required by love, then x cannot be required by love to jettison x's important beliefs about what is good for y. Indeed, the concern of love would seem to require the opposite: if x strongly believes (not whimsically, but with good reason) that promoting y's good in y's sense would be a disaster for y, x would be violating, with weak knees, x's concern for y were x to assimilate x's beliefs to y's. X's ability to promote what is objectively good for y depends on x's remaining at least partially detached from y's perspective.

It is true that if x loves y, x comes to believe much that y believes. But this does not happen, either at all or predominantly, because x's wanting for y what is good for y in y's sense requires x to take on y's beliefs. X's taking on y's beliefs, and vice versa if the love is reciprocal, is partially the result of the admiration and esteem commonly found in love. Further, when people interact they naturally have an effect on their respective beliefs—both inside and outside love. One might even argue that since x and y (can be expected to) know, in advance of any love that arises between them, that the intimacy of their relationship (for example, sharing experiences) will affect their respective beliefs, they must be able to foresee with pleasure having their beliefs modified by interacting with this particular person.[28] Further, I am doubtful about Fisher's claim that a necessary condition of x's desiring for y what y sees as good for y, is that x believes what y believes. Remember that Fisher equates x's desiring whatever y desires (version [i] of carte blanche) with x's desiring for y whatever is good for y in y's sense (version [ii]). If we take version (i) seriously, we would have some reason for subscribing to the thesis that if x is concerned for y, x will assimilate x's beliefs to y's in such a way that x will view as good for y what y sees as good for y. For on version (i), x's desiring what y desires sometimes means that x literally incorporates y's desires into x's system of desires. Since x now has these desires for the things that y desires, x can hardly avoid incorporating y's values that attach to the things y desires: if y's desiring these things implies that y believes they are good, x's now desiring them implies that x now believes they are good.

Perhaps Fisher thought that x's being concerned for y in version (ii) of carte blanche also implies that x will assimilate x's beliefs to y's or incorporate y's values. But x's desiring the good for y in y's sense does not entail that x must modify x's values. X's being able to imagine how y feels requires only that x know y well, not that x psychologically incorporate y's perspective. Hence, x's viewing as bad what is good for y in y's sense does not force x to have contradictory beliefs, because x's wanting for y what is good for y in y's sense does not automatically translate into x's believing it is good. (This applies to hate as well. X must be able to understand how x's behated y sees things, but having this understanding does not require that x psychologically incorporate y's beliefs and values.) Notice that if x wants to do for y what is good for y in x's sense, x must again have an accurate understanding of y's nature; x must still be able to understand how y sees things. But x's needing to understand how y experiences things in some situation does not entail that x must have qualitatively identical experiences in the same situation. Similarly, when x desires to benefit y in y's sense of what is good for y, x need only understand y's values and how they cash out in practical life; but x's needing to understand them does not mean that x must incorporate them into x's own mental life. To assert otherwise would be to claim that x could never empathize with y, and be concerned for y's well-being, without in part *becoming* y. In a sense, we have confirmed an earlier conclusion (9.7 and 10.7): absolute openness and the sharing of all experiences cannot be requirements of love.

8. SPECIAL CONCERN

The lover's concern for the beloved's well-being is not expected to extend to the point of the lover's obliteration. This does not mean that the lover is ultimately self-interested in any exciting sense, for the lover's concern is still expected to extend beyond the point of doing only for the beloved what is compatible with the lover's own good. At the same time, the lover's concern for the beloved's well-being is limited by other considerations, in particular the well-being of persons the lover does not love or, more generally, the demands of morality. Even if y, especially in a reciprocal love relationship with x, deserves to be treated with special concern by x, nevertheless y cannot think, in all fairness, that y's good takes priority over every other good that x could promote. Kierkegaard goes even further. His notorious statement that "your spouse is first and foremost your neighbor" might not mean that the lover must treat the beloved at least as well as required by morality. Instead, as one neighbor among indefinitely many neighbors, one's beloved is not to be treated in a discriminatory fashion but as one equal among other equals: special concern for one's beloved is morally wrong. Even if Kierkegaard should not be read as saying that the ethics of neighbor-love always trump the preferential concern of personal love, the view that the preferential concern of love is always in conflict with the requirements of morality has not escaped the attention of philosophers.

W. Newton-Smith asks us to "suppose that someone has the unhappy choice of saving either his putative beloved or an arbitrary stranger from drowning."[29] About this case Newton-Smith says, "If the putative lover elects to save the stranger, then . . . the relation is not one of love." For, which is plausible, if x loves y and is therefore concerned for y's well-being, x must favor y's well-being over the well-being of other persons whom x does not love. (This is not to say that x favors y's well-being over others' well-being ultimately for egoistic reasons.) But Newton-Smith's case can be analyzed three different ways. First, we could say that x's loving y does require x to save y, that x's saving the stranger negates x's claim to love y. Thus, what is required by love conflicts with what is required by morality, which would have x decide whom to save at least by a random procedure that acknowledges the equal worth of all persons. Second, we could say that morality itself permits or obliges x to choose to save y, because morality countenances special concern directed at those with whom we have close ties. Thus, in this case there is no conflict between love and morality. Third, we could say that x's saving the stranger, or deciding between y and the stranger by using a random procedure, does not negate x's claim to love y. There is no conflict between love and morality because the concern of love does not require x to treat y preferentially; love requires that x be concerned for y, but it does not demand that x favor y's good over anyone else's good.

Perhaps we should say about Newton-Smith's hypothetical case that when x's choice is between x's beloved and a solitary stranger, no interesting question arises because x can save only one person, no matter what x decides to do; no view of the requirements of morality could plausibly expect x to overcome x's inclination to save y merely to give one stranger a fair break by tossing a coin. The obvious interpretation of this case, then, is that x's saving y is required by love and permitted by morality. For this reason Newton-Smith asks us to "suppose the . . . lover has to choose between saving his beloved and a group of strangers"; the dilemma is between saving only y and saving, say, ten others. Were y just another stranger, x's decision would not be difficult; both utilitarian and Kantian moral theories require or permit x to save the ten and allow the one to die (except the deontological view that would have x save none if not all can be saved). But when y is x's beloved the case is not as easily handled. Again there are three interpretations: love and morality conflict with each other, love requiring x to save y, morality requiring x to save the ten strangers; morality permits x to save x's beloved y, because special relationships have their own significant value; or there is no conflict between love and morality, since love does not require x to favor y's good over the good of other people. It is interesting that when the beloved's life is opposed to the lives of ten strangers, the apparently right answer for the "one-stranger" case—that x's saving y is required by love and permitted by morality—is less plausible. Both the first and the third interpretations gain credibility as the number of other lives at stake increases: were x to choose to save a large number of people at y's expense, there would be less reason to bring x's love for y into doubt; and even if saving the group of strangers does negate x's claim to love y, it makes more sense here to say that x ought to jettison x's beloved for their sake.

Newton-Smith remarks that "these examples are not meant to imply any thesis to the effect that in 'true' love, commitment to the beloved must take preference over all other commitments."[30] Of course not. Yet the question remains: To what extent do the demands of morality limit the loving concern x may show toward y? Newton-Smith's conclusion is that these examples make "the significant conceptual point . . . that in the case of love there are these tensions, and this displays the extent to which love involves a commitment," as opposed to "liking," which does not generate any "tension." But this is not convincing; even if x only likes y and has to choose between y and *one* stranger, x is in the same dilemma. And depending on the strength of x's liking for y, x's inclination in the "ten-strangers" case might very well be to save y. So the "tension" remains. Perhaps we have to increase the number of strangers required to generate a dilemma for the x who loves y more so than we have to in the case of the x who only likes y, but this fact does not mark a conceptual distinction between loving and liking. Both loving and liking involve commitments as well as inclinations. Actually, the point of these examples might not be that the tension shows that we take the committed concern of love seriously enough that it challenges morality, but instead that the lack of tension in these examples—our reluctance, except when the number of strangers is very large, to say that x ought to abandon y to the deep—shows how unseriously we take morality when it conflicts with our personal lives and loves.

The thesis that love *always* conflicts with morality has been advanced by Robert Ehman. "The fundamental requirement of love is to raise the beloved above others and to give her a privileged status in our life," he writes. This claim is incredible. Does love demand that x's beloved spouse y be raised above even the children of x and y? If so, love conflicts with one principle of morality—that one must show responsible concern for one's offspring. Or would Ehman conceptualize this conflict as between the demands of x's love for his spouse y and the demands of x's love for his children? Regardless, I do not immediately see how Ehman's claim gives us reason to think that "there is always something immoral in the privilege and attention that the lover gives to the beloved." Making myself privileged in my life, if carried to extremes, is morally suspicious as a significant kind of self-interest; but what moral objection could there be to making someone else privileged? Ehman explains: "The fundamental requirement of morality . . . is to treat all persons as having equal worth and to justify all special treatment of a person by reference to universally valid principles."[31] Thus, x's treating y as special violates the moral requirement that each person be treated as having equal worth. Are we supposed to assume that treating all persons as having equal worth means that each person must be treated the same? That assumption is implausible, and it is not exactly what Ehman has in mind. Rather, x's treating y as special is morally wrong because it is dissimilar treatment that cannot be justified by "universally valid principles"; the lover "singles out an individual for special concern simply on the basis of her personality and of the delight [he] take[s] in being close to her."

Treating all persons as having equal worth does not require that each be treated the same, when morally relevant differences among people justify special treatment (this is consistent with appealing to some universally valid principle). But the fact that x is delighted by y's presence is not, for Ehman, a morally relevant difference between y and other people; it lacks the power to justify x's special treatment of y. Thus, on Ehman's view, love always conflicts with morality, since x treats y as special only because y has the irrelevant property "delights x." But Ehman has not considered other ways to understand x's special concern for y. If x loves y not merely because x takes delight in y's presence but because x finds value in y via y's properties, and if x's concern for y is directed at preserving and enhancing this value, x cannot so quickly be accused of focusing on morally irrelevant differences between y and others. Wanting to preserve the value one finds in the world is not to make an arbitrary distinction. And self-interest in some significant sense does not necessarily underlie x's valuing y's properties, so that reason for charging x with immoral discrimination does not hold. It might be true that all people have the same value as people, but x finds in y not only this value but additional value that distinguishes y from others and that is worth preserving by preferential treatment. Further, if x shows special concern for y because y has the property "is loved by x" (and not merely "delights x"), does this automatically mean that no "universally valid principle" is at work? There might be no contradiction in supposing that preferential concern for beloveds is permitted by morality, ceteris paribus.

The second point is made rather strongly by Edward Sankowski in his discussion of Ehman: "Certain sorts of love constitute such a ponderable human value that one criterion for an adequate account of morality is precisely that it does not say or imply such affections conflict with morality."[32] What is this "ponderable" value? If personal love were a basic human good, something that humans could not do without for a minimally decent life, then the preferential treatment involved in love is easily justified, and no mention need be made of significant self-interest. But there are other moral justifications for love and the preferential concern it involves. Elizabeth Telfer's account of friendship can be applied unchanged to love:

> Friendship . . . promotes the general happiness by providing a degree and kind of consideration for others' welfare which cannot exist outside it, and which compensates by its excellence for the 'unfairness' of the unequal distribution of friendship. For even those who have no friends are . . . better off than they would be if there were no . . . friendship, since the understanding developed by it and the mutual criticism involved in it will improve the way friends deal with people outside the relationship.[33]

The preferential concern of love, then, is morally permissible because this concern itself could not exist without love or without love's being focused preferentially; the world and indefinitely many people would be much poorer without love. The justification of preferential concern, that is, lies in itself: there can be no powerful general moral objection to love and its special concern precisely because the beneficial works of love are good things. And the benefit obtained by the world and its inhabitants is not restricted to the beloveds who are the direct beneficiaries of love's concern but extends indirectly to others: when x and y love each other and promote each other's welfare, their flourishing will have morally valuable effects on other people. But notice that this justification provides little help in setting appropriate limits to the concern x should show toward y at the expense of the concern shown toward others. In particular, to tell the stranger who is drowning, while x preferentially saves x's beloved y, that the special concern of love is justified in part by the beneficial effects it has for other people, is worse than a bad joke. And it is not convincing at all if x's choice is between saving y and saving ten strangers; here the special concern of love is unlikely of benefit to others. This is a typical quandary for utilitarians: behavior that usually maximizes well-being is, in particular situations, counterproductive of well-being. As an alternative, others have sought deontological justifications of friendship and love; for example, their "ponderable" value lies in their recognizing the "deep" value of the person who is their object.[34] But because it is precisely the fact that all persons have the same deep value as persons that conflicts with the special concern of love, this deontological justification needs as much work in achieving consistency as does the utilitarian. And any deontological argument that love must be, for moral reasons, exclusive (since only then can x recognize y's deep value as a person) must be reconciled with the claim that the moral obligation to recognize deep value in all persons prohibits x's focusing on y to the exclusion of others.

We have, then, reached a precarious situation. The weakness of both the utilitarian and the deontological justifications of love and its concern, combined with Ehman's denial that x's delighting in y is a reason powerful enough to justify x's preferential treatment of y, imply that the special concern of love is a moral fault. My suggestion—that it is not x's delighting in y but x's finding y valuable and, as a result, wanting to preserve this value, that justifies special concern by pointing out a morally relevant difference between y and others—probably cannot by itself do the trick. Merely the fact that x finds value in y or y's properties could not be sufficient; we must be able to place some restrictions on x's valuing y in order that such valuing justifies preferential concern. I will soon return to this task.

9. LOVE, JUSTICE, AND MORALITY

Suppose that a personnel director (p.d.) has reviewed the applications for one available position and has eliminated all but two of the applicants, whose resumés are equivalent. The p.d. cannot offer the job to both finalists (multiple, cotemporaneous hirings are impossible, since only one slot is available), although the p.d. might be able to hire both serially. If the p.d. offers the position to one finalist but not the other, the p.d. (like Gellner's E-type lover) might have to deny the generality of reasons: while hiring one finalist on the basis of qualifications Q, the p.d. must ignore these same qualifications in the other. The p.d. already deliberated in a property-based manner while eliminating all but the final two applicants. Thus, the p.d. realizes that having a reason to select one finalist implies that some difference in their resumés allows the p.d. to judge one superior to the other. But there is no job-relevant difference for the p.d. to latch on to. Race and sex, for example, are ordinarily job-irrelevant properties (as wealth is irrelevant to love), so a decision made on this basis is arbitrary. Tossing a coin, or relying on randomly trivial or superficial differences (for example, height or zip code), is also arbitrary and not commensurate with the significance of the outcome. The fact that one finalist applied for the job earlier, or was interviewed ("encountered") first, is not a relevant difference. To claim that there *must* be some difference between the two finalists (because people are unique) is to retreat from, not solve, the problem. Nor are the properties that make one finalist unique relevant to job performance. Yet, it is as morally permissible for the p.d. to hire only one person as it seems to be for x to select some persons, even only one person, to be the recipient of x's love and preferential concern.

There are disanalogies between the situation of this personnel director and the lover x who encounters two (potential) beloveds, both of whom have attractive properties S; but these disanalogies do not amount to much. The p.d. is forced into making an exclusive appointment, not as a matter of logic or morality but as a practical matter. Hence, the p.d. is not like an E-type lover, because the p.d. can admit that if another position were available, the p.d. would hire both finalists. We always have the option, in Gellner's paradox, of rejecting the claim that love is by nature exclusive, while the hands of the p.d. are absolutely tied. But the lover's hands are also tied if the lover *believes* that love must be, for conceptual or moral reasons, exclusive. And the lover may be forced into exclusivity by practical considerations if, for example, the lover's other commitments and non-negotiable responsibilities prevent multiple love or if x's beloveds, out of a desire to be loved exclusively, issue ultimatums.

Perhaps the lover, if affection is primarily under the sway of nonreason-causes, does not (unlike the p.d.) deliberate about whom to love. Consider love at first sight: all in a rush, x is passionately enchanted. Even though x might later look back on the experience and be able to explain in virtue of what properties y (and not z) was the object of x's attention, while it is happening the phenomenon seems not to involve a decision based on reasons. Such thoughts might underlie the resistance to conceiving of love as reason-dependent. But if we leave aside love at first sight, the disanalogy does not run very deep. The p.d. weighs various factors, comparing the applicants on different scales, and decides whom to hire. Lovers go through a similar process of comparing possible beloveds, weeding out those that will not do for some reason or another (8.7), even if they do so less systematically. In surveying the field, lovers make decisions about whom to get to know better or at all (just as the p.d. decides whom to interview), and this reasoned choice in part determines whom they will love—and they know it will have that consequence. The lover in one sense has more power than the p.d.: once the lover has identified and acknowledged the nature of those preferences that causally determine a choice, the lover can allow the preferences to be influential, can refuse to act on them, or can change them (8.4). The p.d., however, cannot change the job description and is stuck looking for an applicant who has Q.

Further, the p.d. must be able to justify the selection of an employee—to others in the firm, to the rejected finalist, even to the hired finalist. When the p.d. is forced to select only one of two equally qualified finalists, the p.d. has a mess of intellectual and psychological problems to deal with. Lacking a definite reason for hiring one finalist and rejecting the other, the p.d. might imagine that there is some real difference between the two or rationalize some small, insignificant difference into a major difference. The p.d. might even claim that the decision was easily made, because one finalist turned out to be uniquely qualified. Similarly, the lover is called upon to justify loving this particular beloved when pressed by the question "why *me*?" and must provide both to beloveds and to those not loved something more convincing than "that's just the way I feel." How would a rejected potential beloved or rejected job applicant respond if told that the lover's or p.d.'s decision had been made by tossing a coin or was otherwise reason-independent? Indeed, how would the actual beloved or employee respond? The lover and the p.d. might be happy if they could announce to all concerned that they had tossed a coin, thereby taking the blame from their shoulders. But those selected and rejected, expecting some rational explanation based on merits or demerits, would be dumbfounded if the lover or p.d. tossed a coin.

But "Which person should I hire?" is a straightforward question and, exceptional circumstances aside, a relatively simple one to answer, whereas "Whom should I love?" seems incomprehensible. The question seems far removed in logical space from "Should I have sex with y or z?" "Should I go to the movies with y or z?" and even "Whom should I marry?"—all of which are similar to "Whom should I hire?" These activities have a specifiable purpose that indicates the properties of persons to be taken into account. The question "Whom should I hire?" is, when unpacked, "Given that the task to be performed is J, that having Q is required to perform J, and that I want J performed well, which applicant has Q to the highest degree?" If I want the job done efficiently, I hire a person who has Q. Similarly, choosing a movie companion, a sex partner, even a spouse, depends on ascertaining the properties relevant to the purposes of these activities; there are no technical job descriptions for movie companions or spouses, but these activities have purposes that we give to them or have by their nature.

For example, "Whom should I marry?" can be unpacked "Given that the meaning or purpose of marriage (for me) is M, that I want to be married, and that a person's having S is required for the achievement of M, which person has S?" Many people today answer this question by saying that marriage is a lifelong relationship between two people who want to achieve certain shared goals (raising children, writing a history of Europe). And they believe that a necessary condition for fulfilling this purpose is that both persons have the property "loves the other person." In different times and places the important S might have been "can contribute to my family's fortune and power" or "will milk the cow every morning," either because marriage was given a different purpose or because it had roughly the same purpose (the achievement of shared goals), but different properties were believed to be essential for its fulfillment. Today, when the Sinatran philosophy ("love and marriage go together like a horse and carriage") is popular in the West, we can still hear whispers of "she only married him for his money" and "he only married her to advance his career." The "only" is revealing, as if people never had a wide variety of purposes in marrying, as if marriage should mean only one thing. (The whispers may have a different point: not to alert us to deviations from the Sinatran philosophy but to suggest that deception is occurring within it; she really married him for his money while he—or she—believed falsely that she did it out of love.) In 1800, would anyone have gossiped, "he brought her in from St. Louis just to milk the cow"? And in Europe a few hundred years ago, did not "he actually married her for *love*" speak of scandal? The conclusion is not that marriage has no purpose and therefore no "job description." To be sure, the properties relevant in choosing between y and z as a spouse are limited only by the purposes one has in marrying; but they *are* limited and they follow from these purposes.

"Whom should I love?," by contrast, resists this kind of analysis.[35] Love seems to have no purpose, either by its nature or by our assigning one to it, but is something whose point resides in itself. If we cannot specify any purpose of love, that method of ascertaining the relevant properties of beloveds is not available. "Why do I want love?" unlike "Why do I want to marry?" has no clear answer that tells us what properties to look for. Or if we want love because we think that love contributes to a full life lived well, this reason is still not powerful enough to generate a list of specific relevant properties. Of course, we prefer happy to unhappy love; but that we should seek a love-partner with whom we can be happy, as Aristophanes says (5.5), is trite advice. One understands, then, why philosophers have claimed that there are few if any logical limits on what sort of person can be the object of love or on what beliefs the lover must have about the beloved's properties—although it is a non sequitur to conclude that love is, therefore, reason-independent. If love has no purpose, or only a very amorphous purpose, this does not rule out an answer to "Whom should I love?" An activity's having a discrete or assignable purpose is sufficient, but not necessary, for ascertaining relevant properties. "Why should I hate?" is as queer a question as "Why should I love?"—yet that does not make incomprehensible the questions "Should I hate y or z?" and "Is my hate for y in virtue of P justifiable?" We do not know exactly why we should practice legal punishment (to deter? to put the universe back in order? to control yet satisfy a desire for revenge?), but we know whom we ought to punish: those who have the property "is guilty of the crime."

Moral judgments, moreover, can be made about x's selecting a beloved (or a behated) on the basis of some properties; the logical "anything goes" does not entail a moral "anything goes." It is difficult to decide for which properties people ought to love others, and in this area one can easily slide from doing philosophy into blandly moralizing. But there are several suggestions worth considering. Even if x's loving y in virtue of those properties that constitute y's identity is not a logical requirement for x's emotion to be love, x's loving y as a person in this sense might be a moral ideal. Or if this is too stringent, either Kantian or perfectionist ethics might imply that loving people for their trivial or superficial properties (like hiring an employee for a superficial reason) is morally objectionable. Even if morality requires recognizing the equal value of all persons, and the special concern of love is justifiable only if there are morally relevant differences between one's beloved and other persons, the valuable properties x finds in y, besides y's value as a person, could be such a morally relevant difference—*if* the properties that x values in y are not superficial but are genuine values worth preserving and enhancing. The worry that x's special concern for y violates morality's injunction against arbitrarily discriminatory treatment might only be the worry that some loves are grounded on the superficial or silly properties of love's object, which properties *are* morally irrelevant and cannot justify preferential concern. Identity properties might seem to fit the bill, but I doubt it; our characters are filled with silly properties from the moral point of view. Of course, some agapists maintain that the only nonsuperficial value—literally and metaphorically—of a person is his or her "deep" value as a person and which all persons have equally;[36] but if this is right, x's focusing on this nonsuperficial value could not justify preferential concern. I have never seen it explained adequately how, after this agape is infused into personal love, the agapized love is justifiably preferential (see 9.9).

In addition, we can appeal to the fact that the best erosic love is based on x's autonomously chosen or formed preferences (8.4); instead of justifying the special concern of love only in terms of x's loving y in virtue of y's properties that are not superficial, it can be justified if x also loves y in virtue of y's properties that mesh with x's preferences that are not superficial, that is, are not unreflectively and uncritically allowed to operate in x's choice.[37] The morality of the preferential choice flows from the value of autonomy, not only from the value of the object of that choice. The suggestion is that as long as lovers have some control over their preferences and over their ability to distinguish worthy from unworthy objects of love, the responsibility for making justifiable distinctions between the beloved and others is the lover's. This, however, is not merely a matter of inner strength; social and economic conditions must be such as to encourage lovers to develop and modify their preferences freely as well as to allow beloveds to develop properties that are not superficial. It is, of course, no easy matter to determine what genuine autonomy amounts to, or what social and economic arrangements are conducive to it, but regardless of the details the analysis remains the same: x's special concern for y is justifiable only if x loves y in virtue of properties that are not superficial and that x finds valuable as a result of x's autonomously formed preferences. Thus, we might say that a property that it is morally permissible for x to love y in virtue of, is a property that x would love y in virtue of if both x and y were free to develop nonsuperficial properties and nonsuperficial preferences.

Hence, love becomes a problem of distributive justice.[38] Applicant selection is already broadly a moral problem within distributive justice. To claim that the choice of beloveds is a similar issue, since social and economic factors impinge on, or can be arranged not to impinge on, the development of preferences and qualities, is to tighten, not loosen, the analogy with applicant selection. One argument against doing so is that distributive justice applies only to economic items (jobs) or hard goods (dollars, wheat). But we can coherently talk about a just (and unjust) distribution of health, even though it is not a standard hard good, and this talk is not merely elliptical for talk about the distribution of its foundation, namely health-care provision and surgical supplies. And a major question of John Rawls' *A Theory of Justice* is how to guarantee, as well as such things can be guaranteed, an equal distribution of self-respect, which is also not a hard good. The question of this distribution is, again, not merely elliptical for questions about the distribution of the economic goods that are the foundation for self-respect, for we are concerned with the distribution of that hard foundation only because it is the means, in part, by which other goods (liberty and then self-respect) are secured, and it is the distribution of the latter that we are really concerned with. If it makes sense to adjust, according to the precepts of justice, the social bases of self-respect, then it must make sense to talk about the social conditions that promote or hinder the ability of persons to engage in well-grounded love relationships.[39] This would hold especially within Rawls' framework, with its emphasis on the basic good of self-respect, if there are (as I have claimed; see 8.3 and 9.8) important links between erosic love in particular and self-respect.

Reflecting on the reasons for or causes of one's attachments, loving on the basis of autonomously formed preferences and focusing on the significant properties of beloveds are not the only requirements for avoiding defective, shallow love. A love may be irrational, as I have argued (7.4), if x's belief that y has S is irrational, that is, not well founded on the evidence. This irrationality is not merely a cognitive fault of love; it can also be a moral fault. Hence, loving the person, in the sense of having well-grounded and accurate knowledge of one's beloved, is both an ontological and a moral dimension of love. Let us try to make this idea more precise. Pausanias, in Plato's *Symposium,* says that it is "discreditable" for a pursued beloved to give in too quickly to his lover (184a5). The beloved must discern, with adequate evidence, whether the lover is motivated by vulgar or by heavenly eros and whether the lover is even feigning the heavenly to hide his vulgar eros. If the beloved gives in too quickly, he has only himself to blame; he has allowed himself negligently or recklessly to be someone's beloved in not waiting to make sure that he has rational and true beliefs about the lover's motivation. Aristotle, too, thinks that the beloved is to blame if "a person has erroneously assumed that the affection he got was for his character, though nothing in his friend's conduct suggested anything of the sort" (*Nicomachean Ethics* 1165b7–9).

Pausanias also says that if y, the beloved, gives in to x, the lover, because y believes that x is rich, y is proceeding incorrectly whether y's belief is rational or irrational, true or false; y in this case is "disgraced" in showing himself to be the sort of shallow person attracted to superficial properties. On the other hand, if y gives in to x believing that x is wise and virtuous, "it does him credit," regardless of the rationality and truth of the belief (184e–185a). But Pausanias here contradicts his earlier claim about y's negligent irrationality. What he should say is that if y believes falsely but on good evidence that x is wise, y's giving in is still praiseworthy, since y's giving in reveals y's commendable motivation (to become virtuous); but that if y believes falsely, due to the negligence in not waiting long enough for the evidence, that x is wise, then despite y's motivation y is a "discreditable" beloved. For y has not attempted to sort out the genuine heavenly erosic lovers from the pretenders.

What Pausanias and Aristotle assert about the beloved applies mutatis mutandis to the lover, and this suggests the additional sense in which a lover can be morally superficial. Suppose that x loves y believing that y has S and that this belief was formed carelessly. In some cases of this sort, x knows (or can be expected to know) that x has not had enough opportunity to gain the knowledge of y required for a rational belief that y has S (or that y's S outweighs y's D). X's loving y on the basis of negligent beliefs about y is a moral fault. In doing so, x leads y to believe that x loves y, makes conditional commitments to y, and creates expectations in y about x's future behavior (even if love is only indefinitely constant). X leads y to believe that x now has certain love-related desires: to spend time with y, to share some delicacies and experiences exclusively with y, and so forth. Further, x creates in y the expectation that y is and will be an object of x's special, preferential concern. Creating all these beliefs in y on the basis of negligently false beliefs is a moral injury to y, since x will likely discover later that x's beliefs that y has S are false, and the love-related desires and concern will dissipate. Indeed, it is plausible to claim that if x does want to be able to justify x's special, preferential concern for y, x is under an obligation to ascertain without negligence that y does have the S that grounds x's love.

Surely, the fact that the end of love might cause the beloved pain is not, in general, a moral defect of love. Love is risky business, and ordinarily beloveds know in advance that they might get hurt. So creating not-to-be-fulfilled expectations by loving, or by declaring one's love, is not in itself morally questionable. Not even when x loves y because x believes falsely that y has S, is it necessarily a moral fault if x hurts y when x's love ends upon the discovery that y does not have S. Consider two cases. First, if x loves y because x believes falsely that y has S, and x has this belief as a result of y's deliberate deception, then of course x's withdrawing love upon the correction of x's beliefs cannot be criticized, even if y is thereby hurt; y has brought it on herself. But compare this case with another: x believes falsely and recklessly that y has S. This situation is somewhat different; here, at least, it makes sense to say that x is at fault morally for hurting y. What is it about the first case that justifies the judgment that x is blameless for hurting y? It is that y knows that x believes falsely that y has S, and so y knows that y should not have the expectations ordinarily associated with being loved. Even though y will be distressed at the loss of x's love, a rational y cannot even think that y has been hurt *by x* in this case, since y knows that y should not take x's declaration of love seriously.

If this is right, we have to be more careful about the second case. For if x loves y because x believes falsely and recklessly that y has S, then if y also knows that this is why x loves y, again y has reason not to take x's love seriously. If y is doing what is demanded by the rationality of love—discovering not only why y loves x but also why x loves y (8.6)—then y, as much as x, is to blame for any pain that y experiences if x's love ends. In this case, too, a rational y might be distressed but cannot think that x is fully to blame for y's pain. Thus, x's loving y because x recklessly believes falsely that y has S is a moral fault only of x, when y not only does not know but also could not be reasonably expected to know that x's love for y is grounded this way. Perhaps y has good evidence that x's love for y is well grounded, even if it is not. Or perhaps x's demeanor is misleadingly suggestive or deliberately deceptive; in these cases the moral defect resides precisely in the deception, a sort of thing that when it arises or exists in a loving relationship is especially objectionable.[40]

CHAPTER 13

The Object of Love

"I heard an old religious man
But yesternight declare
That he had found a text to prove
That only God, my dear,
Could love you for yourself alone
And not your yellow hair."

—W. B. Yeats, "For Anne Gregory"

In an authentic recognition of her individuality, her blondeness would be loved, but in a different way: She would be loved first as an irreplaceable totality, and then her blondeness would be loved as one of the characteristics of that totality.

—Shulamith Firestone, *The Dialectic of Sex*

1. THE BLONDE'S COMPLAINT

Does Firestone believe that human personal love might accomplish what Yeats' theologian proves only God can do?[1] If what God is capable of doing— loving someone for herself alone—is to love humans not in virtue of their properties, and if x's loving y "as an irreplaceable totality" is equivalent to x's loving y for herself, then Firestone is claiming (plausibly) that it is neither a conceptual truth nor a fact of human psychology that personal love is property-based and (implausibly) that in authentic love x values y's properties only because x loves y. These expressions, loving someone "for himself" and loving someone "as an irreplaceable totality," even if not equivalent, have in common the implicit claim that x's loving y because y is blonde is second-rate love. Yeats and Firestone do not mean that blondeness is a silly love-grounding property. If that were the point, then Yeats would be praising God (falsely) for being the only one capable of loving humans in virtue of their significant properties; and Firestone would mean only that loving for significant properties is loving someone as a "totality." Yeats' intended contrast, instead, is between loving on the basis of properties *simpliciter* and loving agapically. And Firestone's is between x's loving y's properties and x's loving y the totality and only derivatively y's properties. Whereas Yeats' poem is about the basis of love, Firestone is making a point about the object of love.

Several expressions are often used to describe first-rate or genuine personal love: x loves y "as person," x loves y "for herself," x's love is "love for the person," x loves y "the whole person." "Personal love" (in its nontechnical sense) is claimed to be, when genuine, "love for the person." These expressions are also often used in asserting that the attractive properties of the beloved play no role in love as either its basis or object. Of course, people say that they want to be loved "for themselves." They frequently use that expression, which is part of our natural language and not merely philosophical jargon. The question, however, is whether love for the person must be understood as love in which properties are neither the basis nor object. Can it be analyzed erosically? I begin by examining a view suggested by Firestone: "loving the person" is loving someone "irreplaceably." Then I turn to "as a totality" (sect. 5).

2. NONFUNGIBLE ATTACHMENT

In discussing love, Ronald de Sousa employs the notion of "non-fungibility."[2] If you loan me a dollar, I can erase my debt by returning *any* dollar bill. I do not have to give you the same bill you gave me; in this context all dollars are identical, that is, dollars are fungible or interreplaceable. But if I steal your rare U.S. Bank Note (with a face value of one dollar) and later give you a one-dollar Federal Reserve Note, I have not made proper restitution; in this context, your Bank Note is nonfungible since no other dollar bill will do in its place. De Sousa notes that I might be able to discharge my debt by "offer[ing] an adequate *substitute*," say, by giving you several hundred Federal Reserve notes. But these are "mere" substitutes that are not commensurate, for you, with the original.

De Sousa claims that in our culture, the nonfungibility of the beloved "is part of the ideology of love." To show that in some cultures the concept of love does not include nonfungibility, he provides this example (borrowed from J. A. Lee via Morton Hunt):

> Dr. Aubrey Richards, an anthropologist who lived among the Bemba of Northern Rhodesia in the 1930's, once related to a group of them an English folk tale about a young prince who climbed glass mountains, crossed chasms, and fought dragons, all to obtain the hand of a maiden he loved. The Bemba were plainly bewildered, but remained silent. Finally an old chief spoke up, voicing the feelings of all present in the simplest of questions: "Why not take another girl?" he asked.

The prince's loving just this maiden, being either unable or not willing to transfer his affections to a more accessible maiden, illustrates the beloved's nonfungibility. The Bemba, de Sousa implies, do not have a concept of love in which the beloved is not fungible; a Bemban prince, faced with these obstacles, could easily replace one beloved with another maiden. Or the Bemba have no concept of love at all, but only a concept of "fungible sexual satisfaction."

The illustration, however, does not clearly show that the Bemba have no concept of nonfungibility. The perplexed and unromantic question "Why not take another girl?" might indicate, instead, that the value of love for the Bemba does not justify taking large risks. Better, the old chief's question shows that he sees through the folk tale and the assumption that the anthropologist packs into it; why describe the prince as motivated by *love* in the first place? What is really going on, the old chief hints to the anthropologist, is that the prince is under the spell of purely erotic desire, and even if the object of sexual desire is itself nonfungible, taking large risks for sexual pleasure is plain stupidity. Let the dragon have its meal and find another maiden. Indeed, we often ask the Bemban chief's question when x loves y but it is a lost love, not because y is stashed away on a mountain but because y does not welcome x's attention and does not reciprocate: "Every one is apt to say, if he cannot obtain the affections of one person, why doth he not apply his to another which is more kind?"[3]

Let us refine the notion of nonfungibility with this analysis of irreplaceability or nonfungible attachment. An item φ is irreplaceable for x if and only if two conditions are met: (I) x deeply values φ and (II) nothing can take φ's place. Both conditions are necessary. For even if x deeply values φ, yet something else could take its place, x's attachment is transferable to the something else. And even if nothing could take φ's place, yet x has no appreciation for φ, x is not nonfungibly attached simply because x has no attachment. In this analysis φ's uniqueness is necessary, but not sufficient, for irreplaceability. Something's being unique does not entail that it will be irreplaceable for someone; even if everything is unique, not everything is valued by someone. But something's being irreplaceable does entail or presuppose that it is unique. Suppose that I possess and value deeply the only 1902 gold coin in existence. Were you to lose that coin through carelessness, nothing you could give me would make me happy; you could only soothe my wounds, not heal them, by giving me twenty newer gold coins. But if the coin I deeply value is not unique, I have no reason to complain if you replace the lost coin with another token of the same type, a 1902 gold coin indistinguishable in the relevant ways from mine. At least, I should not complain if I am rational; if I know that in the significant respects the two coins are identical, I cannot accuse you of failing to make perfect restitution. If I insist, in my misery, that my coin is irreplaceable, I must exhibit a difference between the two coins. I *might* be able to do so: my father gave me the coin you lost. But in stating this difference I am asserting that the coin is irreplaceable after all in virtue of both its uniqueness and my valuing it deeply. Uniqueness is necessary for *rational* irreplaceability, while uniqueness and being deeply valued are jointly sufficient.

Something's being nonfungible is not equivalent to its being valued exclusively. If I am nonfungibly attached to my 1902 gold coin, it does not follow that the only thing I value is that coin; I might also value a 1903 gold coin that is irreplaceable for me. Hence, exclusive valuing is not necessary for irreplaceability. But exclusive valuing is sufficient for irreplaceability. Suppose that the *only* thing I value, among all the things in the world, is my 1902 coin. If I lose or you steal this coin, nothing is capable of being adequate compensation; for, by hypothesis, nothing else in the world has any value for me. Of course, it would be odd if the only thing I valued was my 1902 coin. Normally we value many things, which is why things of different types are adequate (and not "mere") substitutes for each other. Given, however, that I do value only ϕ, it will be irreplaceable; for ϕ's being deeply valued and its being unique are jointly sufficient for it to be irreplaceable, and my valuing ϕ exclusively makes it (derivatively) unique. Strictly speaking, however, exclusive valuing entails irreplaceability only if (1) I do not now value anything but ϕ and (2) I am unable to come to value anything else. If the only thing I now value is my coin, and you lose it, I could be perfectly satisfied with a 1903 coin if I am able to develop an appreciation for it. Although initially the 1903 coin is not adequate restitution, with time I value it as much as I valued my 1902 coin, and I no longer feel the pain of its loss. Hence, my 1902 coin is only temporarily irreplaceable, not absolutely so.[4]

If my 1902 coin is to be absolutely irreplaceable, I must be a rigid person who is unable to come to value other things. Or I must value this coin so deeply that I am unable to value anything else; I am thereby permanently nonfungibly attached to it. Because my deeply valuing something can lead me to not value anything else, one might (mistakenly) think that the whole story to nonfungible attachment is deep valuing. But deep valuing does not yield irreplaceability unless the item cannot be replaced because it is unique. Deep valuing *can* make something unique, so in some cases deep valuing alone will appear to yield irreplaceability; in these cases the satisfaction of condition (I) guarantees the satisfaction of condition (II). Yet this does not mean irreplaceability is just deep valuing. Similarly, if an item's being on its own merits unique is precisely why it is deeply valued, then in some cases the satisfaction of (II) guarantees the satisfaction of condition (I). Yet this does not mean irreplaceability is just uniqueness.

I find no reason to alter the analysis of irreplaceability or nonfungible attachment when speaking about persons as beloveds: y is irreplaceable for x if x deeply values y and no person can take y's place. If so, the irreplaceability of the beloved is only a contingent and perhaps infrequent feature of love. For if x loves (deeply values) y in virtue of y's commonly shared love-grounding properties, these properties do not make y unique enough to prohibit z's taking y's place. If x does value y for y's trivial uniqueness-making properties, or if x perceives (falsely) that y is significantly unique, x might be nonfungibly attached to y. Or y might be unique in the sense that x loves only y; but if the exclusivity of x's love makes y irreplaceable, irreplaceability can be no more frequent than exclusivity. Finally, x might value y so profoundly that x cannot value persons other than y; lovers of long standing often do become nonfungibly attached, even permanently: having loved and valued this one person y for decades, x is unable to love and value z (see 10.3 on self-reinforcing constancy). But in other cases—of which there are enough to show that love is neither essentially nor only at its best nontransferable—irreplaceability is only temporary. "The terrible thing, . . . but the good thing too, the saving grace, . . . is that if something happened to one of us . . . I think the other one . . . would grieve for a while . . . but then . . . would go out and love again. . . . [A]ll of this love we're talking about, it would just be a memory."[5] Knowing this, how could a rational beloved feel irreplaceable, or how could a rational lover consider the beloved permanently irreplaceable? They do not. It is no wonder that we (like the solid, unromantic Aristophanes, for whom only first-generation half-persons are permanently irreplaceable) tell the x who has been abandoned or whose beloved has died to find another sympathetic and congenial partner, at least in part in order to erase the pain of terminated love. De Sousa is right: irreplaceability is only part of our *ideology* of love.

3. PHENOMENOLOGICAL IRREPLACEABILITY

Nevertheless, the idea that "to love someone [is] . . . to value the person . . . as irreplaceable"[6] is often asserted. Neera Badhwar's account of love rests upon the "widely-held intuition" that in the "best" loves, x loves y as an "irreplaceable individual."[7] Because in Badhwar's view irreplaceability "most obviously marks off"[8] what she calls "end love" (the best love) from "means love" (that is, instrumental love), her Aristotelian account is especially pertinent. For it fills out the suggestion that love for the person (in the sense of end love) conceptually involves irreplaceability. Further, in Badhwar's end love, x loves y in virtue of y's attractive identity properties; hence, end love is an erosic love for the person.

The beloved is *phenomenologically* irreplaceable, says Badhwar, "in the precise sense that loving and delighting in her are not completely commensurate with loving and delighting in another." This seems to be a robust sense in which the irreplaceability of the beloved could be a characteristic feature of love. But what is it about loving in virtue of identity properties, or about not loving because the beloved, as a means, provides some specific good, that makes the beloved in end love, but not the beloved in means love, irreplaceable$_p$ in Badhwar's "precise" sense? The answer, I think, should be "nothing"—for loving in virtue of identity properties, or not loving in virtue of a good provided by the beloved, do not obviously necessitate that love has any particular phenomenal feel or that the lover has a specific feeling toward the beloved. Further, if x loves y for y's identity properties, and y dies or leaves, x might come to love z in virtue of z's identity properties; hence, that x end-loves y does not mean x's attachment to y is permanently nonfungible. But even if Badhwar's irreplaceability$_p$ is not the same as nonfungible attachment, why think that x's loving y is "not completely commensurate" with x's loving z and, hence, that y is irreplaceable in this narrower sense?

Immediately after defining irreplaceable$_p$ in terms of "not completely commensurate," Badhwar writes: "This is confirmed by the fact that if the happiness we got from different friends were completely commensurate, there would be no qualitative differences among our friendships, and we would not . . . desire to spend an evening with x rather than with y, but rather only 'with a friend'." Since the sentence begins with "this is confirmed by," Badhwar intends the subsequent "fact" as evidence that in end love the beloved is irreplaceable$_p$ in the sense that x's loving y is "not completely commensurate" with x's loving z. Yet the sentence also functions to explain what Badhwar means by "not completely commensurate" and hence by irreplaceability$_p$. If y and z are irreplaceable$_p$ in the sense that x's loving y is "not completely commensurate" with x's loving z, then there is a qualitative difference between x's loving (or delighting in) y and x's loving z such that x desires to be with y in particular, or with z in particular, but x does not desire to be with some beloved or another, that is, y or z or. . . . But this will not work; it fails to distinguish end love from means love. For x's instrumentally loving both y and z is compatible with there being a qualitative difference between these two loves. Consider the case in which loving y promotes good G_1 for x and loving z promotes G_2 for x: x could very well want to be with not just any old means-friend but with either y in particular or z in particular, depending on whether x now wants G_1 or G_2. So how does irreplaceability "most obviously" mark off the "best" love?

Badhwar's second defense of her claim (or her second explication of "not completely commensurate") is that "when someone who is loved as an end ceases to be loved, the loss cannot be completely made up by acquiring a new friend." It sounds here as if Badhwar understands irreplaceability$_P$ as permanent nonfungible attachment, so that means love is distinguished from end love by its lacking permanent nonfungible attachment. But if x deeply values y because y provides G, and as a result x cannot value anyone else, x's instrumental love for y is permanently nonfungible. Further, Badhwar's elaboration of why in end love "the loss cannot be completely made up by acquiring a new friend" is inadequate to show that end love and means love can be distinguished by irreplaceability$_P$: "The loss of the old friend is a distinct loss, the gain of the new friend, a distinct gain." But the loss of a means-friend can be a distinct loss. Of course, there are senses in which x's loving y is "distinct" from x's loving z (sect. 4), so in some senses the two loves are "not completely commensurate"; for example, x's love for y is spatiotemporally a different love from x's love for z. But in this sense of "distinct"—a sense in which any two things are distinct—x's loving z instrumentally is also a distinct gain whether or not x still loves y for G_1. And in this sense a new end love is also, and only trivially, a distinct gain.

Badhwar undoubtedly means more than this by "distinct"; in a footnote she writes that "unique, irreplaceable values" are irreplaceable in that "they have a different *meaning* to the valuer, are *experienced* differently. Thus x has a value to me for being the person he is that is different, phenomenologically, from the value of y."[9] Being with or loving a given person means something different, or feels different, from being with or loving some other person. But it is illicit for Badhwar to smuggle in "for being the person he is" in this explanation of irreplaceability$_P$, as if only when x end-loves y ("for being the person he is" = "for his identity properties") does x's love have a distinct meaning or feeling. If x loves y instrumentally for G_1 and z for G_2, there is no reason to deny that the meaning of these two loves is different for x or that x experiences the loves, or y and z, differently, depending on the difference between G_1 and G_2. If end love is characterized by irreplaceability$_P$ in this sense, so too is means love, and neither love has been shown generally to involve nonfungible attachment. Badhwar, however, does not understand irreplaceability$_P$ as nonfungible attachment, for even in end love "one ceases to *feel* the loss [of the beloved], because of the passage of time . . . and the presence of other enriching activities and experiences in one's life."[10] But if x is no longer disturbed by the loss of the end love for y *because* x now end-loves z—one of x's later "enriching experiences" that does make up the loss, after all—then to assert "it remains true that different end friendships engender different forms of love and happiness" is dogmatism. Irreplaceability$_P$ has no cash value in distinguishing between end love and means love, and it has no practical implications for the course of x's loves and life. Badhwar's "intuition" that in end love the beloved is irreplaceable has no interesting content; it is simply another piece of the ideology to which de Sousa alerted us.

Even though Badhwar claims that her theory of end love is superior to Plato's theory of eros and to the Christian theory of agape, on the grounds that only her view can account for the irreplaceability$_P$ of the beloved (p. 6), she also employs another notion of irreplaceability to describe end love and distinguish it from means love. If x loves y because y promotes G for x, this is a means love in which y is *numerically* replaceable by anyone who can also promote G. By contrast, in end love the beloved is irreplaceable$_N$: "Friends are not . . . means to each other's ends, they cannot—logically cannot—be replaced by more efficient means" (p. 3). Taken literally, this claim is true; from the fact that y is not loved as a means, it surely follows that y cannot be replaced *as* a means. But it just as surely does not follow that y cannot be replaced *at all*. Hence, if y's not being loved as a means is going to imply that y is irreplaceable$_N$, we have to treat (which I think Badhwar does) "numerically irreplaceable" as by definition "not loved as a means." The beloved's irreplaceability$_N$ in end love is not a separate phenomenon that results from the beloved's not being loved as a means but is entirely exhausted by her not being loved as a means. If this is right, the notion of irreplaceability$_N$ is empty: to say that irreplaceability$_N$ "most obviously" marks off end love from means love is to utter the tautology that what marks off end love from means love is that in the former one is not loved as a means while in the latter one is.

4. IRREPLACEABILITY BY INDIVIDUATION

Thomas Nagel argues that a desire for an omelet is conceptually different from sexual desire: the object of omelet-desire, but not of sexual desire, is replaceable. X might desire an omelet for its "combination of aroma and visual aspect," and any other "omelet with the crucial characteristics would do as well."[11] In contrast, "it is not similarly true that any person with the same flesh distribution"—and now we expect Nagel to complete the sentence with "would do as well." But Nagel says instead: "can be substituted as object for a particular sexual desire that has been elicited by those characteristics." Now, is "cannot be substituted" equivalent, for Nagel, to "would not do as well," so that x will scarf down the second omelet but will not be happy with, or even refuse, the second person? No. As I will show, Nagel means "logically" cannot be substituted, which does not amount to an interesting irreplaceability.

Nagel is concerned to make a point about the individuation of desire: "It may be that" the crucial flesh characteristics "will arouse attraction wherever they recur, but it will be a new sexual attraction with a new particular object, not merely a transfer of the old desire to someone else." Omelet-desire is *not* individuated by its object (x's desire for the second omelet is not a new omelet-desire, but the same desire transferred), but sexual desire *is* individuated by its object (hence, x's desire for the second person, should it exist, is a new sexual desire). I cannot agree that there is necessarily this difference between omelet-desire and sexual desire. It is not obviously wrong to say that x's desire for the second omelet is historically or spatiotemporally a new desire; and x's sexual desire for the second person may simply be a continuation of x's desire for y. How we individuate these desires is a function not merely of the nature of their respective objects but also of what is happening, psychologically, in the subject. Hence (my first objection), Nagel has not shown that we must count two sexual desires and only one omelet-desire.

Furthermore (my second objection), even if x's sexual desire for the second person is a new desire, that does not mean that x will not be equally as happy with the satisfaction of that desire as x would be with the satisfaction of x's original desire. True, x has not transferred one sexual desire from y to z, if we individuate sexual desire as Nagel recommends; yet x *has* transferred sexual attention from y to z, has transferred the goal of achieving satisfaction with y to achieving it with z. Since x might be just as happy satisfying x's sexual desire for z as x would have been satisfying x's sexual desire for y, the individuation of sexual desire places no limit on what might "do as well." Yet if there is going to be an interesting distinction between omelet-desire and sexual desire, it would have to be that the second omelet will, but the second person will not, "do as well," that is, that the object of sexual desire is irreplaceable. And that cannot be shown by individuating desire as recommended by Nagel. (This, I think, is what is wrong also with Badhwar's attempt to analyze irreplaceability$_P$ as implying "distinct" gains and losses. She would like to individuate end loves and means loves in different ways. Not only is such a task probably hopeless, but it is also irrelevant: that we might count end loves and means loves differently does not entail any difference between the two kinds of love in terms of the fungibility of their objects.)

My first objection to Nagel is expressed by Roger Scruton as a question: "Is it not merely a convention that leads us to say that, when I transfer my appetite from this dish of carrots to that [dish], there is only *one* appetite, with two successive objects, while, when I transfer my attention from Elizabeth to Jane, there are two desires, differentiated precisely by their successive objects?" Scruton immediately proceeds to respond to the objection: "Sexual desire is unlike my appetite for these carrots, in being *founded upon* an individuating thought. It is part of the very directedness of desire that a *particular* person is conceived as its object." To defend this claim Scruton points out that there can be "mistakes of identity" about the object of sexual desire, but not about the object of carrots-desire.[12] Suppose that x sexually desires y, but spends the evening in bed with z believing that z is y. A desire of x's has been satisfied, but how is this to be described? "In a crucial sense," says Scruton, x "does not desire [z], but the other" person. Hence, x's evening with z has not satisfied x's desire for z, since x has no such desire. But x does have a desire for y, and we can say either that (1) z has helped x satisfy x's desire for y (since during the evening x believed z was y) or that (2) x's desire for y was not satisfied by x's evening with z (since x did not sleep with y). If we assume some desire of x's has been satisfied, we should take route (1). Route (2) claims that x's desire for y has not been satisfied, and we already know that x has no desire for z that could have been satisfied, so (2) forces us to say that no desire of x's has been satisfied.

Scruton does opt for (1): x's "desire for [y] seemed to be satisfied by his night with [z], only to the extent that, and for as long as, [x] imagined it was [y] with whom he was lying." Thus, x's desire for y *is* satisfied when x does not know that z, instead of y, is in x's bed (or x believes z is y); and x's desire for y is *not* satisfied when x knows that z is slipping into bed with x, or x will in retrospect say that x's desire for y had not been satisfied when x finds out that z was x's partner. By contrast, "the desire for a dish of carrots is not similarly dependent upon an individuating thought, and does not therefore give rise to errors of identity. To eat the wrong dish of carrots may be a social howler, but it is not a mistaken expression of desire—I really did desire the dish of carrots I consumed," while x did *not* desire the z that x by mistake slept with. Scruton claims that the possibility of mistaken identity in sexual desire, and its absence from carrots-desire, can "dispel [the] immediate force" of my first objection to Nagel.

Scruton's argument, however, does not show that when x sexually desires y and then *later* sexually desires z, we should individuate x's states in such a way that x's sexual desire for z is a new desire. For in Scruton's mistaken identity example, x never sexually desires z at all. X has only one sexual desire to begin with—for y; x never has a sexual desire toward z about which we could ask, "Is this the same or a new sexual desire?" Scruton's question was about how to individuate (count) x's sexual desires when x *knowingly* is first attracted to Elizabeth and later to Jane, but in the mistaken identity case x never desires z, so there is nothing to count. Hence, since Scruton's example does not establish that sexual desire must be individuated by its object, it does not confirm the "particularity" of the object of desire or establish that an "individuating thought" plays a role. Note that Scruton equivocates on "individuation"; he uses it both to refer to the counting of desires and to express a thesis about the "particularity" of the object of desire.

Perhaps satisfied that he has established his thesis about the individuation of desire, Scruton also claims that "the person in love wishes his beloved to want him as the unique irreplaceable individual that he is,"[13] and in another passage he rejects, consistently, the Bemba's response to the folk tale: y in particular "is wanted, and not just any person. . . . If John is frustrated in his pursuit of Mary, there is something inapposite in the advice 'Take Elizabeth, she will do just as well'."[14] But why "inapposite"? Perhaps immediately giving that advice is irrelevant to what John is experiencing, but eventually the advice is excellent (with "she will do just as well" tactfully omitted) if John, lonely and depressed, is still pining away for the unattainable Mary. Sure, John's desire for Elizabeth, if it develops, is not the same desire as John's desire for Mary, but that it is a new desire means *not* that the old desire has not been replaced by the new one, but that it *has* been replaced—along with its object. Scruton continues: "Of course, Elizabeth can *console* John . . . [which] consolation consists precisely in extinguishing John's present desire in the flood of another." But it is not correct to say that Elizabeth has merely "consoled" John if she has extinguished his desire for Mary (proving it to be, by making it, a fungible attachment). Elizabeth is not merely holding his hand and offering sympathy but is now the full-blown object of John's attention.

It comes as some surprise to discover that Scruton thinks that the belief that the object of sexual desire or of love is an irreplaceable particular is a metaphysical illusion. "We regard each other as irreplaceable in arousal, just as we do in love, and individualising thoughts are in each case central to our endeavor. . . . [T]hose thoughts have a large illusory component. . . . Individualising thoughts are . . . mystifications."[15] But then the advice "Seek Elizabeth, she will do as well" should be quite acceptable to Scruton. He still resists, arguing that the illusion is beneficial. "It is by such mystifications that we live. They are the necessary salve to the pain of incarnation. . . . In so far as we could give an explanatory account of what one person gains from another in love and desire, it is clear that he might have gained that benefit equally from someone other than the person to whom he directs his attentions. But it is imperative that we do not think of this. If we do so, our enterprise is jeopardised." Scruton is not claiming that x loves y primarily because x gains something from y or that x's love involves a give-to-get attitude, and that as a result of having this questionable motivation x (and y) must "not think of this" to protect their love (6.3). Rather, what must not be thought is that the beloved is replaceable, that someone else could do as well. "By such thoughts we threaten the possibility of any lasting human attachment." But why not claim, instead, that all sorts of things threaten love's constancy and that a rational recognition of replaceability is the salve to the pain of abandonment or lost love?

Scruton claims that believing the other is irreplaceable is crucial not only for love but also for relationships with those who are only, for example, our movie companions. X selects y as a movie companion, says Scruton, because y has certain "relevant properties"; as a result x's "attitude is transferable." Nevertheless, "you would be insulted to learn that you were wanted as a companion *merely* as the instantiation of a universal. It is quite important that I hide from you (and from myself) the idea that someone else might 'do just as well'."[16] Not much difference remains, then, between beloveds and movie companions: the latter are surely replaceable, but the irreplaceability of the beloved is an illusion; in both cases we must "hide" the fact that people are replaceable. Movie companions and beloveds (friends, too) also have in common their being the subjects and objects of personal relations, in contrast to those we interact with impersonally in the public domain. One might think, then, that in the personal domain in particular, but not in the public, maintaining the illusion that people are irreplaceable is important. Yet even though employees, for example, *are* replaceable (ceteris paribus), jobs might not be performed well, or little satisfaction derived from them, unless the illusion is carried into the public domain as well. No one likes to be told or to believe, no matter how true, that they are gears in the economic machine. Job-replaceability is so obvious, however, that no attempt to urge the illusion on us could erase the thought from consciousness. No wonder the personal domain is conceived of, or billed, as a haven from the public domain, the one area in which we can sustain the illusion of irreplaceability.

There is something strange, however, in Scruton's *telling* us that he must "hide from you (and from myself)" the fact that as a movie companion you really are replaceable, and that "it is imperative that we do not think" the destructive thought that our beloveds are replaceable. For if there are thoughts that must not be thought (which Scruton himself thought), these thoughts must not be spoken or written: maintaining the illusion requires silence. Of course, Freud's *The Future of an Illusion* did not destroy religion, but he let the cat out of the bag for anyone willing to listen. Exposing illusions, even to defend them as necessary, is risky business. How can Scruton think and write that irreplaceability is an illusion, yet press us—and himself—to believe it anyway? Like all illusions, the belief in the beloved's irreplaceability requires self-deception or other mental tricks.[17] As I suggested earlier: there are no grounds, or very few, for a rational belief in permanent nonfungibility.

The proposal that we should think of replaceable persons as irreplaceable for the sake of lasting human attachments is quite different from Plato's program. One might become enraptured with, and nonfungibly attached to, a particular person in virtue of her superior human merits. But, for Plato, becoming attached to people is to be avoided, since it impedes one's progress toward Beauty and Goodness; loving imperfect humans is hardly an adequate substitute for infinite bliss. Humans are only replaceable depositories of hints of Beauty and not irreplaceable items (like the Forms) in their own right. According to Martha Nussbaum, a Platonic lover realizes that "it is prudent to consider these related beauties [in various people] to be 'one and the same', that is, qualitatively homogeneous."[18] Nussbaum's Platonic reason, however, is not precisely that in seeing people as replaceable, the lover more readily makes his way up the Ascent; rather, viewing persons as replaceable removes the pain from turbulent human attachments. "This strategy is adopted at least in part for reasons of mental health, because a certain sort of tension has become too risky or difficult to bear. A kind of therapy alters the look of the world, making the related the same, the irreplaceable replaceable," writes Nussbaum. I doubt, however, that Plato believes people *are* irreplaceable and that we have to deny or suppress this truth in order to make progress in the Ascent. When Nussbaum asks, "Why does he [that is, the Platonic lover] think it foolish not to see things in a way that appears, *prima facie,* to be false to our ordinary intuitions about the object of love?" she implies that the Platonic lover knows (and Plato, too) that beloveds are irreplaceable, or at least knows it as well as any "ordinary intuition" can be known. But Plato is not Scruton in reverse; Plato does not argue that irreplaceability is the truth, replaceability the illusion, yet an illusion that is necessary for the sake of the Ascent. For Plato, viewing persons as replaceable is prudent because true, not "true" because prudent. The ordinary intuition is merely an ordinary intuition, a bit of ideology about love.

5. LOVING THE "WHOLE" PERSON

We have investigated irreplaceability at length because one proposal for what it means for x to love y as a person or for herself claims that it is just x's loving y irreplaceably. Except under special circumstances, I have argued, irreplaceability (that is, nonfungible attachment) is not an element of personal love; hence, if we often do love another "as a person," that must amount to something else. There is another reason we should look elsewhere for an account of loving the person. Irreplaceability is the result of love in special circumstances; first x loves y, and then perhaps y becomes irreplaceable. Since x's loving y precedes y's irreplaceability, the issue of y's irreplaceability has only a tenuous connection with the issue of the basis or object of x's love: as soon as x loves y, the basis and object of x's love are already in place (even if they might change), before the history of the love makes y irreplaceable. And if x is already loving y, x might be loving y as a person prior to loving y irreplaceably. Further, the notion "loving the person" is usually used to express a thesis about either the basis or object of love.

Even though x's loving y exclusively is not equivalent to x's loving y as a person, the problems of exclusivity and loving the person can arise in similar ways. Suppose that x loves y in virtue of y's having S but y insists to x that x must "love *me*." Y's demand can be understood in two ways. If y's demand "love *me*" is short for "love only me, not him," y is worried that x's loving y in virtue of S means that x will love someone else who also has S. But if y's demand "love *me*" is short for "love me, not my S" or "love me for myself, not for my S," y is worried about being loved as a person.[19] As I mentioned earlier (9.10), the first horn of Gellner's paradox might be defended either with a claim about exclusivity or with a claim about loving the person. If x loves y for having S and also loves z for having S, then x actually loves neither, goes the argument, either because love by its nature is exclusive or because in such a situation the object of x's love is not y but S itself. The tension between exclusivity and reason-dependence does not destroy the eros tradition, at least because x's loving y agapically no more reliably secures exclusivity; but perhaps the tension between reason-dependence and loving the person does—if loving the person is a mark of genuine love. But note that the present argument does not show that if x loves y erosically, then x cannot be loving y the person. If it is true that the object of x's love (that which is loved) is y's properties, then x's erosic love takes no person as its object. But it is wrong to infer from "x loves y in virtue of S" that "x loves S"; that is a non sequitur. When x loves y (or both y and z) for having S, as a matter of x's psychology x might be loving only S, but not necessarily and not simply because x's love is erosic.

Plato's love in the *Symposium* is often taken to be a prime example of an erosic love that focuses on properties as object rather than on persons. Irving Singer, for example, claims that when x Platonically loves y, y is only the apparent object of x's love. The Platonic lover does not "love another person for himself, but only as a vehicle and partial embodiment of . . . the Good. . . . Plato would say, to love anyone is really to love the goodness which is in him."[20] Singer claims that Plato arrives at this view about the object of love (at *Symposium* 206a) by committing a "glaring" non sequitur:[21] from "men love only what is good" Plato illegitimately infers that "love is exclusively directed toward *the* Good."[22] Singer protests, "It might be true that love never happens unless one person discovers goodness in another; but this gives us no basis for concluding that the object of love is goodness itself." Singer is right, I think, that there is some sort of mistake here, but he is right for the wrong reason. The passage Singer quotes (*Symposium* 206a) does not begin with any statement about the basis of love, but with "the only object of men's love is what is good."[23] Indeed, there is no argument at all in 206a. The passage only asserts that the object of love is goodness and that lovers desire its "perpetual possession." The actual argument is contained in 205e, where Diotima asserts that (a) x does not love x's other half y unless y is good, and (b) men do not love what is theirs unless what is theirs is good. Diotima persuades Socrates to agree with her that, given these premises, what men love is the good. Now, if assertions (a) and (b) are about the basis of love (x loves y because y is good), then Diotima commits the non sequitur mentioned above. But to point out that x does not love what is x's unless what is x's is good might be to say only that in this case the *object* of x's love is that goodness. Hence, the argument of 205e is only an overgeneralization or a weak abduction; from some examples of x's loving goodness, Diotima concludes that men always and only love goodness.

The most well-known criticism of Platonic eros derives from precisely this feature. Gregory Vlastos claims that in Plato's view

> What we are to love in persons is the "image" of the Idea in them. We are to love the persons so far, and only insofar, as they are good and beautiful. Now since all too few human beings are masterworks of excellence, and not even the best of those . . . are wholly free of streaks of the ugly, the mean, the commonplace, the ridiculous, if our love for them is to be only for their virtue and beauty, the individual, in the uniqueness and integrity of his or her individuality, will never be the object of our love. This seems to me the cardinal flaw in Plato's theory. It does not provide for love of whole persons, but only for love of that abstract version of persons which consists of the complex of their best qualities.[24]

Persons have good qualities, but also bad ones; x might find attractive properties S in y, but also "defect" properties D. No one, says Vlastos, not even the best of us, is "wholly free" of D. If we assume with Plato that the actual object of x's love is y's goodness ("our love for them is . . . only for their virtue"), then automatically x loves only part of y, y's goodness, or that "version of [y] which consists of the complex of [y's] best qualities." Note that Vlastos' criticism seems to allow that x *could* love y the "whole" person were y entirely constituted by good qualities; if so, only the contingent fact that no person y fits the bill undermines Plato's view. Also note that Vlastos is not claiming that for Plato, *because* S is the basis of x's love for y, only S, and not y, is the object of x's love. Rather, from the fact that x loves S in y, it follows for Plato that y *is* the object of x's love, albeit not y the whole person or as a "totality," but only the incomplete version of y that is composed of S.

If Vlastos' complaint is to be damaging, there must be an alternative view of love that avoids Plato's error. Since, for Vlastos, x's Platonically loving only the good part of y means that x does not love the whole person y, we expect Vlastos to assert that x *would* be loving the whole person were x to love not only the good part but also the defective part of y. Loving the whole person, then, would be loving everything about one's beloved or *all* her properties. This alternative satisfies Vlastos' criterion that in an adequate theory of love x should be able to love the whole person even when y has defects; this alternative does not require y to be like God or perfectly virtuous in order to be loved as a whole person. But the alternative view is unconvincing. A theory of love should not imply that x *must* love y's defects; for x's only tolerating y's impatience and corns does not negate x's claim to love y. And note that even if this alternative were correct, erosic love could meet its stringent requirement. For if x loves y in virtue of y's having S, as a result x might come to love everything about y, including D. The beloved's defects can be transformed into valuable (or neutral) aspects of y by love's eye—by a love that is already rationally well grounded in S.

Even though Vlastos begins his essay with praise for philia, Aristotle's conception of love is not his own alternative to Plato, since Aristotle "does not repudiate—does not even notice—what I have called . . . 'the cardinal flaw' in Platonic love."[25] Vlastos' own alternative derives from "the image of the diety in the Hebraic and Christian traditions: that of a Being whose perfection empowers it to love the imperfect." Vlastos does not mean that when x loves the whole person y, x loves the imperfections of the imperfect y. Rather, x loves y the whole person when x loves the imperfect y despite y's imperfections or when x "does not proportion affection to merit."[26] "I love you, corns and all" reflects Vlastosian love for the whole person, but the corns are not loved. Y is loved with and despite the corns, because x's love is independent of both y's attractive and unattractive properties.

Vlastos criticizes Plato on the grounds that the ontological object of love on Plato's view turns out to be only part of y. Yet Vlastos' account of love for the whole person has nothing to do with the ontology of the object of love. To claim that x loves the whole person when x agapically loves y despite y's defects is to analyze love for the whole person in terms of the basis of love, not in terms of its ontological object. Thus, "whole" in Vlastos' account is in a different category from "whole" in Vlastos' criticism of Plato; we can therefore accuse Vlastos of equivocation. Further, if love for the whole person is a matter of love's basis, agapic love is not the only kind in which x can love y despite y's defects ("I love you, corns and all"). For x can erosically love y despite the fact that y, being imperfect, has defects; all that is required is that x judge that y's valuable properties outweigh y's defects. Indeed, even Platonic eros has room for x's loving y despite y's defects. As long as x finds sufficient goodness or beauty in y, x has adequate reason to love y; the fact that y has imperfections makes no difference. And were Vlastos to respond that x loves y the whole person only if x loves y regardless of how greatly y's defects (for example, y's abusiveness) outweigh y's attractiveness, then loving the whole person cannot be a requirement of genuine personal love (8.8).

A. W. Price has also argued that erosic love is not necessarily incompatible with loving the person.[27] He writes, "Loving another for himself is not to be set against loving him for some qualities of his . . . so long as he too cares for these qualities, and it is at least partly because of this that I care about his having them." X's loving y for having P can be x's loving y for himself only if (a) y, too, values P in y and (b) x values P in y partially because y values P. Thus, x fails to love y for himself if x loves y for having P, but either y does not value P or x values P independently of y's valuing P. Clause (a) has some affinity with several theses about the properties in virtue of which x appropriately loves y (10.6): x should love y in virtue of properties for which y wants to be loved, or x should love y for properties that are part of y's self-concept. Making the satisfaction of this kind of condition necessary for x to love y the person is an interesting idea: x loves y the person only if x loves y in virtue of that part of y that y considers the best part. In this way, even x's loving only a part of y, in the style of Plato, does not look as bad as Vlastos claimed it was; the truncated version of the person y that is the object of x's love is simply that version of y blessed by himself. Nevertheless, Price's condition (a) is too strong (and note that if clause [a] is rejected, clause [b] goes as well).[28] The reason is similar to the reason x's seeking the good for y only in y's sense is not exactly the concern of love (12.6): that which y values in y might not, from a more detached perspective, be what is actually best about y. We are often as blind to our own virtues as we are to our vices. Consider "I am fond of you because you are humble about your accomplishments"—said when the beloved is not aware of her own humility or even does not think she is accomplished. X might very well find value in y that y is oblivious to and love y in virtue of properties that y herself does not value. Hence, x can love the best part of y without y's knowing or agreeing that this is the best part; and x's doing so is no reason to deny that x loves y the person or for herself.

If x's loving y the person is not ruled out by x's valuing that which x believes is best in y even though y might not agree, that will be true only if x's perception of y is not only detached but also accurate. It will detract from x's loving y the person or for himself if x falsely detects a virtue in y that y knows does not exist. This suggests that a necessary condition for x's loving y the person is that x's beliefs about the properties of y in virtue of which x loves y are true. Of course, x *loves* y whether x believes truly or falsely that y has the S that grounds x's emotion. But one difference between x's believing truly and believing falsely that y has S might be that only in the former case could x be loving y the person: when x's belief that y has S is false, the object of x's love is not y but a person that x imagines exists.[29] In one sense, when x believes falsely that y has S, y is still the object of x's love: x showers affection, attention, and concern on *y*. But in another sense, y is not the object of x's love; the person x actually showers attention on is significantly different from the person x believes x is showering attention on. If x believes truly that y has S, or if x generally has accurate knowledge of y's properties and history, there is no difference between the person x actually loves and the person x believes that x loves; there is one and only one person on which x showers attention. For this reason it may not be too bold to propose that y is the object of x's love, or x loves y the person, precisely when x has sufficiently comprehensive and accurate knowledge about y. X fails to love y the person when x's knowledge of y is deficient and there is thereby a sizeable discrepancy between the person x showers attention on and the person x thinks x showers attention on. That is, x's having true beliefs about y is not merely necessary but also sufficient for x to be loving y the person.

People hope they will be loved "for myself," loved for who they "really" are, and accepted "just the way" they are.[30] It is wrong, however, to think that "this demand that we be loved for ourselves . . . is itself selfish."[31] That claim would be true if the demand to be loved for oneself was motivated by a Balint-desire to be loved unconditionally (see 8.3), but not if motivated by a desire to be loved erosically for S, which outweighs D, when x sees both S and D clearly. Thus the hope that one be loved "for myself" might amount to wanting to be loved without having to deceive one's lover about one's virtues and faults and without one's lover showering attention only on a product of her imagination. Wanting one's "real" self to be loved is wanting the lover not to touch some deep metaphysical level or to focus on identity properties but to have true and extensive knowledge of oneself—and to continue to love while having that knowledge. But there is nothing in erosic love that prevents x from loving y the person in this sense. As long as x judges y's attractiveness to outweigh y's faults, y need not worry that the mere presence of faults will bring love to an end (and x thereby succeeds in loving the whole person). And as long as x perceives y's properties accurately, y need not worry that x is loving a fantasy (and x thereby succeeds in loving y for himself). If this is right, Vlastos will have to concede that Plato's theory of love is not as flawed as he thought. In fact, Vlastos does praise Plato's theory in one regard. Plato's theory is not one of those romantic views that countenance or excuse x's having illusions about the attractiveness of y in order to secure love for the "whole" person (x imagines that every part is perfect and the beloved thereby becomes like God). For Plato, "there is no magnification of [y's] moral or intellectual virtues."[32] By rejecting idealization as a part of love, Plato's theory "makes for a more truthful vision of that part of the world which we are all most tempted . . . to falsify—the part we love." If this is the best that erosic love can do in allowing love for the person, we are not too cynical in thinking that that is enough.

6. LOVING LOVE

Although Robert Solomon thinks we love for erosic reasons,[33] he has a peculiar animosity toward the philosophical concepts that arise in the eros tradition. In the first view of personal love, x's loving y is x's having an emotion that is directed at y (the object of x's emotion), and this emotion is grounded in x's belief that y has certain attractive properties. Solomon dislikes this way of characterizing love. It is wrong, he says, to think of "love [as] an attitude *toward* someone," the emotion's "object."[34] For Solomon, if one says that when x loves y, y is the "object" of x's love, one mistakenly "leaves out half of the picture. An equally essential component of the loveworld is *oneself*."[35]

What is the upshot of Solomon's forcing us to acknowledge the trivial fact that when x loves y, the existence of two people is presupposed? "Love is not just an emotion directed toward another person. . . . I am not just the person who *has* the emotion; I am also part of it." Love is "a world with two people."[36] I find this bewildering. If love is a world composed of two people x and y, and x is part of this love-item, then it makes no sense to say that x is a lover who loves y; and the "beloved" y cannot be the object of love, because y too is part of this love-item. Perhaps this is precisely Solomon's point. Thus, when he says that love "is not an emotion 'about' another person so much as . . . a world," the implication is that y is not the object of love *because* y is part of the love itself. This conception of love as a shared entity (embraced also by Karol Wojtyla; 11.2) runs into problems with reciprocity. Solomon writes, "Love is not just an attitude directed toward another person; it is an emotion which, at least hopefully, is *shared with* him or her."[37] Interpreted innocuously, this just means that when x loves y, x hopes that y also loves x. But it is inconsistent with love's *being* a world composed of x and y. All x can hope for is that y joins with x in creating a shared loveworld; x cannot hope out of *love* for y that y loves x. For there is no love until that loveworld is created.

Further, if Solomon (like the rest of us) does want to speak of x as a lover who loves y, yet y is part of the love-item, then x actually loves the love-item itself, or at least the part of it that is y. This awkward consequence—x loves love—is actively advanced by Robert Brown in his account of the object of love. Brown claims that we can love a person yet "dislike some, or even many, of the properties that the person exemplifies."[38] Hence, he rejects the view that x loves y the whole person when x loves everything about y. And because Brown denies that love is reason-based (8.8), he must reject the view that x loves the whole person y if x loves y in virtue of y's attractive properties that outweigh y's defects. Nor does he claim that loving the whole person is to love an especially important set of y's properties, for example, y's identity properties. What, then, does Brown invoke in characterizing the object of love?

"In part," says Brown, "when the agent loves another person . . . the agent is cherishing . . . a particular complex of instantiated qualities."[39] But this complex is not the object of love, because there is more to a person than *these* properties and because the lover is committed to the object regardless of what properties it might come to have.[40] In order to "contrast . . . love of some of a person's qualities with love of that person as an individual,"[41] Brown proposes that the additional item that comprises the object of love is the love relationship itself: "In claiming to love the whole person . . . the lover . . . is actually claiming also to love . . . their unique relationship with each other. . . . [W]hat helps to constitute his love, and is also part of what he loves, is their unique relationship." But it is strange that Brown solves the problem about love's object—in what sense is y the object of x's love, rather than y's properties—by invoking the relationship as an object of love. The task was to give an account of y as the whole object of love *within* the relationship. Brown can try to handle this objection by claiming that the relationship is part of the object of x's love insofar as the relationship is part of y. Indeed, when Brown says that the relationship is "part of what he loves," he might be claiming that x loves the relationship because (a) x loves y and (b) the relationship is part of y, that is, part of what x loves. This remarkable view is different from saying that x loves y because (c) x loves the relationship and (d) y is part of the relationship—which is inconsistent with the relationship's being *only* "part of what he loves." The remarkable claim is also different from saying that x loves y and x *also* loves the relationship, where y and the relationship are two separate items; this is another sense in which the relationship could be "part of what he loves" (that is, one of the two things loved). Deciding whether Brown means that the relationship is part of y, or vice versa, is not easy, for what he says is obscure: "[Y's] life is entwined with [x's]; any attempt to individuate her as one of the partners in that life will result in characterizing their relationship in contrast to other relationships." The idea seems to be that the history of the x-y relationship—all its details—individuates not only the relationship (trivially) but also the beloved. Y cannot be picked out *as* y, as a distinct person, without referring to the history of y's relationship with x. In this sense the relationship is part of y.

To say that y is individuated by the history of the x-y relationship, however, is just to say that y is individuated by the pieces of y's life, which is irrelevant. From y's being individuated by the history of the x-y relationship, it does not follow that y is even partially constituted by the relationship. In the absence of other reasons to think that y is in part composed of the relationship, invoking this ontology to solve the problem of love's object is no more satisfying than conceiving of y as a transcendental self. Brown's proposal is also weak because if loving the whole person is necessary for genuine love, invoking the x-y relationship as part of love's object is to assert that love is necessarily reciprocal: x logically cannot love y if y does not love x, since if y does not love x there is no complete object for x to love, there is no unique relationship that in part comprises what x loves. This is too high a price to pay for a solution to Vlastos' puzzle.

7. PERSONS AS PROPERTIES

Martin Warner claims that the Platonic and the Christian conceptions of love derive from the difference between conceiving of a person as properties (the eros tradition) and conceiving of a person as more than this, as a transcendental self (the agape tradition).[42] As a matter of historical fact, proponents of erosic love may have held that a person is just his properties, while agapists have embraced a notion of the soul. The interesting issue, however, is whether any logical connection exists between a theory of love and an account of the ontology of the person. Does it follow from love's being erosic (agapic) that the object of love, the person, is his properties (a transcendental self)? Conversely, does it follow from a person's being his properties (a transcendental self) that love must be erosic (agapic)?

Assume that x's loving y erosically and x's loving y agapically are exhaustive and mutually exclusive; and that y's being only her properties and y's being, instead of or in addition, a transcendental self are also mutually exclusive and exhaustive. Then the answer to both questions about the logical connection between the structure of love and the nature of the person is no. It is possible that (A) x loves y erosically even if y is a transcendental self and that (B) x loves y agapically even if y is her properties. Situation (B) is possible just because x might love y for reasons having nothing to do with y's properties, even if y is her properties. Situation (A) is possible just because x might love y in virtue of y's attractive properties, even if these properties are not equivalent to what y fully is. The reason that (A) and (B) are possible and that there is no necessary connection between the structure of love and the nature of the person, is that the theories of erosic and agapic personal love are about the basis of love, while theses about the nature of the person are about its object.

How, then, should we understand Warner's claim that "given Diotima's account of the self, the Christian . . . conception of love's being 'for the person, and not for his qualities' is simply incoherent," that is, to assert that the object of love is the person and not the person's qualities is contradictory?[43] Working out what he takes to be Diotima's view, Warner presents this argument: "If there is no more to the person than his qualities, then in loving a person we are loving (some at least of) his qualities" (p. 339). The Christian falls into "incoherence" because to claim that the object of love is the person and not her qualities is to claim that the object of love is the first rather than the second; yet the two are equivalent, given Diotima's conception of the person. Hence, the Christian must postulate a transcendental self in order to drive a wedge between loving a person and loving properties. Hence, also, Warner's claim that theories of love are logically connected to conceptions of the person: if a person is her properties, then the object of love must be properties, and only if a person is a transcendental self is there logical room for the object being a person as distinct from properties. Warner has not established, however, that there is a connection between the ontological nature of the person and the basis of love; the logical connection, instead, is between the ontology of the person and the ontology of the object of love. Warner's argument yields the conclusion that x loves "some at least of y's qualities," but this does not entail that x loves y in virtue of y's qualities; indeed, the argument is compatible with love's ground being either erosic or agapic.

Warner's argument suggests that we are faced with an unappetizing choice about love's object: when x loves y, either x is "really" loving only the properties y reduces to, or x is loving the transcendental self that y expands to. In neither case does x love y the person in any satisfying sense; if x loves y's properties, y the person who has these properties drops out, and if x loves the transcendental self, y the embodied person drops out. The impression we get from Warner is that x's loving y amounts only to x's loving y's eyes, y's beautiful feet, and y's courage; otherwise, x must be loving something emphemeral. There seems to be no room, in particular, to claim that x loves y the person in virtue of y's attractive properties, even if x must be loving, out of ontological necessity, "some at least of y's qualities."

But Warner has not bequeathed us an insoluble dilemma. If x loves y and y is her properties, it does follow that x loves properties. But what follows about the object of love must be stated carefully; it does not follow that x necessarily loves individually any or each of y's properties, but only that x loves the collection of properties that y is. Having a relation (love) to a collection as object is one thing, and having that same relation to the items in that collection is quite another thing. Hence, x can love y in virtue of y's attractive properties that outweigh y's defects, and the object of x's love is the collection of properties that y is, yet none of these properties is necessarily also an object of love for x. In this sense x's loving y erosically, where the object y is a collection of properties, is compatible with x's loving y the person. At the same time, even on Diotima's conception of a person, admonishing x to love the person, not the person's properties, is after all not incoherent, as long as the contrast drawn is not between loving a transcendental self and loving properties, but between loving a collection of properties and only loving individually any or each property in that collection.[44]

I am not claiming that when x loves y, x never loves y's properties individually; to the contrary, x's erosic love for y is ordinarily, and unobjectionably, both love for y in virtue of S and love for at least some members of S. I have been arguing, instead, that x's directly loving properties does not follow from x's loving y in virtue of S (sect. 5), nor does it follow from y's being a set of properties. Would anyone accept Warner's argument for other emotions? From the facts that I fear or hate you and that you are a set of properties, it does not follow that what I "really" fear or hate are your individual properties. To be sure, we speak of a person's "dangerous temper" and "loathesome irresponsibility." We do so not only because properties can be the objects of emotions, but also because it is shorthand for saying that our emotions directed at the person are erosic and we displace the dangerousness or fearfulness of the person onto the properties. But properties are not literally dangerous. Not even Diotima asserts that necessarily when x loves y, x loves only y's properties. For Diotima, coming to love only the goodness and beauty of a person, and then loving these properties wherever they are found, is an achievement. Diotima urges us to progress from loving a particular person in virtue of his attractive properties to loving the properties themselves.[45] This progression requires that we be able to alter our phenomenological attitude toward things, persons, and properties. On the one hand, we might interpret the progression as involving merely a Gestalt switch in our vision. The fluid or ambiguous underlying reality can be seen however we like, and we learn or decide to see persons as replaceable, goodness as irreplaceable. On the other hand, we might interpret the progression as involving a mistake: we turn genuinely irreplaceable people into the replaceable, thereby demeaning them and our relations to them, while enthroning a metaphysical illusion (the Good or God) and enshrining our relationship to it as the pinnacle of human experience. Plato's (or Diotima's) view, however, is different: we should transfer our love from people, who really are replaceable, and turn to that which is irreplaceable, the Good. But that we are urged to reserve our affections for a thing, or for properties, presupposes that nothing in love or ontology forces that on us.

8. PERSONS ARE NOT PROPERTIES

One of Pascal's *Pensées* is relevant to the issue of what it is to love the person. In Brunschvicg no. 323 he wrote:[46]

> What is the *me*?
>
> A man is at his window watching the passers-by: if I go by, am I entitled to say that he put himself in this position in order to see me? No; for he was not specifically thinking about me. But does the one who loves someone on account of her beauty love her? No; since small pox, which will kill beauty without killing the person, will make it so that he will no longer love her.
>
> What if someone loves me for my judgment, my memory, does that person love *me*? No; since I can lose these qualities without losing myself. Where then is this *me* if it is neither in my body nor in my soul? And how is one to love the body or the soul, if it is not for these qualities, which are not that which constitutes the *me*, since they are perishable? For would it be possible for one to love a person's soul *in abstracto*, and with no regard for its qualities? This is not possible,[47] and moreover would be unfair. Thus, one does not ever love anybody, but qualities only.[48]
>
> Let's not therefore poke fun of those who seek public functions and honors, since we only love another for borrowed qualities.

Is Pascal defending a thesis about the ontology of the person by appealing to claims about love (in the manner of Mark Fisher, who relies on the substitution argument in arguing that a person is a transcendental self; 2.5 and 3.6) or defending a thesis about love by invoking an ontology of the person (in the manner, but not the substance, of Warner's Diotima)? Note that the passage begins with the supposition that x loves y erosically and ends with what apparently is Pascal's conclusion, that no one ever loves another person, but only properties. So it seems as if Pascal commits the non sequitur of arguing that x loves S if x loves y for having S. But Pascal does not make this mistake; he arrives at his view that we love only properties some other way.

Pascal begins by asking: If x loves y for y's physical beauty, does x love y? It is important to realize that Pascal is not asking: Does x *love* y?—that is, is x's emotion love? To that question we might answer that physical beauty by itself is logically irrelevant to love or that if x loves y for only this reason, x is a superficial lover. But Pascal is asking, instead: If x loves y for y's beauty, is y the *object* of x's love? His answer is no, in light of these claims: (1) y can lose y's physical beauty and remain y and (2) if y loses her beauty, x will no longer love y. But does it follow from claims (1) and (2) that x does not love y but only y's beauty? No. That x's love is gone when y's beauty is gone but y remains can mean *either* that the beauty had been the object of x's love *or* that the beauty had been its basis. Pascal would have to add that y is the object of x's love only if x's love for y is constant, but there is no reason to think that he assumes this. Actually, as we shall see, claim (2) is superfluous to Pascal's argument, while claim (1) does all the work.

Pascal immediately asks another question, but not: If x loves y for y's judgment (a mental rather than a physical quality), does x *love* y? Rather, his question is: If x loves y for y's judgment, is y the object of x's love? As above, his answer is no, but now his grounds involve *only* (1*): y can lose y's judgment and remain y. Pascal does not say here that when y loses y's judgment, x no longer loves y; Pascal here does not rely on x's love dying to derive the conclusion that x loves only y's mental property. What the two arguments have in common is the claim that y remains even when y loses a property; Pascal is trying to answer his opening question—"What is the *me*?" He argues that the "me" is not any of its properties, since the "me" remains even when any of its properties are imagined to be absent. (Note the Cartesian methodology. Is Pascal claiming that we can imagine that y remains without even being the *res cogitans* of the *Meditations*? I wonder why, in this passage, Pascal does not draw Descartes's conclusion about the self. Or does he?) All of y's properties are perishable even as y would remain through any of these changes, so the self that is y is something beyond y's properties. Having established to his satisfaction this thesis about the ontology of the person, Pascal then derives his conclusion that x never loves y but only y's properties.[49] If y is something beyond y's properties, then y cannot be the object of x's love if (this step is crucial) the soul or transcendental self that is y is beyond the reach of the emotions. ("This is not possible.") Therefore, x could only be loving y's properties when x loves y.

Note several things about Pascal's argument. First, it is a cute twist on the argument of Warner's Diotima, who argues that x loves y's properties because y is *nothing but* y's properties; for Pascal, x loves y's properties because y is something *beyond* y's properties. (Does this mean that Pascal can love only God's properties, and not God directly?) Second, if we add that genuine love (*pace* Wojtyla; 10.2) must be love for y the person qua transcendental self, then genuine love is impossible. Genuine love *would* be loving the "me," but that is not possible. Hence either there is no genuine love, or if there is, properties are its object. Third, Pascal's conclusion has nothing to do with whether x's love for y dies when y loses one of y's properties. Even if x's love for y is perfectly constant—x loves y after y grows ugly and becomes senile—x is still on-tologically prevented from loving y's real self, since the soul, he claims, is inaccessible to the emotions. Thus, Pascal is not arguing from the vicissitudes of love to a conclusion about the object of love or the ontology of the person. He first defends a thesis about the person and on that foundation argues that the object of love is not the person, but only properties.

Pascal's mistake, of course, occurs precisely where he argues that since y can lose the specific property P_1 and remain y, and also lose (instead!) the particular property P_2 and remain y, and so on, y can lose all y's properties and remain y. That y's existence does not depend on y's retaining any one perisha-ble property does not mean that y can lose all y's properties and still exist (or even that y can lose some set of them and remain y); it is a non sequitur to argue that if y is not P_1 and not P_2 (and so on) individually, then y is something beyond properties altogether. Of course, there is another weakness in his argument: Pascal never explains why the emotions cannot latch on to the transcendental self. *That* is merely assumed. Yet, without including some reason for thinking that the metaphysics of the transcendental self makes it inaccessible, Pascal's argument threatens to beg the question by assuming that emotions can attach only to properties. But our question about the object of love is precisely whether that is true.

9. ENDING A REGRESS

If x loves y erosically, x loves y the "whole" person when x loves y for y's attractive properties S that outweigh y's defects D, and x loves y "for himself" when x's beliefs about S and D are accurate. X might have good reason to tolerate D quietly because x considers D insignificant in comparison with the value of S, while hoping that no new vice arises, or no old vice finally shows itself, that might outweigh S. Or x might tolerate D in y less well than x would tolerate D in a stranger, just because x loves y and is concerned that y be as good or virtuous as possible; so x might attempt to eliminate D not only to make x's love more secure but also to help y improve himself. Or x might come to cherish some of D simply because x loves y in virtue of S or, less rationally, come to see D as good even though at some level x regards it as bad. All these erosic possibilities indicate that x has not lost sight of y the "whole" person, even if x does not love everything about y. They also suggest that x might dislike some of y's properties without disliking y; and if it is conceptually possible for x to dislike, even hate, individual properties of y, it must be conceptually possible for x to like, even love, individual properties.

Could it be argued that loving a person's properties is, nevertheless, not conceptually possible? Since a property (the blondeness of y's hair) is an inanimate thing, properties can be loved only if inanimate things can be loved. A common argument against the possibility of loving mere things (derived from Aristotle [*NE* 1155b26–32] and often repeated) is that things have no interests of their own to take into account in our treatment of them. Since we cannot be concerned for the welfare of a thing for *its* sake, if love necessarily includes that sort of concern, we cannot love things. Or we could love them only instrumentally. I doubt, however, that this argument is powerful enough to overcome our tendency to think that we do love things (recall the 1902 gold coin I cherish).[50] But there is another argument. Suppose that when x loves y, x does so in virtue of y's attractive properties; that is, x's loving y (the object) is based on something other than y himself, namely, some of y's properties. Y is the object of x's love just because there is a valuable tertium quid in virtue of which x loves y; x's emotion is tied to the object of that emotion by something other than the object. Similarly, x loves x's gold coin just because the coin too has attractive properties; these are its tertium quid. To claim that x can love a property, however, then amounts to asserting that something other than the beloved property, a valuable tertium quid, grounds x's love for the property, and this must be a valuable property that the property has. Things have attractive properties that make them lovable, and persons have attractive properties that make them lovable—but is it not absurd to think that properties have attractive properties that make them lovable?

If we suppose that a property is valuable by virtue of its having another property that is valuable, we are thrust into an infinite regress. The problem is not only that we thereby presuppose a neverending hierarchy of properties of properties of properties of . . . . In addition, if when explaining why x finds P_1 attractive, we appeal to P_1's having P_2, then in explaining in turn why x finds P_2 attractive, we have to appeal to P_2's having P_3, and so on. Hence, we can never fully understand x's finding the original P_1 attractive. The conclusion seems to be that properties are not the sort of thing that can be loved. Or love for properties cannot be accounted for erosically; some other basis of love for properties must exist if they are to be objects of love. Actually, this argument can be construed as exposing yet another incoherence in the first view of personal love. For if x loves y because y has attractive properties S, then in explaining why x finds S valuable we now have to mention S's own valuable properties. The regress arises not only when properties are the object of love, but also when a person is the object *and* the person is loved in virtue of her properties. This is embarrassing to an account of love that prided itself on picturing love as comprehensible rather than a mystery.

Both Plato and Aristotle recognized this regress and argued that it is avoided by positing the existence of things that could be loved or desired for their own sake (for example, *Symp.* 205a).[51] Thus, x's loving something, or finding it valuable, must at some point lead to x's valuing something else for itself, which something must be valuable in its own right. The implications of this way of avoiding the regress are enormous. If x loves a property P or finds it attractive, but not because P has valuable Q, then x's valuing P seems to be more an agapic than an erosic phenomenon. If so, there can be no erosic love for persons or properties without agapic love existing at some point—the point at which the regress ends. The upshot is not that there is no erosic love at all, but that all erosic love depends on, and hence "ultimately" is, agapic love; or that all personal love is a mixture of reconciled eros and agape. And if all erosic love for a person is, or reduces to, agapic love for a property, then it becomes more plausible to claim that x's love for a person y is straightaway agapic: since agapic love must occur at some point to end the regress, why not suppose that it occurs at the very beginning and prevents the regress from getting under way? If the theory of erosic love must posit that at some point x must value something for itself and not in virtue of further qualities, then why not suppose that valuing something for its own sake occurs at the very beginning, that is, that x loves a person y simply for himself? Using Irving Singer's terminology (1.7), we might say that in love x immediately bestows value on y rather than (only) on y's properties.

Note that if something is valuable in its own right, then for this thing the distinction between the basis and object of love collapses; there is no distinction precisely because the object provides (or is) its own basis. That love involves somewhere a collapse of the basis-object distinction should not come as a surprise; indeed, we have already encountered this idea. Recall the proposal that x loves y the person when x loves y in virtue of y's identity properties (10.5). Since y is identical to her identity properties, loving y for those properties means that the basis and object of love are the same, and y is literally loved for herself. This erosic view, I have argued, is unacceptable, but its failure does not mean that the eros tradition cannot accommodate in this one context the collapse of the basis-object distinction.

Persons are attractive precisely because they are composites, composed of and having valuable properties. Any properties of persons that are similarly composites are attractive also in virtue of the valuable properties they have. Thus, both persons and composite properties feed the regress. But noncomposite properties (perhaps goodness and beauty) cannot be valued in virtue of their properties; hence, noncomposite properties end the regress. These properties are valued for themselves in the sense that they cannot sustain the distinction between basis and object. If this picture is coherent, there is less philosophical motivation for understanding x's love for a person y as loving y directly for himself: since y is a composite, comprehending x's love for y erosically is possible; and since the regress can be ended with noncomposite properties, there is no reason to prevent it from beginning by implausibly assuming that y is a noncomposite particular straightaway loved for himself. The erosic picture makes more sense than saying that "the beloved is reason enough"[52] for the love. We are not forced to put a mystery into love at the very beginning, by supposing that the beloved is, strangely enough, a noncomposite particular (8.2), when we have the alternative of appealing to the beloved's properties as the reason for love. If it is mysterious that some properties are valuable in themselves, or that *they* are "reason enough" for their being valued, at least it is a mystery that occurs at a place where there are bound to be mysteries. The metaphysics underlying love might be mysterious, but not love itself.

10. SMALL CAUSES

If mysteries at the surface of love are what we want, they are not hard to come by. In love, Kierkegaard tells us, "There seems to be something wrong with cause and effect. . . . [T]hey do not rightly hang together. Tremendous and powerful causes sometimes produce small and unimpressive effects, sometimes none at all; then again it happens that a brisk little cause produces a collosal effect."[53] A heavy rock is heaved at a window, but it bounces off, leaving only a scratch; the same window is tickled with the beat of a fly's wings and it shatters—mysterious occurrences (even miracles) that make the world of the laws of nature as baffling as the geometry of round squares. "I used to fall in love all the time. . . . Didn't take much, either. A smile, something about the eyes. . . . A flower in the hair."[54] The mystery of sweet love: a momentous occurrence based on so little about the beloved that it is impossible (or just embarrassing?) for the lover to retrieve these reasons; the causes are so tiny that the lover believes there are none except the beloved herself.

In his account of love, John McTaggart takes very seriously the idea that love may be based on very little about the beloved: "Love is not necessarily proportional to the dignity or adequacy of the qualities which determine it. A trivial cause may determine the direction of intense love. . . . And yet it may be all that love can be. . . . To love one person above all the world for all one's life because her eyes are beautiful when she is young, is to be determined to a very great thing by a very small cause."[55] McTaggart's scenario is weird; x loves y timelessly exclusively and strictly constantly just because of the young y's beautiful eyes. Sure, this is a "very small cause," but where is the "very great thing"? X's loving y *because* the young y's eyes are beautiful is hardly momentous; the whole—the cause and its effect—seems silly, if not irrational. Yet McTaggart relies on this discrepancy between cause and effect (as a common feature of love) to support his major thesis about love, that it is anomalous in being "more independent than *any other* emotion of the qualities of the substance towards which it is felt."[56] Using his special terminology, McTaggart expresses his thesis that love is "more independent" of the beloved's qualities this way: "Love may be *because* of those qualities, [but] it is not in *respect* of them."[57] Hence, for McTaggart, love is independent of qualities not in the "because of" sense but in the "in respect of" sense.

McTaggart's meaning is very clear when he says that emotions (including love) can exist *because of* qualities: the qualities of the object are part of the causation ("determination") of the emotion. For example, y's P causes x to believe that y has P, and this belief in turn causes x to love (admire, resent) y; for McTaggart, y's P is the ultimate cause of x's emotion, while y's property "is believed by x to have P" is its immediate cause. Or if y does not have P, x's emotion toward y is caused by x's false belief that y has P. Thus, McTaggart holds that love is erosic in the narrow sense that x's believing y to have P causally grounds x's love. Then in what sense is love independent of qualities? McTaggart is much less clear when he says that other emotions, but *not* love, are also "in respect of" qualities.

One interpretation is that x's emotion toward y is "in respect of" P when x's emotion is directed at P itself, so that P is the object of x's emotion, not y.[58] Thus, the distinction between "because of" and "in respect of" marks the difference between the causal basis and the object of an emotion. In the case of admiration, then, to say that it is both because of and in respect of P is to say that P causes x's admiration for y and that P is also the admired object. In contrast, love is not in respect of properties, so P is the cause of x's love but not its object. This interpretation, however, is not very satisfying. Since x's being determined to admire y by x's belief that y has P does not entail that x admires P itself (recall the non sequitur), I find little reason to suppose that for erosic emotions other than love P is usually the actual object. Hence, love could hardly be alone in being "because of" and not "in respect of" qualities. Further, McTaggart summarizes his view with "love is for the person, and not for his qualities," immediately adding, "*nor* is it for him in respect of his qualities."[59] Hence, love's not being in respect of qualities is, for McTaggart, something other than its not being love for the qualities themselves.

A second interpretation is that x's emotion is in respect of P when x's *reason* for the emotion is that y has P. Thus, the distinction between "because of" and "in respect of" marks a difference between two separable bases for x's emotion: x's belief that y has P is the causal basis, while y's having P is x's reason for the emotion. To say that admiration is both because of and in respect of P, then, is to say that y's P figures into both the cause of the emotion and x's reason for it. In contrast, P figures into the causal basis for love but plays no role in x's reasons for loving y; indeed, that love is not in respect of P may mean exactly that no reasons at all are involved in x's love for y. If so, McTaggart is claiming that love, in contrast to the other erosic emotions, is property-based but not reason-dependent, that is, that love by its nature, and not merely in isolated cases, is a nonideal erosic phenomenon.

At the very beginning of his discussion, McTaggart inserts a footnote that suggests a third interpretation of "in respect of":

> Love and hatred are varieties of liking and repugnance. . . .[60] Approval and disapproval are distinguished from liking and repugnance by the fact that they are . . . for substances in respect of their possession of . . . qualities, while liking and repugnance are for particular substances as wholes, though they may be *determined* by the qualities of the substances.[61]

Hence, x's having an emotion (for example, admiration) toward y that *is* "in respect of" P is x's *not* having that emotion toward a particular "substance as a whole."[62] In contrast, even though x's love toward y is caused by x's belief that y has P, x's love is *not* in respect of P in that x's love *is* directed at y the particular (y the noncomposite thing) or at y as a whole. McTaggart certainly believes that (i) love is not directed at P as an object, (ii) y's P is part of the cause of, but not a reason for, x's love, and (iii) the object of love is a particular whole. Interpretation (iii) seems to be (later I show it is not) the meaning of McTaggart's thesis that love is independent of qualities in that it is not in respect of them. Obviously, to say that the object of love is a particular whole is to deny that qualities are the object of love, so claim (i) is a consequence of love's not being in respect of qualities. Further, if y is loved qua whole, rather than qua composite of attractive properties, then x loves y for himself, which is to say that if x has a reason, y is the reason (8.2). Hence, (iii) is the central thesis, from which (i) and (ii) are derived.

McTaggart claims that the fact that love, a great effect, can be brought about by a tiny cause supports his thesis that love is more independent of qualities than other emotions. Note that his argument is not: because the cause that can bring about the emotion is so slender, love is more independent of qualities *as causes* (that is, in the "because of" sense) than other emotions. Rather, McTaggart means that the discrepancy between cause and effect shows that love is independent of qualities in not being in respect of them. Now, McTaggart does provide an argument, or an explanation,[63] that ties together the discrepancy between cause and effect and love's not being in respect of qualities. Before we look at it, let us consider this question: Given the three interpretations of what it means for love not to be in respect of qualities, what *should* the argument for that thesis be?

Suppose that x's love not being in respect of qualities means that even though x is caused to love y by P, x does not love P itself. If so, the discrepancy argument makes little sense; the fact that P is a tiny thing about y gives us no reason to think that x does or does not love P itself. The x who loves y exclusively and constantly, causally determined to do so by y's beautiful eyes, might very well, for all we know, be loving those eyes. Or suppose that love's not being in respect of qualities means that even though x is caused to love y by P, either x has no reason for loving y or P does not figure into the reason. Again, it does not follow from the discrepancy that x has no reason that includes P for loving y. Because the cause is tiny, x might not want to admit that this cause is also x's reason, but that is a different matter. We shall have some luck in constructing an argument, however, by supposing that love's not being "in respect of" qualities means that the object of love is a particular whole. If x is caused to love y by just a small part of y, and yet x ends up loving y as a whole, then x has been determined to a thing greater than its cause. The discrepancy is between the magnitude of the effect, x's love for the *whole* person, and the magnitude of its cause, that *small part* of y. If x ends up loving everything (individually) about y, just because x finds y's eyes attractive, then a tiny cause has produced a greater thing; or if x ends up loving the whole set of y's properties, again the effect is greater than the cause. Perhaps x ends up loving y qua transcendental self or as a particular. Then an ontological leap has occurred; the discrepancy between the tiny cause and the effect is qualitative, not quantitative. Either a small material thing (y's eyes) causes love for a nonmaterial thing (y's soul), or x has jumped from the general (the beauty of y's eyes) to the particular (the noncomposite y).

The problem with the argument is that it is inconsistent with McTaggart's claim that love is anomalous in being more independent of qualities than all other emotions. X might come to hate, resent, or admire y as a whole person in response to a tiny cause; for example, x might develop a strictly constant hatred for y "the person" even when the initial cause of x's emotion (say, the young y's ugly eyes) has disappeared. Although McTaggart does not advance the argument I constructed above, he does respond to this objection while providing his own argument:

Other emotions . . . may be determined by causes not proportioned to them in dignity or adequacy. . . . But the difference is that, in the case of the other emotions . . . we condemn the result [as unjustified] if the cause is trivial and inadequate. . . . But with love . . . we judge differently. If the love does arise, it justifies itself, regardless of what causes produce it. . . . [I]f what is caused is really love . . . it is not condemned. . . .[64] This would seem to indicate that the emotion is directed to the person, independently of his qualities, and that the determining qualities are not the justification of that emotion, but only the means by which it arises.[65]

In light of this passage, I conclude that "in respect of" must mean something different from any of the three interpretations already considered.

We know that, for McTaggart, repugnancy and its "variety," hatred, are for the person as a particular whole. Yet McTaggart quite sensibly claims that hate is justified only "when it is grounded on qualities in the person hated, and on qualities which afford an adequate ground for hate. If B hated F on no grounds at all . . . B would certainly be condemned."[66] Now, if both love and hate take a particular as their object, yet only love is independent of qualities, then love's not being in respect of qualities must mean that (iv) love does not require justification by an appeal to the object's qualities. Note that interpretation (iv) is not the same as (ii), above; love's not being in respect of qualities does not mean that y's properties are not the reason for x's love. More precisely, love is independent of qualities in the sense that y's properties do not figure into the justificatory reasons for x's love, since love requires no justification.

When McTaggart writes that hate is justifiable only by appealing to the qualities on which it is "grounded," I think he wants to say (plausibly) both that x is caused to hate y by believing that y has P and that the same P figures into x's justifying reason. To claim, then, that love is because of properties yet independent of them, is to claim that the causes of love need never be brought forth as justifying reasons for the emotion, and that love cannot be criticized just because a small cause has brought love about or because there is a disproportion between the intensity of love and its cause. Indeed, since love cannot be criticized, we are barred from saying that a small cause, that is, a silly reason for love, *is* a silly reason. When hate, admiration, resentment (and so forth) exhibit disproportion, they are condemned (even by McTaggart) as either irrational or morally defective.[67] For McTaggart, the mere fact that x is causally determined to have the emotion is no bar to condemnation, quite because the causally relevant P can be summoned by x as also the emotion's justifying reason, which is open to evaluation as being either good or not good enough. Thus, McTaggart does not claim that x is logically or metaphysically prevented from treating the causes of x's love also as x's justifying reasons, but only that x is not required to do so.

But the disproportion argument, it is clear, has taken a queer turn. I had thought that McTaggart was arguing from the ontological relationship between love and the cause of love to a conclusion either about the nature of the object of love or about the ground of love. Instead, he is arguing from what he assumes is the usual response people have to cases of disproportionate love (and hate) to the conclusion that love is "more independent" of qualities than other emotions. This argument is weak. From our typical evaluation of cases of disproportionate love and hate, it could not follow that love *is* more independent of qualities than other emotions, but at the most that those people who make these evaluations treat or conceive of love as being independent of qualities. I have argued—in precisely the way McTaggart handles hate—that any disproportion between love and its basis can be plausibly viewed as a way in which love is irrational (7.4–7.5), morally questionable, or superficial in its quality (12.9). When the feather brushes the window and it shatters, or when x experiences a terrible hate for y for no reason at all (or for a very small reason), we know that something has gone wrong. I have found little reason to think differently about love.

Perhaps it would be hasty to complain, in terms of either rationality or morality, about disproportionate love, if love had some great, offsetting value. If love has some profound value, then it might not be objectionable to *treat* love as being independent of qualities by never requiring justificatory reasons for it. Thus, it is surprising that McTaggart never claims that love has some special value in virtue of which it is anomalous and that distinguishes it from, say, approval and admiration—a value that implies that love, but not approval or admiration, is properly treated as being independent of justificatory reasons. When McTaggart writes that love might have a tiny cause, yet "may be all that love can be," I at first suspect that McTaggart puts so much into the "all" that love can be that love's value does trump its disproportionate origin. But it is hard to see that in McTaggart's view love has any or much value. "The essence of love," for McTaggart, is a *feeling,* "a sense of union" that is both necessary and sufficient for love.[68] But if love is only a feeling, then love has too little value to overcome accusations of irrationality. And love's being a sense of union does not entail that it has any significant value.

It is interesting that McTaggart's view of love as a feeling leaves no room for including concern as a part of the emotion.[69] For if anything could justify disproportionate love, it would have to be the concern feature of love. We might say (in patching up McTaggart) that the great thing that love is—great in virtue of its concern for the well-being of the beloved—justifies love even when love is irrational in being brought about by a trivial cause (the young y's eyes). Or love is "all that love can be"—it can generate powerful concern—no matter what its cause happens to be. (See the end of 10.3.) The general question that arises here is whether some properties are a better or more appropriate basis of love because love grounded on them is more likely to generate high-quality or intense concern for the beloved's well-being. Thus, some might find it plausible to claim that if x loves y for y's eyes, or wealth, or the sexual pleasure y affords x, there is no reason to complain as long as x's love yields superlative concern for y and as long as x's concern is not of the give-to-get variety. It is not clear, however, that aside from the odd case love's being grounded on any of these properties will satisfy these two conditions. Further, even if it were true that regardless of its cause, love could be all it can be, there are moral reasons to object to disproportionate love. Since the concern of love is preferential, lavished on some persons (or only one person) to the exclusion of others, x will have to do better than simply appeal to the beauty of y's eyes in order to justify being specially concerned for y's well-being. And if those eyes cannot justify love's preferential concern, neither could the reason-independent "because you're you" or "because I just do."

NOTES

PREFACE

1. *Harvard Classics,* vol. 39 (New York: P. F. Collier, 1910), p. 3.
2. Sigmund Freud, *Three Essays on the Theory of Sexuality,* part I, chapter 1, section B, n. added in 1910. In the following sentence Roger Scruton either agrees, providing his own version of Freud's thesis about contemporary sexual psychology, or he exhibits the flaw that Freud lamented: "In my desire I am gripped by the illusion of a transcendental unity behind the opacity of flesh, the repository of infinite moral possibilities, and the promise of that perfect enfolding presence that would—if it could be obtained—justify the turmoil of sexual pursuit" (*Sexual Desire,* p. 130).
3. Gay, *The Tender Passion,* p. 80.
4. Here and in the text I use "claim" and "argue" in the following senses: "x claims that *p*" means that the person x asserts the sentence *p*, while "x argues that *p*" means that x defends *p*, or gives a reason for claiming *p*, by providing a formal or semiformal argument. I do not use "argues" in the loose sense "asserts." In many cases, arguments are more interesting than claims.

CHAPTER ONE: TWO VIEWS OF LOVE

1. Capellanus, *The Art of Courtly Love,* p. 2. (Full information on works cited in the endnotes can be found in the Bibliography.)
2. Descartes, *The Passions of the Soul* (*Philosophical Writings,* vol. 1, p. 356).
3. *The Four Loves,* p. 63.
4. Weston, "Toward the Reconstruction of Subjectivism," p. 182.
5. See C. S. Lewis, *The Four Loves,* pp. 81–82, 124, 154, 160–166; Smedes, *Love Within Limits,* pp. 6, 92–93; and de Rougemont, *Love in the Western World,* p. 311f.
6. See Martha Nussbaum on the distinction between the "basis" and the "object" of love (*The Fragility of Goodness,* p. 355).
7. Robert Musil, "Tonka," in *Five Women,* p. 113. He continues: "But whereas in dreams there is still a hair's-breadth margin, a crack, separating the love from the beloved, in waking life this split is not apparent; one is merely the victim of *doppelgänger*-trickery and cannot help seeing a human being as wonderful who is

not so at all." See also George Eliot, *Daniel Deronda*, p. 658: "We may learn from the order of word-making, wherein *love* precedeth *lovable*." The view that x finds S in y valuable only because x loves y is also mildly suggested in Carson McCullers's *The Ballad of the Sad Café*, pp. 26–27.

8. Barry, *French Lovers*, p. 195.
9. One might read Pascal's remark (*Pensées* no. 423, p. 154)—the lover's "heart has its reasons of which reason knows nothing"—agapically. It is apparently a retraction of an earlier claim of his: "We have unaptly taken away the name of reason from love, and have opposed them to each other without good foundation. . . . Let us not . . . exclude reason from love, since they are inseparable. The poets were not right in painting Love blind" ("Discourse on the Passion of Love," pp. 522–523). A modern version of this "inseparability" thesis is defended by Nakhnikian, "Love in Human Reason."
10. Niklas Luhman claims that the second view of personal love historically postdates the first view. In the theory of courtly love, "A knowledge of the object's characteristics was essential." Later, "in the field of paradoxical codification" [romantic love], "love [was] justified . . . by means of imagination" (that is, x's perceiving S in y, even falsely imagining S, sufficed for love). But "once the autonomy of intimate relations had finally been established, it was possible to justify love simply by the inexplicable fact that one loved. . . . The beauty of the beloved . . . now no longer had to be in evidence, nor did it have to be imagined; this had ceased to be a reason for love, and rather was seen by the lovers as a consequence of their love" (*Love as Passion*, p. 44, italics deleted; see also p. 166: "The lover himself is the source of his love"). But also, of course, Plato preceded Paul.
11. See Davidson, "Reasons as Causes."
12. In "The Justification of Attitudes" (p. 148), J. N. Findlay claims that the object of love (y, or even y's property S) does not itself cause x's emotion; it is caused, instead, by x's beliefs about y. Surely this holds when the object of love does not exist, since a nonexistent object cannot cause anything, while beliefs about this nonexistent object can be efficacious. (See William Lyons' discussion of x's love for a dead grandmother, which he says has no "material" object but is not "illusory"; *Emotion*, p. 109.) And in general, Findlay is right; for objects that do exist, it is not exactly y's having S that causes the emotion but x's mediating belief that y has S. Nevertheless, y's having S is the cause of x's love one step removed, if y's having S is why x believes that y has S. Further, what Findlay claims about the causal role of beliefs may not apply to x's perceiving that y has S. If x's loving y is caused by x's perception that y has S, we need not always invoke a mediating belief (x's belief that y has S) that comes between y's having S (the cause) and x's loving y (the effect).
13. C. D. Broad ("Emotion and Sentiment," pp. 206–207) considers a matrix that crosses "actually motivated" and "actually unmotivated" emotions with "ostensibly motivated" and "ostensibly unmotivated." Broad's point is that there might be divergence between the reasons one consciously believes are operative and the (unconscious) reasons that are really operative.
14. I am not committing myself (or my interlocutor) to the view that these properties are objective; to understand the objection, just assume they are. The issue here is

not about the distinction between objective and subjective but about how such properties fit into the two views of love.

15. Woody Allen, *Without Feathers*, p. 110.

16. For this reason John Brentlinger claims that "the issue of whether *eros* or *agape* is the correct conception of love reduces to the question of whether values are objective or relative" ("The Nature of Love," p. 126).

17. Comparisons of eros and agape have been enormously influential in my thinking; for example, Kierkegaard's *Works of Love*, Anders Nygren's *Agape and Eros*, and Gene Outka's *Agape: An Ethical Analysis*. Robert Solomon, in contrast, believes that this literature is dispensable: "Much of the history of Western love, written primarily by theological scholars and German philologists, has consisted in the mock battle between these two Greek words. . . . But all of this has nothing to do with love. . . . [I]t is rather a technique to indulge in scholarship and avoid looking at any actual experience. . . . Indeed, rather than clarify the issues, this scholarly piddling is itself another political move, a way of making an ordinary emotion sound impressively profound" (*Love: Emotion, Myth and Metaphor*, p. 9).

18. Nygren, *Agape and Eros*, p. 78. See also Helmut Thielicke, *The Ethics of Sex*, p. 33.

19. Douglas Morgan, *Love: Plato, the Bible, and Freud*, p. 74.

20. Nygren, *Agape and Eros*, p. 75.

21. Quoted by Nygren, *Agape and Eros*, p. 654.

22. See Outka, *Agape*, pp. 158–160.

23. See Nygren, *Agape and Eros*, pp. 96–98, and Morgan, *Love*, p. 123, n. 74.

24. The similarity between Plato's eros and a neighbor-love that loves God-in-the-human is suggested by Shirley Letwin ("Romantic Love and Christianity," p. 133): "The object of Diotima's love is real, not an illusion. But this real object of love is neither a human being nor a human quality. It is the divine spark in all men." This spark is not a piece of the Christian God but the "participation" of a human in the Form of Beauty.

25. Fromm, *The Art of Loving*, pp. 33–37.

26. See Judith Van Herik, *Freud, Femininity, and Faith*, for a discussion of similar theses in Freud.

27. Singer, *The Nature of Love*, vol. 1, pp. 300–301.

28. Aristotle, *Nicomachean Ethics*, 1155b15–20. In this translation, Martin Ostwald reluctantly uses "lovable"; see p. 217, n. 11. Both Gregory Vlastos ("The Individual as an Object of Love in Plato," p. 4, text and n. 4) and Nussbaum (*The Fragility of Goodness*, p. 354) think that *philia* is best translated as "love," not "friendship."

29. Montaigne, *Complete Essays*, book I, chap. 28, "Of Friendship," p. 139. Even though I am interpreting Montaigne as claiming that personal love has no reasons, other readings are possible: (1) Montaigne does have reasons, of which he was unconscious; or (2) Montaigne is claiming that all Boétie's properties, taken together, provided his reason for loving. "Because it was he," then, means "because he was the sum of all his properties." See notes 69 and 71, below.

30. Rogers, *Matrimoniall Honour* (1642); quoted by Leites, *The Puritan Conscience and Modern Sexuality*, p. 101.

31. Leites, *The Puritan Conscience*, p. 101.

32. Quoted by Aldous Huxley, *The Perennial Philosophy*, p. 83.

33. Baxter, *A Christian Dictionary* (1678); quoted by Leites, *The Puritan Conscience*, p. 176, n. 82.

34. Singer, *The Nature of Love*, vol. 2, p. 49.

35. Gay, *The Tender Passion*, p. 65.

36. Stendhal, *Love*, p. 60.

37. Ibid., p. 59: "Why does one enjoy and delight in each new beauty discovered in the beloved?"

38. Ibid., pp. 45, 50.

39. See Russell Vannoy, *Sex Without Love*, p. 157, n. 3.

40. See my article, "The Unity of Romantic Love," pp. 388–395. George Eliot wrote that admiration was, fortunately, only a necessary condition for love: "Care has been taken not only that the trees should not sweep the stars down, but also that every man who admires a fair girl should not be enamoured of her. . . . [N]ature's order is certainly benignant in not obliging us one and all to be desperately in love with the most admirable mortal we have ever seen" (*Daniel Deronda*, p. 85). If we read this serious passage in a way unintended by Eliot, it will sound like Woody Allen's "Not only is there no God, but try getting a plumber on weekends" (*Getting Even*, p. 25).

41. Singer, *The Nature of Love*, vol. 2, p. 361.

42. Ibid., p. 365.

43. For an example of deriving some features of love from more fundamental features, see my "Unity of Romantic Love." Nakhnikian derives five features of "undemanding love" from its two defining features in "Love in Human Reason" (p. 301).

44. Kierkegaard, *Works of Love*, p. 74.

45. William Dunbar, *The Merle and the Nychtingail*, l. 16.

46. Nygren suggests (*Agape and Eros*, p. 157) that for John the distinction between the lower and the higher eros was not between lower and higher human objects of love, as in Pausanias, but between love of anything worldly and the love for God.

47. Freud wrote that some people direct "their love, not to single objects but to all men alike" (that is, exhibit neighbor-love) precisely to avoid "the uncertainties and disappointments of genital love" (*Civilization and Its Discontents*, p. 49). These people replace erosic love with agapic rather than with a higher erosic love.

48. Pascal, *Pensées*, no. 396, p. 145.

49. An obvious rebuttal to Pascal's view that we should love God but not humans (because they die) is Louise Glück's: "Why love what you will lose? / There is nothing else to love" (*The Triumph of Achilles*, p. 56). That there might be no God must deflate J. M. Stafford's sigh of relief that "instances of people claiming to be in love with non-existent individuals are fortunately very rare" ("On Distinguishing Between Love and Lust," p. 300).

50. Capellanus (*The Art of Courtly Love*, p. 52) warns young men not to love women; they will not reciprocate as surely as God will.

51. *Confessions*, p. 55 (book 3, para. 1).

52. Graves, "Symptoms of Love," in Stallworthy, *A Book of Love Poetry*, p. 45.

53. For some brief remarks on this idea, and on the "rivalry," see Outka, *Agape*, pp. 44–45, 52–53.

54. Greeley, *Bottom Line Catechism for Contemporary Catholics,* quoted by Peter Gardella, *Innocent Ecstasy,* pp. 150–151.
55. Quoted by Singer, *The Nature of Love,* vol. 1, p. 195.
56. Nygren, *Agape and Eros,* p. 213.
57. Lewis suggests that "by a high paradox, God enables men to have a Gift-love towards Himself." We can "withhold," or not withhold, "our wills and hearts, from God" (*The Four Loves,* p. 177).
58. Nygren, *Agape and Eros,* p. 127.
59. Ibid., p. 95. There is a question, in my mind, whether Nygren is substituting "faith" for the human love for God (which drops out altogether) or analyzing the human love for God as *pistis.* Outka glosses over this distinction; contrast p. 47, 1.6, to p. 48, 1.5, in his *Agape.*
60. Nygren, *Agape and Eros,* p. 127.
61. Ibid., p. 213.
62. Ibid., pp. 213–214.
63. Tillich, *Love, Power, and Justice,* p. 31.
64. Nygren actually claims that humans *must* love God: "All choice on man's part is excluded" (*Agape and Eros,* p. 213). See my discussion of Wojtyla and Fromm on Nygrenian reciprocity in human personal love (11.2): x's loving y *causes* y to love x.
65. Kierkegaard, *Works of Love,* pp. 156–157, italics added.
66. Singer, *The Nature of Love,* vol. 1, "Appraisal and Bestowal," pp. 3–22; vol. 3, "Toward a Modern Theory of Love," pp. 389–406.
67. Singer's distinction between appraisal and bestowal had earlier been made by Emil Brunner (*Justice and the Social Order,* 1945). See Outka, *Agape,* pp. 81–83, 157–158.
68. Vlastos, "The Individual as an Object of Love in Plato," p. 33.
69. Singer, then, here distances himself in this regard from the second view of personal love. He rejects Montaigne's reason also on p. 14 of vol. 1: "For what then does a man love a woman? For being the person she is, for being herself? But that is to say that he loves her for nothing at all. Everyone is himself. Having a beloved who is what she is does not reveal the nature of love." (See n. 71, below.)
70. See also vol. 3, p. 399: "Persons we appraise highly . . . are easier to love."
71. If bestowal is ungrounded, then love is, after all, "for nothing at all" (see n. 69, above). Indeed, in vol. 3 Singer asserts, rather than repudiates, Montaigne's reason: "A person acquires this gratuitous value [of bestowal] by being whatever he is. Therein lies the rich absurdity of love; for everyone . . . is what he is" (p. 393).
72. See vol. 1, chap. 13, "Agapē: The Divine Bestowal."
73. The bestowal that occurs in the human love for God, then, is apparently only the deep-level bestowal. Hence, x's bestowing value in loving God is quite different from x's bestowing value on a human—which is a top-level bestowal.
74. Himmelfarb, *On Liberty and Liberalism,* p. 225.
75. Ibid., p. 209.

CHAPTER TWO: LOVE AT SECOND SIGHT

1. Gellner, "Ethics and Logic" (page references are in the text).
2. Newton-Smith, "A Conceptual Investigation of Love," p. 124.

3. One might interject here that x is not faced with "the same situation," and therefore z's having S need not have the same effect on x as y's having S. But given that the situations are in one salient way precisely the same (both y and z have S), the burden of proof, to state how the situations are different, is carried by those who would solve Gellner's paradox this way. We shall consider solutions of this sort later. (See 3.4, 4.2, and 6.1.)

4. As Nygren wrote about agape, "When it is said that God loves man, this is not a judgment on what man is like, but on what God is like" (*Agape and Eros*, p. 76). Thus Gellner in the second horn rejects the subject-centricity of the second view of personal love in favor of the object-centricity of the first view (1.3).

5. Slater, *The Pursuit of Loneliness*, p. 87.

6. The thesis that love is out of proportion to the properties of the object is advanced by John McTaggart; see 13.10.

7. Slater, *The Pursuit of Loneliness*, p. 87. Does this apply also to Freud's love for Martha Bernays, "who despite all my resistance [!] captivated my heart at our first meeting"? (See epigraph.)

8. Singer, *The Nature of Love*, vol. 1, p. 32.

9. Robert Ehman argues that "we can never in the strict sense love a person at first sight," because the basis of love is the beloved's unique character and that is not yet available to the lover ("Personal Love," p. 123). I discuss Ehman in 3.6.

10. Descartes, *Philosophical Letters*, pp. 224–225.

11. See Descartes's definition of love, p. 1.

12. If Gellner's dilemma shows that love is impossible, it might be seen as the *reductio ad absurdum* of the thesis that love is property-based. I think Bernard Mayo would interpret Gellner that way; he claims, barely providing a shred of argument, that love "has nothing to do with reasons" (*Ethics and the Moral Life*, p. 199; see 8.7).

13. For Plato, the E-type lover is irrational. "Then he must see that the beauty in any one body is family-related to the beauty in another body; . . . it is *great mindlessness* not to consider the beauty of all bodies to be one and the same" (*Symposium* 210a5ff; italics added to Martha Nussbaum's translation, *The Fragility of Goodness*, p. 179). Other translations: "great folly" (Hamilton), "utterly senseless" (Groden), "altogether mindless" (Stanley Rosen, *Plato's Symposium*, p. 265).

14. Bernstein, "Love, Particularity, and Selfhood"; Fisher, "Reason, Emotion, and Love." Outside philosophy, see Emily Brontë's *Wuthering Heights* (the passage just before Catherine declares "I *am* Heathcliff"), Balzac's *Sarrasine*, and Mozart's "Cosi Fan Tutti." Kierkegaard plays with substitutions in "First Love," *Either/Or*, vol. I. The problem has an analogue in aesthetics. A good forgery has the properties in virtue of which the original elicits aesthetic approval, so it should elicit the same approval. See Francis Sparshott, "The Disappointed Art Lover," pp. 254–255.

15. Bernstein, "Love, Particularity, and Selfhood," p. 287. For Nancy's reply (in a sense) to Mark, see her letter to the editor, *Proceedings of the APA* 62, 4 (March 1989), pp. 718–720.

16. Job suddenly and inexplicably lost his wife, but was quite happy with the nonidentical replacement God later gave him. Perhaps Bernstein's unhappiness with the identical Nancy* means that he has a much more refined notion of personal love than the Hebrews. (Note that Job's replacement wife might have been identical for *him*.)

17. Bernstein, "Love, Particularity, and Selfhood," p. 288.
18. Ibid. Yet Bernstein admits that if asked why he loves Nancy, he would say "because . . . she is kind, sensitive, intelligent, and beautiful." Is love, then, reason-dependent, but its reasons are nongeneral? Is this why Bernstein would not love the identical Nancy*? If so, this is nongenerality at its worst.
19. Ibid., p. 291.
20. W. B. Yeats, "The Three Bushes," *The Collected Poems,* p. 294; see also Gen. 30:23–25: "In the evening [Laban] took his daughter Leah and brought her to Jacob. . . . And in the morning, behold, it was Leah," not Rachel.
21. Fisher, "Reason, Emotion, and Love," p. 201.
22. Fisher argues that x's not loving the empirically indistinguishable y*, even though x loved y, entails that the object of love is a transcendental self (3.6). In a later paper ("Love as Process," p. 7), Fisher provides a reinterpretation of his earlier argument: "A lover who discovered that for his beloved had been substituted a [perfect copy] . . . would be far more likely to feel bitter at the deception than to concede that he did love the substitute . . . , which is what he would have to concede" if love were property-based. Surely, x would be bitter. But whether or not x "concedes" that he loved y* for five years, x did love y* for five years. Further, why does x justifiably feel bitter, if not because x was tricked for five years into loving y*? Fisher does say, in "Love as Process," that his earlier substitution argument was "bad," but for a different reason: "the basis of the resentment and the non-appearance of love of the substitute [when discovered] can be . . . the shared history." (See 3.4.)
23. Another variant, suggested by Norton Nelkin.

CHAPTER THREE: THE UNIQUENESS OF THE BELOVED

1. Scruton, *Sexual Desire,* pp. 96, 98–99, 232. (See 8.5 and 13.4.)
2. Nussbaum, *The New York Review of Books,* Dec. 18, 1986, p. 50.
3. "Everyone is unique" is not self-contradictory if "x is unique" = "x has at least one property no one else has":
$$Ux = (\exists P)[Px \ \& \ (y)(y \neq x \rightarrow -Py)].$$
"Everyone is unique" is then trivially true, because every x has the property "self-identity," and no one else is identical to that person. "Everyone is unique" is not even a contradiction if "x is unique" = "x has only properties no other person has," that is,
$$(P)[Px \rightarrow (y)(y \neq x \rightarrow -Py)],$$
as long as a theory of types distinguishes "unique" from lower-level predicates.
4. See Lyons, *Emotion,* pp. 74–75; Norton and Kille, *Philosophies of Love,* p. 11; and especially Robert Ehman, "Personal Love," p. 120: "In the measure that a person's love . . . focuses on a single person to the exclusion of others, he will feel that the basis is something unique to his beloved and goes beyond all repeatable qualities that the person shares with others."
5. In Barry's *French Lovers* (p. 94), we learn that Molière rejected Chapelle's advice to "have Armande [M's wife] shut up in a convent, as did other husbands with unfaithful wives"; instead, Molière gave her money and did not interfere with her

freedom of conduct. In response to Chapelle, Molière wrote: "I can see that you have never loved. . . . [I]f you knew how much I suffered, you would pity me. My feeling reached such a height that I began to sympathize with *her;* and when I think how difficult it is for me to overcome my passion for her, I tell myself that perhaps she has the same difficulty in vanquishing her penchant for being a coquette."

6. "I was struck too by the way in which her nose, imitating in this the model of her mother's nose and her grandmother's, was cut off by just that absolutely horizontal line at its base, that same brilliant if slightly tardy stroke of design. . . . [I]t seemed to me wonderful that at the critical moment nature should have returned . . . to give to the granddaughter, as she had given to her mother and her grandmother, that significant and decisive touch of the chisel" (Marcel Proust, "Time Regained," *Remembrance of Things Past,* vol. 3, p. 1088). "Decisive," yet hardly unique.

7. Fromm, *The Art of Loving,* pp. 11–12, 72.

8. Ibid., p. 23.

9. Fromm does draw the conclusion, but on the different grounds that people lack the capacity to love (Ibid., p. 111).

10. Galston, *Justice and the Human Good,* p. 154.

11. In aesthetics, we might speak of "syndromes." See Sparshott, *The Structure of Aesthetics,* pp. 172–173, 186–189.

12. Lewis, *The Four Loves,* pp. 58–59.

13. Singer, *The Nature of Love,* vol. 3, p. 391.

14. Meager, "The Uniqueness of a Work of Art," pp. 69–70. The claim that works of art are unique is common in aesthetics; see Prall, *Aesthetic Analysis,* pp. 186–188, and Macdonald, "Some Distinctive Features of Arguments Used in Criticism of the Arts." For a sober appraisal, see Sparshott, *The Structure of Aesthetics,* p. 10; Wellek and Warren, *Theory of Literature,* pp. 5–8.

15. Consider Mark Bernstein's substitution argument (2.5). Bernstein wonders whether he can explain his love for Nancy not in terms of intelligence but in terms of "intelligence-in-Nancy." He remarks that this property is "non-repeatable, . . . it's conceptually impossible for another person to exemplify intelligence-in-Nancy" ("Love, Particularity, and Selfhood," p. 289). Remember, however, that Bernstein has dreamed up Nancy*, who is qualitatively indistinguishable from Nancy. What are we to say about "intelligence-in-Nancy*"? Intelligence-in-N is different from intelligence-in-N*, but only numerically; intelligence-in-N is qualitatively identical to intelligence-in-N*, because N and N* are qualitatively identical. Hence intelligence-in-N, contrary to Bernstein, is repeatable. Intelligence-in-N is nonrepeatable only if N and N* are not qualitatively identical. Hence, prior differences (if any) between N and N* explain the difference between P-in-N and P-in-N*, and not vice versa.

16. Quinton, "The Soul," pp. 402–404. Consider Milan Kundera: "What is unique . . . hides itself in what . . . cannot be guessed at or calculated, what must be unveiled, uncovered, conquered" (*The Unbearable Lightness of Being,* p. 199). "The millionth part dissimilarity is present in all areas of human existence," but for Tomas "in all areas other than sex it is exposed and needs no one to discover it. . . . One woman prefers cheese . . . , another loathes cauliflower, . . . [but this] originality . . . demonstrates its own irrelevance. . . . Only in sexuality does the mil-

lionth part dissimilarity become precious, because . . . it must be conquered" (p. 200). We understand, then, why for Tomas the anus "is the spot he loved most in all women's bodies" (p. 205): the least exposed, the most difficult to conquer. The details of a woman's anus: uniqueness-making but trivial; and not even for Tomas the basis of love.

17. Kierkegaard thinks that if a wife "were to adorn herself merely to please" the husband, what he should take as valuable is not her first-order property of looking pretty but only her trying to please him: "If he with a single nerve of his eye were to see amiss and admire [her beauty], instead of comprehending love's correct expression, that it was to please him, already he is on a false track . . . of becoming a connoisseur" (*Stages on Life's Way,* p. 157). Of course, if she tries to look pretty but fails to do so, then he can love her for the attempt. But why protest, if x loves y both because y tries to please x and succeeds in doing so?

18. Do not confuse this claim—the uniqueness of the x-y relationship means that y will have uniqueness-making properties that serve as the basis of love—with the claim that the uniqueness of the x-y relationship makes y unique as the object of love (see Robert Brown, *Analyzing Love,* pp. 106–108; 13.6).

19. Newton-Smith, "A Conceptual Investigation of Love," p. 124.

20. Sylvia Walsh ("Women in Love," p. 360) finds this view in D. H. Lawrence, but I wonder. Birkin says, "There is . . . a final me which is stark and impersonal. . . . So there is a final you. And it is there I would want to meet you. . . . There we are two stark, unknown beings, two utterly strange creatures." Ursula responds "in a mocking voice": "But don't you think me good-looking?" (*Women in Love,* pp. 137–138.)

21. Fromm, *The Art of Loving,* p. 47.

22. "Only God sees the most secret thoughts. But why should these be all that important?" (Wittgenstein, *Zettel,* no. 560, p. 98e.)

23. Kierkegaard wrote, "Sometimes when in my drawing room there is carried on by a connoisseur . . . a grandiloquent discourse about . . . the importance of the lovers learning to know one another thoroughly, so that in choosing one can be sure of choosing a faultless mate, . . . I say 'Yes, that is the difficulty. . . . [I]n the case of corns, how is anybody to be sure whether one has them, or has had them, or whether one may not get them?' " (spoken as Judge William, *Stages on Life's Way,* p. 131). This is a caricature of erosic personal love, but it does raise a serious question. See 8.8.

24. Early on, what lovers "do know is genuine and enough to sustain their conviction that they can bear coming to know one another better" (Letwin, "Romantic Love and Christianity," p. 144).

25. Medawar, *The Uniqueness of the Individual,* p. 143.

26. Ibid., p. 155. Another biologist, F. Gonzales-Crussi, rejects the medical proof of uniqueness; see *Notes of an Anatomist,* pp. 69–71.

27. MacLagan, "Respect for Persons as a Moral Principle—I," pp. 204–205.

28. Buscaglia, *Love,* pp. 19–20. Or she read M. Scott Peck, *The Road Less Traveled* (p. 151); or even worse, Dominitz, *How to Find the Love of Your Life: 90 Days to a Permanent Relationship,* chap. 4, "Thrive on Your Uniqueness."

29. Ehman, "Personal Love and Individual Value," p. 92. In an earlier paper, "Person-

al Love," Ehman claimed that the beloved's uniqueness is the "basis" of love (pp. 118–120, 124), although he seemed to mean an empirical rather than a metaphysical uniqueness.

30. Fisher, "Reason, Emotion, and Love," pp. 201–202. See also Jacques Maritain: "Love does not look to qualities. . . . [W]hat I love is the deepest, most substantial and hidden, most existential reality of the beloved being—a metaphysical center" (*La personne et le Bien commun;* quoted by Johann, "The Problem of Love," p. 242).

31. Ehman, "Personal Love and Individual Value," pp. 94–95, italics added.

32. Quoted by John Bayley, *The Character of Love,* p. 226.

33. "For he who would end with the inexplicable had best begin with it and say not a word more, so as not to become an object of suspicion" (Kierkegaard, *Stages on Life's Way,* p. 50). Look who's talking.

34. Solomon, *Love: Emotion, Myth and Metaphor,* p. 94.

35. Ehman, "Personal Love and Individual Value," p. 98.

36. Ibid., p. 93. Ehman's argument must proceed from the uniqueness of art to the uniqueness of its creator (because nothing is in the product that is not already in the producer?), rather than from the latter to the former (as in Edmund Wilson, *Axel's Castle,* pp. 21–22); after all, the uniqueness of the person is what he needs to establish.

37. Ehman, "Personal Love and Individual Value," p. 98, italics added.

38. Fisher, "Reason, Emotion, and Love," p. 201.

39. Ibid., p. 198.

40. Quinton's account in this regard may be better (see text at n. 16, above). For Quinton, the self that is loved is the unique empirical cluster of character and recollections, and this self is repeatedly identified and distinguished from other selves by the empirical body with which it is associated; bodies are "convenient recognition devices" ("The Soul," p. 402). Roger Scruton, in effect, claims that Quinton understates the case; the body is more than a recognition device—it constitutes the self. "I *am* my body. . . . [E]xcretion is the final 'no' to all our transcendental illusions" (*Sexual Desire,* p. 151). This is as funny as Samuel Johnson's "refuting" Berkeley by kicking a rock.

41. Fisher, "Reason, Emotion, and Love," p. 202.

42. Ibid.

43. Ibid., p. 201.

44. Fisher recognizes all three, but not the implication.

45. Gellner, "Ethics and Logic," p. 161.

46. Thanks to Edward Johnson for the example. (See 8.7 on reasons *not* to love.)

47. Firestone, *The Dialectic of Sex,* p. 154.

CHAPTER FOUR: COMING FIRST

1. Such high standards would generate a social foundation for pedestalism. Consider:

> You meaner beauties of the night,
>   That poorly satisfy our eyes
> More by your number than your light,

> You common people of the skies;
> What are you when the moon shall rise?

These are the words of Sir Henry Wotton in his poem "Elizabeth of Bohemia," who was for Wotten "By virtue first, then choice, a Queen . . . Th' eclipse and glory of her kind" (Stallworthy, *A Book of Love Poetry,* pp. 61–62). So much for a thousand points of light.

2. See Luhmann, *Love as Passion,* pp. 30–31. This also holds for love in aristocratic Athens: "The perfect form of friendship is that between good men. . . . Such friendships are of course rare, since such men are few" (Aristotle, *Nicomachean Ethics,* 1156b6, b25).

3. The actual historical connection between courtly love and love for God might have been just the reverse: "The love religion [courtly love] can become more serious without becoming reconciled to the real religion. Where it is not a parody of the Church it may be . . . her rival—a temporary escape, a truancy from the ardours of a religion that was believed into the delights of a religion that was merely imagined" (Lewis, *The Allegory of Love,* p. 21).

4. The problem of choice arises also regarding marriage. According to Erich Fromm (*The Art of Loving,* p. 3), the change from arranged marriages to "free choice" in partner-selection necessitated the invention of selection principles. Parents had used certain principles in deciding on mates for children, but these principles could not or would not be employed by emancipated choosers. Persons living within Western capitalism devised property-based selection principles that mirrored the principles of the market; they had nowhere else to turn in filling in the lacuna left by the abandonment of arranged marriages. Note the irony. Freedom of choice comes at a time when, due to the homogenization of personality, there are insufficient differences among people to make freedom of choice meaningful. For the view that social conventions concerning love generally limit "free choice," see Goode, "The Theoretical Importance of Love," pp. 131–132, 135.

5. Gellner, "Ethics and Logic," p. 160.

6. Place is the same sort of factor as time; they interact inseparably. "The woman whose face we have before our eyes more constantly than light itself, . . . this woman who is to us unique might well have been another if we had been in another town from the one in which we met her, if we had explored other quarters of the town, if we had frequented a different salon. Unique, we suppose? She is legion" (Marcel Proust, "The Fugitive," *Remembrance of Things Past,* vol. 3, p. 513).

7. The concept of the "accidental" is tricky. R. W. England ("Images of Love and Courtship in Family-Magazine Fiction," p. 164) distinguishes between x and y meeting because they live on the same street, attend the same school, work for the same business, belong to the same club, or are introduced by mutual friends, on the one hand, and encountering "each other anonymously as complete strangers." The former result from "patterned social relationships," the latter from "chance." But all these meetings involve chance. See Kierkegaard: "The occasion is always the accidental, and this is the tremendous paradox, that the accidental is just as absolutely necessary as the necessary. . . . The occasion is at one and the same time the most significant and the most insignificant. . . . Without the occasion, precisely nothing at all happens, and yet the occasion has no part at all in what does happen" (*Either/Or,* vol. 1, pp. 232, 236).

8. Stallworthy, *A Book of Love Poetry*, pp. 50–51.
9. Berger and Kellner claim that "the couple . . . construct not only present reality but reconstruct past reality as well, fabricating a common memory that integrates the recollections of the two individual pasts ("Marriage and the Construction of Reality," p. 15).
10. See Fromm, *The Art of Loving*, pp. 47–48. This might be what Kierkegaard, for whom personal love is agapic, had in mind when he wrote that the world "is like a play. . . . [W]hen the curtain falls, the one who played the king, and the one who played the beggar, . . . they are quite alike, all one and the same: actors. And when in death the curtain falls on the stage of actuality . . . then they also are all one; they are human beings. . . . [T]he distinctions of earthly existence are only like an actor's costume" (*Works of Love*, p. 95).
11. Is neighbor-love, as a form of agape, restricted by time and place factors? On this question see Outka, *Agape*, pp. 12–13; Bishop Butler, *Five Sermons*, p. 58; and Kilpatrick, *Identity and Intimacy*, pp. 227–228.
12. In romantic love, "the symbolic marker 'chance' was . . . used to socially differentiate at the very beginning of a love relationship. . . . The combination of chance and fate . . . did not affect the significance of the love relationship negatively; on the contrary, being independent of any external moulding, this enhanced the significance the relationship bore, making it absolute in and of itself" (Luhmann, *Love as Passion*, p. 143).
13. Gellner, "Ethics and Logic," p. 162.
14. Scruton, *Sexual Desire*, p. 81.
15. Empirical evidence that this phenomenon occurs is provided by Ellis, "A Study of Human Love Relationships," p. 69.
16. Gareth Evans, "The Causal Theory of Names," p. 191.
17. "Could the fact that you were born on December 2 be a reason for loving you? Certainly those who write the astrology columns believe that it is" (Robert Solomon, *Love*, p. 167). Those who write or read astrology columns believe no such thing; they do not believe that time per se is a reason for loving. Rather, date of birth is (purportedly) nomically tied to other factors (personality traits) that are the reasons.
18. Newton-Smith, "A Conceptual Investigation of Love," p. 124.

CHAPTER FIVE: ARISTOPHANIC LOVE

1. Plato, *Symposium*, 191a–d (translations Hamilton's unless indicated otherwise).
2. See also Gen. 2:18–24.
3. Tillich, *Love, Power, and Justice*, pp. 28, 27.
4. Nussbaum, *The Fragility of Goodness*, p. 173.
5. Saxonhouse, "The Net of Hephaestus," p. 28.
6. Ibid. This is Nussbaum's point, when she says that Aristophanic humans love "whole people . . . with all their idiosyncrasies, flaws, and even faults" (*The Fragility of Goodness*, p. 173).
7. Diotima in effect criticizes Aristophanes at 205e: "Love is not desire either of the half or of the whole, unless that half or whole happens to be good." She immedi-

ately continues, "People are not attached to what particularly belongs to them, except in so far as they can identify what is good with what is their own." This is ambiguous. She wants to say (I think) that x loves that which is x's only if that which is x's is independently good (eros), but she can be read as saying that x judges that which is x's to be good just because it is x's (agape).

8. "Forced" is the key. These half-persons have no freedom of choice in selecting a beloved. But exactly because they lack this freedom, their loves are exclusive, constant, and reciprocal.

9. Saxonhouse, "The Net of Hephaestus," p. 28.

10. Nussbaum, *The Fragility of Goodness,* pp. 172, 174.

11. Nussbaum is right that "reason and planning" play no role in Aristophanic love, but for the wrong reason. Reason plays no role not because reason cannot help x to find y (which it can), but because reason is not required and is, indeed, irrelevant for x to select a beloved. See n. 8, above.

12. See Stanley Rosen, *Plato's Symposium,* p. 151.

13. In Aristophanes, no; in Freud, yes: every person is born as a sexually polymorphous and psychically androgynous whole. Freud's project was to explain how some people turn out heterosexual, others homosexual, in both cases losing a chunk (a "half") of natural sexual potential. Aristophanes also explains why some are heterosexual and some homosexual, not by working out the changes induced in an identical originating material but by postulating three different originating materials. In Aristophanes' view: different starting stuffs, same cause (fission); in Freud's: same starting stuff, different causes, that is, different psychogenic histories.

14. David Hume, "Of Love and Marriage," *Essays,* p. 555, italics added.

15. Morton Hunt identifies (c) as one of "the articles of faith in the American credo of romanticism," along with the belief that we "choose the right one on the basis of feeling 'the real thing'" (*The Natural History of Love,* pp. 363–364). Hunt doubts that the ideology is seriously embraced: "Americans, even young ones, are not utter fools." But see Slater, *The Pursuit of Loneliness,* p. 86.

16. Kierkegaard bitingly criticized the ideal mate theory: "Again and again we hear this story in poetry: A man is bound to one girl whom he once loved or perhaps never loved properly, for he has seen another girl who is the ideal. A man makes a mistake in life; it was the right street but the wrong house, for directly across the street on the second floor lives the ideal. . . . A lover has made a mistake, he has seen the beloved by artificial light and thought she had dark hair, but . . . on close scrutiny she is a blond—but her sister is the ideal. This is supposed to be a subject for poetry" (*Fear and Trembling,* p. 91). Thurber and White's humor is a nice contrast to Kierkegaard's sarcasm: "Every man entertained . . . the suspicion that if he waited twenty-four hours, or possibly less, he would likely find a lady even more ideally suited to his taste than his fiancée. . . . He was greatly strengthened in his belief by the fact that he kept catching a fleeting glimpse of this imaginary person— in restaurants, in stores, in trains. To deny the possibility of her existence would be, he felt, to do a grave injustice to her, to himself, and to his fiancée. Man's unflinching desire to give himself and everybody else a square deal was the cause of much of his disturbance" (*Is Sex Necessary?* pp. 96, 98).

17. Descartes, *The Passions of the Soul* (*Philosophical Writings,* vol. 1, p. 360). Annette

Baier says that Descartes here "seems to endorse Plato's theory in the *Symposium*" ("The Ambiguous Limits of Desire," p. 51). Does Baier believe Descartes misread Plato as speaking only about heterosexuality? See n. 20, below.

18. See Karol Wojtyla, *Love and Responsibility*, p. 48. Of course, sexual desire is hard to quiet even with the cooperation of another person.

19. Rosen, *Plato's Symposium*, p. 150.

20. Hume reads Aristophanes' myth as being entirely about heterosexuals descended from androgynes: "each individual person was a compound of both sexes" ("Of Love and Marriage," p. 555). In *Three Essays on the Theory of Sexuality*, Freud wrote: "The popular view of the sexual instinct is beautifully reflected in the poetic fable which tells how the original human beings were cut up into two halves—man and woman—and how these are always striving to unite again in love" (p. 2). Freud's editor claims that this sentence is "no doubt an allusion to . . . Aristophanes in Plato's *Symposium*" (p. 2, n. 1), thereby accusing Freud of Hume's mistake.

21. Fromm, *The Art of Loving*, pp. 6–8, 15.

22. Reik, *Of Love and Lust*, pp. 52–53. Diotima also says that love is the child of Poverty (*Symposium*, 203b).

23. Bellah, *Habits of the Heart*, p. 98 (chapter written by Ann Swidler).

24. See also M. Scott Peck, *The Road Less Traveled*, p. 82.

25. Anders Nygren, *Agape and Eros*, p. 101. Compare this Christian view with the Hebrew view endorsed by Irving Singer: "By interpreting love of self as self-affirmation, we . . . see the wisdom in the psychiatric (and Hasidic) insistence that no one can love another unless he loves himself" (*The Nature of Love*, vol. 3, p. 434). Is "self-affirmation" simply what the Christian calls "pride"?

26. The state of the art is represented by this summary: "We have found that those high in genuine self-acceptance and self-actualization, respectively, reported more frequent love experiences and derived greater personal satisfaction and enjoyment from their relationships; however, it was the persons lower on these personality dimensions who were fonder of their partners, esteemed them more highly, and had a stronger love for them" (Dion and Dion, "Romantic Love," in Sternberg and Barnes, *The Psychology of Love*, pp. 284–285; see also pp. 268–270).

27. "Love as *erōs*," says Tillich, "strives for a union with that which is a bearer of values because of the values it embodies" (*Love, Power, and Justice*, p. 30). Note that Tillich asserts that the human love for God is a desire for union with that from which humans have been separated (see text at n. 3, above) *and* (here) that the human love for God is a desire for union with that which has value (pp. 30–31). Tillich thus overdetermines the desire to merge. He might as well have tossed in that when we compare ourselves with God, we feel deficient and want to merge for this third reason.

28. Another nonideal agapic scenario: the love we desire to receive is agapic, and we desire this kind of love because we had it earlier, when cared for by our mothers. Separation from her is traumatic; we attempt to ease this pain by merging with a substitute who in this reunion will love us as she did.

29. This seems to be Rosen's reading; see *Plato's Symposium*, p. 158.

30. In Hamilton's translation, the similarity of lover and beloved is often asserted by Aristophanes; see 192b (male homosexuals seek men, always cleaving "to what is

akin to themselves") and 193d (love leads "us toward what is akin to us"). But then in what sense would heterosexuals be "akin"?

31. See Foucault, *The Use of Pleasure*, p. 232.
32. Nussbaum claims that "there is nothing like a general description of a suitable . . . lover, satisfiable by a number of candidates, that could serve as a sufficient criterion of suitability" (*The Fragility of Goodness*, p. 173). But more precisely, we should say that Aristophanes' description is *too* general.
33. Barthes, *A Lover's Discourse*, p. 20.

CHAPTER SIX: THE SATISFACTION OF DESIRE

1. "There is no stopping because the object pursued [at lower levels] is an illusion instead of the good which the lover's soul really craves, and therefore the lover can never be satisfied" (Letwin, "Romantic Love and Christianity," p. 133).
2. On the disappointment of loving "lower things," in both Plato and Augustine, see Annette Baier, "Caring About Caring," p. 276.
3. See Singer, *The Nature of Love*, vol. 3, p. 46.
4. Helmut Thielicke, *The Ethics of Sex*, p. 30. See also L. A. Kosman, "Platonic Love."
5. Singer claims, to the contrary, that "through appraisal we establish what an object is worth on the basis of its . . . capacity to satisfy needs within ourselves" (*The Nature of Love*, vol. 3, p. 157; see also pp. 360, 390).
6. Vannoy, *Sex Without Love*, p. 217.
7. Ibid., p. 134.
8. See Seligman et al., "Effects of Salience of Extrinsic Rewards on Liking and Loving."
9. The difference between x's satisfying y's desires (1) because y will satisfy x's and (2) because y has satisfied x's desires is important. If both x and y will not give until they already get, the x-y relationship never gets off the ground. Hence, x or y must give before getting, without any guarantee that the giving will lead to getting. Thus, at least one of them must be willing to give even if the giving is never returned. If so, why not allow, contrary to the D-S model, that some people sometimes give just for the sake of giving?
10. Levy, "The Definition of Love in Plato's *Symposium*," p. 286.
11. Ibid., pp. 286–287.
12. Freud's writings on love illustrate this similarity. His methodology, postulating that libido underlies all forms of "Liebe," is exactly Diotima's. See Singer, *The Nature of Love*, vol. 3, p. 126.
13. Baier argues, on the ground that the logic of love and the logic of desire are different, that love cannot be a desire: "To desire something is to want that desire to be satisfied, but not necessarily to want the desired [object] to reciprocate the desire (this makes no sense for most desires), nor to want the desire to recur. But to love someone is necessarily to will that love to continue and to hope for return love" ("The Ambiguous Limits of Desire," p. 55). Baier is right, I think, that love is not identical to any specific desire; but love still might include desires as components. Nevertheless, her argument is questionable: some desires may entail a desire for their own continuation (see de Sousa, "Desire and Time," in Marks, *The Ways*

of Desire, p. 91); and to love might not necessarily be "to will" love's constancy or its reciprocity (see chaps. 10, 11).

14. Robinson, "Emotion, Judgment, and Desire," p. 736.
15. Ibid., p. 737. See Iris Murdoch, *Bruno's Dream,* pp. 59–60.
16. Robinson, "Emotion, Judgment, and Desire," p. 738.
17. Ibid. Robinson also intends this claim to counter William Lyons' view that if x loves y for S, then x will love anyone who has S (*Emotion,* p. 73). Lyons solves Gellner's paradox by appealing to y's uniqueness (ibid., pp. 74–75).

CHAPTER SEVEN: HATE, LOVE, AND RATIONALITY

1. Wittgenstein, *Zettel,* #488, p. 86e.
2. Ibid., #504, p. 89e.
3. To paraphrase Auden: thou shalt not commit an erosic analysis of love. See Halmos, "Psychologies of Love," p. 61.
4. Roger Scruton suggests that the *emotions* (love, for example) "do not in general exhibit the coherence and rationality" of *attitudes,* because emotions "are directed towards things as particulars" while attitudes "are directed towards things as . . . instantiations of some . . . property" ("Attitudes, Beliefs, and Reasons," pp. 41–42). But Scruton's argument for the claim that love, as an emotion, is directed at a person as a particular and is not grounded in x's belief that y has P is odd. "We can know that X loves Y without identifying any quality of Y on the basis of which X loves him. . . . On the other hand we cannot say that X despises Y unless it is possible to refer to some quality of Y towards which X's emotion is directed." The fact that we might know that x loves y without knowing ("identifying") why x loves y is irrelevant. (See my chap. 8, n. 36.)
5. Thanks to Archie Bunker for the example.
6. See Ortega y Gasset, *On Love,* p. 17.
7. Brown, *Analyzing Love,* p. 115.
8. Woody Allen's film "Everything You Wanted to Know About Sex."
9. Stallworthy, *A Book of Love Poetry,* p. 65.
10. But we do not judge x's hate for y irrational merely because y does not reciprocate. This difference between our attitudes toward unreciprocated love and unreciprocated hate results either from the belief that reciprocity is axiomatic of love (chap. 11) or the belief that reciprocated love is better than unreciprocated love.
11. Hamlyn, "The Phenomena of Love and Hate," p. 9, italics added.
12. Hamlyn also says of love "full-stop" that "there is likely to be some explanation why the love came into being" (p. 12), but this does not mean, for Hamlyn, that love "full-stop" is erosic. First, Hamlyn immediately adds, "But there seems to be no necessity that it should be like that," that is, that love "full-stop" does have an explanation. Second, even if love "full-stop" has an explanation, Hamlyn does not claim that the explanation must be erosic (see n. 14, below).
13. William Lyons handles fear without its characteristic belief differently: it is, for him, not even an emotion, for "an emotion is based on knowledge or belief about properties" (*Emotion,* p. 71). Lyons' definition has the interesting implication that Hamlyn's love "full-stop" is neither love nor an emotion. Of course, many have

claimed (for example, Kant and Kierkegaard) that agape itself is not an emotion, at least not an emotion understood as a feeling or inclination. But that Lyons' account entails further that agapic personal love is neither love nor an emotion makes his view seem wrong. C. H. Whiteley ("Love, Hate and Emotion") responds to Hamlyn's claim—that love and hate can be belief-independent emotions—by drawing a distinction between emotions (which are belief-dependent) and "sentiments" (hate and love); this is close to Scruton's distinction (n. 4, above) between emotions and attitudes.

14. Here is confirmation that Hamlyn's hate "full-stop" (and love "full-stop") is agapic: in these cases "the only place to look for an explanation . . . is in something about the [hater] himself, not in any . . . significance that the object may have that makes hate appropriate" (p. 16). This is to say that in these cases the emotion is fully subject-centric (1.3).

15. Pitcher, "Emotion," p. 331; see also pp. 337, 340.

16. Elizabeth Telfer writes, "a sufferer [of love] may intelligibly say 'I don't know what it is about him/her that draws me, but I cannot be without him/her'" ("Friendship," pp. 225–226). She calls love in such a case irrational because it is not well grounded in beliefs, whereas Pitcher withholds "irrational" for the same reason.

17. Note that when Hamlyn argued that love can be reason-independent he did not appeal to the subjectivity of evaluations. He claimed that because x can love y while believing that y was worthless (*not* while having a different or subjective idea of "worth"), love has no characteristic belief such as "y is valuable."

18. Taylor, "Love," p. 147.

19. Now we can see why claim (2) is untenable—the claim that one feature of those emotions having a φ is that φ will place limits on Ψ. Consider fear, which has a φ ("dangerous") and various Ψ's (for example, "has sharp claws") and is a paradigm case of an emotion. I will argue that for fear φ places no limit on Ψ at all. The restriction that φ ("dangerous") is supposed to place on Ψ is that x's believing y to have Ψ (sharp claws) explains why x believes y to have φ. But to say that some cases of x's believing y to be φ ("dangerous") *because* x believes y to have Ψ (sharp claws) are rational, while other cases of x's believing y to be φ ("dangerous") *because* x believes y to be Ψ (cuddly) are irrational, is to say that every (or any) Ψ can explain why x believes y to be φ. X's believing that y is cuddly still explains why x believes y is dangerous, even though the fact that this explanatory relationship holds *for x* shows that x, or x's emotion, is irrational. The point: once we say that for some Ψ's the explanatory relationship holds, yet is irrational, there is no logical room for nonexplanatory relationships between the belief in φ and the belief in Ψ. Any time we find a Ψ that apparently does not explain φ, it can get handled as a Ψ that explains φ irrationally.

20. Jerome Shaffer's view is that *unlike* hate, "love is an anomalous emotion. . . . It does not admit of the full range of assessments with respect to rationality." His view is based on the claim that "the belief element [of the emotions] plays no essential role [in love], so that the standard criteria for evaluating beliefs in terms of truth and justification cannot apply" ("An Assessment of Emotion," p. 170). But what does Shaffer mean by "no essential role"? He writes that "the element of belief essential to love appears to be very weak. . . . [O]nce there are enough beliefs to specify the object . . . there are no further beliefs necessary to make the object

loved" (p. 169). As I have argued, however, that beliefs play "no essential role" in this sense (that is, that reason-independent love is conceptually possible) does not entail that we cannot judge cases of love to be irrational. Surely, if belief plays "no essential role" in love in this sense, then belief can play "no essential role" in hate in the same sense (see Hamlyn); yet we would judge x's hate for y, when "there are no further beliefs" about y that ground x's hate, to be irrational. "Love has been known to persist through incredible alterations in belief," says Shaffer, even "the discovery that the loved one is very different from what one thought" (p. 169). But from the fact that x loved y at t_1 because x believed that y had P, yet x continues to love y at t_2 after x realizes that y does not have P, it does not follow that belief plays no role in love; indeed, x's earlier belief did play a role, and at least x's earlier love can be assessed as rational or irrational. Perhaps Shaffer means that the persistence of love when x's beliefs dramatically change (or when y's properties dramatically change) shows that even originally x's love was not belief-dependent. The inference, however, is fallacious; see my discussion of the O-lover in sect. 4. Shaffer's argument is hardly enough to show that love is so belief-free as not to admit of being judged irrational, nor does it drive any wedge at all between love and hate.

21. Plato opts for (4) in *Euthyphro*, as he opts for (1) in *Symposium*. Saint Paul opts for both (2) and (3).

22. Whereas Frankfurt justifies (6) and (2) by invoking the value of caring, or of love, Freud justifies (5) and (1) in the same way: "A love that does not discriminate . . . forfeit[s] a part of its own value, by doing an injustice to its object. . . . [N]ot all men are worthy of love" (*Civilization and Its Discontents*, p. 49; see also p. 56).

23. Frankfurt, "The Importance of What We Care About," pp. 271–272.

24. Baier, "Caring About Caring," p. 277.

25. Were Frankfurt to conceive of caring more agapically he could respond to the objection that no selection principle is available by saying that none is needed: we should care about everything.

26. Kraut, "Love *De Re*," p. 423. Consistently, Kraut also claims "it is hardly clear that emotions like love are based upon reasons" (p. 417).

27. Ibid., p. 416. Kraut draws the conclusion, based on assuming the agapic order, that "we cannot explain the intentionality of [love] in terms of the intentionality of the judgments that caused it, since no judgments caused it." But in the second view of personal love, there is little or no intentionality to be explained.

28. MacLagan, "Respect for Persons as a Moral Principle—I," p. 205.

29. Brentlinger, "The Nature of Love," p. 124 (see also p. 117).

30. Groden's translation of "To Anactoria in Lydia," *The Poems of Sappho*, p. 7.

31. Note that in Sappho's poem Helen abandons home and child, in high romantic fashion, for her beloved; here love is irrational in virtue of the desires and acts it causes. I am therefore perplexed that anyone could write: "Since ancient times, erotic love has been praised and analyzed in two distinct traditions, one ethereal, sentimental, uncritical and soft on specifics, the other tough-minded, hard-headed, practical and attentive to details and difficulties. The first is mainly male and dates back to Socrates' effete philosophizing in the *Symposium*. The second is often female and traces its lineage to the nitty-gritty observations of Sappho" (Robert Solomon, "Separating Love into His and Hers"). In particular, Solomon's claim

that men are more romantic, and women "less rhapsodic and more practical" about love, may be true, but it is not borne out by a comparative reading of Plato and Sappho.

32. Gould, *Platonic Love*, p. 166.
33. Ibid.
34. Kierkegaard, *Works of Love*, p. 158, italics deleted.
35. Ibid., pp. 342–343; p. 377, n. 78.
36. The neighbor (that is, everyone but myself) is "the least lovable object" (ibid., p. 117)—because my own inclination is toward self-love.
37. Hamlyn, "The Phenomena of Love and Hate," p. 13.
38. Annis, "Emotion, Love and Friendship," p. 1.
39. The second view of personal love can rely on the agapic order to differentiate love and hate. When x loves y, x is caused to evaluate y positively; when x hates y, x is caused to evaluate y negatively. This tactic is unavailable to the first view with its erosic order, because x's *first* perceiving y as attractive may lead to x's loving *or* hating y. But the agape tradition succeeds in differentiating love and hate only because it cannot explain why these emotions arise in the first place.
40. Brown, *Analyzing Love*, p. 30.

CHAPTER EIGHT: DEFENDING AND REFINING EROSIC LOVE

1. In de la Mare, *Love*, p. 387.
2. F. T. Prince, "The Question," in Stallworthy, *A Book of Love Poetry*, p. 101.
3. "Being able to love on the basis of pictures or stories and then only having to make contact with the beloved was a constantly recurring motif in novels of the seventeenth century. This presumed implicitly the existence of a relatively small upper class" (Luhmann, *Love as Passion*, p. 229, n. 48; see also pp. 138, 143).
4. Brown, *Analyzing Love*, p. 122.
5. Kierkegaard, *The Sickness Unto Death*, p. 104.
6. Burch, "The Commandability of Pathological Love," p. 138. "Genuine love has got to be without any motives at all," he says. But Burch never explains why. (For one answer, see Nakhnikian's criticism of Aristotle's philia, which I discuss below, 12. 3.) Burch uses this claim as a premise in arguing that one logically cannot undertake to love. Hence it makes sense, in contrast to Burch's agapic picture of love, that from an erosic perspective one *can* undertake to love (see 8. 4).
7. At the other extreme, William Galston claims that love is necessarily erosic: "A love no grounds of which can be described or identified is almost certainly some other sentiment masquerading as love" (*Justice and the Human Good*, p. 152). One point of chapter 7 is that both Burch and Galston are wrong.
8. Gilbert, "Friendship and the Will," p. 67.
9. Ehman, "Personal Love," p. 120.
10. Hardwig, "Should Women Think in Terms of Rights?" p. 444. The possibility that "x loves y because y is y" means "x loves y in virtue of y's identity properties" is explored in 10.5.
11. Barthes, *A Lover's Discourse*, p. 19. See also Telfer, "Friendship," pp. 226, 228.

12. Barthes, *A Lover's Discourse,* p. 222.

13. Vacek, "Scheler's Phenomenology of Love," p. 160.

14. Johann, "The Problem of Love," p. 229.

15. Ibid., p. 230.

16. Galston remarks that "Why do you love me?" is "the most natural and inevitable of all lover's questions" (*Justice and the Human Good,* p. 152).

17. "How could anything be called love which was not based on delight? Or even if it were possible, who wants to be loved like that? We want to be loved because we please our lovers; nobody wants to be loved in spite of being *un*pleasing" (Richards, *The Sceptical Feminist,* p. 187).

18. Pascal, "Discourse on the Passion of Love," p. 519.

19. Sartre, *Being and Nothingness,* p. 370.

20. Freud, *Civilization and Its Discontents,* p. 49.

21. Ibid., p. 90. Kierkegaard objects: "Because the highest good is now offered to everyone, men take it as nothing, discern nothing in it, to say nothing of becoming personally aware of its extraordinary quality, just as if the highest good had lost something because every man has or may have the same" (*Works of Love,* p. 41; see also pp. 334–335).

22. "Charity . . . , though a sort of love we need, is not the sort we want. We want to be loved for our cleverness, beauty, generosity, fairness, usefulness" (Lewis, *The Four Loves,* p. 181).

23. Vonnegut, *God Bless You, Mr. Rosewater,* pp. 65, 183. If Vonnegut is right that we presently love others only because they are useful to us, we would be approximating the society described by Plato in the *Republic.* See Gregory Vlastos, "The Individual as an Object of Love in Plato," pp. 11–19.

24. Sociobiologists explain this pattern as largely genetic; see Symons, *The Evolution of Human Sexuality.*

25. Fromm, *The Art of Loving,* p. 35.

26. Gaylin, *Rediscovering Love,* p. 43, italics added. I disagree with Gaylin's suggestion that *receiving* unconditional love is less painful and difficult: being infinitely attended to can be a psychological burden.

27. Balint, "Critical Notes on the Theory of the Pregenital Organizations of the Libido," p. 50, italics deleted.

28. Kosman, "Platonic Love," p. 57.

29. Sartre, *Being and Nothingness,* p. 367.

30. Lyons, *Emotion,* p. 122.

31. See Charles Taylor, "What is Human Agency," *Philosophical Papers,* p. 42. Also see Sankowski ("Love and Moral Obligation," p. 110): "Love can . . . be an achievement of a . . . significant sort, since in creating oneself as a person who loves in a certain way, one creates the self."

32. Neu, "Jealous Thoughts," p. 442. Lyons lists nine ways "a person can exercise control over his emotions and . . . be held responsible for them" (*Emotion,* pp. 196–202).

33. Suppose, instead, that x decides to alter x's preferences by freely taking a potion, thereby causing love for y. Since x is bringing it about that x is able to love y, and since x is doing it freely, should y complain? Yes; the change in x's preferences still results from an artificial process. Only certain mechanisms for changing our prefer-

ences are acceptable, for the same reasons that we object to potion-induced love in the first place.

34. Brown, *Analyzing Love,* p. 124; see also p. 57.

35. Scruton, *Sexual Desire,* p. 96.

36. In earlier work (see my chap. 7, n. 4), Scruton did argue that the particularity of the beloved ruled out love's being reason-dependent. He also distinguished between attitudes and emotions, classifying love as an emotion. In *Sexual Desire* he abandons that distinction.

37. "Since a lover often helps to create in his beloved the features that the lover hopes to find, . . . the agent's love can both precede and produce the belief that the partner is loved because of those features. . . . [W]e quite commonly first love a person and then find in him . . . some instantiated qualities that we can offer as explanation and justification of our love" (Brown, *Analyzing Love,* pp. 102–103). We can read this as saying: x loves y, and as a result x finds value in y; being reason-hungry, x offers as x's reasons the very value x has attributed to y in virtue of loving y. This love is a crazy version of agapic personal love (1.3).

38. Isaiah Berlin, "On the Pursuit of the Ideal," p. 11.

39. *Ethics and the Limits of Philosophy,* p. 102. Thanks to Carolyn Morillo for bringing this passage to my attention and for discussing it with me.

40. Wojtyla, *Love and Responsibility,* pp. 54–57.

41. Was G. B. Shaw serious when he wrote (*Man and Superman,* p. 32): "This is the true joy in life, the being used for a purpose recognized by yourself as a mighty one; the being thoroughly worn out before you are thrown on the scrap heap"? I prefer: "To be a marionette in the service of some inexplicable power is comic" (Kierkegaard, *Stages on Life's Way,* p. 54).

42. Baier, "Caring About Caring," pp. 284–285.

43. Capellanus, *The Art of Courtly Love,* pp. 42, 28.

44. Mayo, *Ethics and the Moral Life,* p. 198.

45. Ibid., p. 199, italics added.

46. The argument can also be found in Mayo (ibid., pp. 195–196).

47. Mendus, "Marital Faithfulness," p. 248.

48. Brown, *Analyzing Love,* pp. 106–107, italics added.

49. For example, x might know in advance that if y later expresses odd sexual tastes, x will be repulsed and no longer be able to love y. The thought, that this unpredictable possibility of an open-ended relationship might happen, is so horrifying that x does not formulate its not happening as an explicit condition of love. Still, x's love is conditional at the very start.

50. See Downie, "Forgiveness," p. 133.

CHAPTER NINE: EXCLUSIVITY

1. Gellner, "Ethics and Logic," p. 195.

2. Symbolically, we can render the ambiguous "love is exclusive" by (E1):
$$(x)(y)[(xLy \ \& \ (x \neq y)) \rightarrow (z)(((y \neq z) \ \& \ (x \neq z)) \rightarrow -xLz)].$$
The clause "$(x \neq y)$" is essential, otherwise the definition of exclusivity entails that if x loves himself, then x loves no one else.

3. Taking time into consideration in this way, the ambiguous (E1) becomes (E2):

$$(x)(y)[(\exists t)(xLyt \& (x \neq y)) \rightarrow (z)(t)(((x \neq z) \& (y \neq z)) \rightarrow -xLzt)].$$

4. The lady on the train in Tolstoy's "The Kreutzer Sonata" tries valiantly to hold fast to her belief that true love is timelessly, constantly exclusive, despite the objections of the cynic in her compartment.

5. (E2) adequately symbolizes timeless nonconstant exclusivity. To (E2) timeless constant exclusivity adds (let t′ range over all times later than t):

$$CON: (x)(y)[(\exists t)xLyt \rightarrow (t')xLyt'].$$

6. Discontinuities in love do occur, for example, x's emotion toward y vacillating between love and hate. Capellanus says that it is unlikely, but not impossible, for x's love to revive if it stops in response to a "misdeed" or "defect" in y (*The Art of Courtly Love*, p. 29).

7. Symbolically, timed exclusivity is rendered by (E3):

$$(x)(y)(t)[(xLyt \& (x \neq y)) \rightarrow (z)(((y \neq z) \& (x \neq z)) \rightarrow -xLzt)].$$

Capellanus claimed, "an old love . . . ends when a new one begins, because no one can love two people at the same time" (*The Art of Courtly Love*, p. 29). His argument was psychological, not conceptual: "He who shines with the light of one love can hardly think of embracing another woman, even a beautiful one. For when he thinks deeply of his beloved the sight of any other woman seems . . . rough and rude" (p. 4).

8. In "A Study of Human Love Relationships," Albert Ellis reported that college women of the 1940s (1) tended to think of their loves as serial and bracketed, while their infatuations overlapped, and (2) perceived longer time gaps between loves than between infatuations.

9. By incorporating a constancy condition, timed exclusivity would mimic timeless constant exclusivity. Indeed, if timed exclusivity incorporates *CON* (see n. 5), it is almost equivalent to strict exclusivity: since *CON* entails that if xLy at t, xLy at all later times, there is only one bracket available to x, so x could not love y and z during different brackets. (However, note that *CON* and (E3) do not entail that x cannot love z after y dies.) Similarly, by incorporating a constancy condition, timed exclusivity also mimics *non*exclusivity: if x could love both y and z during different brackets, yet *CON* is true, these brackets must overlap as long as y and z are alive at the same time. To be a plausible doctrine, however, timed exclusivity must deny *CON*, so that x can love y at t_1 and z at t_2, even if y is still alive.

10. Gellner has difficulty with the case in which xLy for S, later xMz and xLz for S, and xLy ends when or before xLz begins; he cannot say that this serial exclusivity is exactly what is predicted by x's being an E-type lover. Gellner invoked love's being an E-type emotion to explain why x does not have the same attitude toward a later-encountered z who also has S, that is, why x does not *extend* the attitude toward an additional person. But this does not explain why the attitude is not directed toward both of two relevantly similar people rather than being *withdrawn* from the first and directed instead toward the second. Once x has developed love for y, it makes some sense that xLz never occurs if x is an E-type lover. But x's being an E-type lover does not make comprehensible x's withdrawing love from y and directing it at z instead.

11. Luhmann, *Love as Passion*, p. 97.

12. Ibid., p. 213, n. 2.
13. Brown, *Analyzing Love*, p. 33.
14. "My love is something valuable . . . which I ought not to throw away without reflection. It imposes duties on me for whose fulfillment I must be ready to make sacrifices. [Hence] if I love someone, he must deserve it" (Freud, *Civilization and Its Discontents*, p. 56). Why is my love valuable? Because it is in short supply. "Since a man does not have unlimited quantities of psychical energy at his disposal, he has to accomplish his tasks by making an expedient distribution" (p. 50). What is interesting about the argument is that in effect it reconciles reason-dependence and exclusivity by first defending exclusivity and then deriving reason-dependent selection from exclusivity.
15. Ehman, "Personal Love," p. 119. See also Bayles, "Marriage, Love, and Procreation," p. 135.
16. Newton-Smith, "A Conceptual Investigation of Love," pp. 134, 135, italics added.
17. Stafford, "On Distinguishing Between Love and Lust," p. 297.
18. Bernstein, "Love, Particularity, and Selfhood," p. 291.
19. Berger and Kellner, "Marriage and the Construction of Reality," p. 14.
20. Ibid., p. 15.
21. See Ethel Person, "Love Triangles," p. 47.
22. Hegel, "On Love," in *Early Theological Writings*, p. 306.
23. Ibid., p. 307. "As long as love was . . . understood to form a mystical losing of oneself in the other person, . . . exclusivity had a clear place. . . . [H]ow was someone supposed to be able to lose himself in more than one person without having to multiply himself?" (Luhmann, *Love as Passion*, p. 97).
24. Hunter, *Thinking about Sex and Love*, pp. 75–76.
25. Fried, *An Anatomy of Values*, p. 142.
26. Neu, "Jealous Thoughts," p. 430.
27. He who has secrets shouldn't marry, says Kierkegaard (*Either/Or*, vol. 2, p. 119). See Watson, "The Seducer and the Seduced," p. 358; and my chap. 8, n. 49.
28. Maybe this is Neu's point, since he says that "the second relationship would inevitably involve one in *betraying* the intimacies of the first" ("Jealous Thoughts," p. 429, italics added).
29. Sexual activity might serve this function, but when casual sex is commonplace it cannot, or cannot any longer, do so. (An exception: x saves one special, esoteric sexual act for this occasion and is sure to tell her beloved "I've never done this before.") If sexual activity, especially loss of virginity, is considered *the* mark of intimate sharing, timeless exclusivity makes sense; having already shared it with y, x has nothing to share with a later would-be beloved. For the same reason, *CON* would also make sense (see n. 5).
30. Neu, "Jealous Thoughts," p. 432. Neu's reason why x seeks a friendship with z even though x loves y is exactly the reason, according to the desire-satisfaction model, why x will seek a second *beloved* (6.2). Why not say, instead, that x seeks a friend for reasons of autonomy and individuality, without dragging in needs that y cannot or will not satisfy?
31. Reiman, "Privacy, Intimacy, and Personhood," pp. 30–35.

32. See also 1171a12: "Being in love means to have something like an excess of friendship, and that is only possible toward one person." Throughout, the translations are Martin Ostwald's.

33. Hunter, *Thinking about Sex and Love,* p. 76.

34. Montaigne, "Of Friendship," *Essays,* book 1, chap. 28, p. 142. Note the derogatory "fraternity."

35. Ibid., p. 141. He continues: "On the contrary, he is sorry that he is not double, triple, or quadruple, and that he has not several souls and several wills, to confer them all on this one subject." If we could love two persons, we would prefer to love our one beloved twice as much. (See Luhmann, n. 23, above.)

36. Ehman, "Personal Love," p. 119.

37. Spencer, *The Principles of Psychology,* in de la Mare, *Love,* p. 237.

38. W. B. Yeats, "For Anne Gregory," *The Winding Stair,* p. 245.

39. Lessing, *A Man and Two Women,* pp. 83–95.

40. Kierkegaard pokes fun at this escape clause of timeless exclusivity in "The First Love," *Either/Or,* vol. 1, especially p. 252. Yet as Judge William he flirts with timeless exclusivity; see *Either/Or,* vol. 2, pp. 9, 63, and *Stages on Life's Way,* p. 127.

41. See MacLagan, "Respect for Persons as a Moral Principle—I."

42. Kierkegaard's Don Juan makes this speech: "I am no husband who requires an unusual girl to make me happy; every girl has that which makes me happy, and I therefore take them all" (*Either/Or,* vol. 1, p. 96). Given what Kierkegaard says in *Works of Love* (p. 77)—erotic love mistakenly tries (in vain) to achieve perfection through the perfection of its object—and in *Stages on Life's Way* (pp. 127–128, 157)—a man selecting a wife must not be a connoisseur—this Don Juan, who practices a universal eros, appears faultless. Indeed, he is close to the morally virtuous married man who has no need to marry "an extraordinary girl" (*Either/Or,* vol. 2, p. 307). This fellow, even if he does not marry every girl, at least would marry any girl.

43. Wojtyla, *Love and Responsibility,* p. 298.

44. Outka, *Agape,* p. 12.

45. Ibid.

46. Kierkegaard, *Works of Love,* pp. 62–63; see Nordentoft, "Erotic Love," p. 97.

47. Suppose that x says to y "I love you" and y asks "Why?" X might give the erosic answer "because you have S," to which y can respond "then why not also z?" If x instead gives an agapic answer, y's response "then why not also z?" has just as much punch.

48. Ortega y Gasset, *On Love,* p. 94. See Barthes, *A Lover's Discourse,* p. 34.

49. Brown, *Analyzing Love,* p. 45. Why "confine" instead of "extend"?

50. Note that if x loves P and not the person having P, the difference among x's loving y timelessly exclusively for always having P, x's loving y and z serially exclusively because both have P, and x's loving y and z at the same time because both have P, collapses.

51. Descartes, *The Passions of the Soul* (*Philosophical Writings,* vol. 1, p. 360).

52. Lewis, *The Four Loves,* p. 135. See Murdoch, *The Black Prince,* p. 323.

53. See Sternberg and Barnes, *The Psychology of Love,* pp. 75, 90, 94, 104; Symons, *The Evolution of Human Sexuality;* and Comfort, *Nature and Human Nature,* p. 30.

54. Ortega y Gasset, *On Love,* p. 89. See Singer, *The Nature of Love,* vol. 2, p. 323, for a similar thesis in Rousseau.
55. Thurber and White, *Is Sex Necessary?* pp. 62, 67. "The extraordinary intensification of the sexual need that is so often felt . . . has the biological aim of forcibly eliminating the man's scruples, misgivings, doubts, and hesitations. This is very necessary, because the very idea of marriage . . . often makes a man panicky" is not how White continues his joke but was meant seriously by Carl Jung (*Aspects of the Feminine,* p. 37). "It is only to be expected . . . that nature will push him over the obstacle." Is marriage, for the Jungian male, what Shakespeare was referring to by "the edge of doom" (*Sonnet* 116)? By the way, in a letter Rosemary Thurber advised me that E. B. White, and not James Thurber, wrote the passages from *Is Sex Necessary?* that I quoted in the text.
56. See Outka, *Agape,* p. 8 and passim.
57. Does *this* exhaust what it means to "agapize" personal love?

CHAPTER TEN: CONSTANCY

1. Both claims are from Shakespeare, *Sonnet* 116.
2. 1 Cor. 13:8.
3. Newton-Smith, "A Conceptual Investigation of Love," p. 125.
4. Lyons, *Emotion,* p. 90.
5. Symbolically: $(x)(y)[(\exists t)xLyt \to (t')xLyt']$; t' ranges over times after t (this is CON from chap. 9, n. 5). We need not discuss Thorbecke's flamboyant claim: "I believe, my little girl, when people love as I love you, they have always loved each other" (*Lettres à sa fiancée et à sa femme*), or: $(x)(y)[(\exists t)xLyt \to (t)xLyt]$.
6. Kierkegaard, *Works of Love,* pp. 320–322.
7. Brown, *Analyzing Love,* p. 21.
8. Kierkegaard, *Works of Love,* pp. 281–282.
9. Symbolically: $(x)(y)[(\exists t)xLyt \to (\exists t')xLyt']$.
10. Buscaglia, *Love,* pp. 104–105, 108.
11. Respectively, Baier, "Caring About Caring," p. 283 (see her "The Ambiguous Limits of Desire," p. 55); Stafford, "On Distinguishing Between Love and Lust," p. 297; and Bayles, "Marriage, Love, and Procreation," p. 136.
12. Mendus, "Marital Faithfulness, p. 250 (see 8.8).
13. Wojtyla, *Love and Responsibility,* p. 134.
14. Why, for Wojtyla, is a severe test of love the death of sexual desire? Given his project, it makes sense: "There exists . . . a problem which can be described as that of 'introducing love into love'. The word as first used in that phrase signifies the love which is the subject of the greatest commandment, while in its second use it means all that takes shape between a man and a woman on the basis of the sexual urge. We could look at it the other way round and say that there exists a problem of changing the second type of love (sexual love) into the first, the love of which the New Testament speaks" (ibid., p. 17). I find it strange that Wojtyla sets up this dichotomy between agape and sexuality, as if these two exhaust the field. Is personal love part of the "all" that occurs between x and y "on the basis of the sexual urge"?

I smell a Freudo-Reichian mouse here. Now we see why he says that after "sexual values" are gone, *nothing* remains except the value "of the person."

15. Ibid., p. 135.
16. Ibid., pp. 42, 79, 121, 133.
17. When Wojtyla argues that the exclusivity of marital love ("monogamy") entails indissolubility (ibid., p. 211), he apparently means that marital love is strictly constant.
18. Ibid., p. 212.
19. Kierkegaard commented sarcastically on "Christians" relying on the escape clause of Paul's dictum: the priest who gladly marries a couple on the oath of the New Testament is like the policeman who blesses a crook about to commit a theft (*Attack on "Christendom"*, p. 220).
20. "We want continuity [because] we are aware of being constituted by the perceptions of others, particularly . . . of those who love or hate us" (Amelie Rorty, "The Historicity of Psychological Attitudes," p. 405).
21. Brown, *Analyzing Love*, p. 56.
22. Newton-Smith, "A Conceptual Investigation of Love," p. 132.
23. This is Lawrence Blum's term (*Friendship, Altruism and Morality*, p. 77). Recall the notion "conditional unconditionality" (8.8).
24. Carole King, *Tapestry* (Ode Records, 1971). The word "still" is not in the title but in the lyrics (by Gerri Goffin and Carole King, 1960).
25. Vlastos, "Justice and Equality," pp. 44–45.
26. Ibid., p. 43.
27. Ibid., p. 44.
28. For still other analyses, see 13.5.
29. This idea appears also in Plato; Pausanias says "the lover of a noble nature remains its lover for life, because the thing to which he cleaves is constant" (Hamilton, *Symposium* 183e–184a). Groden's translation is more Aristotelian.
30. A few hundred years later Jesus' message would be: since he is unable to save him, he all the more strongly ties his connections with him. *Pace* Wojtyla, he "loves all the more," or Kierkegaard, he loves the unlovable.
31. Martha Nussbaum thinks that "it is not clear whether Aristotle really wants to accord to character the status of an essential property." But Aristotle's treatment of the good y who turns evil upsets one of her arguments: "His discussions of character-change certainly permit some changes without a change of identity, and he never discusses sudden and sweeping changes" (*The Fragility of Goodness*, p. 498, n. 33).
32. See Badhwar, "Friends as Ends in Themselves," p. 14, n. 27.
33. Kosman, "Platonic Love," pp. 56–57.
34. See 8.2 and chap. 1, n. 69 and n. 71.
35. Brown, *Analyzing Love*, p. 105; Solomon, *Love*, p. 163.
36. In Burton, *Written With Love*, p. 35.
37. Nussbaum, *The Fragility of Goodness*, p. 359. She cites *Nicomachean Ethics* 1099b3–4 and *Rhetoric* 1381b1. But in the first, Aristotle only says "a man who is very ugly . . . cannot be classified as altogether happy." And in the second, he only says that friendship is likely to be directed at those who are "clean and pure in appearance and dress."

38. Aristotle expects friends to live together, so x's noticing that y is not clean in appearance might warn x that the x-y household would not be neat. But this does not rule out two virtuous slobs from being friends. Perhaps Aristotle disagrees that ugliness has nothing to do with character. Some ugliness may be due to character defects (y's potbelly is not an incidental feature; it grew out of y's gluttony). But not all ugliness can be understood this way. Recall Alcibiades' swooning over the physically ugly yet virtuous Socrates. (Thanks to Ed Johnson.)

39. See my "Physical Attractiveness and Unfair Discrimination." The nonsense written on this topic is astonishing. Listen to Roger Scruton (*Sexual Desire*, p. 70): "It is well known [*sic*] that a pretty face may compensate for much bodily ugliness . . . [but] a beautiful body . . . will always [*sic*] be rendered repulsive by an ugly face, and can certainly never compensate for it." If that isn't hilarious, consider the sequel: "While I can fall in love on seeing another's portrait, I could not have the same reaction to a photograph of . . . sexual parts." (Is this autobiographical?) "An excitement which concentrates upon the sexual organs, . . . which seeks, as it were, to by-pass the preliminary interest in the face, . . . is perverted." Freud mildly agrees (*Civilization and Its Discontents*, p. 30): "The genitals themselves, the sight of which is always [*sic*] exciting, are nevertheless hardly ever judged to be beautiful; . . . beauty seems, instead, to attach to . . . secondary sexual characteristics," presumably including Scruton's face. Didn't lovers in Vienna in 1910 tell each other that they had a "beautiful cock" or a "beautiful cunt"? (*Oder auch, schön Schwanz.*) For Scruton, the other's face grabs our attention and makes us sense him as a subject, but for Ortega y Gasset the face has the opposite effect (*On Love*, p. 148): "The excessive perfection of a face encourages us to objectify its possessor and to keep at a distance from her in order to admire her as an aesthetic object."

40. Ann Landers, *The Times-Picayune* (New Orleans, La.), April 26, 1988, p. D-6.

41. In "Emotion and Sentiment," C. D. Broad argues, instead, that love based on the physical has the advantage. Regarding "emotions which are felt towards other persons in respect of their . . . mental" properties, "one cannot literally *perceive* another person's mind or . . . his dispositions or his motives"; hence "we are very liable to be mistaken in our beliefs about them, and thus to have misplaced emotions" (p. 209). But if knowing the mental is more difficult than the physical, this would only justify loving first on the basis of the physical and later on the basis of less easily known mental qualities. (By the way, it sometimes works the other way around.) What is odd is Broad's claim that mental qualities cannot be perceived and therefore we are *very liable* to be wrong about them. His Cartesianism entails that it is not merely difficult, but impossible, to know the mental.

42. Newton-Smith, "A Conceptual Investigation of Love," p. 121.

43. I wonder if Newton-Smith's claim that love is properly grounded on the essential is consistent with his solution to Gellner's paradox (4.2): x loves y, who has S, but not z, who also has S, *because* y was the first to elicit x's passion. Y's being the first to elicit passion in x is something extrinsic to or accidental about y.

44. In Plato's theory, x will lose interest in (say) y's beautiful body when x realizes that this beauty is an inferior sort of beauty; in this case x changes—that is, loses interest in one manifestation of The Beautiful—without becoming a different person w. And notice that x's love for the y who has a beautiful body will end *before* y loses y's

beauty. There is no hint in the *Symposium* (see 210b–c) that x's love for y is not constant because the basis of x's love, y's beauty, has faded; rather, x's love is not constant because x realizes that this beauty will fade.

45. McTaggart, *The Nature of Existence*, vol. 2, p. 154; see 13.10.
46. Outka, *Agape*, p. 11.
47. Quoted by Lesser, "Love and Lust," p. 52.
48. Hamlyn even argues that erosic love will be more constant than agapic, since "epistemic factors . . . are . . . the only thing that can give love . . . stability" (*Perception, Learning and the Self*, p. 299).
49. Kierkegaard, *Works of Love*, p. 76.
50. Ibid., p. 47, italics deleted.
51. Compare *Either/Or*, vol. 2, p. 141, and *Works of Love*, pp. 156–157.
52. Kierkegaard, *Either/Or*, vol. 2, pp. 148–149.
53. See Hannay, *Kierkegaard*, p. 275.
54. Wojtyla must be an optimist; he thinks that the will is "the most important element" in love (*Love and Responsibility*, p. 90).
55. Fromm, *The Art of Loving*, p. 33.
56. Galston, *Justice and the Human Good*, p. 152.
57. Kierkegaard, *Works of Love*, p. 124.
58. Ibid., p. 283.
59. Ibid., p. 117. See C. S. Lewis, *The Four Loves*, p. 166.
60. Kierkegaard, *Works of Love*, p. 124.
61. Ibid., p. 118.
62. Ibid., p. 73. But should not a proponent of agape emphasize *its* power? Why isn't agape the water to the fire that is eros? See n. 14, above.
63. *Papirer*, XI² A152, italics added, quoted by Mark Taylor, "Love and Forms of Spirit," p. 108. See Collins (*The Mind of Kierkegaard*, p. 76): "He came to regard married love as that component in ethical existence which converts it into an independent, self-satisfied sphere, and hence which serves as an obstacle to the full development of the existential dialectic. This is the basic theoretical reason behind his later disparaging attitude toward marriage and women." According to Vlastos, there is a similar theme in the *Symposium*: "Conjugal love, however intense, would still remain in Plato's scheme a spiritual dead end" ("Sex in Platonic Love," in *Platonic Studies*, p. 41). In this case a permanent human relationship is inferior to, and would block movement toward, a "transcendental marriage" with Absolute Beauty.
64. But see Kierkegaard on Paul, n. 19, above.
65. Kierkegaard, *Works of Love*, p. 141. X's *spouse* being "first and foremost" x's *neighbor* seems contradictory: "spouse" denotes a preferential relationship, while "neighbor" denotes a nonpreferential relationship.
66. Kierkegaard, *Either/Or*, vol. 2, p. 58.
67. Kierkegaard, *Works of Love*, p. 314.
68. Williams, *The New York Review of Books*, April 25, 1985, p. 37.
69. "Love has a tendency to grow . . . , while [sexual] desire has a tendency to wither. . . . Eventually desire is replaced by . . . trust and companionship. . . . The problem is, how to shut out the third party who will [arouse] . . . a new desire"

(Scruton, *Sexual Desire,* p. 244). Why not invite the third in, rather than shut him or her out?

70. See my essay "The Unity of Romantic Love."

CHAPTER ELEVEN: RECIPROCITY

1. On "reciprocal" versus "mutual" sexual desire, see Sara Ketchum, "The Good, the Bad and the Perverted," p. 147.
2. We can render "love is reciprocal" as:

$$(x)(y)(t)[xLyt \leftrightarrow yLxt]$$

or as:

$$(x)(y)(A)(t)[((-xAyt \text{ v } -yAxt) \& (x \neq y)) \rightarrow A \neq L].$$

3. Aristotle, *Nicomachean Ethics* 1155b27–33.
4. Ehman, "Personal Love," p. 123.
5. Ibid., p. 136.
6. Wojtyla, *Love and Responsibility,* p. 85; see also p. 86.
7. Fried, *An Anatomy of Values,* p. 79.
8. Kierkegaard, *Stages on Life's Way,* p. 56.
9. Kierkegaard, *Works of Love,* p. 66; see also p. 361, n. 44.
10. Ibid., p. 68.
11. Ibid., pp. 320–322.
12. Wojtyla, *Love and Responsibility,* p. 129.
13. Fromm, *The Art of Loving,* p. 21. See also Peck: "Love . . . is invariably . . . a reciprocal phenomenon. . . . Value creates value. Love begets love" (*The Road Less Traveled,* pp. 123, 126); and Vacek: "By its very essence [love] evokes . . . love from the loved one" ("Scheler's Phenomenology of Love," p. 176).
14. Marx, *Early Writings,* p. 379.
15. Kierkegaard, *Works of Love,* pp. 320–321. Kierkegaard is more Marxist than the early Marx: "Deception . . . play[s] the master, just as in the commercial world. . . . One makes a transaction of love; one pays out his love in exchange, but one gets no love in exchange—yes, in this way one is deceived" (p. 223)—instead of impotent. This is the later Marx's Moneybags, who fools wage-laborers into thinking they are receiving equal value for their contribution to production.
16. Baier, "The Ambiguous Limits of Desire," p. 55.
17. Fisher, "Reason, Emotion, and Love," p. 197.
18. Newton-Smith, "A Conceptual Investigation of Love," pp. 126–127.
19. Fisher, "Reason, Emotion, and Love," p. 197.
20. Aldous Huxley, *The Perennial Philosophy,* p. 83.
21. Ibid.
22. "[L]ove proper . . . exists only between living beings who are alike in power" (Hegel, "Love," p. 304).
23. Firestone, *The Dialectic of Sex,* p. 152.
24. Respectively: Nietzsche, *The Joyful Wisdom V,* pp. 321–323; Fromm, *The Art of Loving,* pp. 7 and 13; Wojtyla, *Love and Responsibility,* pp. 81, 107, 110.
25. See Lewis, *The Four Loves,* pp. 105–107.

26. Fromm, *The Art of Loving,* p. 18.
27. In abandoning all y's needs and desires out of love for x, y does not also abandon the desire to benefit x; otherwise y would no longer be altruistic—nor would y any longer love x.
28. See Nietzsche, *The Joyful Wisdom* (p. 322): "If both renounced themselves out of love, there would result—well, I don't know what, perhaps a *horror vacui?*"
29. Ibid., p. 321.
30. See Armstrong, "Friendship," p. 215; Newton-Smith, "A Conceptual Investigation of Love," pp. 114–115, 132.
31. Fill in the blank three hundred ways, but do not forget sex. One standard disagreement in the folklore of heterosexuality is illustrated by a cartoon by Joseph Farris that appeared at least ten years ago in *The New Yorker,* in which a man holds a sign "No sex, no love" and a woman holds up "No love, no sex." One, of course, must give in—to power?
32. Hannay, *Kierkegaard,* pp. 264–265.
33. What if it were true, as a matter of human psychology, that everyone's love was conditional on reciprocity? The pattern of human love would be exactly that entailed by the thesis that love is conceptually reciprocal: there would be cases of xLy and yLx, and cases of −xLy and −yLx, but nothing else. So if love's being conditional on reciprocity were a universal psychological truth, the thesis that love is conceptually reciprocal would *look* true.
34. Ehman, "Personal Love," p. 123.
35. Hannay, *Kierkegaard,* pp. 264–265.
36. What is implied about reciprocity by the theory of difficulties, according to which we love exclusively and unconstantly because we succumb to the obstacles to loving otherwise (10.3)? Which is psychologically more difficult, loving with or without reciprocity? Intuitively, it is difficult for x to love y if y does not love x; hence, our loves will tend to be exclusive, unconstant, and reciprocal. Yet it can be argued that loving with reciprocity is *more* difficult; one must deal on a daily basis with a real person.
37. See Vlastos, "The Individual as an Object of Love in Plato," pp. 29–30, n. 28.

CHAPTER TWELVE: CONCERN AND THE MORALITY OF LOVE

1. Kierkegaard, *Either/Or,* vol. 2, p. 23.
2. Nabokov, *Lolita,* p. 259.
3. Brown, *Analyzing Love,* pp. 29, 30, italics added.
4. See Nakhnikian, "Love in Human Reason," pp. 303–305. The inclusion of the self within the scope of neighbor-love is denied by Kierkegaard (*Works of Love*): x can be expected to be (overly) concerned for *x* naturally (hence, self-concern, unlike neighbor-love, cannot be a duty); practicing neighbor-love therefore demands self-renunciation.
5. This self-love can be erosic or agapic: x might love (that is, respect, like, accept) *x* because *x* has valuable qualities, or x might love *x* because *x*'s nature is to love. In agapic style, x may find *x*'s properties attractive because x loves *x;* or in erosic style x

may love *x* for some of *x*'s properties and find other properties of *x* valuable because x loves *x*. When x agapically loves *x*, x loves *x* regardless of *x*'s defects and in spite of *x*'s sins, which x might see clearly; or x's loving *x* may be an erosic function of a comparison between *x*'s attractive and unattractive properties. If the latter outweigh the former, x might dislike *x*.

6. Vannoy, *Sex Without Love*, p. 137. I replaced "beloved" twice with "lover."
7. See Rawls, *A Theory of Justice*, pp. 396, 440.
8. Nygren, *Agape and Eros*, pp. 175–177; Vlastos, "The Individual as an Object of Love in Plato," p. 30. On Nygren's view, Plato's eros is directed at that which has value *because* eros is (more fundamentally) acquisitive (*Agape and Eros*, pp. 176, 180). But if we characterize erosic love, instead, as love grounded on the object's value, it does not follow from x's loving y erosically that x is acquisitive; it is false to say that eros is acquisitive *because* it is a response to value. For defenses of Plato against Nygren and Vlastos, see Brentlinger, "The Nature of Love" and Levy, "The Definition of Love in Plato's *Symposium*."
9. Nakhnikian, "Love in Human Reason," p. 294.
10. Vlastos, "The Individual as an Object of Love in Plato," p. 33.
11. X's desire must be "effective," that is, not merely one desire in x's repertoire of passing fancies but a desire that motivates x to act. (See Frankfurt, "Freedom of the Will and the Concept of a Person," pp. 9–10.) Even more precisely, we should say that x has an "effective disposition"; x *would* act if x could. This is why x's being in prison prevents x from acting but does not negate x's love.
12. Nakhnikian, "Love in Human Reason," p. 297.
13. Fried, *An Anatomy of Values*, p. 142.
14. See Octavius' love for Ann in Shaw's *Man and Superman* (iv, p. 195).
15. Hannay, *Kierkegaard*, p. 265.
16. Wojtyla, *Love and Responsibility*, p. 138.
17. Kierkegaard, *Works of Love*, pp. 113, 124. See 10.7.
18. Ibid., p. 36. (See Lindström, "A Contribution to the Interpretation of Kierkegaard's Book The Works of Love," p. 5.) Kierkegaard should add: love God in unconditional obedience, even if what He demands of you may seem harmful to others. Abraham is the knight of faith (*Fear and Trembling*), and one's son being first and foremost one's neighbor is not incompatible with intending to kill him.
19. Wojtyla, *Love and Responsibility*, pp. 245–247, 250–252. Wojtyla's claim that if x loves y, x makes a gift of (surrenders) x's self to y (11.2) must not, then, be interpreted to mean that x is concerned for y carte blanche.
20. Fisher, "Reason, Emotion, and Love," p. 196.
21. Ibid., p. 202, n. 8.
22. Ibid., p. 200.
23. Ibid., p. 196.
24. Ibid., p. 202, n. 8.
25. Fisher similarly claims that hatred is "desiring for him whatever he wants not to have, for the reason that he desires not to have it" (ibid., p. 196). This analogue to version (i) of carte blanche will not do, because y might desire not to have something, yet it is good for y; and y might desire to have something, yet it is bad for y. In the latter case, x can harm y by promoting y's having that which y desires but which is bad for y; and in the former, x's promoting for y what y desires not to have

will not harm y, since it is good for y. Instead, the analysis might be analogous to version (ii): if x hates y, x desires the bad for y in y's sense of "bad." But why rule out x's desiring for y, out of hate for y, what is bad for y in x's sense? Here, too, x faces a conflict: to do what is bad for y in y's sense (which might be good for y in x's sense) or to do what is bad for y in x's sense. Can x harm y only if x does what y sees as harmful? No. From the fact that y might not recognize that what x does to y is harmful, it does not follow that y has not been harmed. What likely follows is that x will not have the joy of seeing y recognize x's hatred. X will have to find x's joy, instead, in the silent knowledge that x has harmed y. Hence, if x does for y what is good for y in x's sense but not in y's, it does not follow that x has not shown concern for y, but only that y might not recognize x's intention to benefit y.

26. Ibid., p. 202, n. 8.
27. Ibid., p. 196. He continues: "The blinding power of love . . . is on my analysis to be expected, and so confirms it." I think, however, that the expression "the blinding power of love" refers specifically to the lover's idealizing the beloved, not to the different phenomenon of the lover's incorporating the beloved's beliefs.
28. See Nussbaum on Aristotle (*The Fragility of Goodness,* pp. 362–363); this is a reason for loving the virtuous *because* they are virtuous.
29. Newton-Smith, "A Conceptual Investigation of Love," p. 120.
30. Ibid., p. 121.
31. Ehman, "Personal Love," p. 124–125. Jesse Kalin also claims that "love does not recognize justice as morally central and hence the two are essentially incompatible." His argument is identical to Ehman's ("Lies, Secrets, and Love," pp. 261–262).
32. Sankowski, "Love and Moral Obligation," p. 105. See also Scheffler, "Morality's Demands and Their Limits," p. 537.
33. Telfer, "Friendship," p. 238.
34. Annis, "The Meaning, Value, and Duties of Friendship," p. 351.
35. Nelly Dean's Socratic questioning of Catherine Earnshaw (in Emily Brontë's *Wuthering Heights,* pp. 118–122) reduces the poor girl to a state worse than Glaucon or Agathon, exposing her utter confusion about reasons for love and reasons for marriage.
36. See Kierkegaard (chap. 4, n. 10, above).
37. Mrs. Newhart grilled Michael (the way Nelly Dean grilled Catherine) about his love for the wealthy Stephanie ("The Newhart Show," May 12, 1986): "*Mrs. Newhart:* Michael, why do you love Stephanie? *Michael:* She dresses well, she's pretty, she has that cute little button nose. *Mrs. Newhart:* Would you love her if she weren't pretty? *Michael:* Date a dog? Not in this lifetime! *Mrs. Newhart:* If she was poor? *Michael:* Sure, as long as she dressed nicely. *Mrs. Newhart:* Michael, you're not a golddigger. Just superficial." Later Michael tells Stephanie about Mrs. Newhart's conclusion, which makes Stephanie—herself superficial—deliriously happy. "Nothing is better evidence of a man's true inclinations than the character of those whom he loves" (Rousseau, *The Confessions,* book 7, p. 264; see Ortega y Gasset, *On Love,* p. 86–87).
38. See Diorio, "Sex, Love, and Justice," pp. 231, 234.
39. See *A Theory of Justice,* in which Rawls discusses the goods of "personal affection and friendship" (at p. 425).

40. See Wasserstrom, "Is Adultery Immoral?" Thanks to Norton Nelkin for discussion of this issue.

CHAPTER THIRTEEN: THE OBJECT OF LOVE

1. "Yeats was," says Willard Gaylin, "absolutely correct. What does craving to be loved for ourselves—as distinguished from our traits . . . —what does that mean? There is no inner self independent of . . . our character" (*Rediscovering Love*, p. 122). He is arguing that if being loved "for ourselves" means being loved independently of properties, being loved "for ourselves" is impossible: no basis or object of love remains once our properties are dismissed. But if so, Yeats is not "absolutely correct," for then not even God could love a human "for herself." (Note this too narrow and incorrect interpretation of Yeats: only God could love this particular person for herself alone; or a human could love *this* woman only for her blondeness—since she in particular has no other merit.)
2. De Sousa, "Self-deceptive Emotions," pp. 694–695.
3. Algernon Sidney, "Of Love," in de la Mare, *Love*, p. 252.
4. Thus, when Robert Kraut imagines that Linus' blanket *changes* from being irreplaceable to replaceable for him ("Love *De Re*," p. 428), Kraut is imagining that Linus is temporarily, not absolutely, nonfungibly attached to it.
5. Raymond Carver, *What We Talk About When We Talk About Love*, p. 145.
6. Brown, *Analyzing Love*, p. 24.
7. Badhwar, "Friends as Ends in Themselves," p. 1.
8. Ibid., p. 14; see also p. 3.
9. Ibid., p. 15, n. 29.
10. Ibid., p. 14.
11. Nagel, "Sexual Perversion," p. 80.
12. Scruton, *Sexual Desire*, p. 78. For a similar argument that distinguishes love (an intentional, cognitive phenomenon) from "lust" (a purely sensory phenomenon), on the grounds that the former more clearly involves the possibility of mistakes about its object, see J. M. Stafford, "On Distinguishing Between Love and Lust," pp. 299–301.
13. *Sexual Desire*, p. 163.
14. Ibid., p. 76; on p. 103 Scruton says something similar about love.
15. Ibid., pp. 136–137; see also p. 391: our loves "contain a vast metaphysical flaw," the belief in the transcendental self.
16. Ibid., p. 104.
17. About the "metaphysical flaw" (see above, n. 15) Scruton says: "Although there are such faulty layers in our intentional understanding, there is still a difference in reality between those objects which can, and those which cannot, sustain the transcendental illusions which are built upon them" (ibid., p. 391). I guess he means that there is a real difference between a person and a tree, such that deceiving ourselves into believing that a person is a transcendental self is easier than doing so for trees. (At least for contemporary, Western, enlightened persons?)
18. Nussbaum, *The Fragility of Goodness*, p. 179.

19. John Brentlinger claims that the complaint "you don't love *me*, you just love my *G*" is "perennial but not very bright," at least if meant as a demand that the lover "be indifferent to *all* the beloved's qualities ("The Nature of Love," pp. 122–123). To be sensible, he implies, the complaint must be only a demand that x love y for the right rather than the wrong qualities. But note that this is *not* what the bright blonde woman in Yeats' poem means; clearly she wants agapic love.

20. Singer, *The Nature of Love*, vol. 1, p. 69.

21. Singer attributes the fallacious argument to Socrates during the banquet. But in this section of the *Symposium* Diotima is instructing the young Socrates.

22. Singer, *The Nature of Love*, vol. 1, pp. 68–69.

23. This is Hamilton, the translation Singer used. Other translations agree.

24. Vlastos, "The Individual as an Object of Love in Plato," p. 31. It is curious that for Vlastos this is "the cardinal flaw" in Plato's view, since he had already said that "Plato's theory is not, and is not meant to be, about personal love for persons" (p. 26).

25. Ibid., p. 33, n. 100.

26. Ibid., p. 33. See 10.4 for my discussion of Vlastos' account of love for the "individual" as agapic personal love.

27. Price, "Loving Persons Platonically," pp. 32–33.

28. Price derived from his analysis the conclusion that if x loves y (only) for y's physical properties, x does not love y "for himself" since clause (b) in particular "is seldom met by loving another for his appearance." (It hardly ever happens that x values y's figure *because* y values y's figure.) Thus, if condition (b) is rejected and we still want to claim that x's loving y for y's physical properties is not x's loving y "the person," we have to invoke other considerations—for example, these properties logically cannot be the sole basis of love, or a love based solely on them is inferior, or this basis shows the superficiality of the lover and his love.

29. Lyons, *Emotion*, p. 74. Hence, x's emotion at first sight for y can *be* love, but not always love for "the person" (2.2).

30. Rubin, *Intimate Strangers*, p. 68, and Bellah et al., *Habits of the Heart*, p. 91.

31. Ignatieff, "Lodged in the Heart and Memory," p. 112.

32. Vlastos, "The Individual as an Object of Love," p. 30, n. 88.

33. Solomon, *Love: Emotion, Myth and Metaphor*, chap. 13.

34. Ibid., p. 130.

35. Ibid., p. 132.

36. Ibid., p. 133.

37. Ibid., p. 131.

38. Brown, *Analyzing Love*, p. 105.

39. Ibid., p. 106.

40. Ibid., pp. 45, 105–107.

41. Ibid., p. 108.

42. Warner, "Love, Self, and Plato's *Symposium*," pp. 337–339.

43. An example of what is incoherent, if Warner and Diotima are right that a person is just her properties: "Romeo loves Juliet not for the values . . . she possesses . . . but for herself, without determining in advance the actuality . . . of any such values" (Vacek, "Scheler's Phenomenology of Love," p. 163).

44. From (i) x loves y and (ii) y is the single property P, it does follow that x, in loving y,

is loving a discrete property. But there is no earthly reason to suppose (ii). The inference has an unearthly version: x loves y, y is a transcendental self, so x loves a transcendental self. This inference should neither console nor threaten anyone.

45. Nancy Sherman, "Aristotle on Friendship and the Shared Life," p. 602.

46. This is no. 688 in Krailsheimer's edition. Céline Léon (Grove City College) prepared the translation for me from *Oeuvres Complètes,* no. 306 (Paris: Editions Gallimard, 1954, p. 1165); hers is not appreciably different from the translations of Krailsheimer and W. F. Trotter (*Great Books of the Western World,* vol. 33). The translation quoted by Scruton (*Sexual Desire,* p. 98), which he attributes to J. M. Cohen, is odd; it includes a line that is not in the French: "Or, if one loves the person, it must be said that it is the totality of the qualities which constitute the person." This dubious addition is not entailed by what Pascal wrote; indeed, it seems to contradict the point Pascal is pressing on us in this passage. In *Pensées de Blaise Pascal,* vol. 2 (Paris: Librairie Hachette, 1904), Leon Brunschvicg wrote: "This fragment was not in the edition of 1670; in publishing it, Port-Royal suppressed the title and replaced the last paragraph by a conciliatory thought: 'Or, if one loves the person, we must say that it is the assemblage of qualities which makes the person'" (p. 242). Thanks to Ed Johnson for digging out and translating Brunschvicg.

47. Except for Pascal's God, as Yeats' theologian proved?

48. Here Scruton's translation inserts the line I mentioned in n. 46, above.

49. Singer thinks that "in reaching" his "dire conclusion . . . Pascal assumes that a person is something apart from his 'qualities'" (*The Nature of Love,* vol. 1, p. 94). No. Pascal is arguing, not assuming, that a person is something beyond properties (even if the argument is bad).

50. See Brown, *Analyzing Love,* pp. 20–22; Lyons, *Emotion,* pp. 112–114.

51. See Julia Annas, "Plato and Aristotle on Friendship and Altruism," p. 537; L. A. Kosman, "Platonic Love," p. 60; Vlastos, "The Individual as an Object of Love," p. 34.

52. Vacek, "Scheler's Phenomenology of Love," p. 160.

53. *Either/Or,* vol. 1, "Diapsalmata," p. 25.

54. Ralph Pape, "Girls We Have Known," in Finamore, *First Love,* p. 31.

55. J. M. E. McTaggart, *The Nature of Existence,* vol. 2 (book 5, chap. 41), pp. 152, 153.

56. Ibid., p. 151, italics added.

57. Ibid.; see also p. 152.

58. See Diorio, "Sex, Love, and Justice," p. 233.

59. *The Nature of Existence,* vol. 2, p. 154, italics added.

60. More precisely: "I propose to use the word ["love"] for a species of liking. . . . Love is a liking . . . towards persons, and which is intense and passionate" (ibid., pp. 147, 148). Therefore, in the rest of the passage I quote in the text, what McTaggart says about liking applies to love.

61. Ibid., p. 144, n. 1.

62. Ibid., p. 162, n. 1.

63. Singer claims, rightly I think, that McTaggart's arguments for his thesis are only restatements; see *The Nature of Love,* vol. 3, pp. 397–401.

64. McTaggart's example: "We do not . . . condemn B for being determined to love C

rather than D by the fact that C is beautiful and that D is not" (*The Nature of Existence,* vol. 2, p. 152, n. 1).

65. Ibid., pp. 152–153.
66. Ibid., p. 154, n. 1.
67. See Pitcher, "Emotion," p. 331; Shaffer, "An Assessment of Emotion," p. 164.
68. On love as a sense of union, see *The Nature of Existence,* vol. 2, pp. 150–151; for love as a feeling, see pp. 147, 148, 150, 151.
69. "The difference . . . [between love and] benevolence is fundamental, since benevolence is not an emotion at all, but a desire—a desire to do good to some person, or to all persons" (ibid., p. 148).

BIBLIOGRAPHY

Allen, Woody. *Getting Even* (New York: Vintage, 1978).

———. *Without Feathers* (New York: Ballantine, 1983).

Annas, Julia. "Plato and Aristotle on Friendship and Altruism." *Mind* 86 (1977): 532–554.

Annis, David B. "Emotion, Love and Friendship." *International Journal of Applied Philosophy* 4, no. 2 (1988): 1–7.

———. "The Meaning, Value, and Duties of Friendship." *American Philosophical Quarterly* 24 (1987): 349–356.

Aristotle. *Nicomachean Ethics*. Translated by Martin Ostwald (Indianapolis: Bobbs-Merrill, 1962).

Armstrong, Robert L. "Friendship." *Journal of Value Inquiry* 19 (1985): 211–216.

Auden, W. H. *Another Time* (London: Faber and Faber, 1940).

Augustine. *Confessions* (New York: Penguin, 1961).

Austen, Jane. *Pride and Prejudice* (New York: Avenel, 1985).

Badhwar, Neera. "Friends as Ends in Themselves." *Philosophy and Phenomenological Research* 48 (1987): 1–23.

Baier, Annette. "The Ambiguous Limits of Desire." In *The Ways of Desire,* edited by Joel Marks (Chicago: Precedent, 1986), pp. 39–61.

———. "Caring About Caring: A Reply to Frankfurt." *Synthese* 53 (1982): 273–290.

Balint, Michael. "Critical Notes on the Theory of the Pregenital Organizations of the Libido" (1935). In *Primary Love and Psycho-Analytic Technique* (New York: Liveright, 1965), pp. 37–58.

Balzac, Honoré de. "Sarrasine." In *The Works of Honoré de Balzac,* vol. 16 (Philadelphia: Avil, 1901).

Barry, Joseph. *French Lovers* (New York: Arbor House, 1987).

Barthes, Roland. *A Lover's Discourse* (New York: Hill and Wang, 1978).

———. *S/Z* (New York: Hill and Wang, 1974).

Bayles, Michael D. "Marriage, Love, and Procreation." In *Philosophy and Sex,* 2d ed., edited by R. Baker and F. Elliston (Buffalo: Prometheus, 1984), pp. 130–145.

Bayley, John. *The Character of Love* (New York: Collier Books, 1963).

Beauvoir, Simone de. *The Second Sex* (New York: Bantam, 1961).

357

Bellah, Robert N., Richard Madsen, William M. Sullivan, Ann Swidler, and Steven M. Tipton. *Habits of the Heart* (Berkeley: University of California Press, 1985).

Berger, Peter, and Hansfried Kellner. "Marriage and the Construction of Reality." *Diogenes* no. 46 (Summer 1964): 1–24.

Berlin, Isaiah. "On the Pursuit of the Ideal." *New York Review of Books,* March 17, 1988, 11–18.

Bernstein, Mark. "Love, Particularity, and Selfhood." *Southern Journal of Philosophy* 23 (1986): 287–293.

Berryman, John. *Berryman's Sonnets* (New York: Farrar, Straus and Giroux, 1967).

Blum, Lawrence. *Friendship, Altruism and Morality* (London: Routledge and Kegan Paul, 1980).

Brentlinger, John A. "The Nature of Love," afterword to *The Symposium of Plato,* edited by J. A. Brentlinger (Amherst: University of Massachusetts Press, 1970), pp. 113–129.

Broad, C. D. "Emotion and Sentiment." *Journal of Aesthetics and Art Criticism* 13 (1954): 203–214.

Brontë, Emily. *Wuthering Heights* (New York: Penguin, 1965).

Brown, Robert. *Analyzing Love* (Cambridge: Cambridge University Press, 1987).

Burch, Robert. "The Commandability of Pathological Love." *Southwestern Journal of Philosophy* 3, no. 3 (1972): 131–140.

Burton, Peter Paul, ed. *Written With Love* (New York: Bantam, 1971).

Buscaglia, Leo. *Love* (New York: Ballantine, 1982).

Butler, Joseph. *Five Sermons* (Indianapolis: Hackett, 1983).

Byrne, Donn, and Sarah K. Murnen. "Maintaining Loving Relationships." In *The Psychology of Love,* edited by R. Sternberg and M. Barnes (New Haven: Yale University Press, 1988), pp. 293–310.

Capellanus, Andreas. *The Art of Courtly Love.* Edited by F. W. Locke and translated by John Jay Perry (New York: Frederick Ungar, 1957).

Carver, Raymond. *What We Talk About When We Talk About Love* (New York: Vintage, 1982).

Collins, James. *The Mind of Kierkegaard* (Princeton: Princeton University Press, 1983).

Comfort, Alex. *Nature and Human Nature* (London: Weidenfeld and Nicolson, 1966).

Davidson, Donald. "Actions, Reasons, and Causes." In *Essays on Actions and Events* (Oxford: Clarendon Press, 1980), pp. 3–19.

De la Mare, Walter, ed. *Love* (New York: William Morrow, 1946).

De Rougemont, Denis. *Love in the Western World* (New York: Harper and Row, 1974).

De Sales, Francis. *The Love of God* (London: Sands and Co., n.d.).

Descartes, René. *Descartes: Philosophical Letters,* edited by Anthony Kenny (Oxford: Oxford University Press, 1970).

———. *Meditations* (Indianapolis: Bobbs-Merrill, 1951).

———. *The Philosophical Writings of Descartes,* vol. 1. Translated by J. Cottingham, R. Stoothoff, and D. Murdoch (Cambridge: Cambridge University Press, 1985).

De Sousa, Ronald. "Desire and Time." In *The Ways of Desire,* edited by Joel Marks (Chicago: Precedent, 1986), pp. 83–100.

———. "Self-deceptive Emotions." *Journal of Philosophy* 75 (1978): 684–697.

Dion, K. L., and K. K. Dion. "Romantic Love: Individual and Cultural Perspectives." In *The Psychology of Love,* edited by R. Sternberg and M. Barnes (New Haven: Yale University Press, 1988), pp. 264–289.

Diorio, Joseph. "Sex, Love, and Justice: A Problem in Moral Education." *Educational Theory* 31 (1982): 225–235.

Dominitz, Ben. *How to Find the Love of Your Life: 90 Days to a Permanent Relationship* (Rocklin, Calif.: Prima, 1986).

Donne, John. *The Complete English Poems* (Harmondsworth, Eng.: Penguin, 1971).

Downie, R. S. "Forgiveness." *The Philosophical Quarterly* 15 (1965): 128–134.

Dunbar, William. *The Poems of William Dunbar* (London: Faber and Faber, 1932).

Ehman, Robert. "Personal Love." *The Personalist* 49 (1968): 116–141.

———. "Personal Love and Individual Value." *Journal of Value Inquiry* 10 (1976): 91–105.

Eliot, Charles, ed. *Prefaces and Prologues to Famous Books.* Vol. 39 of *Harvard Classics* (New York: P. F. Collier and Sons, 1910).

Eliot, George. *Daniel Deronda* (New York: New American Library, 1979).

Ellis, Albert. "A Study of Human Love Relationships." *Journal of Genetic Psychology* 75 (1949): 61–71.

England, R. W., Jr. "Images of Love and Courtship in Family-Magazine Fiction." *Marriage and Family Living* 20 (1960): 162–165.

Evans, Gareth. "The Causal Theory of Names." *Proceedings of the Aristotelian Society,* Supplementary Vol. 47 (1973): 187–208.

Finamore, Roy, ed. *First Love* (New York: Stewart, Tabori and Chang, 1986).

Findlay, J. N. "The Justification of Attitudes." *Mind* 63 (1954): 145–161.

Firestone, Shulamith. *The Dialectic of Sex* (New York: Bantam, 1971).

Fisher, Mark. "Love as Process." Paper presented at a meeting of the Society for the Philosophy of Sex and Love, Washington, D.C., December 1985.

———. "Reason, Emotion, and Love." *Inquiry* 20 (1977): 189–203.

Foucault, Michel. *The Use of Pleasure* (New York: Pantheon, 1985).

Frankfurt, Harry G. "Freedom of the Will and the Concept of a Person." *Journal of Philosophy* 68 (1971): 5–20.

———. "The Importance of What We Care About," *Synthese* 53 (1982): 257–272.

Freud, Ernst L., ed. *Letters of Sigmund Freud* (New York: Basic Books, 1975).

Freud, Sigmund. *Civilization and Its Discontents* (New York: W. W. Norton, 1961).

———. *Three Essays on the Theory of Sexuality* (New York: Basic Books, 1975).

Fried, Charles. *An Anatomy of Values* (Cambridge: Harvard University Press, 1970).

Fromm, Erich. *The Art of Loving* (New York: Harper and Row, 1974).

Galston, William. *Justice and the Human Good* (Chicago: University of Chicago Press, 1980).

Gardella, Peter. *Innocent Ecstasy* (New York: Oxford University Press, 1985).

Gay, Peter. *The Bourgeois Experience: Victoria to Freud.* Vol. 2, *The Tender Passion* (New York: Oxford University Press, 1986).

Gaylin, Willard. *Rediscovering Love* (New York: Viking, 1986).

Gellner, E. A. "Ethics and Logic." *Proceedings of the Aristotelian Society* 55 (1955): 157–178.

Gilbert, Paul. "Friendship and the Will." *Philosophy* 61 (1986): 61–70.

Gilligan, Carol. *In A Different Voice* (Cambridge: Harvard University Press, 1982).

Glück, Louise. *The Triumph of Achilles* (New York: Ecco, 1985).

Gonzales-Crussi, F. *Notes of an Anatomist* (New York: Harcourt, Brace, Jovanovich, 1985).

Goode, William J. "The Theoretical Importance of Love." In *The Practice of Love*, edited by A. Montagu (Englewood Cliffs, N.J.: Prentice-Hall, 1975), pp. 120–135.

Gould, Thomas. *Platonic Love* (London: Routledge and Kegan Paul, 1963).

Groden, Suzy Q., trans. *The Poems of Sappho* (Indianapolis: Bobbs-Merrill, 1966).

Hacker, Marilyn. *Love, Death, and the Changing of the Seasons* (New York: Arbor House, 1986).

Halmos, Paul. "Psychologies of Love." *Philosophy* 41 (1966): 58–69.

Hamlyn, D. "The Phenomena of Love and Hate." *Philosophy* 53 (1978): 5–20.

———. *Perception, Learning and the Self* (London: Routledge and Kegan Paul, 1983).

Hannay, Alastair. *Kierkegaard* (London: Routledge and Kegan Paul, 1982).

Hardwig, John. "Should Women Think in Terms of Rights?" *Ethics* 94 (1984): 441–455.

Hegel, Friedrich. *On Christianity: Early Theological Writings.* Translated by T. M. Knox (New York: Harper and Bros., 1948).

Himmelfarb, Gertrude. *On Liberty and Liberalism* (New York: Alfred A. Knopf, 1974).

Hume, David. *Essays: Moral, Political, and Literary* (London: Oxford University Press, 1963).

Hunt, Morton. *The Natural History of Love* (New York: Minerva Press, 1959).

Hunter, J. F. M. *Thinking About Sex and Love* (New York: St. Martin's, 1980).

Huxley, Aldous. *The Perennial Philosophy* (New York: Harper and Bros., 1945).

Ignatieff, Michael. "Lodged in the Heart and Memory." *Times Literary Supplement* (London), April 15–21, 1988, 411–413.

Johann, Robert O. "The Problem of Love." *Review of Metaphysics* 8 (1954–55): 225–245.

Jung, C. G. *Aspects of the Feminine* (Princeton: Princeton University Press, 1982).

Kalin, Jesse. "Lies, Secrets, and Love: The Inadequacy of Contemporary Moral Philosophy." *Journal of Value Inquiry* 10 (1976): 253–265.

Ketchum, Sara Ann. "The Good, the Bad and the Perverted." In *Philosophy of Sex*, edited by A. Soble (Totowa, N.J.: Littlefield, Adams, 1980), pp. 139–157.

Kierkegaard, Søren. *Attack Upon "Christendom"* (Princeton: Princeton University Press, 1968).

———. *Either/Or*, vols. 1 and 2 (Princeton: Princeton University Press, 1959–71).

———. *Fear and Trembling. Repetition* (Princeton: Princeton University Press, 1983).

———. *The Sickness Unto Death* (Princeton: Princeton University Press, 1980).

———. *Stages on Life's Way* (Princeton: Princeton University Press, 1945).

———. *Works of Love* (New York: Harper and Row, 1962).

Kilpatrick, William. *Identity and Intimacy* (New York: Delacorte, 1975).

Kosman, L. A. "Platonic Love." In *Facets of Plato's Philosophy,* edited by W. H. Werkmeister (Amsterdam: Van Gorcum, 1976), pp. 53–69.

Kraut, Robert. "Love *De Re.*" *Midwest Studies in Philosophy* 10 (1986): 413–430.

Kundera, Milan. *The Unbearable Lightness of Being* (New York: Harper and Row, 1985).

Lawrence, D. H. *Women in Love* (New York: Penguin, 1976).

Leites, Edmund. *The Puritan Conscience and Modern Sexuality* (New Haven: Yale University Press, 1986).

Lesser, A. H. "Love and Lust." *Journal of Value Inquiry* 14 (1980): 51–54.

Lessing, Doris. *A Man and Two Women* (New York: Popular Library, 1963).

Letwin, Shirley Robin. "Romantic Love and Christianity." *Philosophy* 52 (1977): 131–145.

Levy, Donald. "The Definition of Love in Plato's *Symposium.*" *Journal of the History of Ideas* 40 (1979): 285–291.

Lewis, C. S. *The Allegory of Love* (Oxford: Oxford University Press, 1936).

———. *The Four Loves* (New York: Harcourt, Brace, Jovanovich, 1960).

Lindström, Valter. "A Contribution to the Interpretation of Kierkegaard's Book The Works of Love." *Studia Theologica* 6 (1953): 1–29.

Luhmann, Niklas. *Love as Passion* (Cambridge: Harvard University Press, 1986).

Lyons, William. *Emotion* (Cambridge: Cambridge University Press, 1980).

McCullers, Carson. *The Ballad of the Sad Café and Other Stories* (New York: Bantam, 1958).

MacDonald, Margaret. "Some Distinctive Features of Arguments Used in Criticism of the Arts." In *Aesthetics and Language,* edited by W. Elton (Oxford: Basil Blackwell, 1954), pp. 114–130.

MacLagan, W. G. "Respect for Persons as a Moral Principle—I," *Philosophy* 35 (1960), 193–217.

McTaggart, John McTaggart E. *The Nature of Existence,* vol. 2 (Cambridge: Cambridge University Press, 1927).

Marx, Karl. *Early Writings.* Edited by Q. Hoare (New York: Vintage, 1975).

Mayo, Bernard. *Ethics and the Moral Life* (New York: St. Martin's, 1958).

Meager, R. "The Uniqueness of a Work of Art." *Proceedings of the Aristotelian Society* 59 (1958–59): 49–70.

Medawar, P. B. *The Uniqueness of the Individual* (London: Methuen, 1957).

Mendus, Susan. "Marital Faithfulness." *Philosophy* 59 (1984): 243–252.

Mill, John Stuart. *On Liberty* (Indianapolis: Hackett, 1978).

Montaigne, Michel de. *The Complete Essays of Montaigne.* Translated by D. M. Frame (Stanford: Stanford University Press, 1958).

Morgan, Douglas N. *Love: Plato, the Bible and Freud* (Englewood Cliffs, N.J.: Prentice-Hall, 1964).

Murdoch, Iris. *The Black Prince* (New York: Warner, 1974).

———. *Bruno's Dream* (New York: Viking, 1964).

Musil, Robert. *Five Women* (Boston: David R. Godine, 1986).

Nabokov, Vladimir. *Lolita* (New York: Berkley, 1977).

Nagel, Thomas. "Sexual Perversion." In *Philosophy of Sex,* edited by A. Soble (Totowa, N.J.: Littlefield, Adams, 1980), pp. 76–88.

Nakhnikian, George. "Love in Human Reason." *Midwest Studies in Philosophy* 3 (1978): 286–317.

Neruda, Pablo. *100 Love Sonnets* (Austin: University of Texas Press, 1986).

Neu, Jerome. "Jealous Thoughts." In *Explaining Emotions,* edited by A. Rorty (Berkeley: University of California Press, 1980), pp. 425–463.

Newton-Smith, W. "A Conceptual Investigation of Love." In *Philosophy and Personal Relations,* edited by A. Montefiore (Montreal: McGill-Queen's University Press, 1973), pp. 113–136.

Nietzsche, Friedrich. *The Joyful Wisdom* (New York: Frederick Ungar, 1960).

Nordentoft, K. "Erotic Love." In *Kierkegaard and Human Values,* edited by N. Thulstrup and M. M. Thulstrup (Copenhagen: C. A. Reitzels Boghandel, 1980), pp. 87–99.

Norton, David, and Mary Kille, eds. *Philosophies of Love* (Totowa, N.J.: Rowman and Allanheld, 1983).

Nussbaum, Martha. "Sex in the Head." *New York Review of Books,* December 18, 1986, 49–52.

———. *The Fragility of Goodness* (Cambridge: Cambridge University Press, 1986).

Nygren, Anders. *Agape and Eros* (Chicago: University of Chicago Press, 1982).

Ortega y Gasset, José. *On Love* (New York: Meridian, 1957).

Outka, Gene. *Agape: An Ethical Analysis* (New Haven: Yale University Press, 1972).

Pascal, Blaise. "Discourse on the Passion of Love." In *The Thoughts, Letters, and Opuscules of Blaise Pascal,* translated by Orlando William Wight (New York: Hurd and Houghton, 1869), pp. 514–525.

———. *Pensées.* Translated by A. J. Krailsheimer (New York: Penguin, 1966).

Peck, M. Scott. *The Road Less Traveled* (New York: Simon and Schuster, 1978).

Person, Ethel. "Love Triangles." *The Atlantic* (February 1988): 41–52.

Pitcher, George. "Emotion." *Mind* 74 (1965): 326–346.

Plato. *Euthyphro.* In *The Collected Dialogues of Plato,* edited by E. Hamilton and H. Cairns (Princeton: Princeton University Press, 1961), pp. 169–185.

———. *The Symposium.* Translated by Walter Hamilton (New York: Penguin, 1951).

———. *The Symposium.* Translated by Suzy Q Groden (Amherst: University of Massachusetts Press, 1970).

———. *The Symposium.* Translated by Raymond Larson (Arlington Heights, Ill.: AHM Publishing Co., 1980).

Prall, D. W. *Aesthetic Analysis* (New York: Thomas Y. Crowell, 1936).

Price, A. W. "Loving Persons Platonically." *Phronesis* 26 (1981): 25–34.

Proust, Marcel. *Remembrance of Things Past* (New York: Random House, 1981).

Quinton, Anthony. "The Soul." *Journal of Philosophy* 59 (1962): 393–409.

Rawls, John. *A Theory of Justice* (Cambridge: Harvard University Press, 1971).

Reik, Theodor. *Of Love and Lust* (New York: Pyramid, 1976).

Reiman, Jeffrey. "Privacy, Intimacy, and Personhood." *Philosophy and Public Affairs* 6 (1976): 26–44.

Richards, Janet Radcliffe. *The Sceptical Feminist* (London: Routledge and Kegan Paul, 1980).

Robinson, Jenefer. "Emotion, Judgment, and Desire." *Journal of Philosophy* 80 (1983): 731–741.

Rorty, Amelie. "The Historicity of Psychological Attitudes: Love is Not Love Which Alters Not When It Alteration Finds." *Midwest Studies in Philosophy* 10 (1986): 399–412.

Rose, Phyllis. *Parallel Lives: Five Victorian Marriages* (New York: Knopf, 1983).

Rosen, Stanley. *Plato's Symposium,* 2d ed. (New Haven: Yale University Press, 1987).

Rousseau, Jean-Jacques. *The Confessions.* Translated by J. M. Cohen (New York: Penguin, 1953).

Rubin, Lillian B. *Intimate Strangers* (New York: Harper and Row, 1983).

Sankowski, Edward. "Love and Moral Obligation." *Journal of Value Inquiry* 12 (1978): 100–110.

Sartre, Jean-Paul. *Being and Nothingness.* Translated by Hazel E. Barnes (New York: Philosophical Library, 1956).

Saxonhouse, Arlene W. "The Net of Hephaestus: Aristophanes' Speech in Plato's *Symposium.*" *Interpretation* 13 (1985): 15–32.

Scheffler, Samuel. "Morality's Demands and Their Limits." *Journal of Philosophy* 83 (1986): 531–537.

Scheler, Max. *Ressentiment.* Translated by W. W. Holdheim (New York: Free Press, 1961).

Scruton, Roger. "Attitudes, Beliefs and Reasons." In *Morality and Moral Reasoning,* edited by John Casey (London: Methuen, 1971), pp. 25–100.

———. *Sexual Desire: A Moral Philosophy of the Erotic* (New York: Free Press, 1986).

Seligman, Clive, Russell H. Fazio, and Mark P. Zanna. "Effects of Salience of Extrinsic Rewards on Liking and Loving." *Journal of Personality and Social Psychology* 38 (1980): 453–460.

Shaffer, Jerome A. "An Assessment of Emotion." *American Philosophical Quarterly* 20 (1983): 161–173.

Shakespeare, William. *The Sonnets* (New York: New American Library, 1964).

Shaw, G. B. *Man and Superman* (New York: Penguin, 1982).

Sherman, Nancy. "Aristotle on Friendship and the Shared Life." *Philosophy and Phenomenological Research* 47 (1987): 589–613.

Singer, Irving. *The Nature of Love.* Vol. 1, *Plato to Luther,* 2d ed.; vol. 2, *Courtly and Romantic;* vol. 3, *The Modern World* (Chicago: University of Chicago Press, 1984–87).

Slater, Philip. *The Pursuit of Loneliness* (Boston: Beacon Press, 1970).

Smedes, Lewis B. *Love Within Limits* (Grand Rapids, Mich.: Eerdmans, 1978).

Soble, Alan. "Physical Attractiveness and Unfair Discrimination." *International Journal of Applied Philosophy* 1 (1982): 37–64.

———. "The Unity of Romantic Love." *Philosophy and Theology* 1 (1987): 374–397.

Solomon, Robert C. "Separating Love into His and Hers," *The Philadelphia Inquirer Book Review Section,* December 28, 1986, 5.

———. *Love: Emotion, Myth and Metaphor* (Garden City, N.Y.: Anchor Press, 1981).

Sparshott, Francis. "The Disappointed Art Lover." In *The Forger's Art,* edited by D. Dutton (Berkeley: University of California Press, 1983), pp. 246–263.

———. *The Structure of Aesthetics* (Toronto: University of Toronto Press, 1963).

Stafford, J. Martin. "On Distinguishing Between Love and Lust." *Journal of Value Inquiry* 11 (1977): 292–303.

Stallworthy, Jon, ed. *A Book of Love Poetry* (New York: Oxford University Press, 1986).

Stendhal. *Love* (Harmondsworth, Eng.: Penguin, 1975).

Sternberg, Robert J., and Michael L. Barnes, eds. *The Psychology of Love* (New Haven: Yale University Press, 1988).

Symons, Donald. *The Evolution of Human Sexuality* (New York: Oxford University Press, 1979).

Taylor, Charles. *Human Agency and Language: Philosophical Papers I* (Cambridge: Cambridge University Press, 1985).

Taylor, Gabrielle. "Love." *Proceedings of the Aristotelian Society* 76 (1976): 147–164.

Taylor, Mark C. "Love and Forms of Spirit: Kierkegaard vs. Hegel." *Kierkegaardiana* 10 (1977): 95–116.

Telfer, Elizabeth. "Friendship." *Proceedings of the Aristotelian Society* 71 (1970–71): 223–241.

Thielicke, Helmut. *The Ethics of Sex* (New York: Harper and Row, 1964).

Thurber, James, and E. B. White. *Is Sex Necessary?* (New York: Perennial Library, 1975).

Tillich, Paul. *Love, Power and Justice* (New York: Oxford University Press, 1960).

Tolstoy, L. *The Novels and Other Works of Lyof N. Tolstoi,* vol. 16 (New York: Scribner's, 1900).

Vacek, Edward. "Scheler's Phenomenology of Love." *Journal of Religion* 62 (1982): 156–177.

Van Herik, Judith. *Freud on Femininity and Faith* (Berkeley: University of California Press, 1982).

Vannoy, Russell. *Sex Without Love: A Philosophical Exploration* (Buffalo: Prometheus, 1980).

Vlastos, Gregory. "The Individual as an Object of Love in Plato." In *Platonic Studies* (Princeton: Princeton University Press, 1973), pp. 3–34.

———. "Justice and Equality." In *Social Justice,* edited by Richard B. Brandt (Englewood Cliffs, N.J.: Prentice-Hall, 1962), pp. 31–72.

Vonnegut, Kurt, Jr. *God Bless You, Mr. Rosewater* (New York: Dell, 1965).

Walsh, Sylvia. "Women in Love." *Soundings* 65 (1982): 352–368.

Warner, Martin. "Love, Self, and Plato's *Symposium.*" *Philosophical Quarterly* 29 (1979): 329–339.

Wasserstrom, Richard. "Is Adultery Immoral?" In *Today's Moral Problems,* 1st ed., edited by R. Wasserstrom (New York: Macmillan, 1975): 240–252.

Watson, Richard. "The Seducer and the Seduced." *Georgia Review* 39 (1985): 353–366.

Wellek, René, and Austin Warren. *Theory of Literature* (New York: Harcourt, Brace and Co., 1949).

Weston, Anthony. "Towards the Reconstruction of Subjectivism: Love as a Paradigm of Values." *Journal of Value Inquiry* 18 (1984): 181–194.

Whiteley, C. H. "Love, Hate and Emotion." *Philosophy* 54 (1979): 235.

Wilde, Oscar. *De Profundis* (New York: Philosophical Library, 1950).

Williams, Bernard. *Ethics and the Limits of Philosophy* (Cambridge: Harvard University Press, 1985).

Wilson, Edmund. *Axel's Castle* (New York: Scribner's, 1931).

Wittgenstein, Ludwig. *Zettel* (Oxford: Basil Blackwell, 1967).

Wojtyla, Karol (Pope John Paul II). *Love and Responsibility* (New York: Farrar, Straus, Giroux, 1981).

Yeats, W. B. *The Collected Poems of W. B. Yeats* (New York: Macmillan, 1956).

———. *The Winding Stair and Other Poems* (New York: Macmillan, 1933).

INDEX

Abandoning love, 223–24, 246, 253, 257
Abelard, 21
Abraham, 351*n*18
Admiration, 107, 129, 315; role in love, 16, 86, 95, 324*n*40
Agapizing personal love, 4, 22–23, 234–35, 282, 345*n*14, 345*n*57
Annis, David, 136
Anomalous emotion, love as, 107, 117–29, 141, 170, 238; due to reason-independence, 119, 125, 153, 163, 314–15, 337*n*20
Appreciation, 57
Aristocratic love, 68, 88, 139, 339*n*3
Aristophanes: theory of love reconstructed, 83; explanation of homosexuality, 85, 89; on love and equality, 88, 250; love by description, 139; on irreplaceability, 290; and Freud, 333*n*13, 334*n*20
Aristotle, 250–51, 284, 312, 323*n*28; on basis of love, 14–15, 222, 261; perfect friendship rare, 88, 187, 331*n*2; wishing y well for y's sake, 100–03 passim, 262; on exclusivity, 186–87; inferior vs. perfect friendship, 186–87, 221–23; on reciprocity, 187, 223, 238; on constancy, 222–26; on ugliness, 226
Auden, W. H., 191–92, 336*n*3
Augustine, Saint, 19, 94–95

Austen, Jane *(Pride and Prejudice)*, 70, 139–40

Badhwar, Neera: on irreplaceability, 290–93
Baier, Annette: immorality of love, 130, 160–61; on desire for reciprocity, 243, 335*n*13; on constancy, 211, 335*n*13
Balint, Michael, 148
Barthes, Roland, 3; on ideal mate, 89; beloved indescribable, 143
Basis of love vs. object of love: 4, 225, 300, 306–07, 313, 321*n*6, 329*n*18
Bayles, Michael, 211
Beethoven Violin Concerto (BVC) lover, 48–49, 72, 153–54, 200
Being loved as a reason for love, 5, 9, 21, 55, 135–36, 241, 254
Bellah, Robert, 86
Bernard, Saint, 15, 246, 249
Bernays, Martha. *See* Freud, Sigmund
Bernstein, Mark: substitution problem, 45–46, 328*n*15
Berryman, John, 163
Bestowal of value, 11, 16–17, 67, 195; agapic, 11, 17, 25–26, 197–98; as the nature of love, 23, 27; erosic, 26, 67, 198; on properties, 28, 313; on God, 325*n*73

Lewis, C. S., 3, 331*n*3, 340*n*22; on subjective preferences, 53; sexual desire exclusive, 200; love for God, 325*n*57

Linus, 353*n*4

Lolita. *See* Humbert, Humbert

Love as shared item, 240, 304

Love begetting love, 19, 21, 96, 135, 238, 241–42, 257, 325*n*64, 349*n*13

Lovelace, Richard, 269

Love potion, 149–53, 243

Loving an abusive person, 112, 124, 127, 135, 136. *See also* Loving the unlovable

Loving the person, 3, 114, 148, 299–303, 305, 354*n*28, 354*n*29; and loving properties, 3, 34, 65, 299, 301, 305, 307–08; and erosic love, 34, 65, 97–98, 199, 220, 225, 299, 302–03, 308, 311; and the transcendental self, 65, 98, 307; in Aristophanes, 79, 81; as incoherent, 98, 307; as loving for identity properties, 219, 225, 229, 290; and agapic love, 220, 225, 233, 301, 313

Loving the unlovable, 104–05, 115, 119, 122, 125, 132–34, 213, 262

Luhmann, Niklas, 171–72, 322*n*10, 339*n*3

Lyons, William: loving the dead, 207, 322*n*12; all emotions belief-dependent, 336*n*13; Gellner's paradox, 336*n*17

MacLagan, W. G., 61, 130

McTaggart, J. M. E.: on constancy, 232; love as anomalous, 314–15; on disproportionate love, 314–16; love requires no justification, 318

Maritain, Jacques, 330*n*30

Marriage, 15, 56, 343*n*27, 346*n*17, 348*n*63; selection of person for, 71, 280–01, 331*n*4; and love, 214, 281; and sex, 214, 345*n*55

Marx, Karl: on unrequited love, 242

Mayo, Bernard, 163, 326*n*12

Meager, R., 54

Medawar, Peter, 60–61

Mendus, Susan, 164–65

Michelangelo *(Sonnet 55),* 145

Mill, John Stuart: and Harriet Taylor, 1, 2, 28–29; on individuality, 51, 53; *On Liberty,* 51, 172; on happiness, 99

Molière, 327*n*5

Montaigne, Michel de, 15; on love at first sight, 31, 35–36; on exclusivity, 188–89

Montaigne's reason for love, 15, 54, 145, 323*n*29, 325*n*69, 325*n*71; as indexed reason, 42; reason for exclusivity, 62; as uniļluminating, 66; and beloved indescribable, 143; as irrational, 144; as loving for identity properties, 225; offered when real reason silly, 314

—"because y is y," 15, 62, 66, 144, 225

—"because you are you," 24, 25, 42, 54, 143, 144

—"y-ness," 143

—beloved herself, 143, 314, 316

Morality: and exclusivity, 33, 109, 178, 181, 198, 201–02; and basis of love, 55, 159, 161, 227, 281–82; and constancy, 109, 201, 208, 232–34; and rationality, 112, 283–85, 318, 320; and agapic love, 120, 146, 343*n*14, 338*n*22

Musil, Robert ("Tonka"), 321*n*7

Mystery in love, 62, 69–70; in erosic love, 5, 312, 314; in reciprocal love, 5, 21, 55, 144; in agapic love, 6, 15–16, 144

Nagel, Thomas: individuation of sexual desire, 293–94

Nakhnikian, George: on Aristotle, 260–62

Neighbor-love, 324*n*47; basis of, 13, 37, 195–96, 199; objects of, 13, 134, 196, 323*n*24; and self-love,